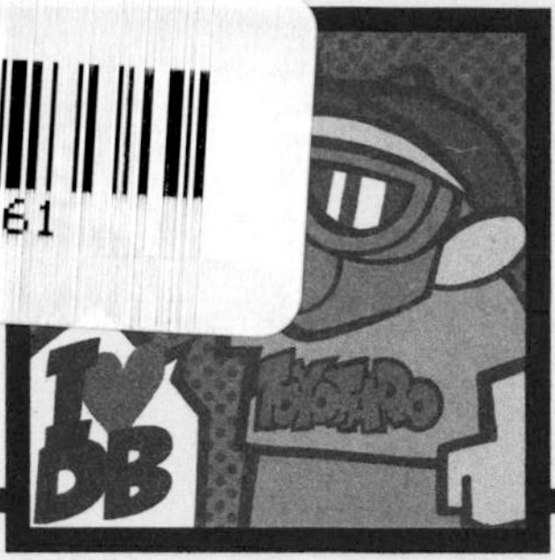
I ♥ DB
TOYOTARO

As a kid, sometimes I would end up going out with my family and forget to record an episode of the anime. I'd say, "What's gonna happen if Goku loses this next battle and I don't see it? Let's go home right now!" My dad would then say, "If he loses, he loses, whether you're there to witness it or not," and I always was at a loss for words. That's not the point!

Yet, even now, I haven't come up with a good comeback...

—Toyotarou, 2018

Toyotarou

Toyotarou created the manga adaptation for the *Dragon Ball Z* anime's 2015 film, *Dragon Ball Z: Resurrection F*. He is also the author of the spin-off series *Dragon Ball Heroes: Victory Mission*, which debuted in *V-Jump* in Japan in November 2012.

Akira Toriyama

Renowned worldwide for his playful, innovative storytelling and humorous, distinctive art style, Akira Toriyama burst onto the manga scene in 1980 with the wildly popular *Dr. Slump*. His hit series *Dragon Ball* (published in the U.S. as *Dragon Ball* and *Dragon Ball Z*) ran from 1984 to 1995 in Shueisha's *Weekly Shonen Jump* magazine. He is also known for his design work on video games such as *Dragon Quest*, *Chrono Trigger*, *Tobal No. 1* and *Blue Dragon*. His recent manga works include *COWA!*, *Kajika*, *Sand Land*, *Neko Majin*, *Jaco the Galactic Patrolman* and a children's book, *Toccio the Angel*. He lives with his family in Japan.

DRAGON BALL SUPER 6

SHONEN JUMP Manga Edition

STORY BY **Akira Toriyama**

ART BY **Toyotarou**

TRANSLATION **Toshikazu Aizawa, Christine Dashiell, and Caleb Cook**
LETTERING **Paolo Gattone and Chiara Antonelli**
TOUCH-UP ART **James Gaubatz**
DESIGN **Shawn Carrico**
EDITOR **Marlene First**

Printed in the U.S.A.

Published by VIZ Media, LLC
P.O. Box 77010
San Francisco, CA 94107

10 9 8 7 6 5 4 3 2 1
First printing, September 2019

viz.com

shonenjump.com

DRAGON BALL SUPER

6

THE SUPER WARRIORS GATHER!

STORY BY
Akira Toriyama

ART BY
Toyotarou

CAST OF CHARACTERS

UNIVERSE 7

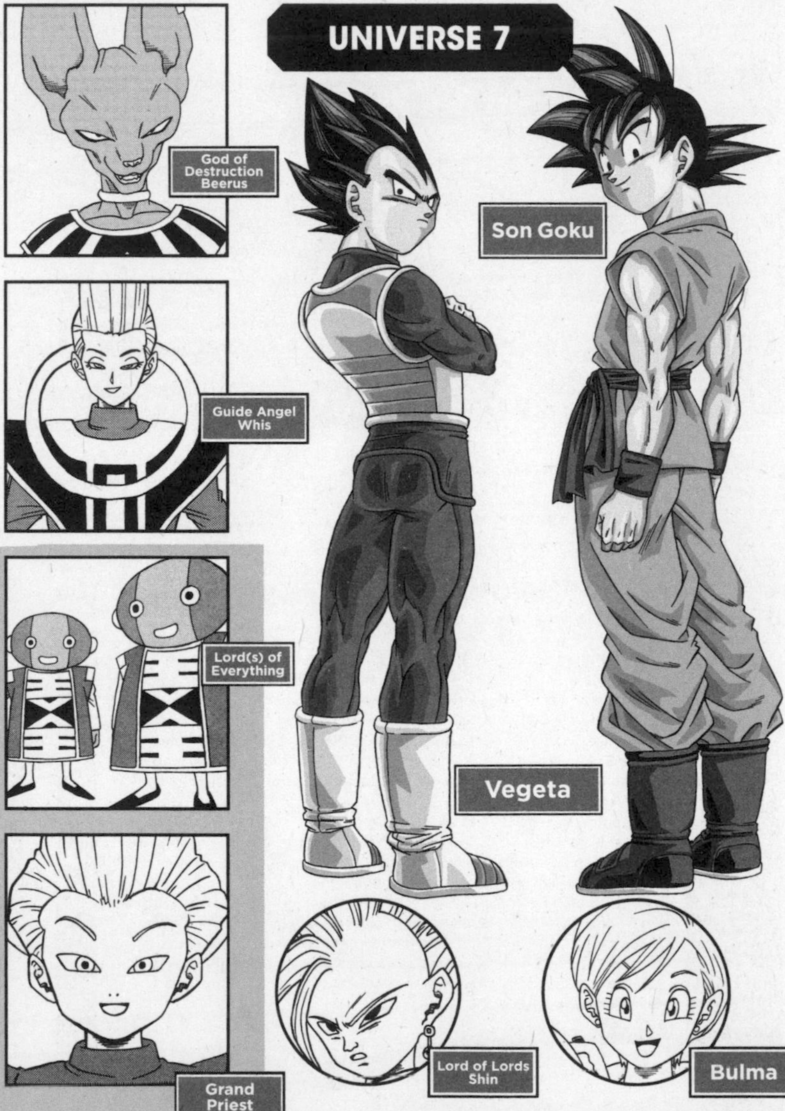
Son Goku
Vegeta
God of Destruction Beerus
Guide Angel Whis
Lord(s) of Everything
Grand Priest
Lord of Lords Shin
Bulma

From Other Universes

God of Destruction Candidate from Universe 11
Toppo

God of Destruction from Universe 11
Belmod

God of Destruction from Universe 6
Champa

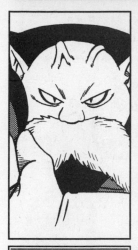

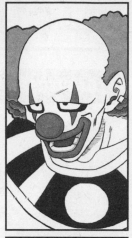

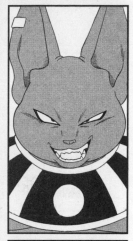

STORY THUS FAR

A long, long time ago, Son Goku left on a journey in search of the legendary Dragon Balls—a set of seven balls that, when gathered, would summon the dragon Shenlong to grant any wish. After a great adventure, he collects them all. Later, he becomes the apprentice of Kame-Sen'nin, fights a number of vicious enemies, defeats the great Majin Boo and restores peace on Earth. Some time passes, and then Lord Beerus, the God of Destruction, suddenly awakens and sets out in search of the Super Saiyan God. Goku, by becoming the Super Saiyan God, manages to stop Beerus from destroying the Earth and starts training under him with Vegeta. One day, Trunks appears hoping to save the future. Goku and Vegeta travel to his future, but they soon find themselves struggling against Goku Black and Zamas from the parallel world. Things get even worse when Goku Black and Zamas perform Potara fusion to become the immortal God Zamas. With little hope remaining, Goku ends up asking for help from the Lord of Everything, who erases the entire future world, along with Zamas. After some time, Goku suggests that the two Lords of Everything hold a Tournament of Power. As such, the Gods of Destruction and Lords of Lords from all the universes are summoned, and the Zen Exhibition Match between Gods of Destruction begins. Goku is on the edge of his seat...

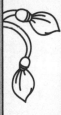

DRAGON BALL SUPER

6

TABLE! OF! CON-TENTS!

DRAGON BALL SUPER

CHAPTER 28: TOPPO, UNIVERSE 11 GOD OF DESTRUCTION CANDIDATE!

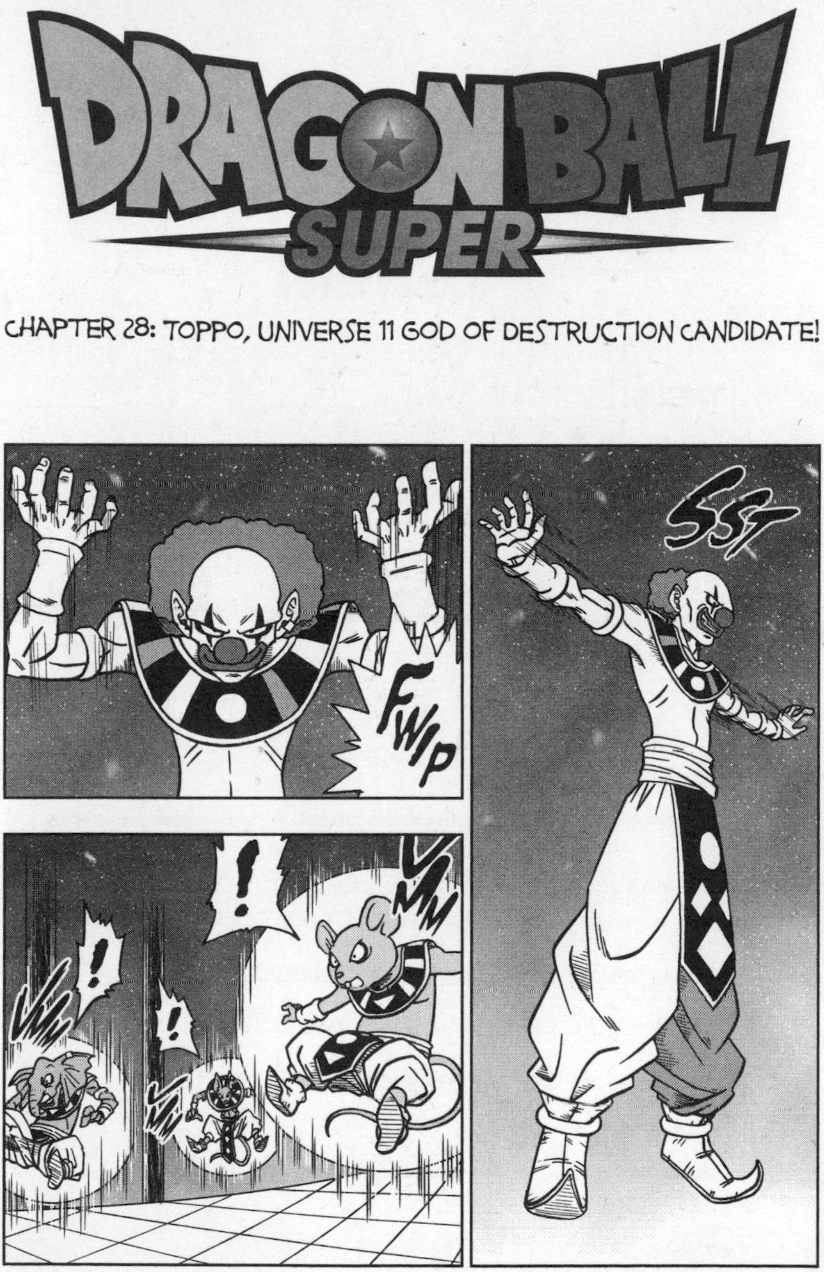
SST
FWIP
!
!
!

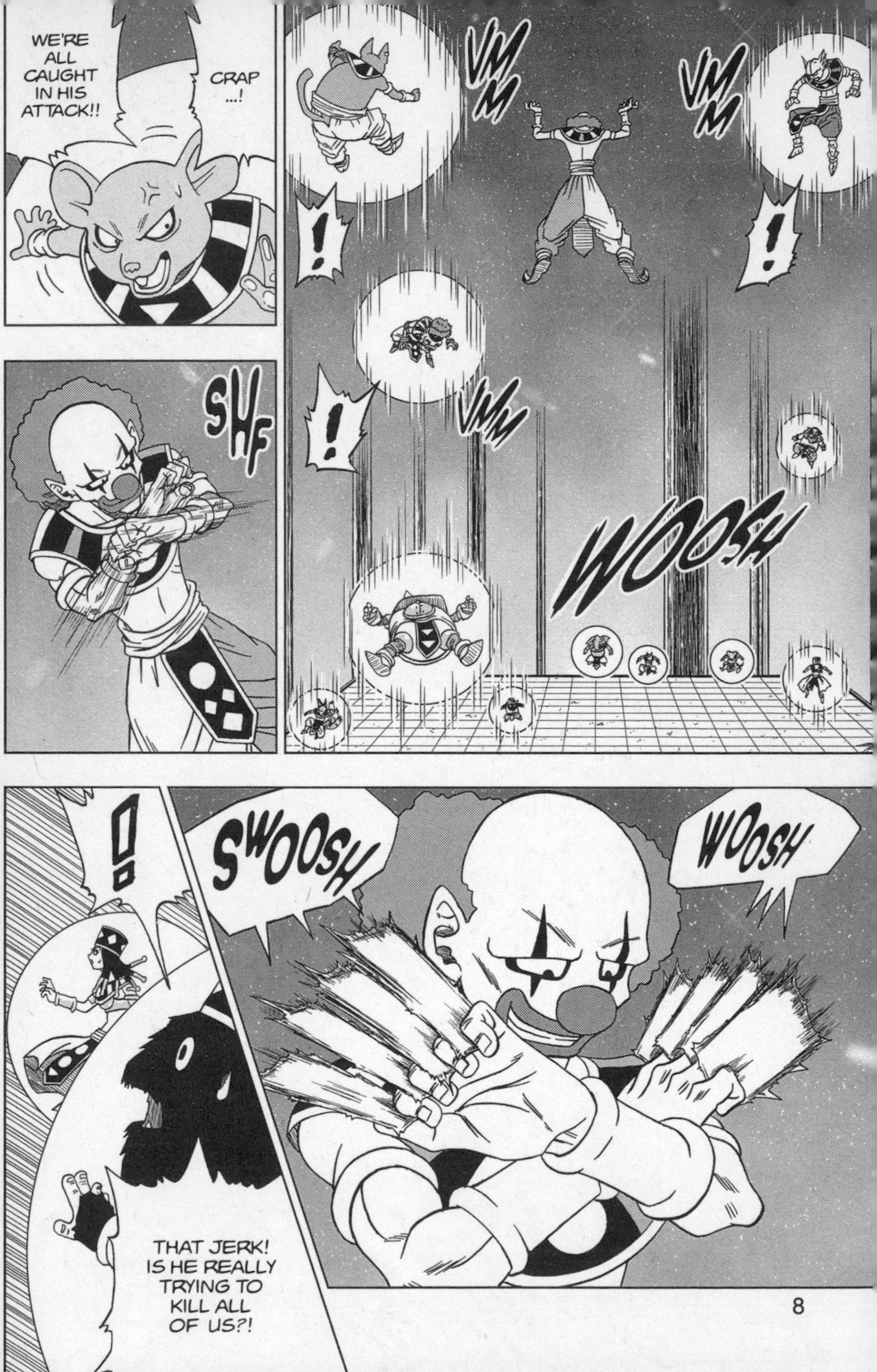
VMM
VMM
!
!
!
VMM
WOOSH
CRAP ...!
WE'RE ALL CAUGHT IN HIS ATTACK!!
SHF
WOOSH
SWOOSH
!
THAT JERK! IS HE REALLY TRYING TO KILL ALL OF US?!

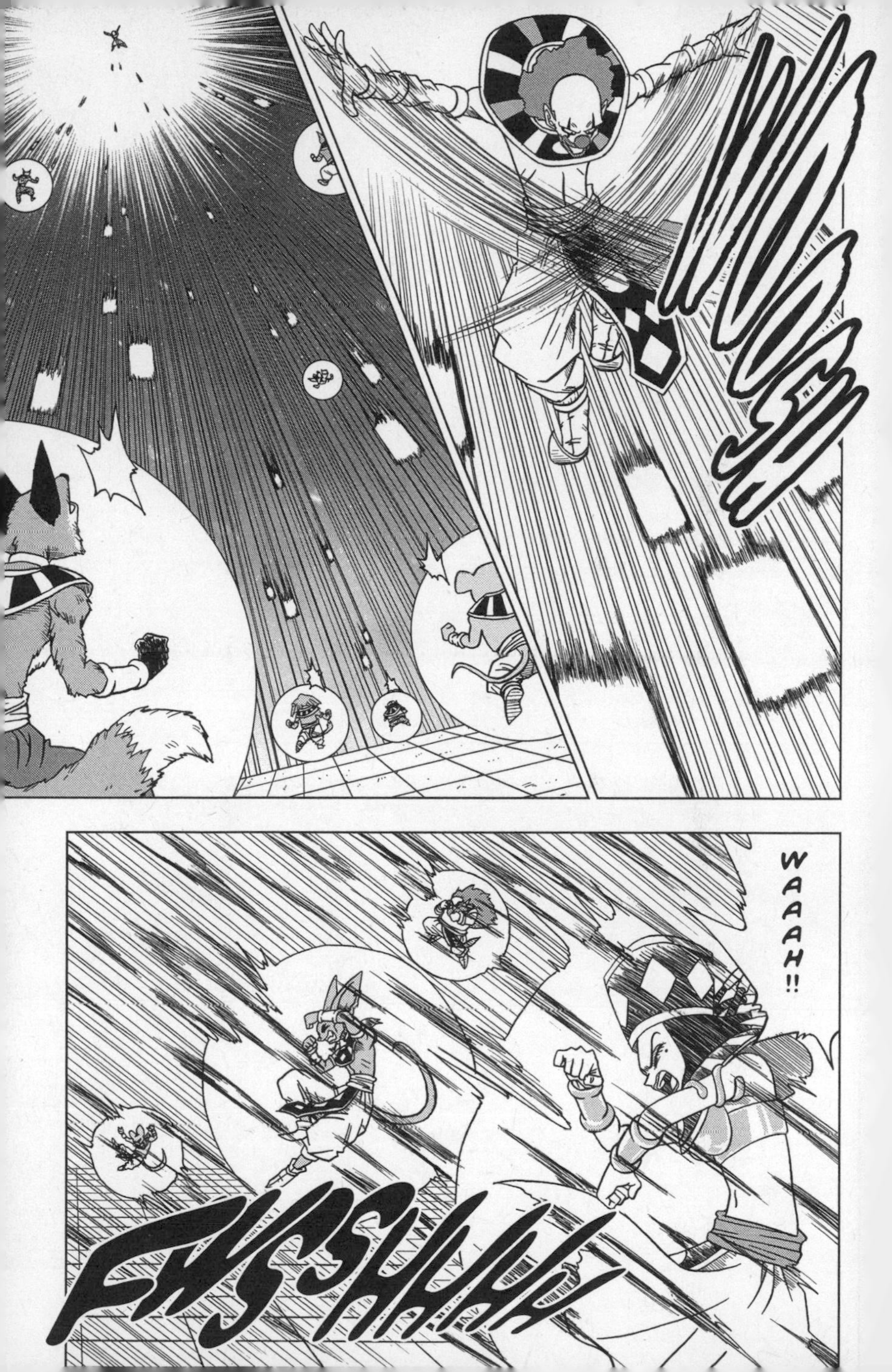
WAAAH!!

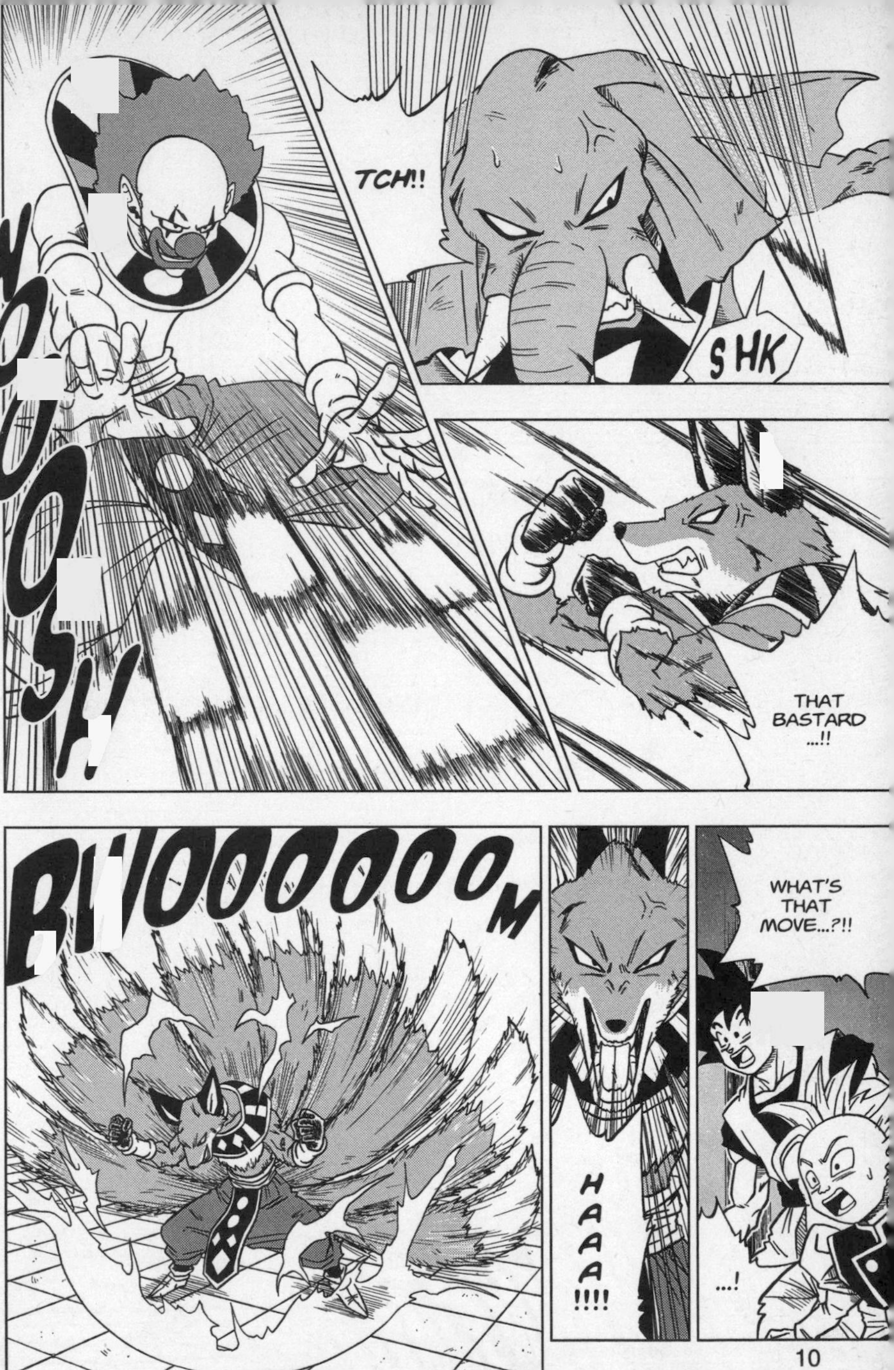
TCH!!
SHK
THAT BASTARD ...!!
WOOOOSH!!
WHAT'S THAT MOVE...?!!
...!
HAAAA!!!!
BWOOOOOOOM

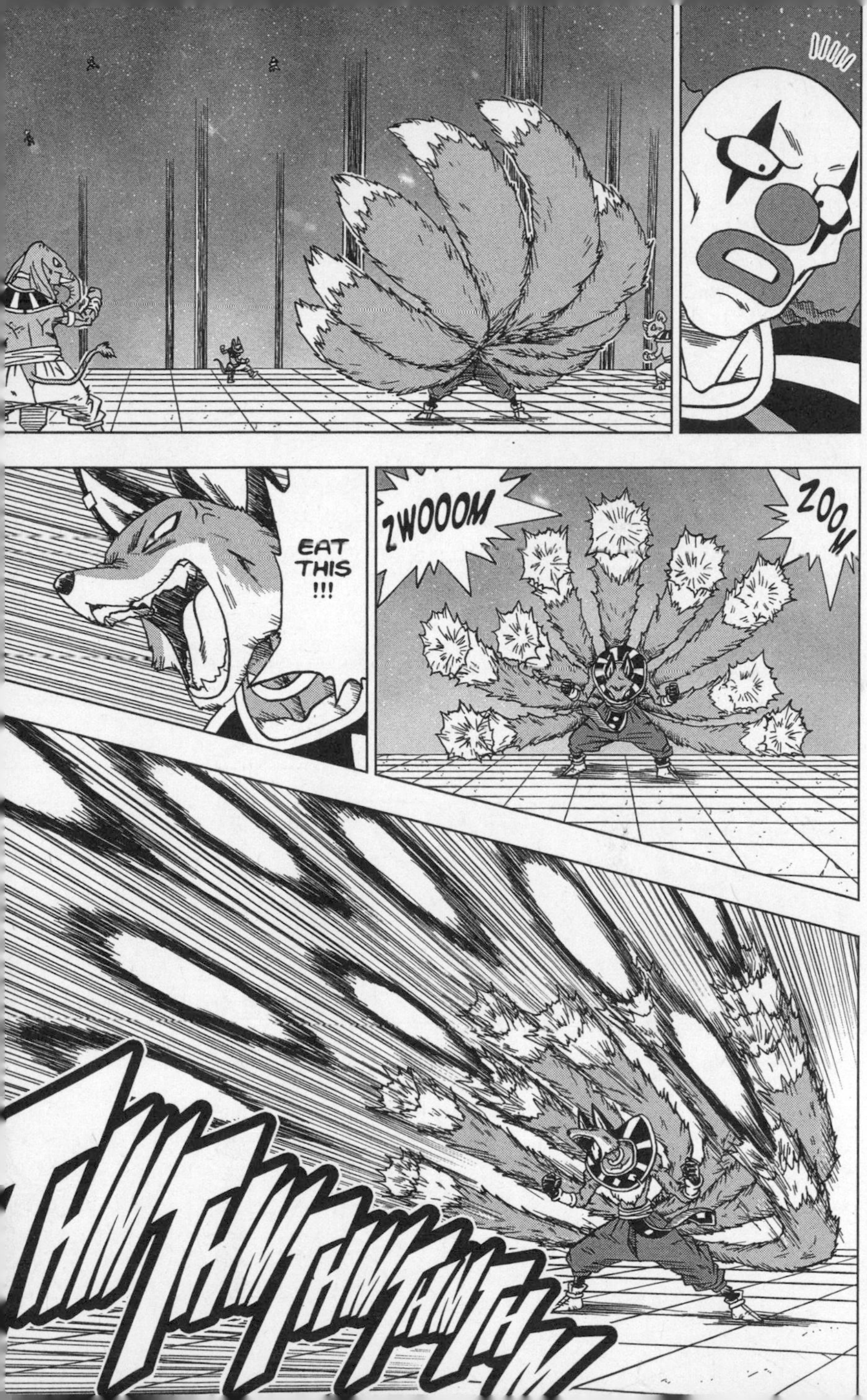
ZOOM
ZWOOOM
EAT THIS !!!
TAM TAM TAM TAM TAM

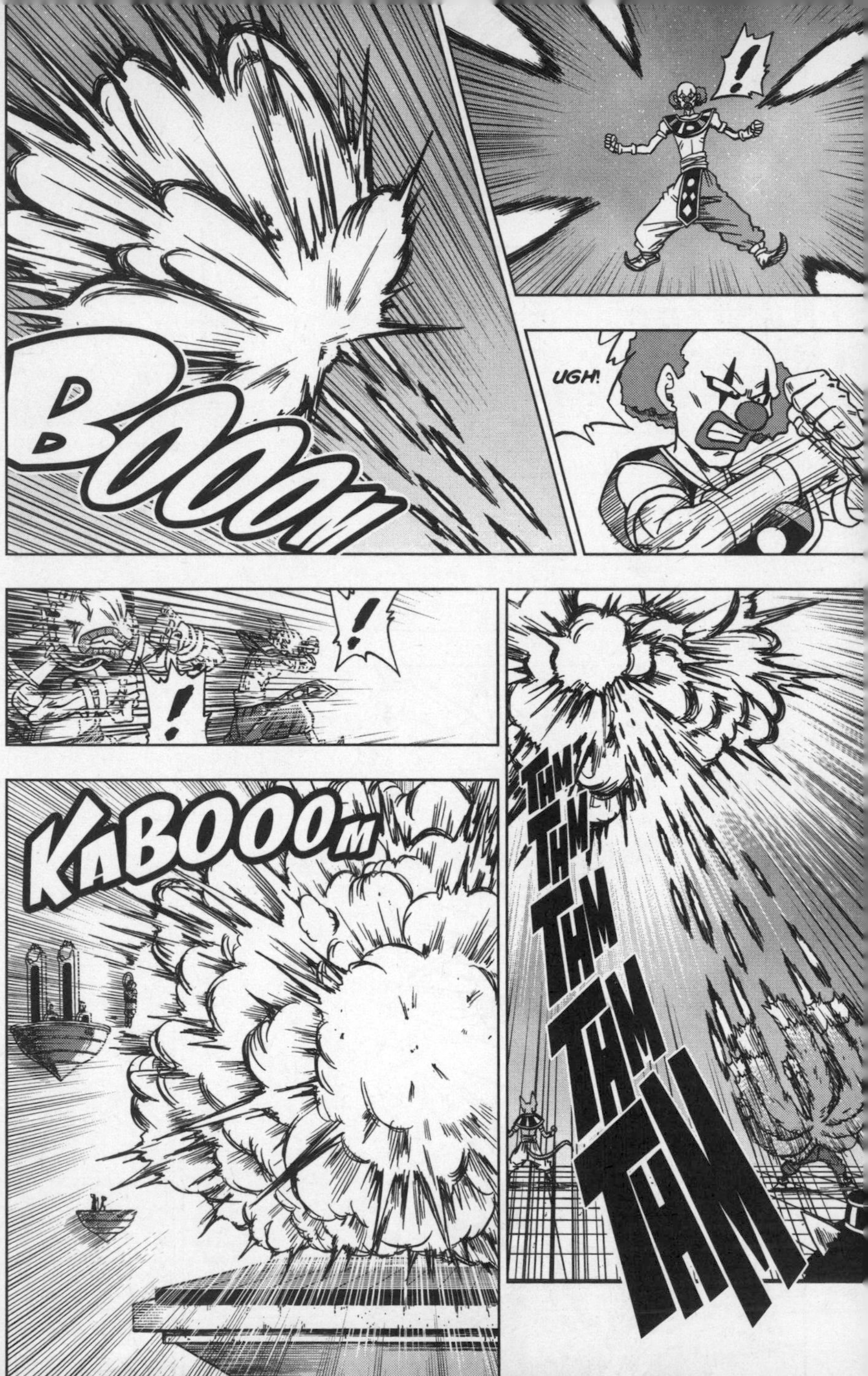
!
UGH!
BOOOM
THM THM THM THM THM THM
!
!
KABOOOM

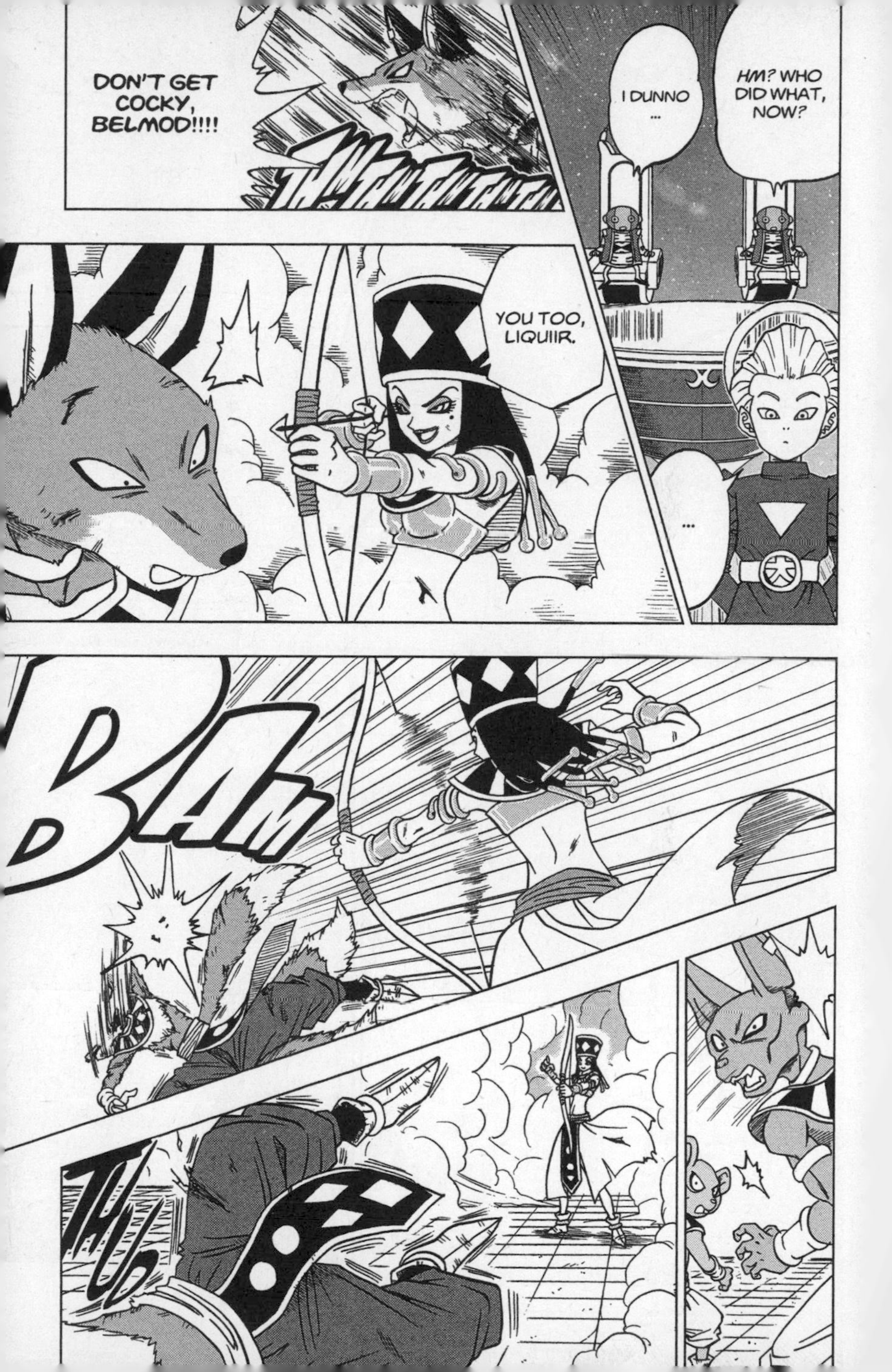
HM? WHO DID WHAT, NOW?
I DUNNO ...
...
DON'T GET COCKY, BELMOD!!!!
YOU TOO, LIQUIIR.
BAM

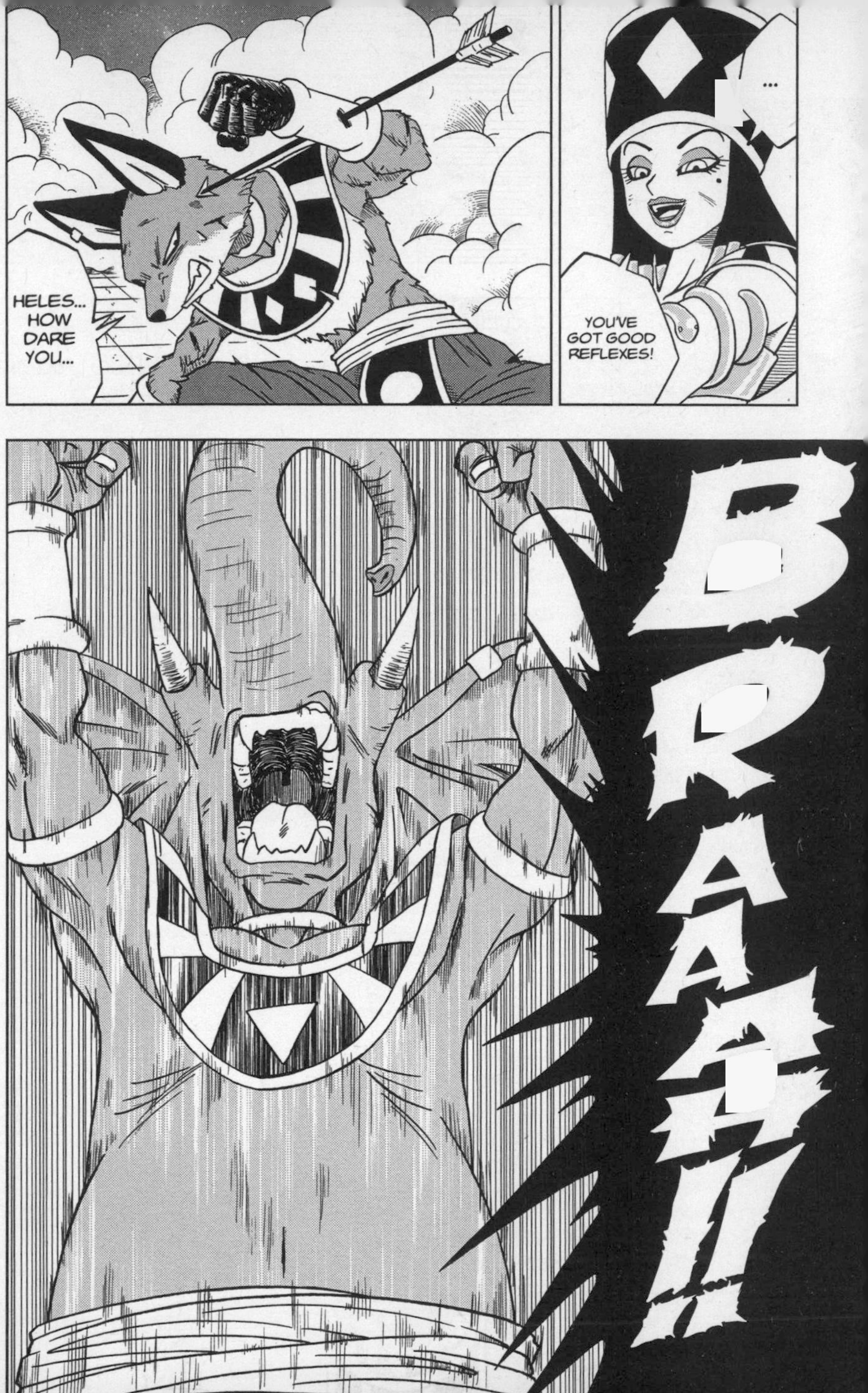
...
YOU'VE GOT GOOD REFLEXES!
HELES... HOW DARE YOU...

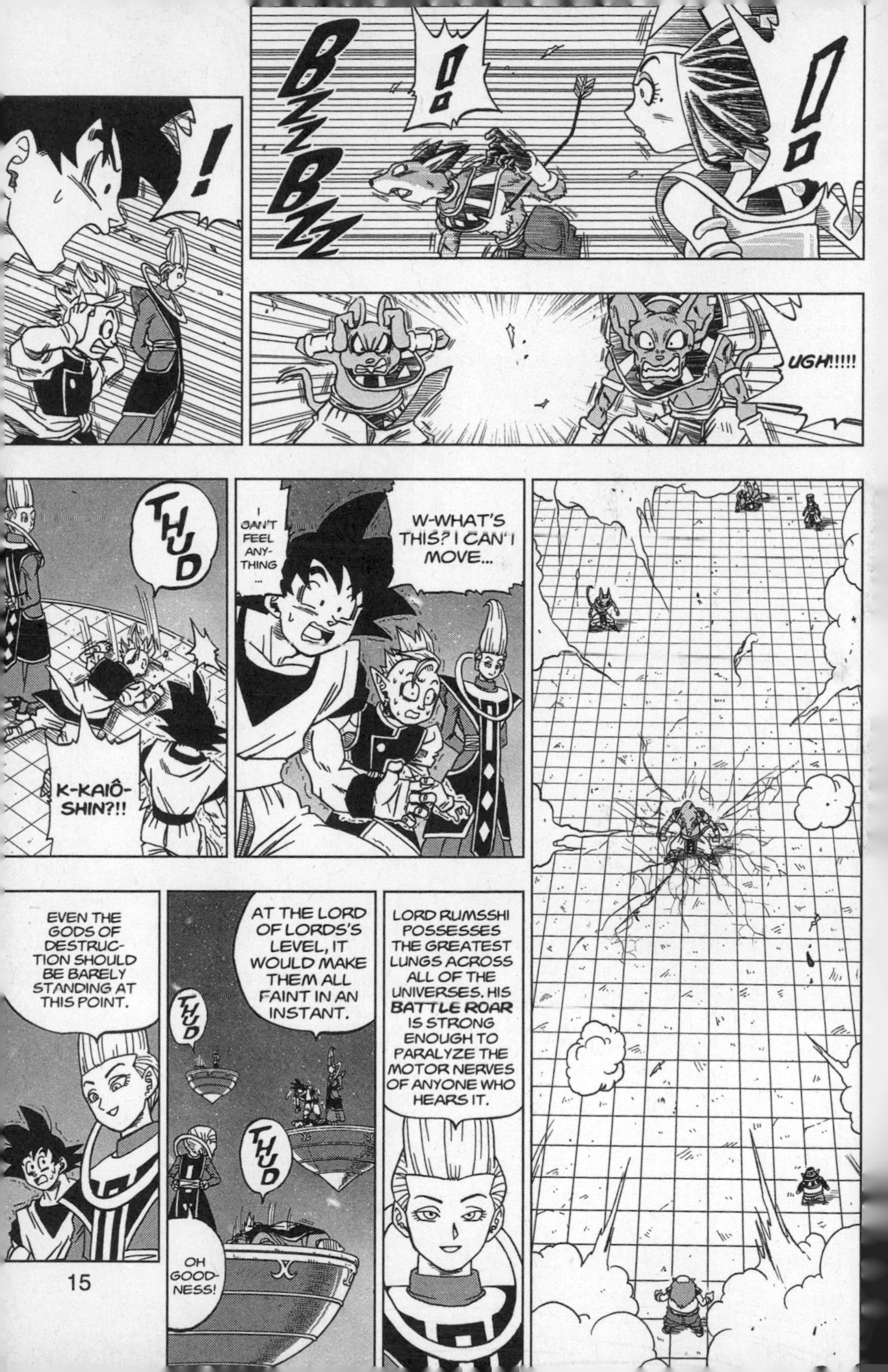
BZZBZZ
!!
!!
UGH!!!!!
!
W-WHAT'S THIS? I CAN'T MOVE...
I CAN'T FEEL ANYTHING...
THUD
K-KAIÔSHIN?!!
LORD RUMSSHI POSSESSES THE GREATEST LUNGS ACROSS ALL OF THE UNIVERSES. HIS BATTLE ROAR IS STRONG ENOUGH TO PARALYZE THE MOTOR NERVES OF ANYONE WHO HEARS IT.
AT THE LORD OF LORDS'S LEVEL, IT WOULD MAKE THEM ALL FAINT IN AN INSTANT.
THUD
THUD
OH GOODNESS!
EVEN THE GODS OF DESTRUCTION SHOULD BE BARELY STANDING AT THIS POINT.

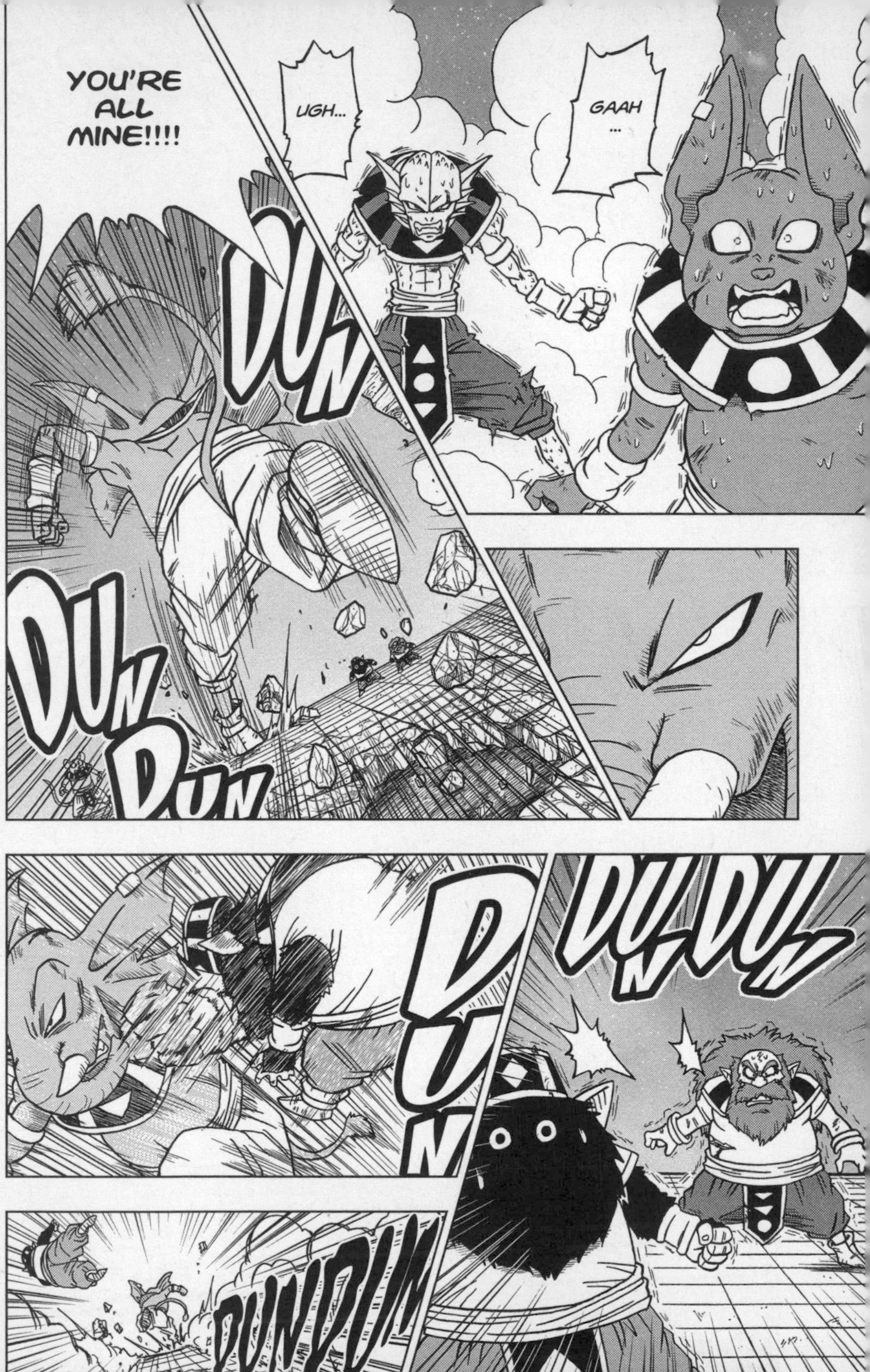

GAAH ...
UGH...
YOU'RE ALL MINE!!!!
DUN
DUN DUN
DUN DUN
DUN
DUNDUN

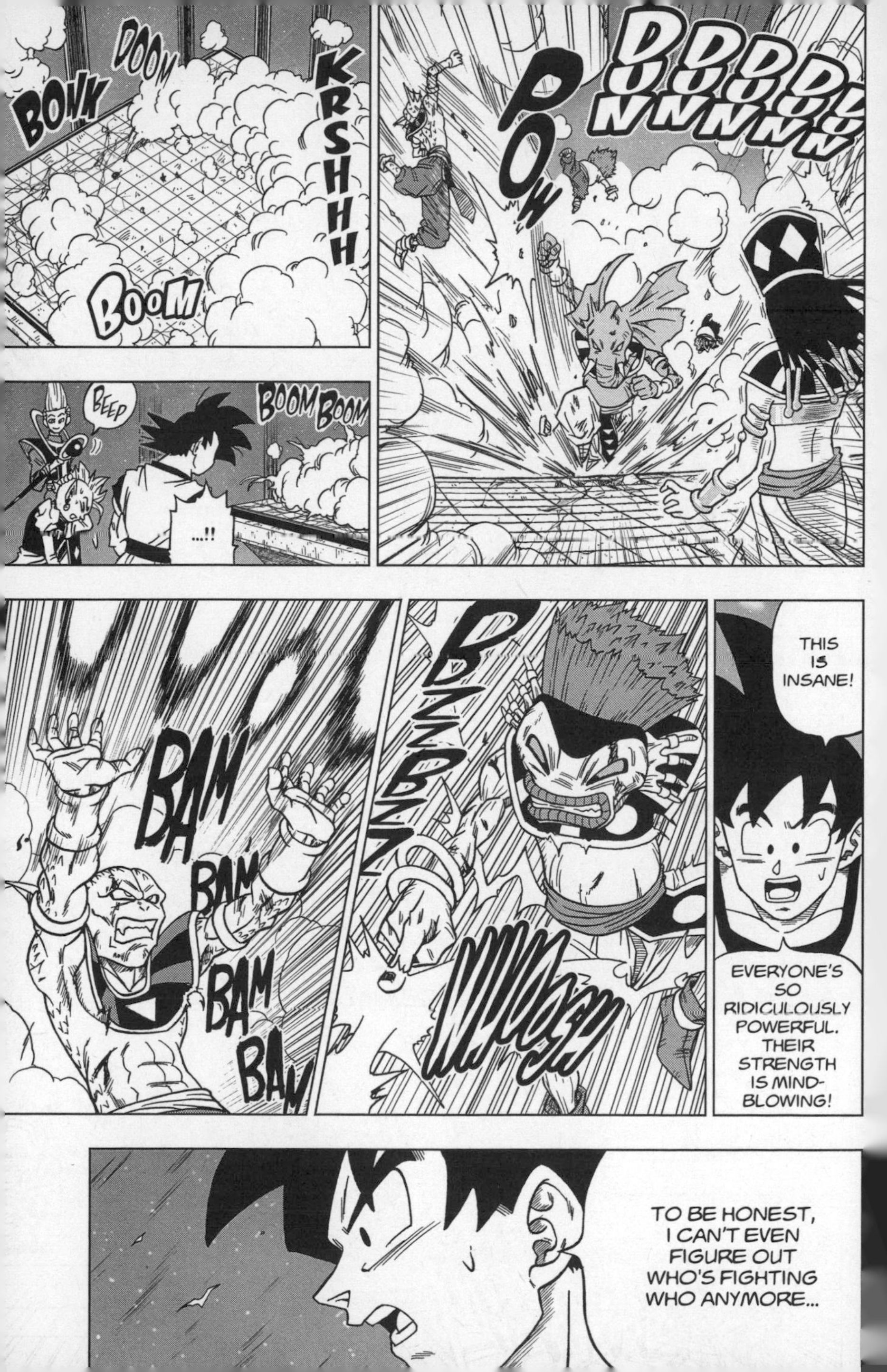
POW
BONK
DOOM
KRSHHHH
BOOM
BEEP
BOOM BOOM
...!!
THIS IS INSANE!
EVERYONE'S SO RIDICULOUSLY POWERFUL. THEIR STRENGTH IS MIND-BLOWING!
BAM BA
BAM
BAM
BAM
TO BE HONEST, I CAN'T EVEN FIGURE OUT WHO'S FIGHTING WHO ANYMORE...

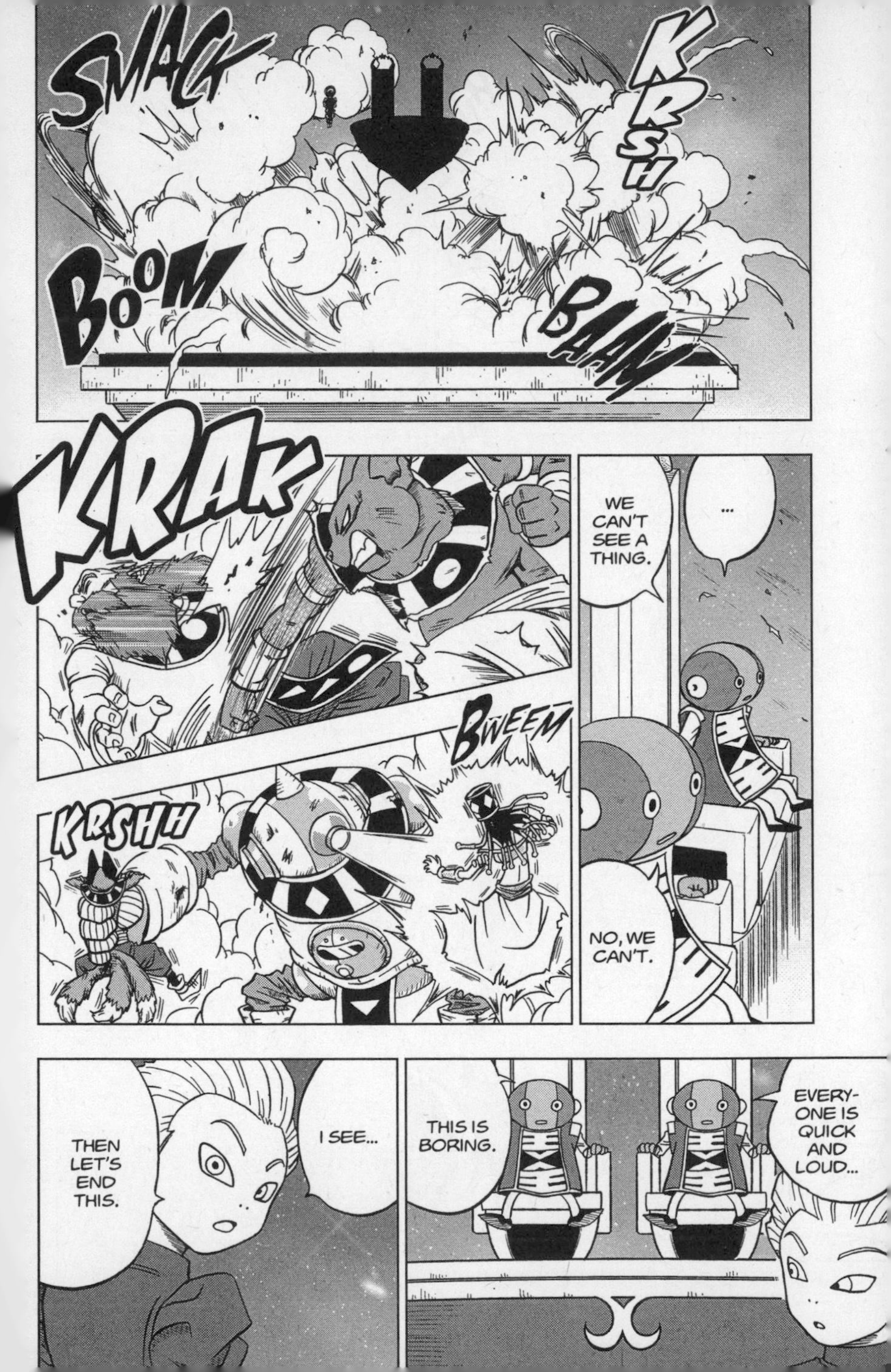
KRSH
SMACK
BAM
BOOM
...
WE CAN'T SEE A THING.
NO, WE CAN'T.
KRAK
BWEEM
KRSHH
EVERYONE IS QUICK AND LOUD...
THIS IS BORING.
I SEE...
THEN LET'S END THIS.

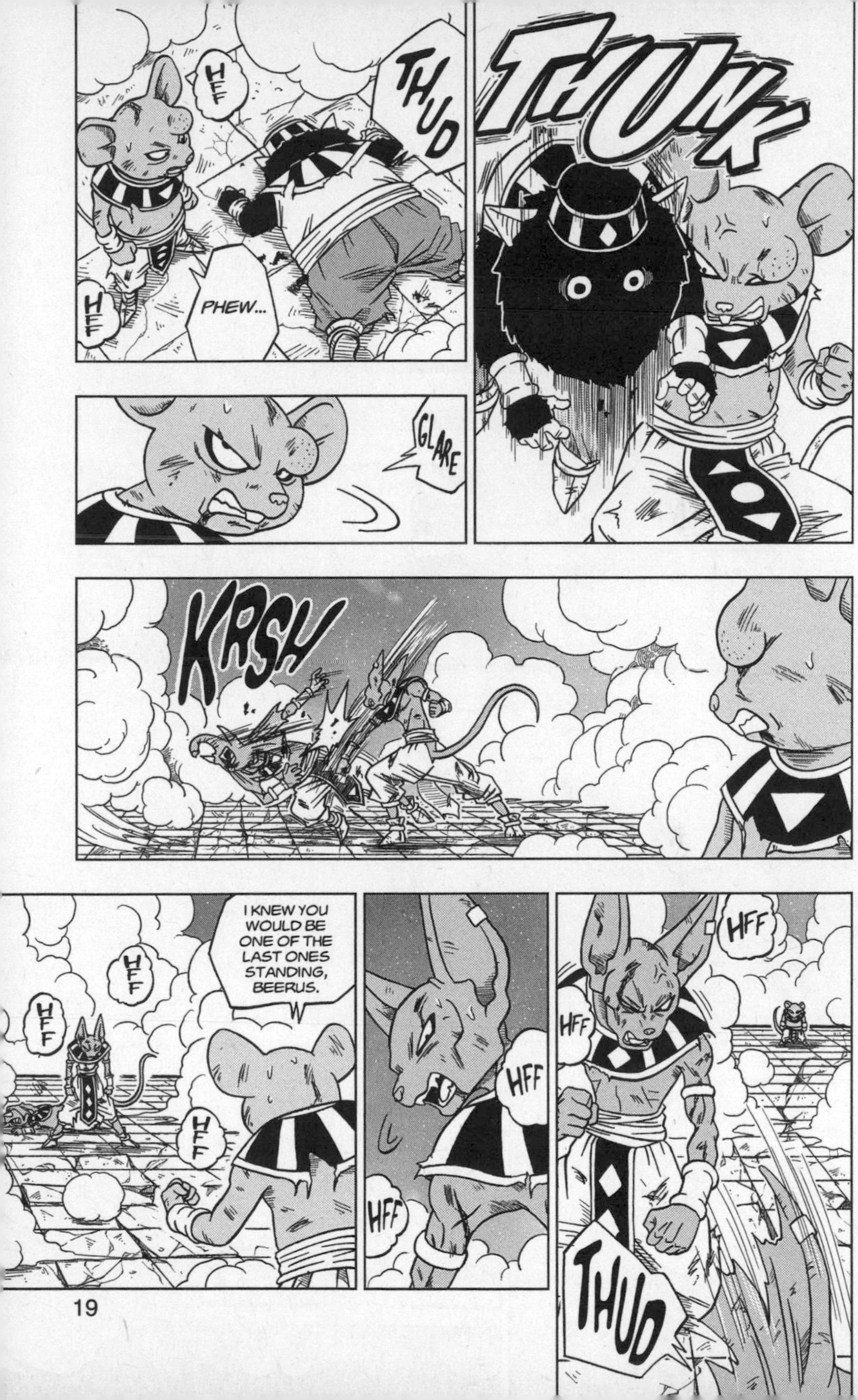
THUNK
THUD
HFF
PHEW...
HFF
GLARE
KRSH
HFF
HFF
THUD
HFF
HFF
I KNEW YOU WOULD BE ONE OF THE LAST ONES STANDING, BEERUS.
HFF
HFF
HFF

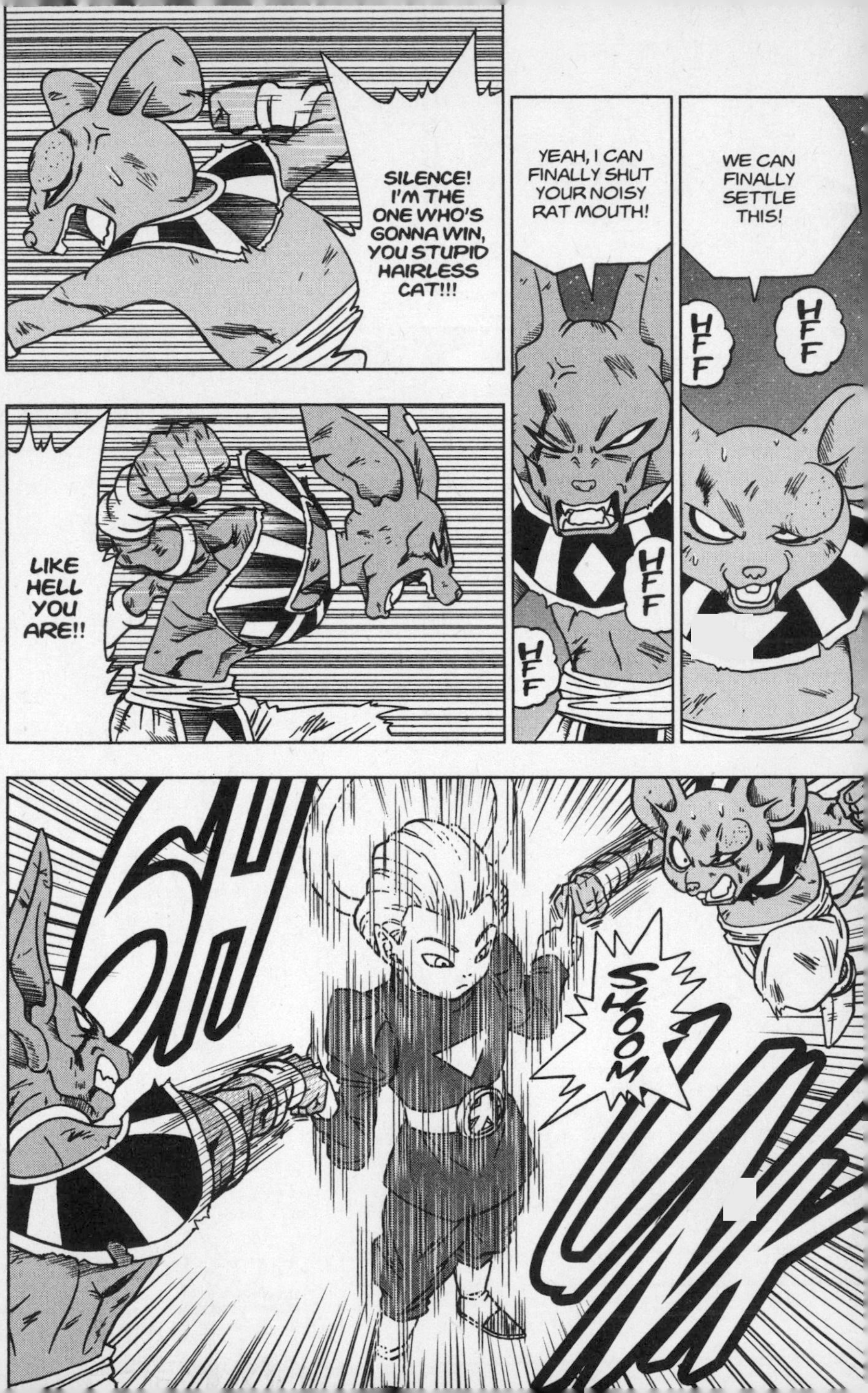
WE CAN FINALLY SETTLE THIS!
HFF HFF
YEAH, I CAN FINALLY SHUT YOUR NOISY RAT MOUTH!
HFF HFF
HFF HFF
SILENCE! I'M THE ONE WHO'S GONNA WIN, YOU STUPID HAIRLESS CAT!!!
LIKE HELL YOU ARE!!
SHOOM

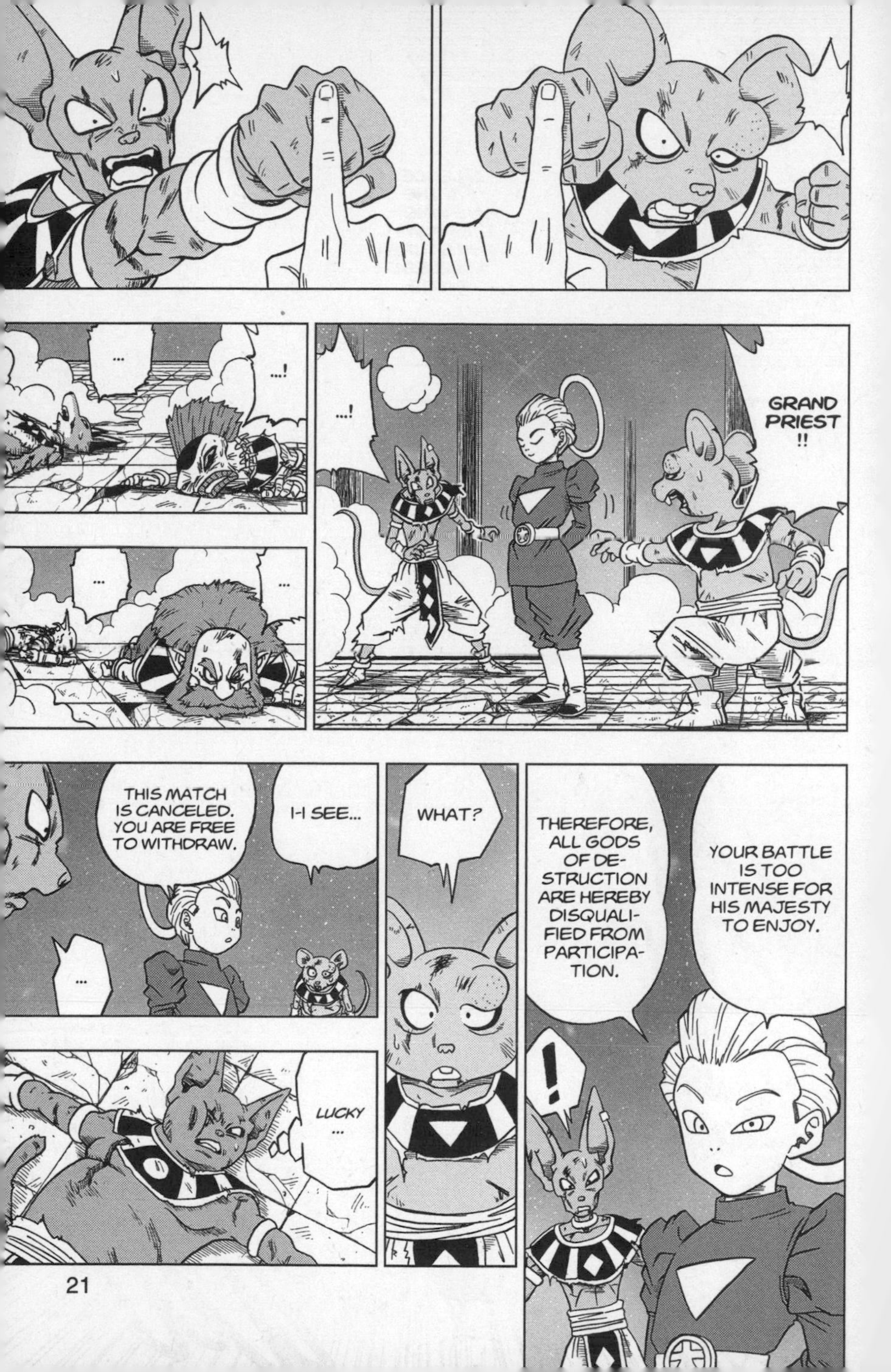
GRAND PRIEST !!
...!
...!
...
...
...
YOUR BATTLE IS TOO INTENSE FOR HIS MAJESTY TO ENJOY.
THEREFORE, ALL GODS OF DESTRUCTION ARE HEREBY DISQUALIFIED FROM PARTICIPATION.
!
WHAT?
I-I SEE...
THIS MATCH IS CANCELED. YOU ARE FREE TO WITHDRAW.
...
LUCKY ...

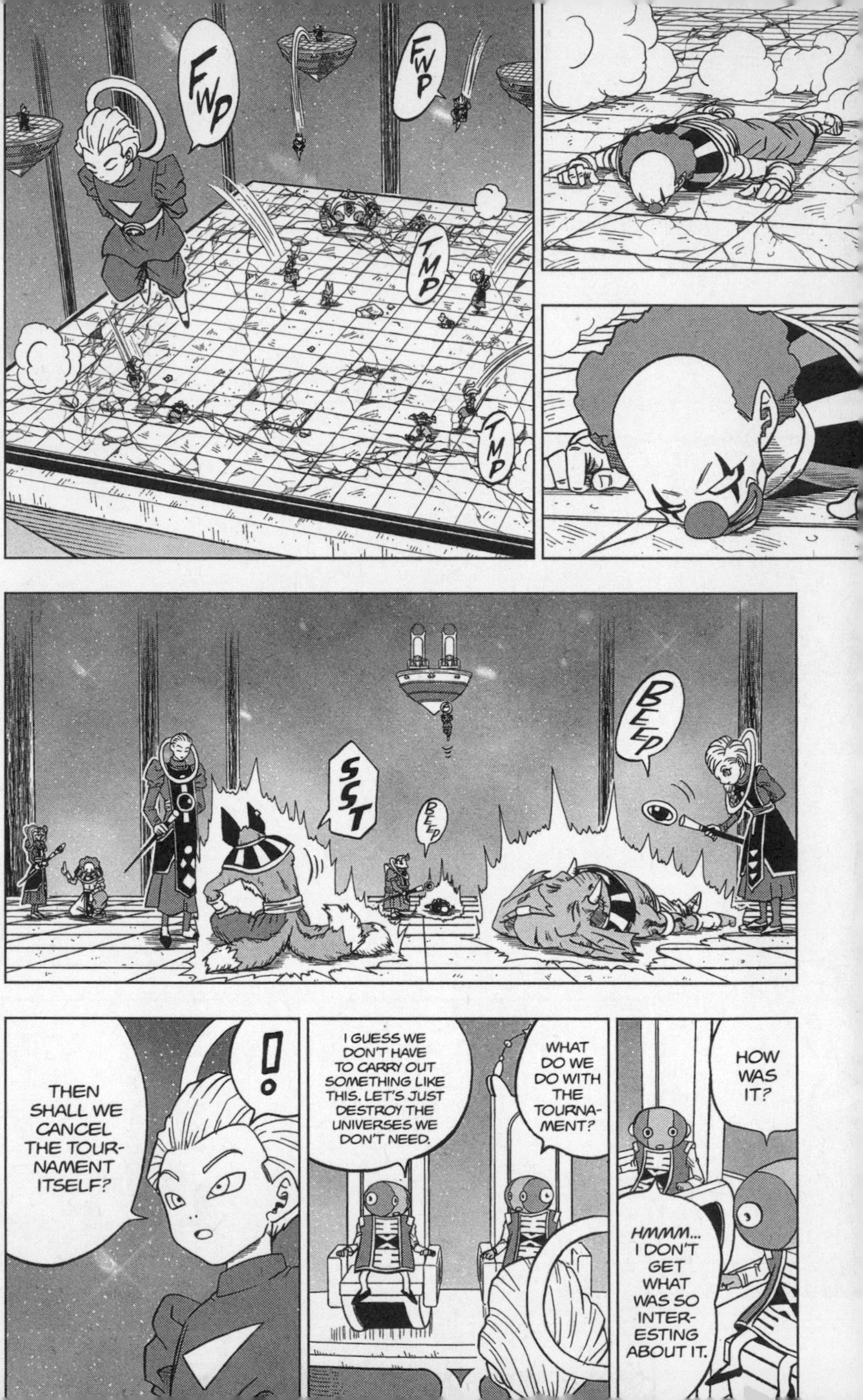
FWP
FWP
TMP
TMP
BEEP
SST
BEEP
HOW WAS IT?
HMMM... I DON'T GET WHAT WAS SO INTERESTING ABOUT IT.
WHAT DO WE DO WITH THE TOURNAMENT?
I GUESS WE DON'T HAVE TO CARRY OUT SOMETHING LIKE THIS. LET'S JUST DESTROY THE UNIVERSES WE DON'T NEED.
!
THEN SHALL WE CANCEL THE TOURNAMENT ITSELF?

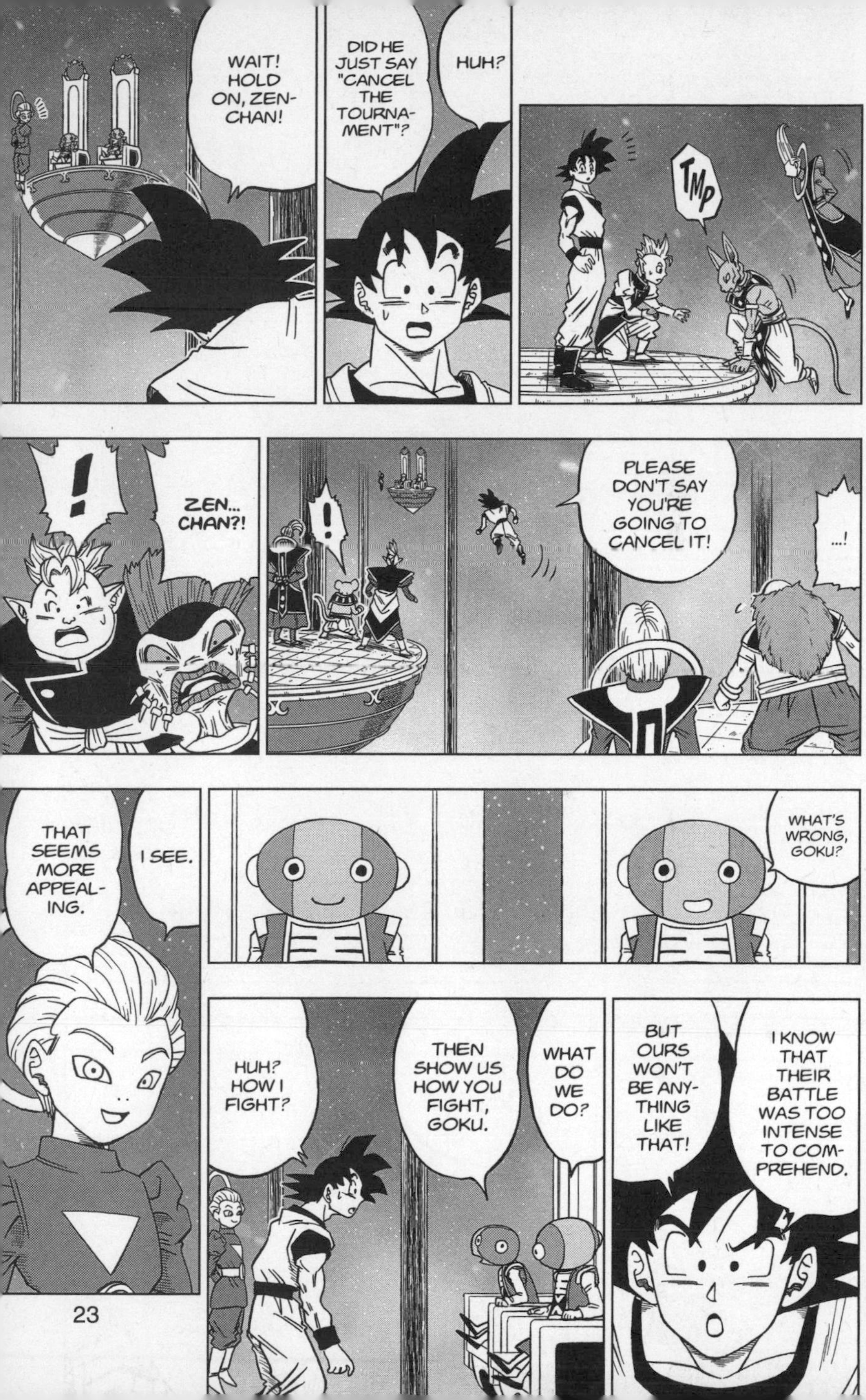
TMP
HUH?
DID HE JUST SAY "CANCEL THE TOURNAMENT"?
WAIT! HOLD ON, ZEN-CHAN!
...!
PLEASE DON'T SAY YOU'RE GOING TO CANCEL IT!
!
ZEN... CHAN?!
!
WHAT'S WRONG, GOKU?
I KNOW THAT THEIR BATTLE WAS TOO INTENSE TO COMPREHEND.
BUT OURS WON'T BE ANYTHING LIKE THAT!
WHAT DO WE DO?
THEN SHOW US HOW YOU FIGHT, GOKU.
HUH? HOW I FIGHT?
I SEE.
THAT SEEMS MORE APPEALING.

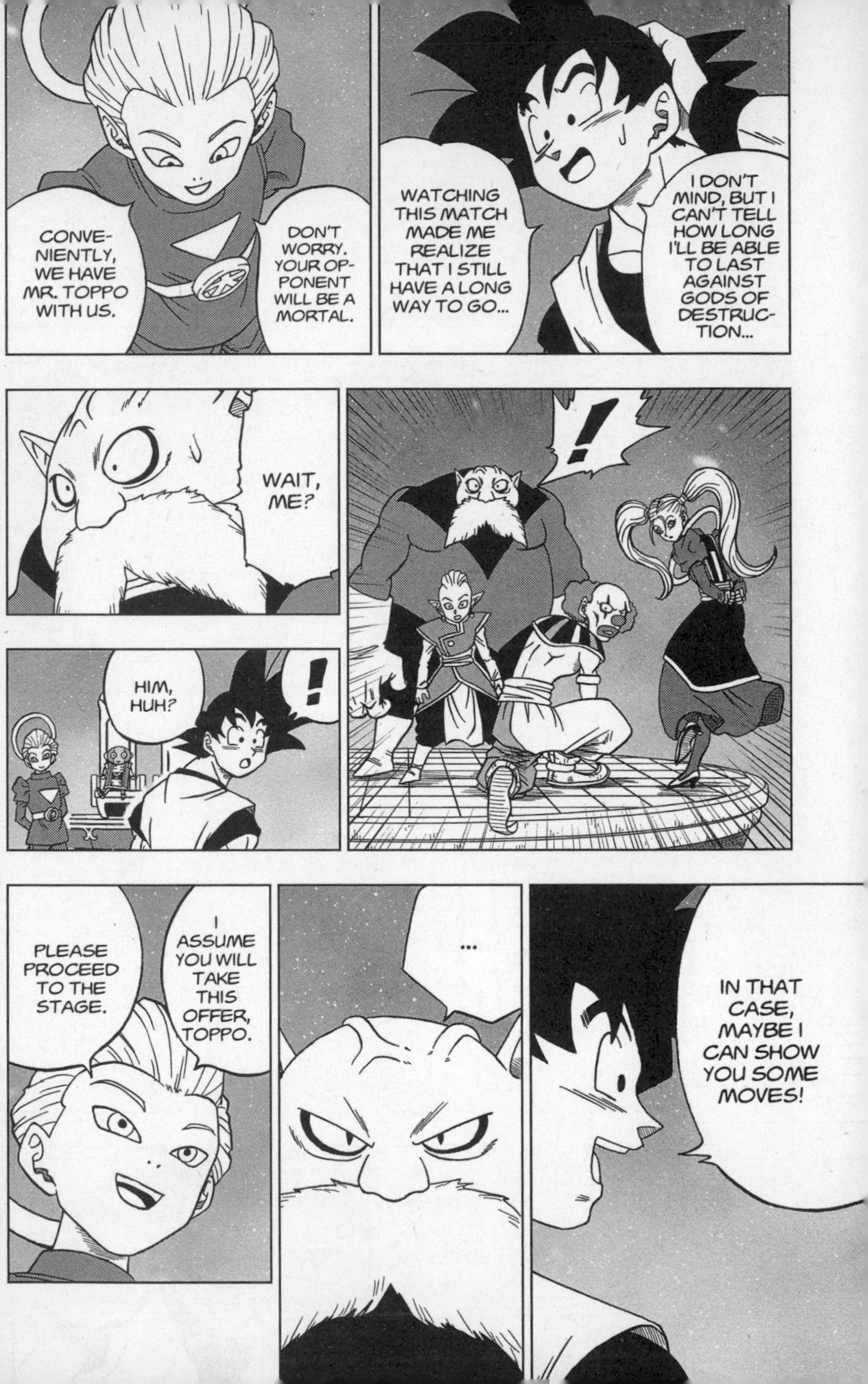
I DON'T MIND, BUT I CAN'T TELL HOW LONG I'LL BE ABLE TO LAST AGAINST GODS OF DESTRUCTION...
WATCHING THIS MATCH MADE ME REALIZE THAT I STILL HAVE A LONG WAY TO GO...
DON'T WORRY. YOUR OPPONENT WILL BE A MORTAL.
CONVENIENTLY, WE HAVE MR. TOPPO WITH US.
!
WAIT, ME?
!
HIM, HUH?
IN THAT CASE, MAYBE I CAN SHOW YOU SOME MOVES!
...
I ASSUME YOU WILL TAKE THIS OFFER, TOPPO.
PLEASE PROCEED TO THE STAGE.

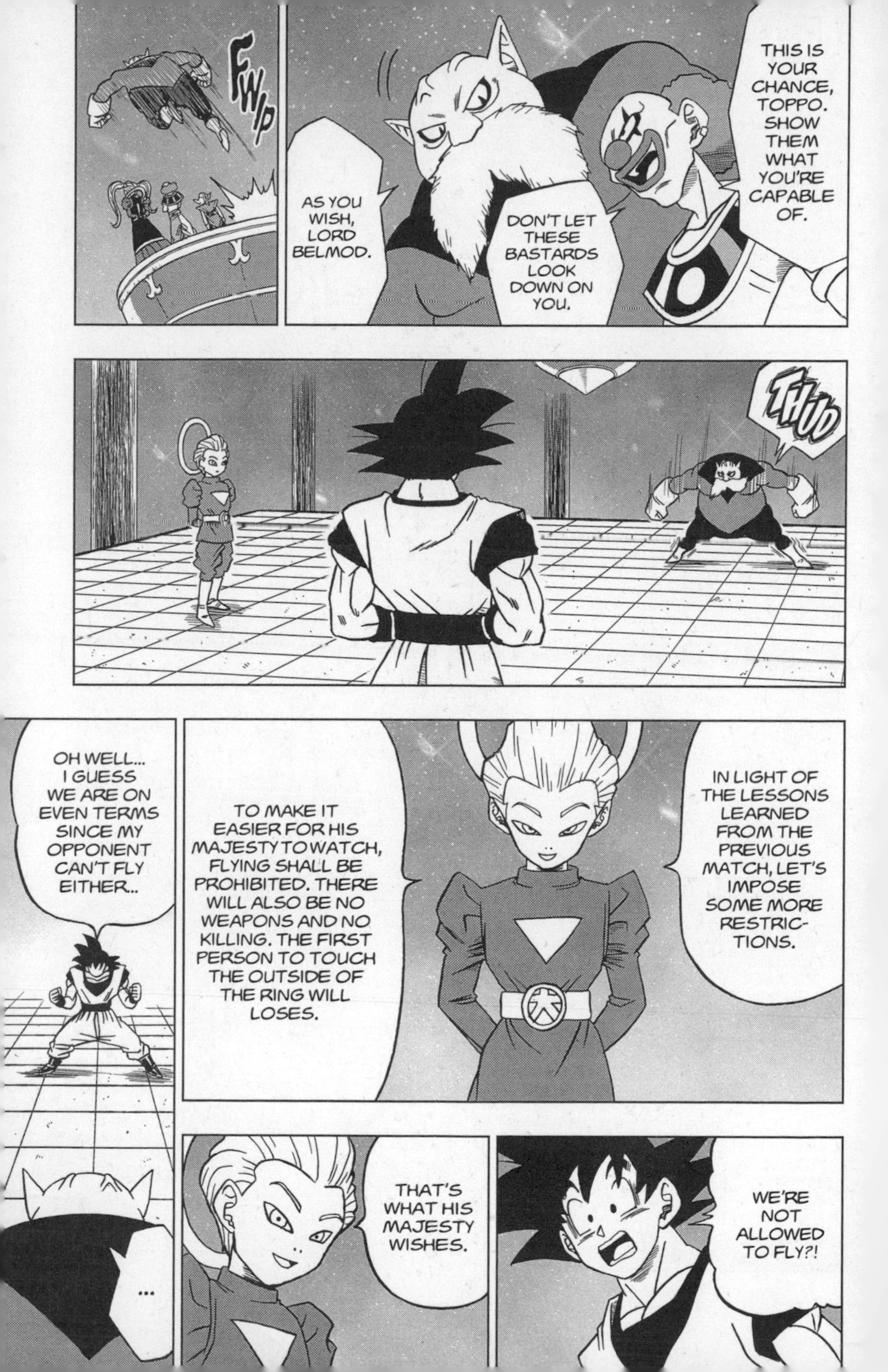
THIS IS YOUR CHANCE, TOPPO. SHOW THEM WHAT YOU'RE CAPABLE OF.
DON'T LET THESE BASTARDS LOOK DOWN ON YOU.
AS YOU WISH, LORD BELMOD.
FWIP
THUD
IN LIGHT OF THE LESSONS LEARNED FROM THE PREVIOUS MATCH, LET'S IMPOSE SOME MORE RESTRIC-TIONS.
TO MAKE IT EASIER FOR HIS MAJESTY TO WATCH, FLYING SHALL BE PROHIBITED. THERE WILL ALSO BE NO WEAPONS AND NO KILLING. THE FIRST PERSON TO TOUCH THE OUTSIDE OF THE RING WILL LOSES.
OH WELL... I GUESS WE ARE ON EVEN TERMS SINCE MY OPPONENT CAN'T FLY EITHER...
WE'RE NOT ALLOWED TO FLY?!
THAT'S WHAT HIS MAJESTY WISHES.
...

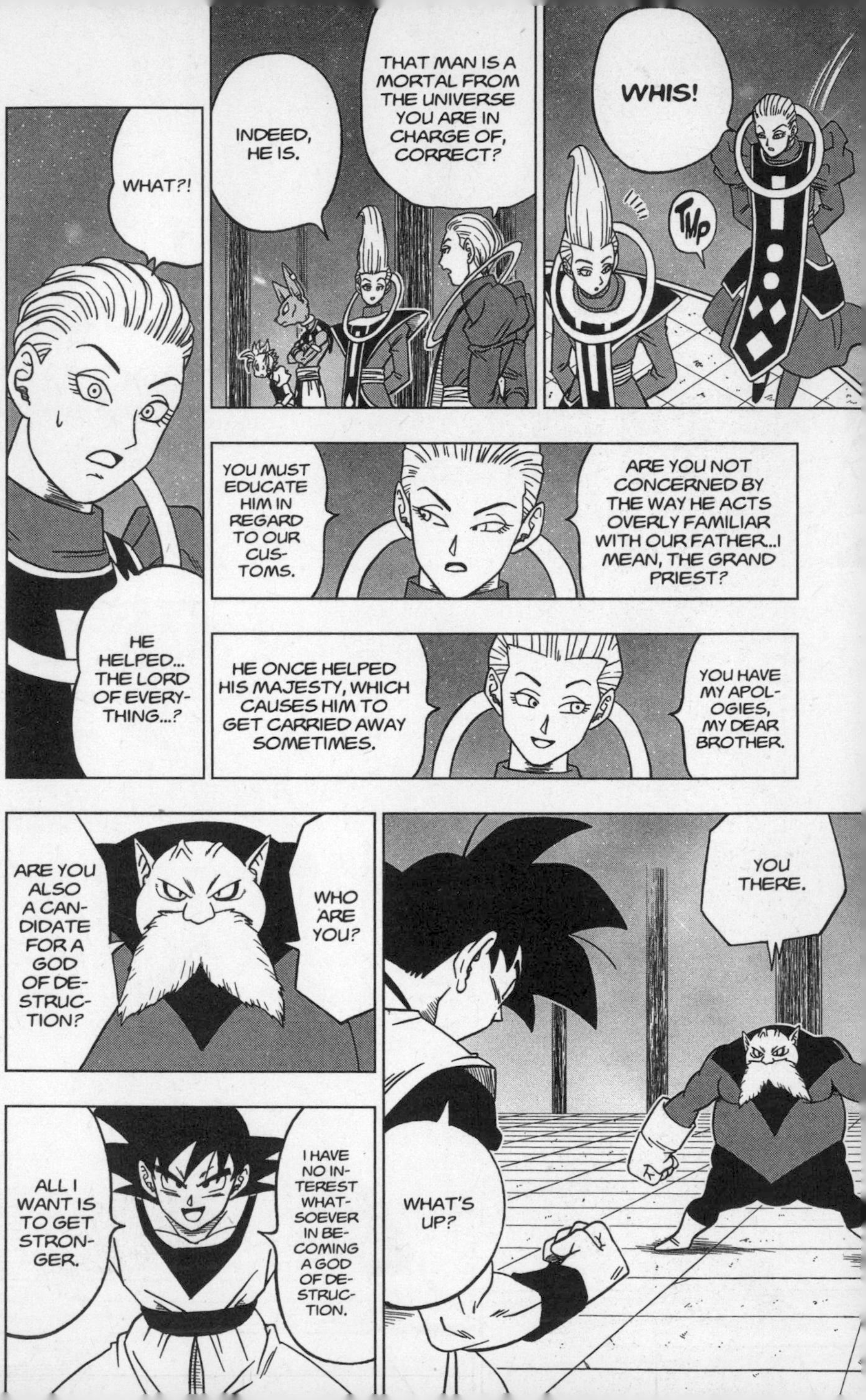
WHIS!
TMP
THAT MAN IS A MORTAL FROM THE UNIVERSE YOU ARE IN CHARGE OF, CORRECT?
INDEED, HE IS.
ARE YOU NOT CONCERNED BY THE WAY HE ACTS OVERLY FAMILIAR WITH OUR FATHER...I MEAN, THE GRAND PRIEST?
YOU MUST EDUCATE HIM IN REGARD TO OUR CUS-TOMS.
YOU HAVE MY APOL-OGIES, MY DEAR BROTHER.
HE ONCE HELPED HIS MAJESTY, WHICH CAUSES HIM TO GET CARRIED AWAY SOMETIMES.
WHAT?!
HE HELPED... THE LORD OF EVERY-THING...?
YOU THERE.
WHAT'S UP?
WHO ARE YOU?
ARE YOU ALSO A CAN-DIDATE FOR A GOD OF DE-STRUC-TION?
I HAVE NO IN-TEREST WHAT-SOEVER IN BE-COMING A GOD OF DE-STRUC-TION.
ALL I WANT IS TO GET STRON-GER.

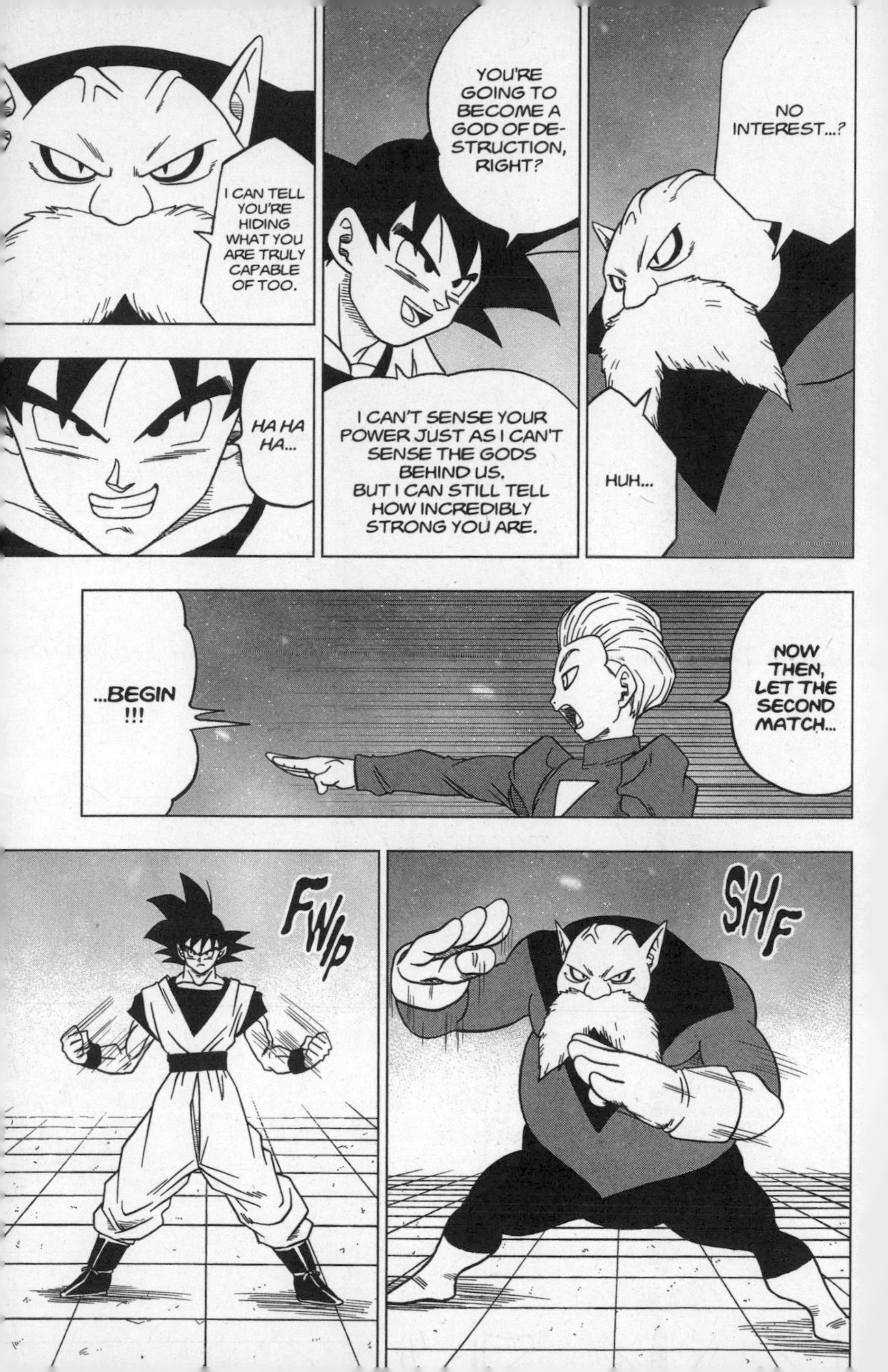
NO INTEREST...?
HUH...
YOU'RE GOING TO BECOME A GOD OF DE-STRUCTION, RIGHT?
I CAN'T SENSE YOUR POWER JUST AS I CAN'T SENSE THE GODS BEHIND US. BUT I CAN STILL TELL HOW INCREDIBLY STRONG YOU ARE.
I CAN TELL YOU'RE HIDING WHAT YOU ARE TRULY CAPABLE OF TOO.
HA HA HA...
NOW THEN, LET THE SECOND MATCH...
...BEGIN!!!
SHF
FWIP

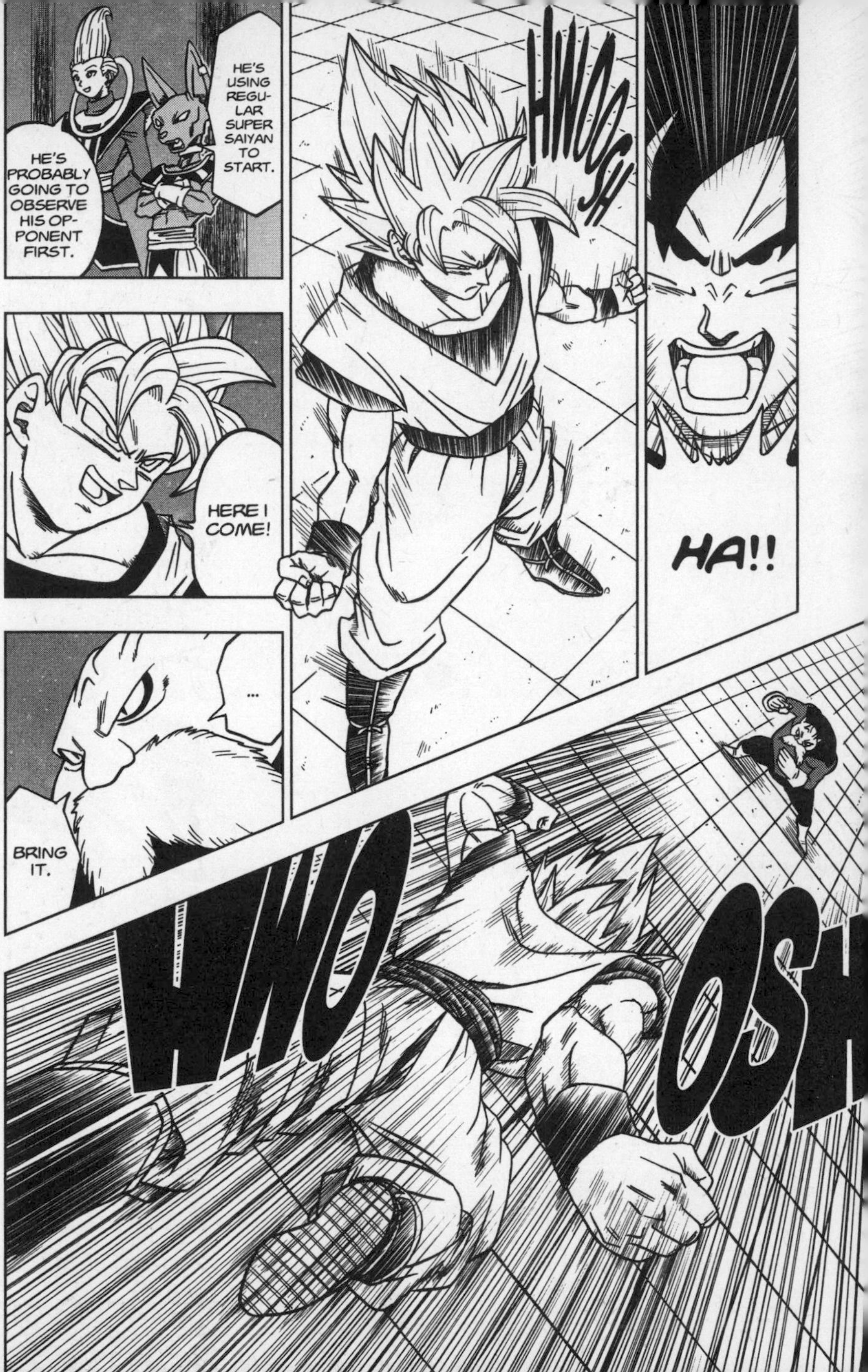
HA!!
HWOOSH
HE'S USING REGULAR SUPER SAIYAN TO START.
HE'S PROBABLY GOING TO OBSERVE HIS OPPONENT FIRST.
HERE I COME!
...
BRING IT.
HWOOSH

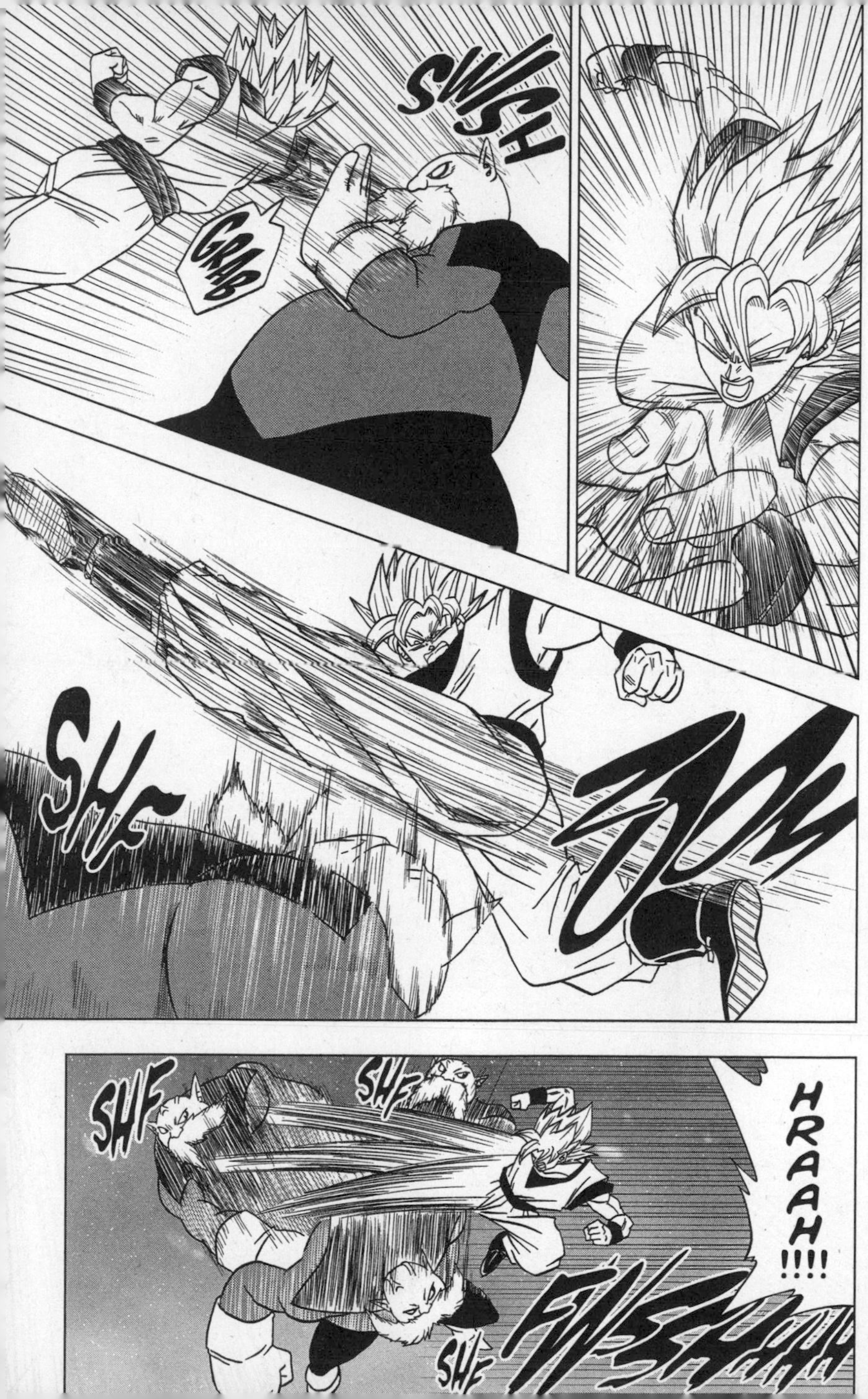
SWISH
GRAB
ZOOM
SHF
HRAAAH!!!!
SHF
SHF
SHF
FWSHHHH

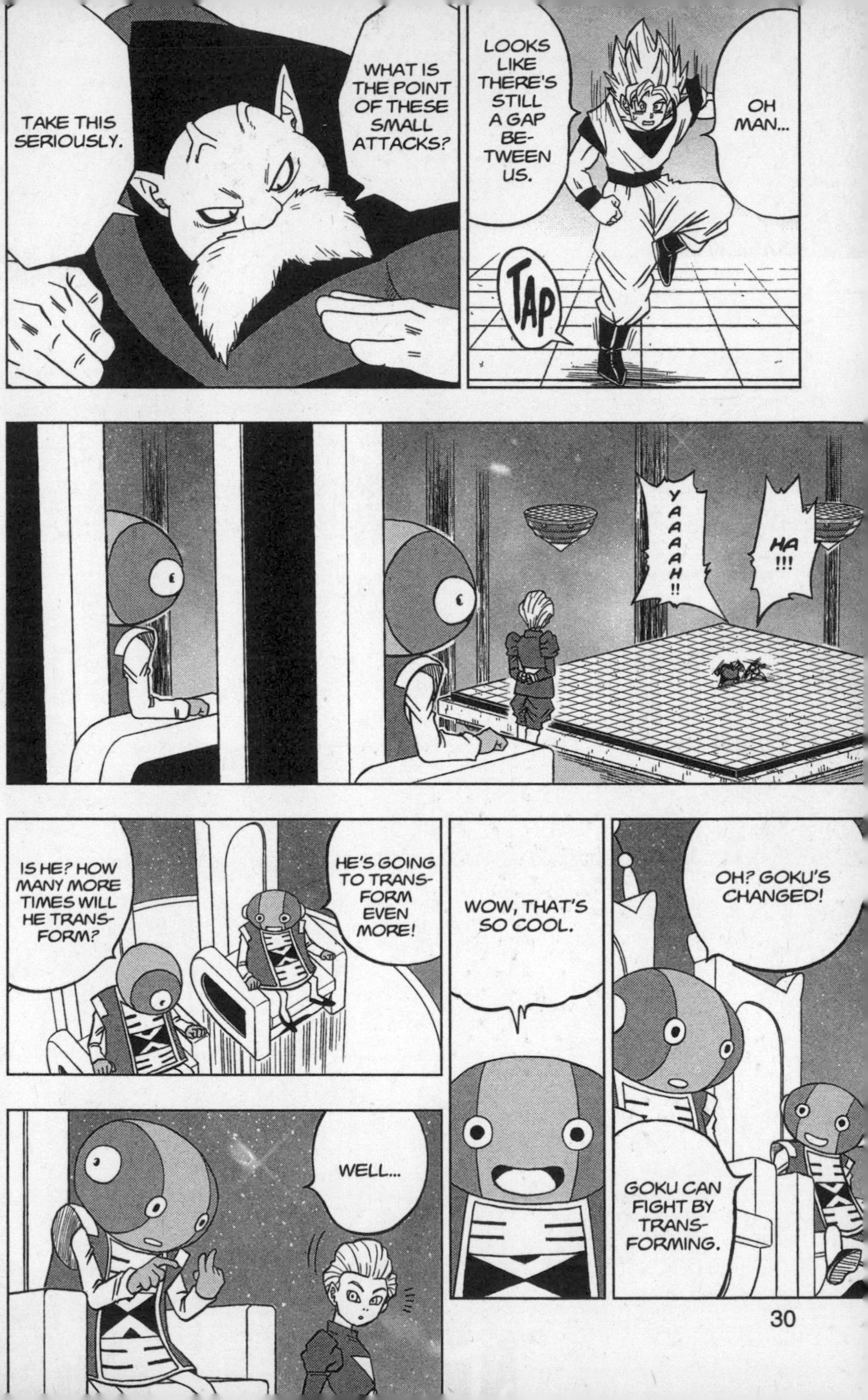
OH MAN...
LOOKS LIKE THERE'S STILL A GAP BE- TWEEN US.
TAP
WHAT IS THE POINT OF THESE SMALL ATTACKS?
TAKE THIS SERIOUSLY.
HA !!!
YAAAAAH!!
OH? GOKU'S CHANGED!
GOKU CAN FIGHT BY TRANS- FORMING.
WOW, THAT'S SO COOL.
HE'S GOING TO TRANS- FORM EVEN MORE!
IS HE? HOW MANY MORE TIMES WILL HE TRANS- FORM?
WELL...

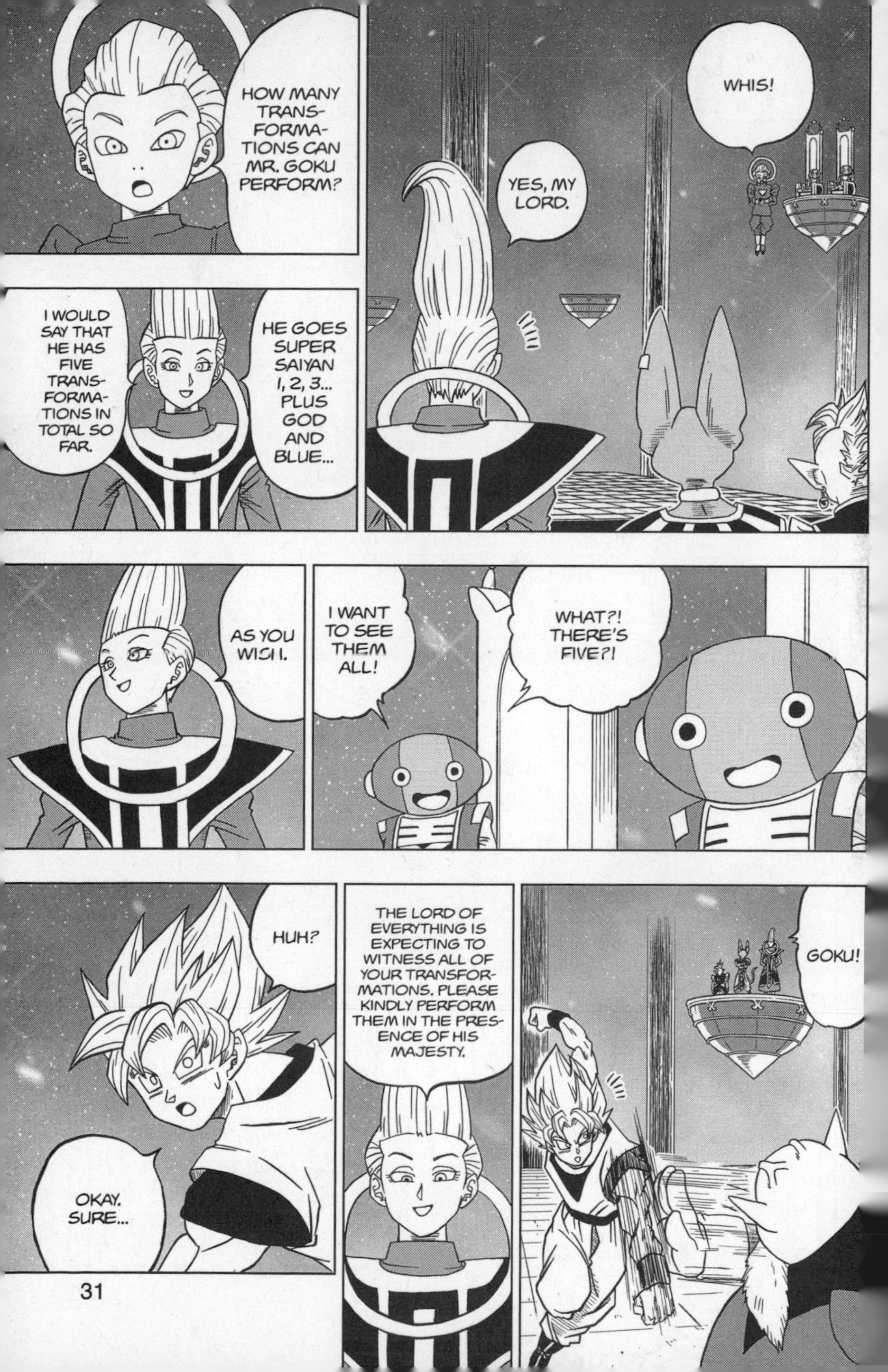
WHIS!
YES, MY LORD.
HOW MANY TRANSFORMATIONS CAN MR. GOKU PERFORM?
HE GOES SUPER SAIYAN 1, 2, 3... PLUS GOD AND BLUE...
I WOULD SAY THAT HE HAS FIVE TRANSFORMATIONS IN TOTAL SO FAR.
WHAT?! THERE'S FIVE?!
I WANT TO SEE THEM ALL!
AS YOU WISH.
GOKU!
THE LORD OF EVERYTHING IS EXPECTING TO WITNESS ALL OF YOUR TRANSFORMATIONS. PLEASE KINDLY PERFORM THEM IN THE PRESENCE OF HIS MAJESTY.
HUH?
OKAY. SURE...

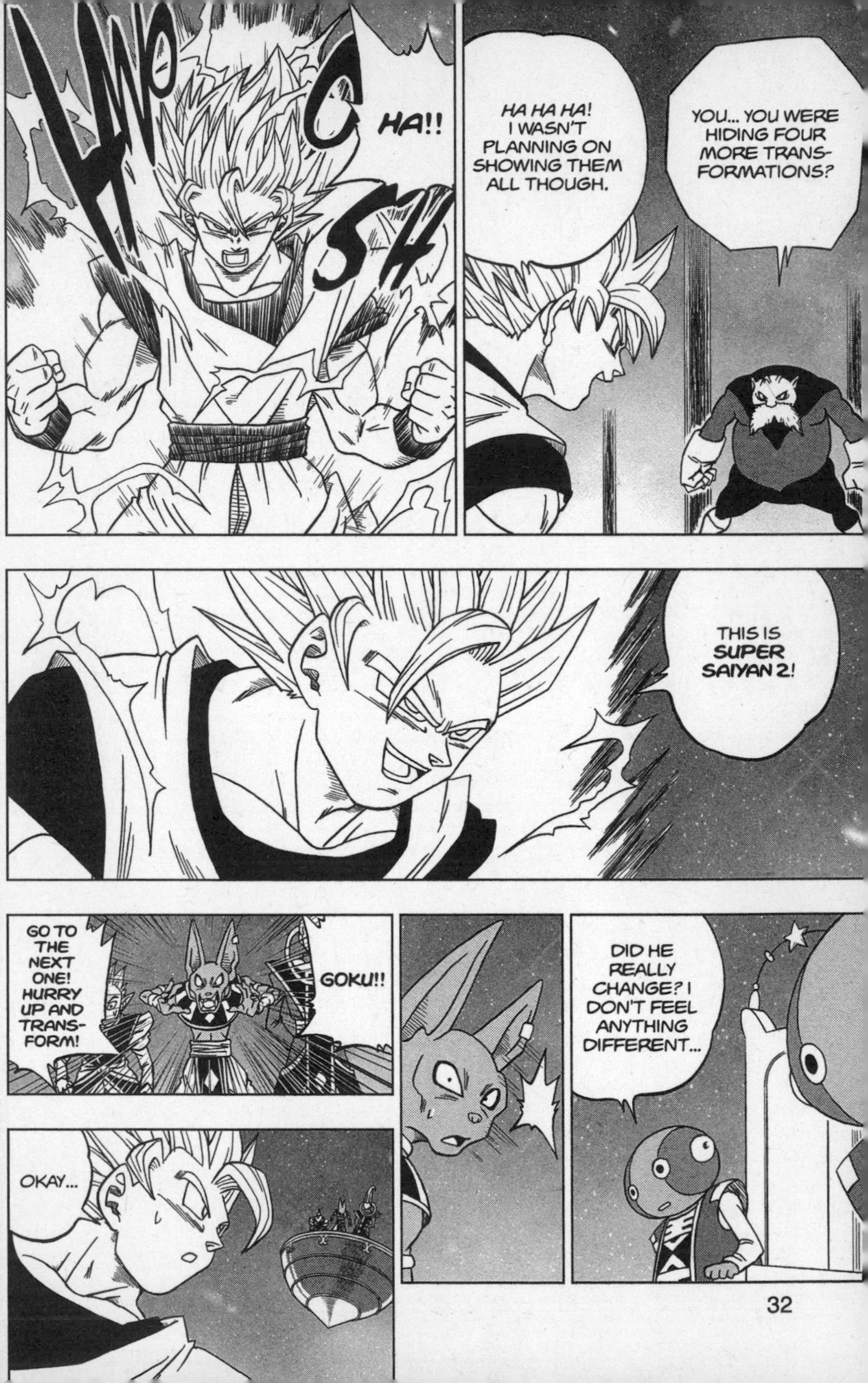
YOU... YOU WERE HIDING FOUR MORE TRANS-FORMATIONS?
HA HA HA! I WASN'T PLANNING ON SHOWING THEM ALL THOUGH.
HA!!
THIS IS SUPER SAIYAN 2!
DID HE REALLY CHANGE? I DON'T FEEL ANYTHING DIFFERENT...
GOKU!!
GO TO THE NEXT ONE! HURRY UP AND TRANSFORM!
OKAY...

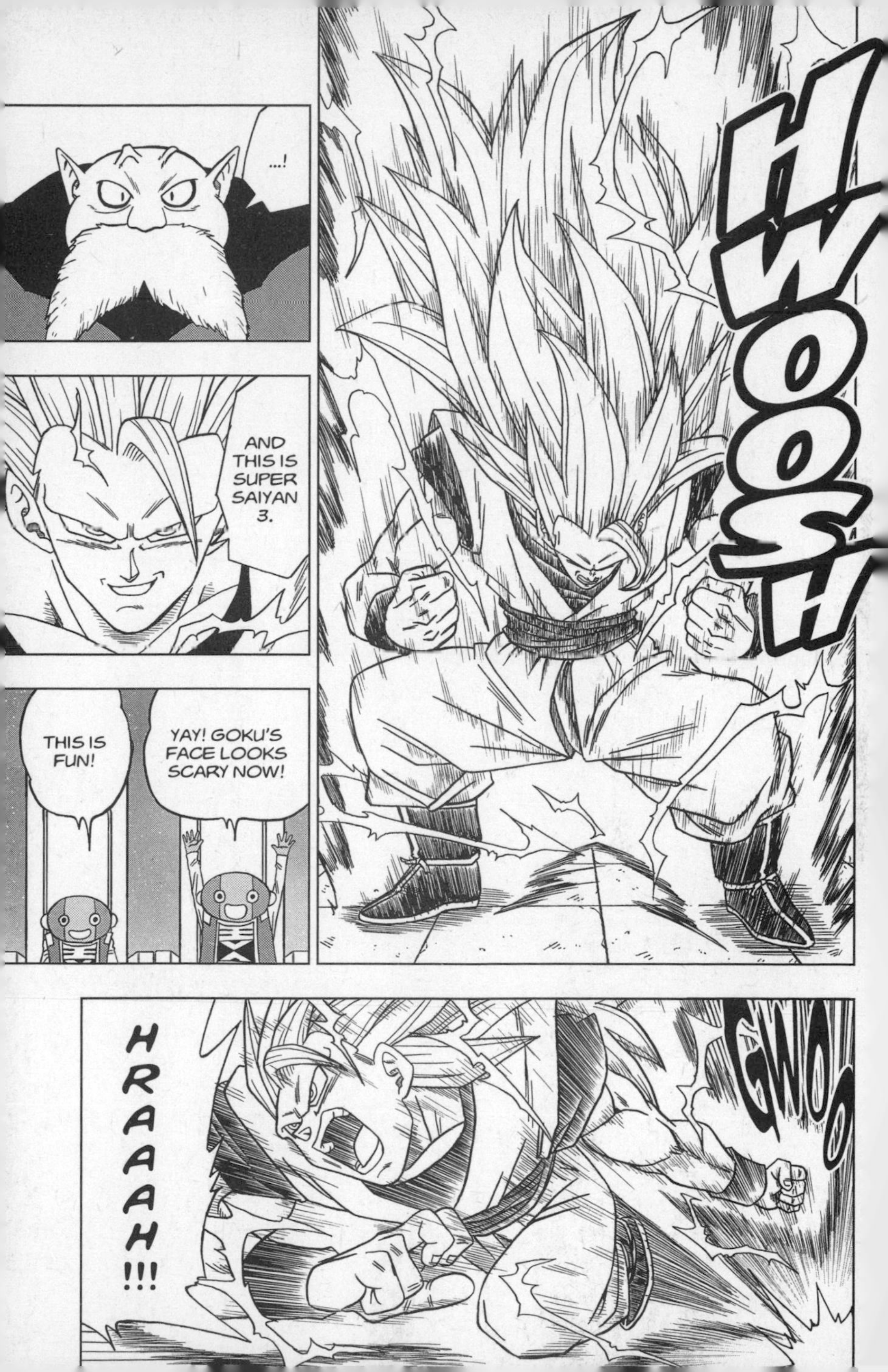
WHOOSH
...!
AND THIS IS SUPER SAIYAN 3.
YAY! GOKU'S FACE LOOKS SCARY NOW!
THIS IS FUN!
GWOO
HRAAAAH!!!

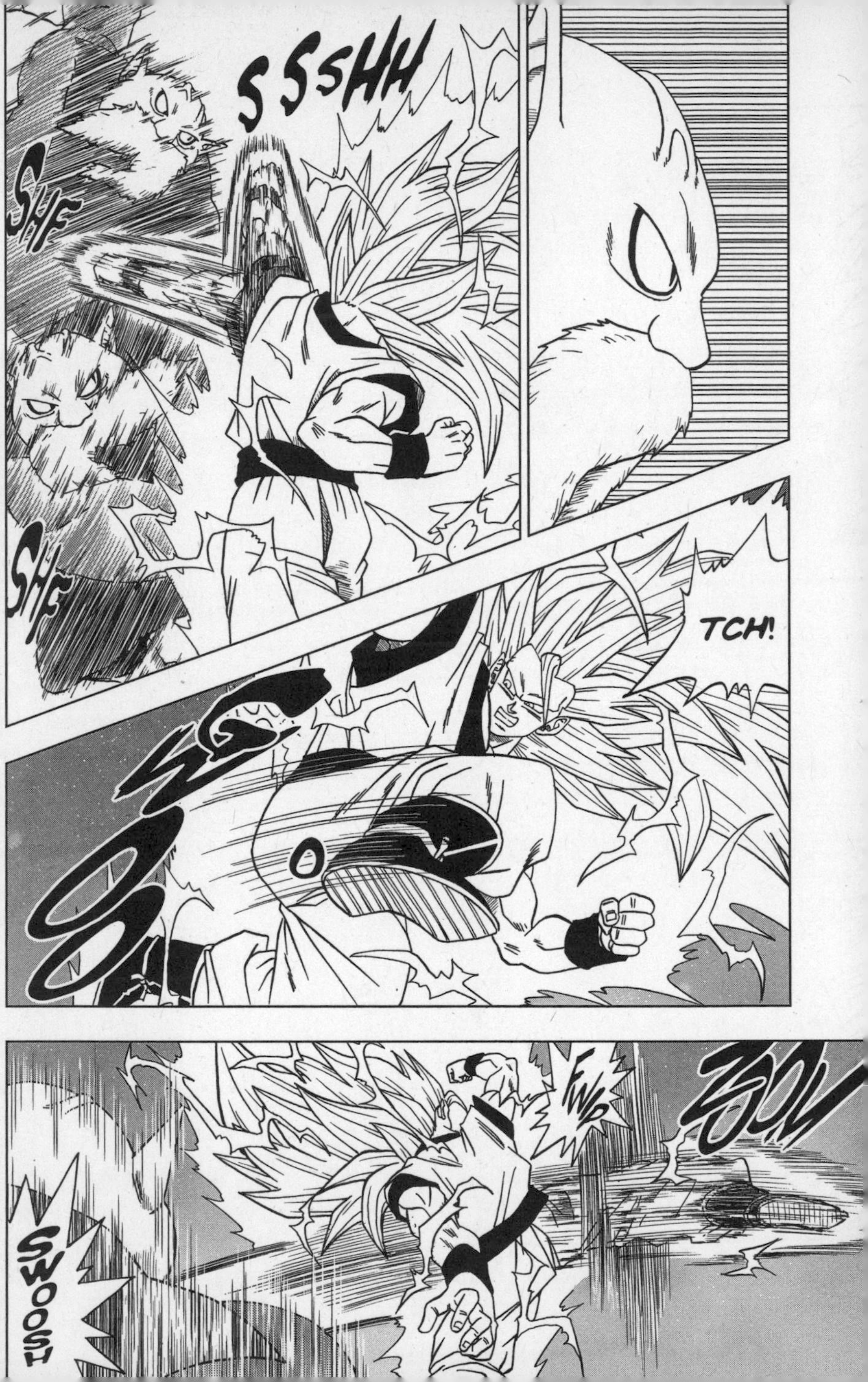
SSSHH
SHF
SHF
TCH!
SWOOSH

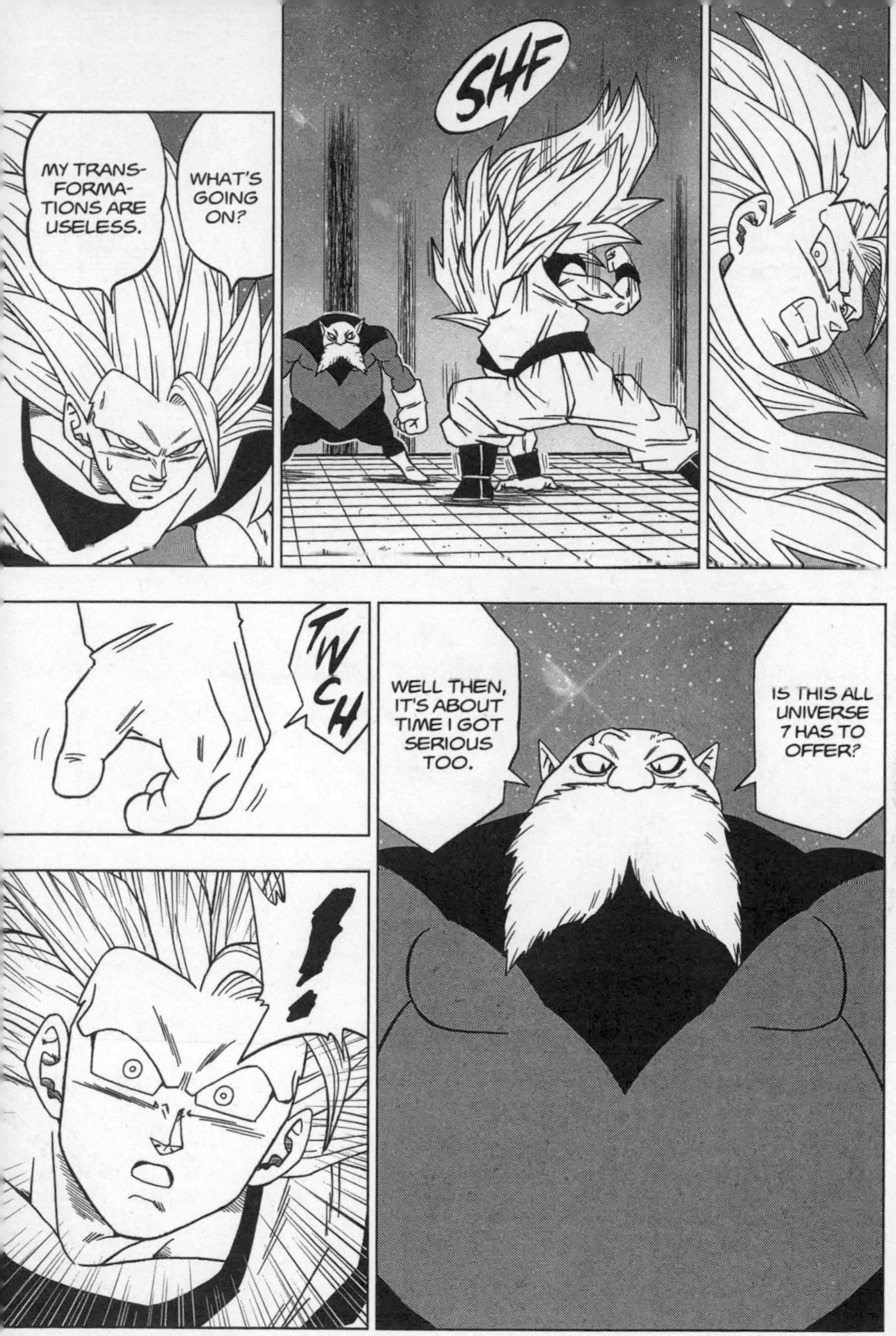

SHF
WHAT'S GOING ON?
MY TRANS-FORMA-TIONS ARE USELESS.
IS THIS ALL UNIVERSE 7 HAS TO OFFER?
WELL THEN, IT'S ABOUT TIME I GOT SERIOUS TOO.
TWCH
!

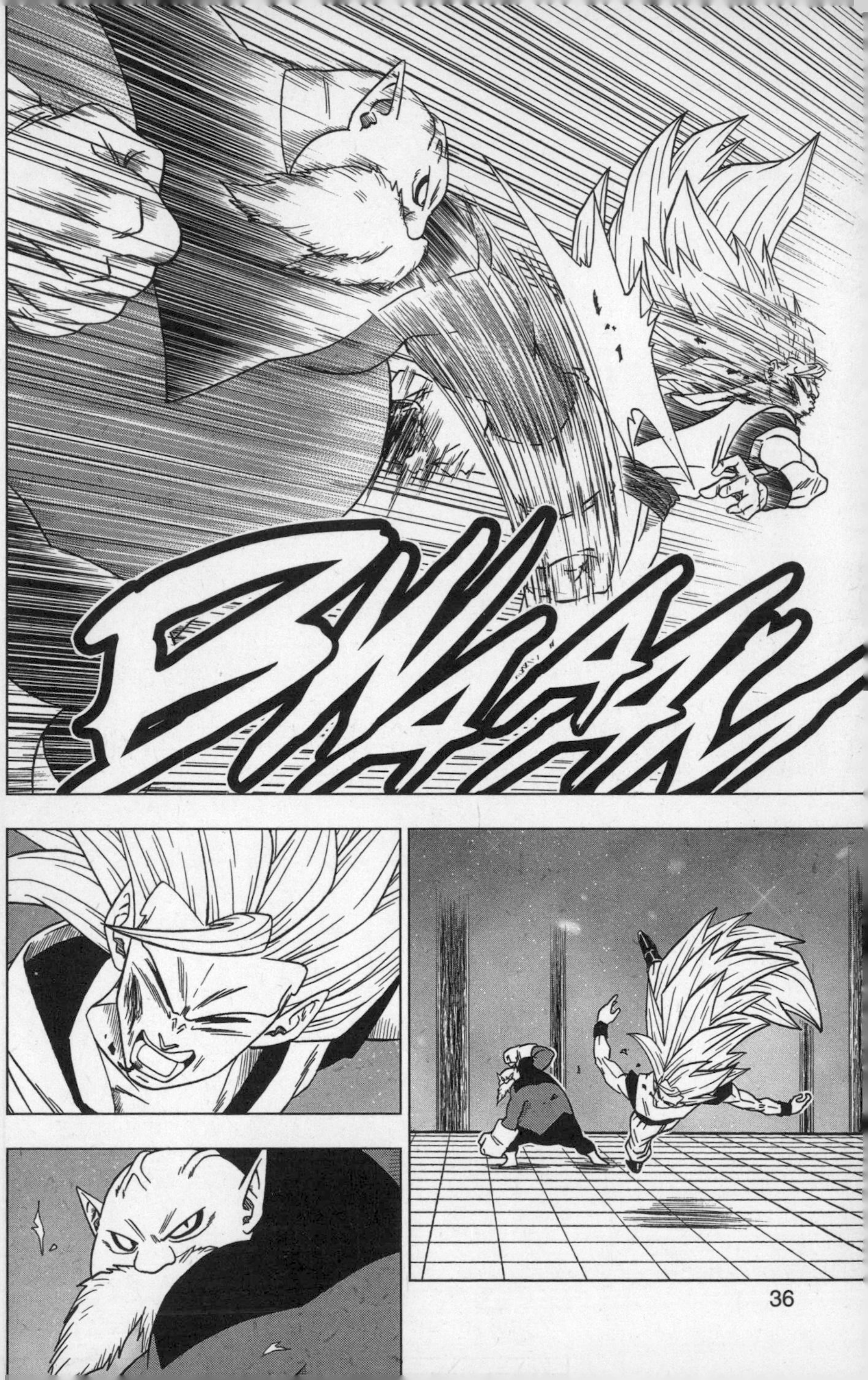

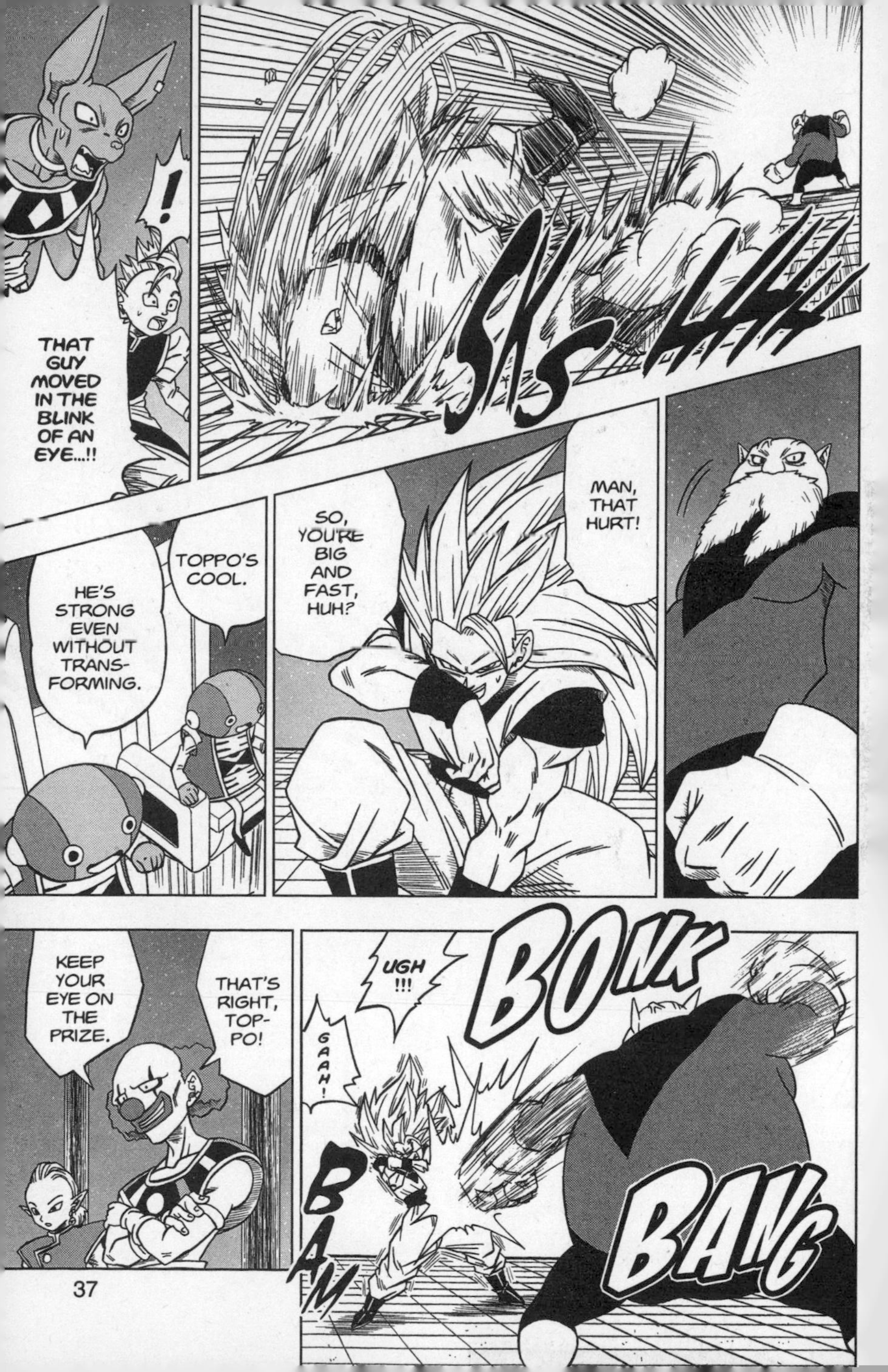
!
THAT GUY MOVED IN THE BLINK OF AN EYE...!!
MAN, THAT HURT!
SO, YOU'RE BIG AND FAST, HUH?
TOPPO'S COOL.
HE'S STRONG EVEN WITHOUT TRANSFORMING.
BONK
UGH !!!
GAAH!
BAM
BANG
THAT'S RIGHT, TOP-PO!
KEEP YOUR EYE ON THE PRIZE.

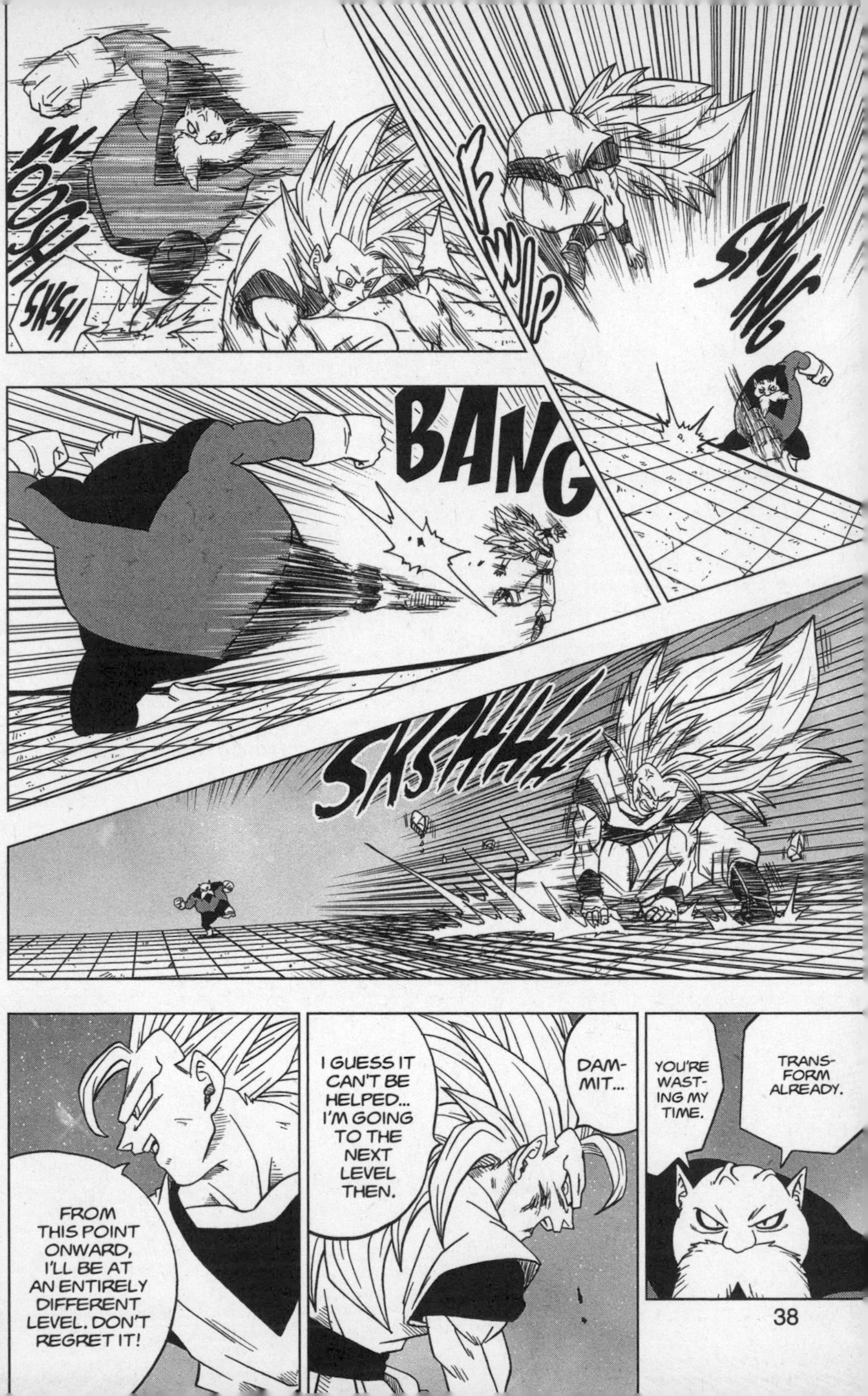
FWIP
SWING
WHOOSH
SKSH
BANG
SKSHHH
TRANSFORM ALREADY.
YOU'RE WASTING MY TIME.
DAMMIT...
I GUESS IT CAN'T BE HELPED... I'M GOING TO THE NEXT LEVEL THEN.
FROM THIS POINT ONWARD, I'LL BE AT AN ENTIRELY DIFFERENT LEVEL. DON'T REGRET IT!

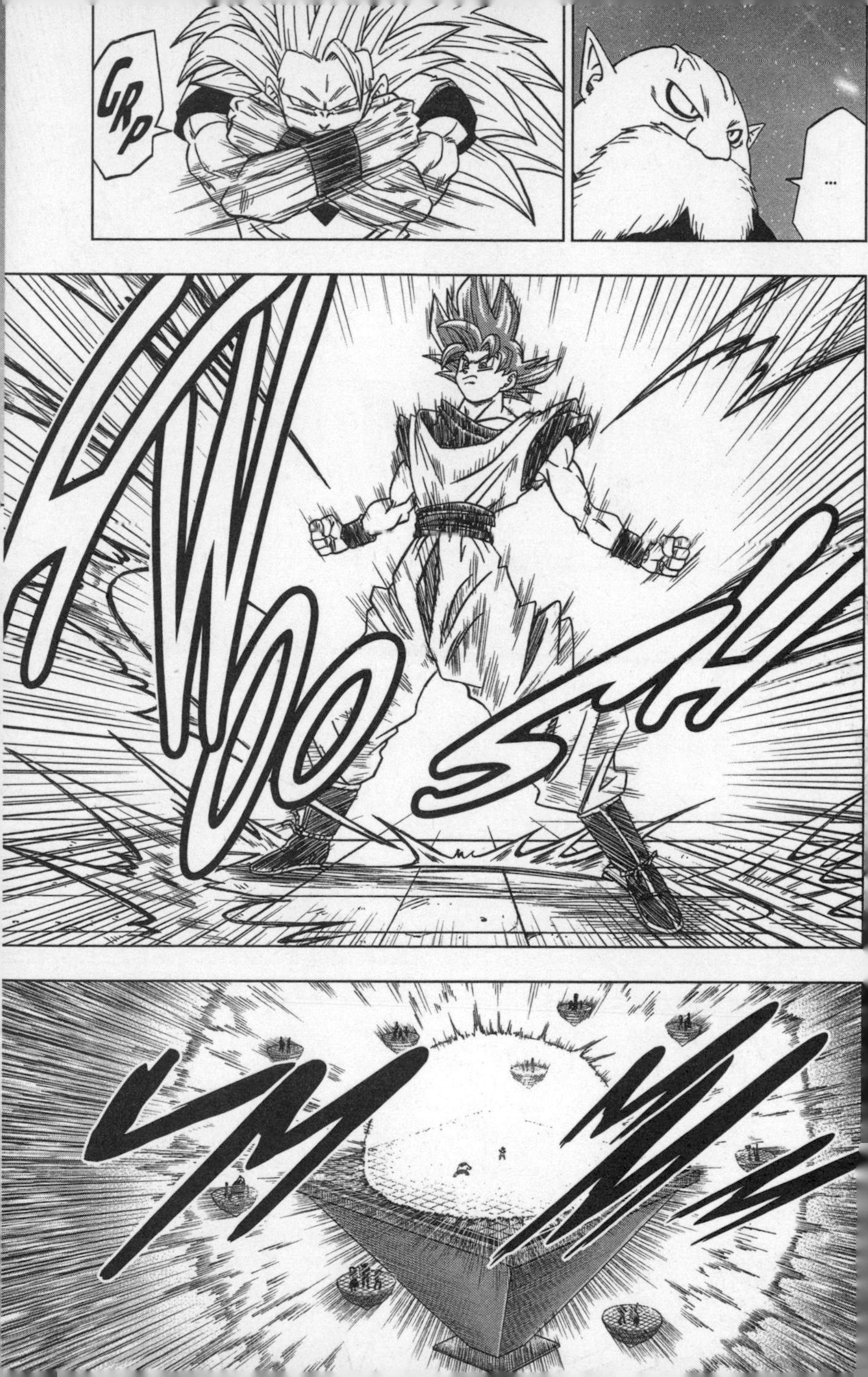
...
GRP
WHOOSH

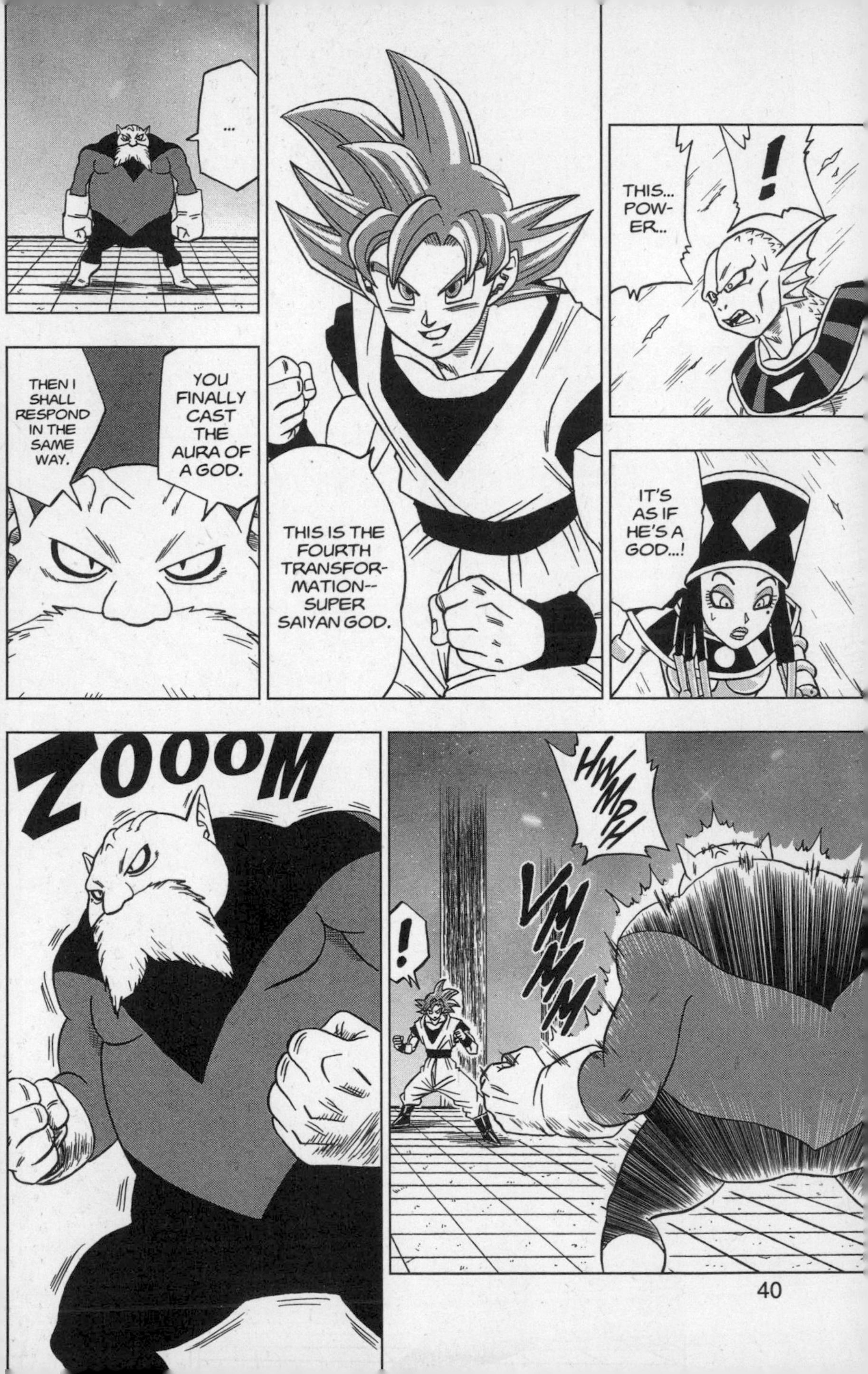
!
THIS... POW-ER...
IT'S AS IF HE'S A GOD...!
THIS IS THE FOURTH TRANSFOR-MATION-- SUPER SAIYAN GOD.
...
YOU FINALLY CAST THE AURA OF A GOD.
THEN I SHALL RESPOND IN THE SAME WAY.
HWMPH
!
VMMMM
ZOOOM

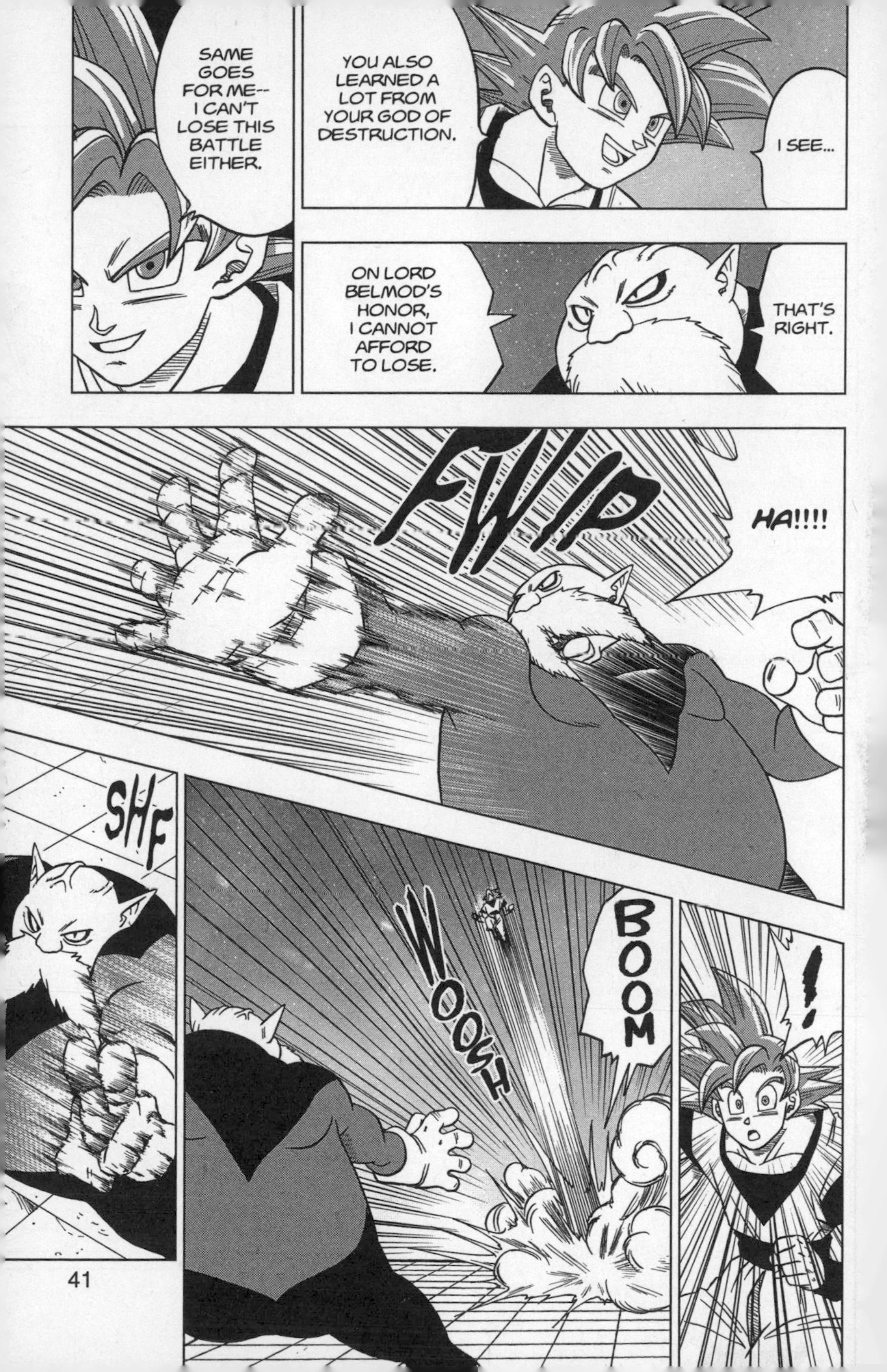

I SEE...
YOU ALSO LEARNED A LOT FROM YOUR GOD OF DESTRUCTION.
THAT'S RIGHT.
ON LORD BELMOD'S HONOR, I CANNOT AFFORD TO LOSE.
SAME GOES FOR ME-- I CAN'T LOSE THIS BATTLE EITHER.
HA!!!!
FWIP
!
BOOM
WOOSH
SHF

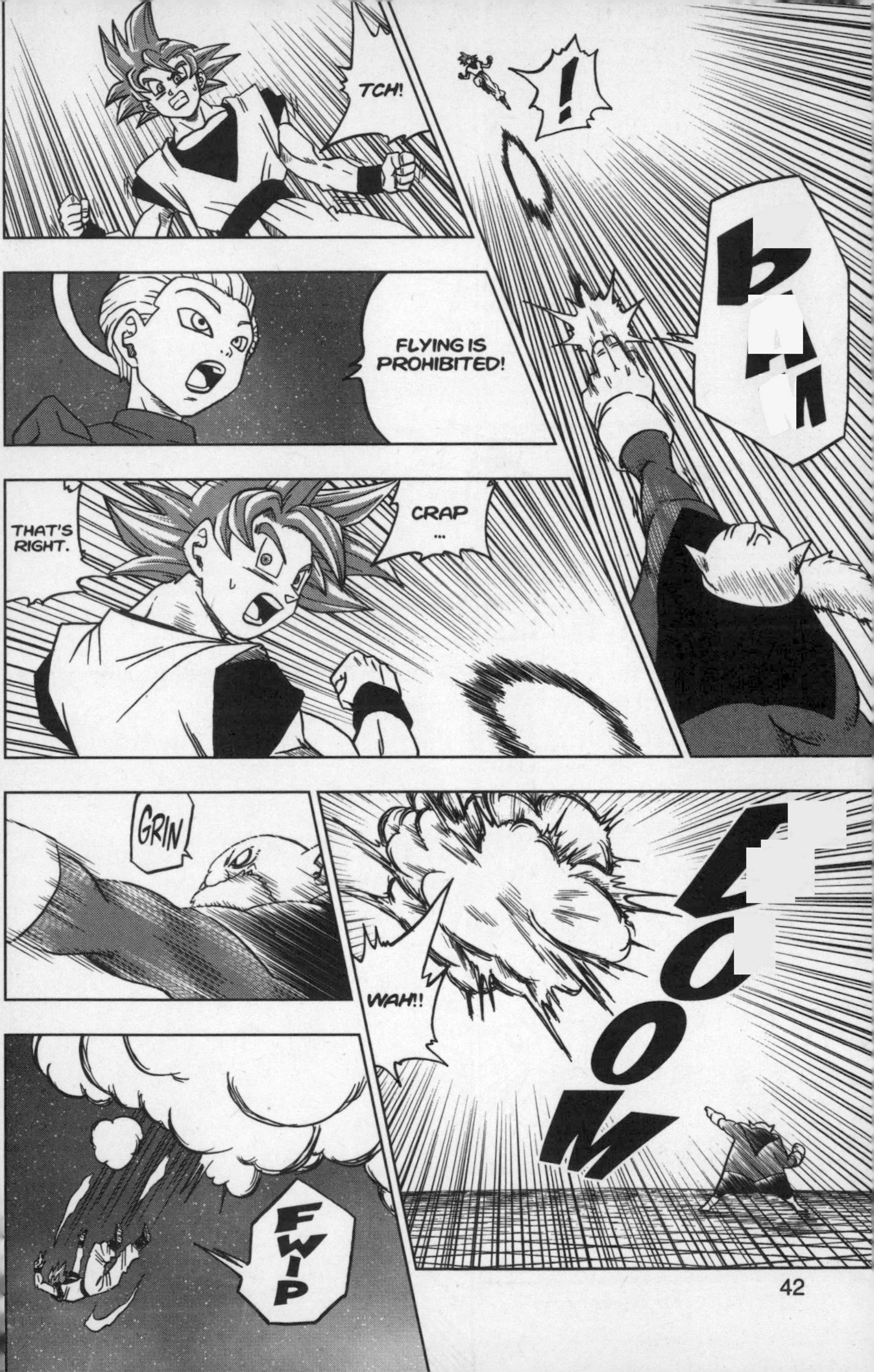

!
TCH!
FLYING IS PROHIBITED!
CRAP ...
THAT'S RIGHT.
WAH!!
GRIN
FWIP

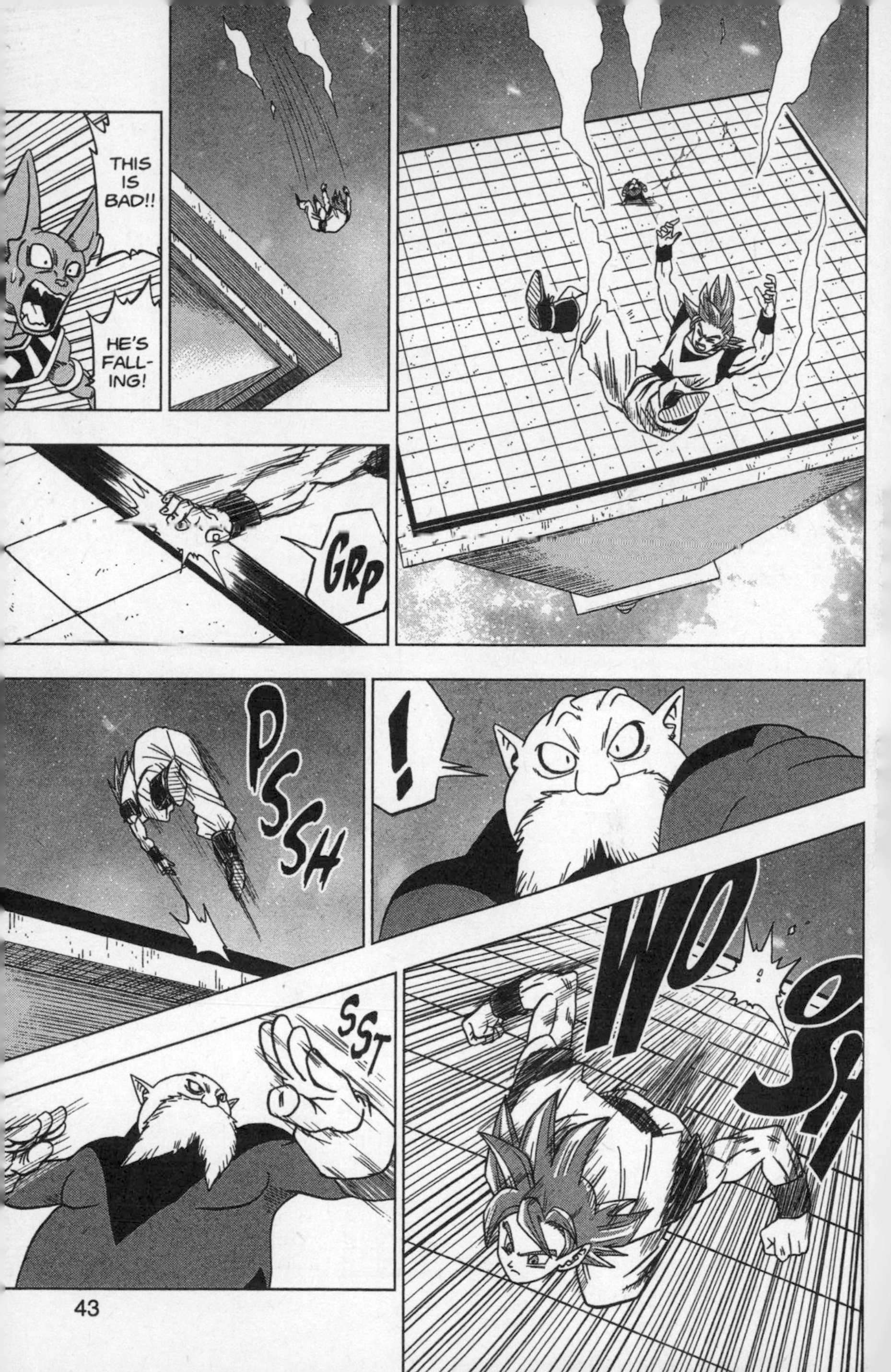

THIS IS BAD!!
HE'S FALLING!
GRP
!
PSSH
WOOSH
SST

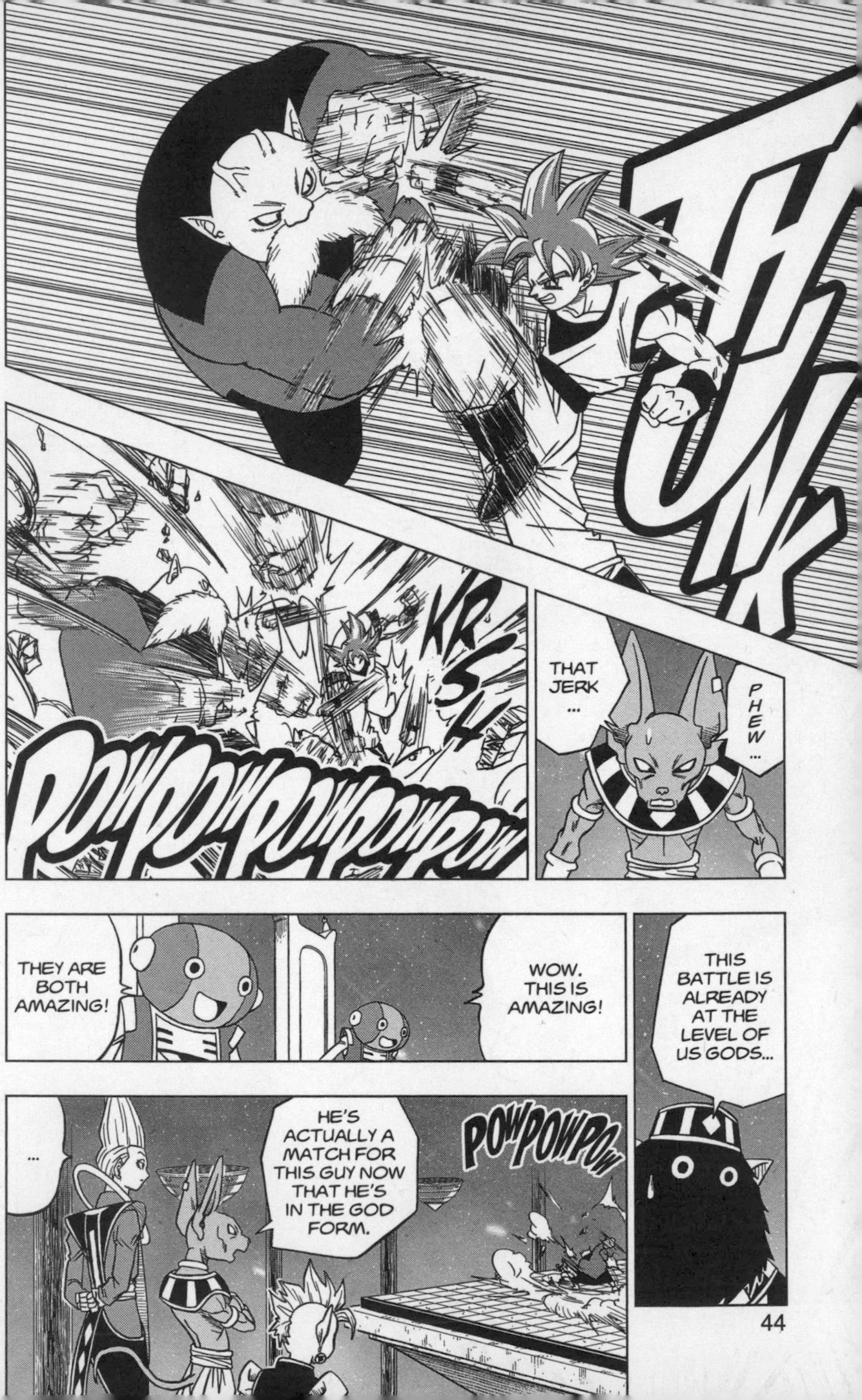
THUNK
PHEW...
THAT JERK...
KRSSH
POWPOWPOWPOWPOWPOWPOW
THIS BATTLE IS ALREADY AT THE LEVEL OF US GODS...
WOW. THIS IS AMAZING!
THEY ARE BOTH AMAZING!
POWPOWPOW
HE'S ACTUALLY A MATCH FOR THIS GUY NOW THAT HE'S IN THE GOD FORM.
...

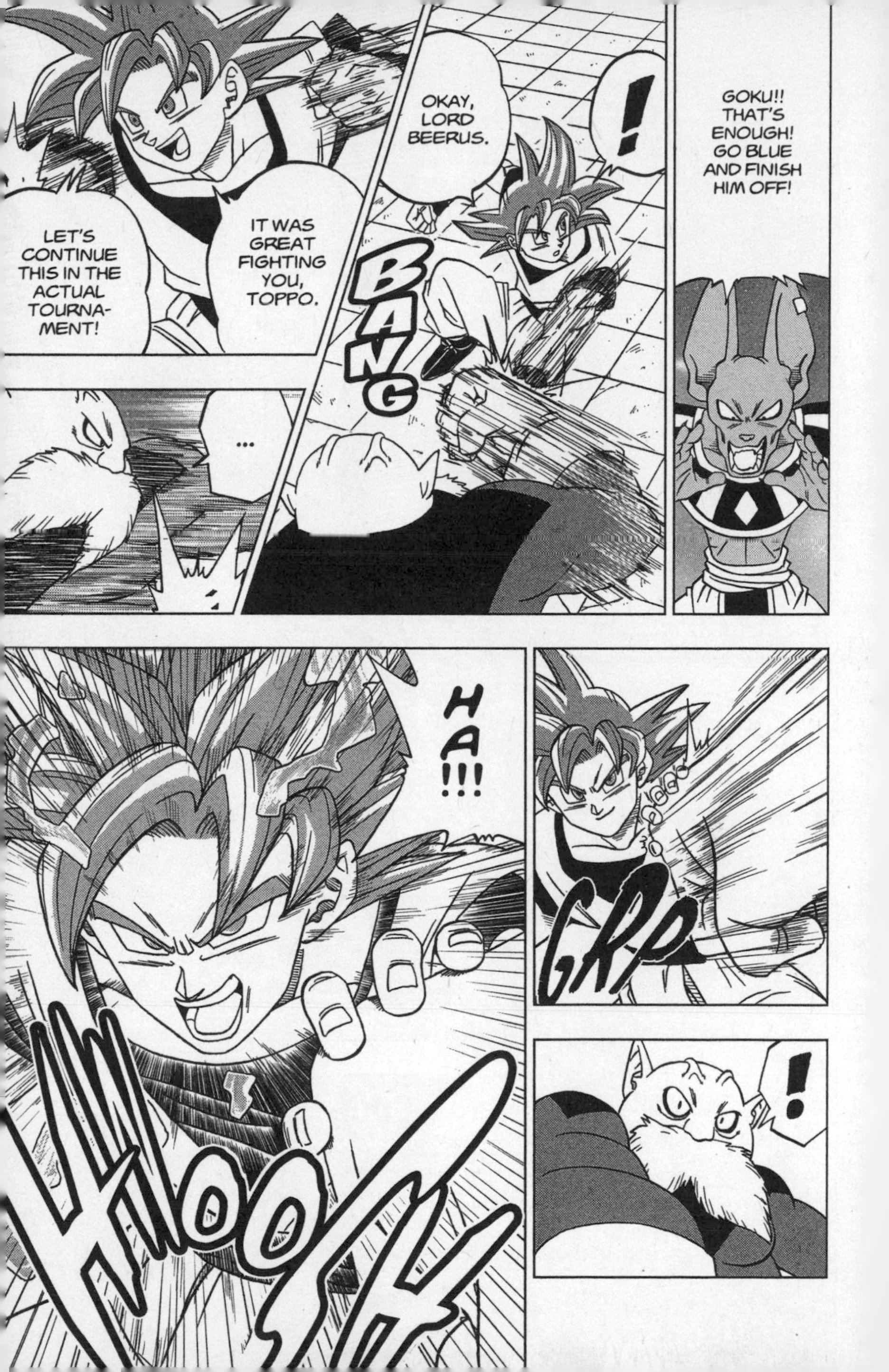
GOKU!! THAT'S ENOUGH! GO BLUE AND FINISH HIM OFF!
!
OKAY, LORD BEERUS.
BANG
IT WAS GREAT FIGHTING YOU, TOPPO.
LET'S CONTINUE THIS IN THE ACTUAL TOURNAMENT!
...
GRP
!
HA!!!
WHOOSH

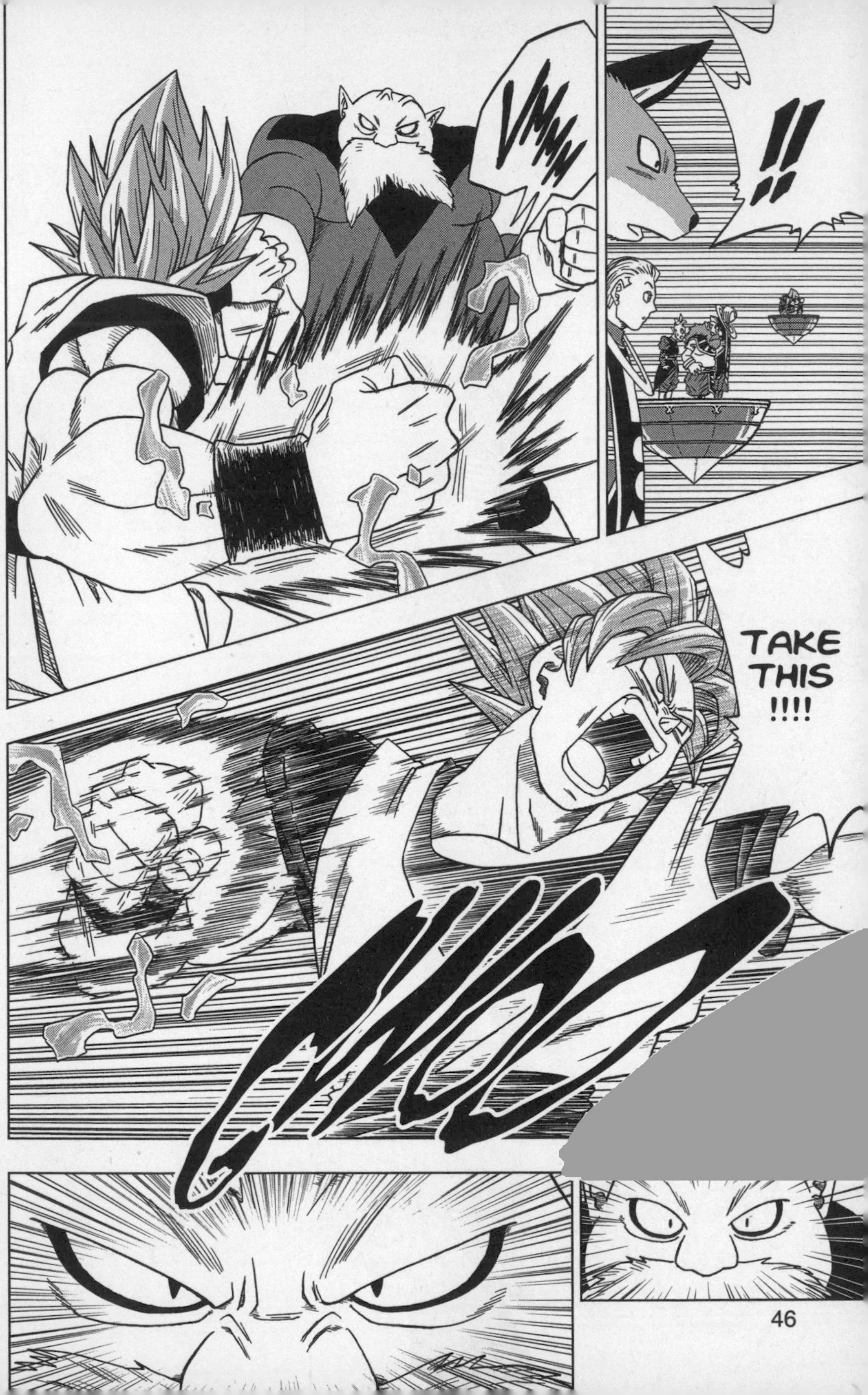
!!
VMMM
TAKE THIS !!!!

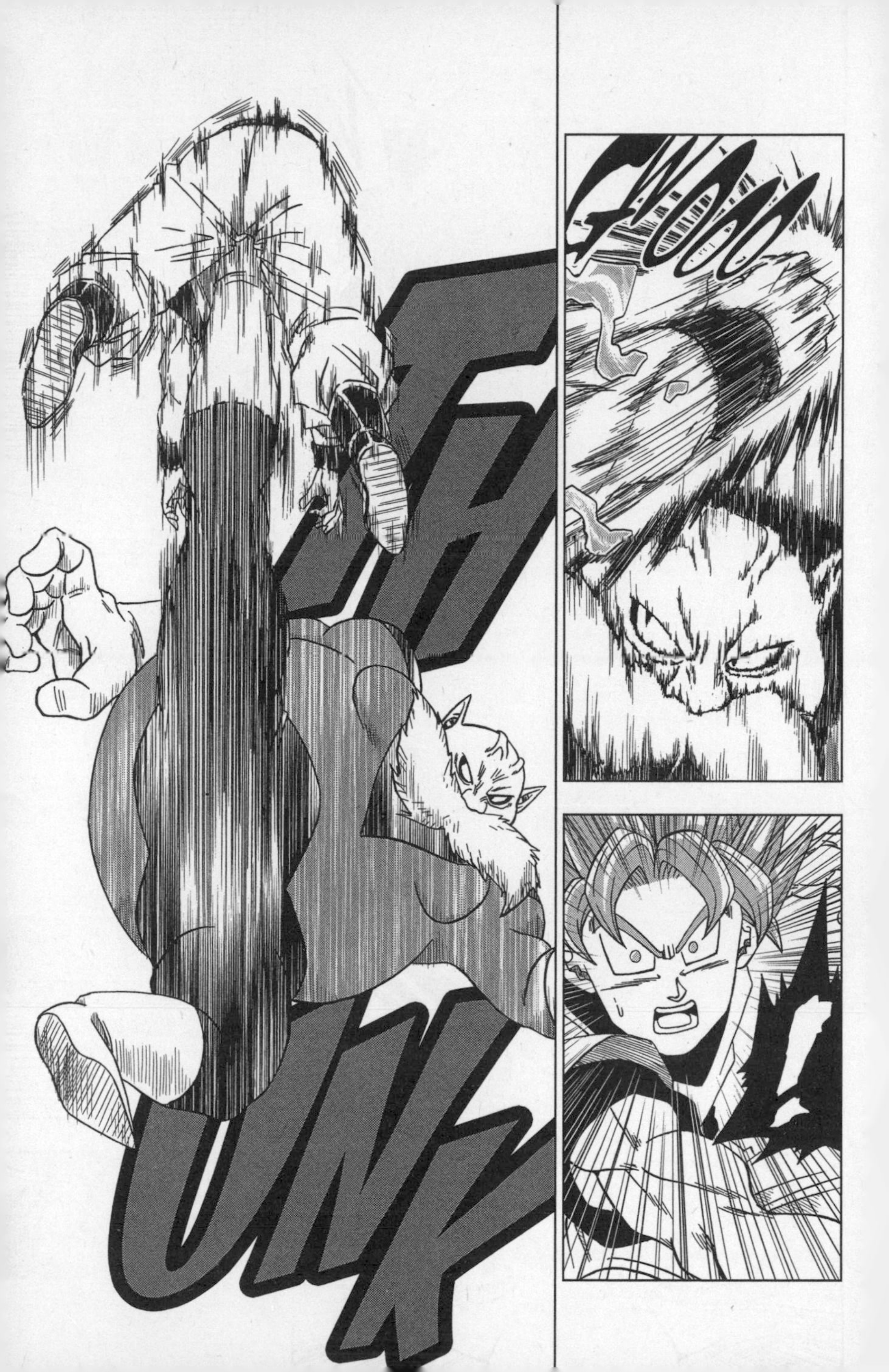
FWOOO
THUNK

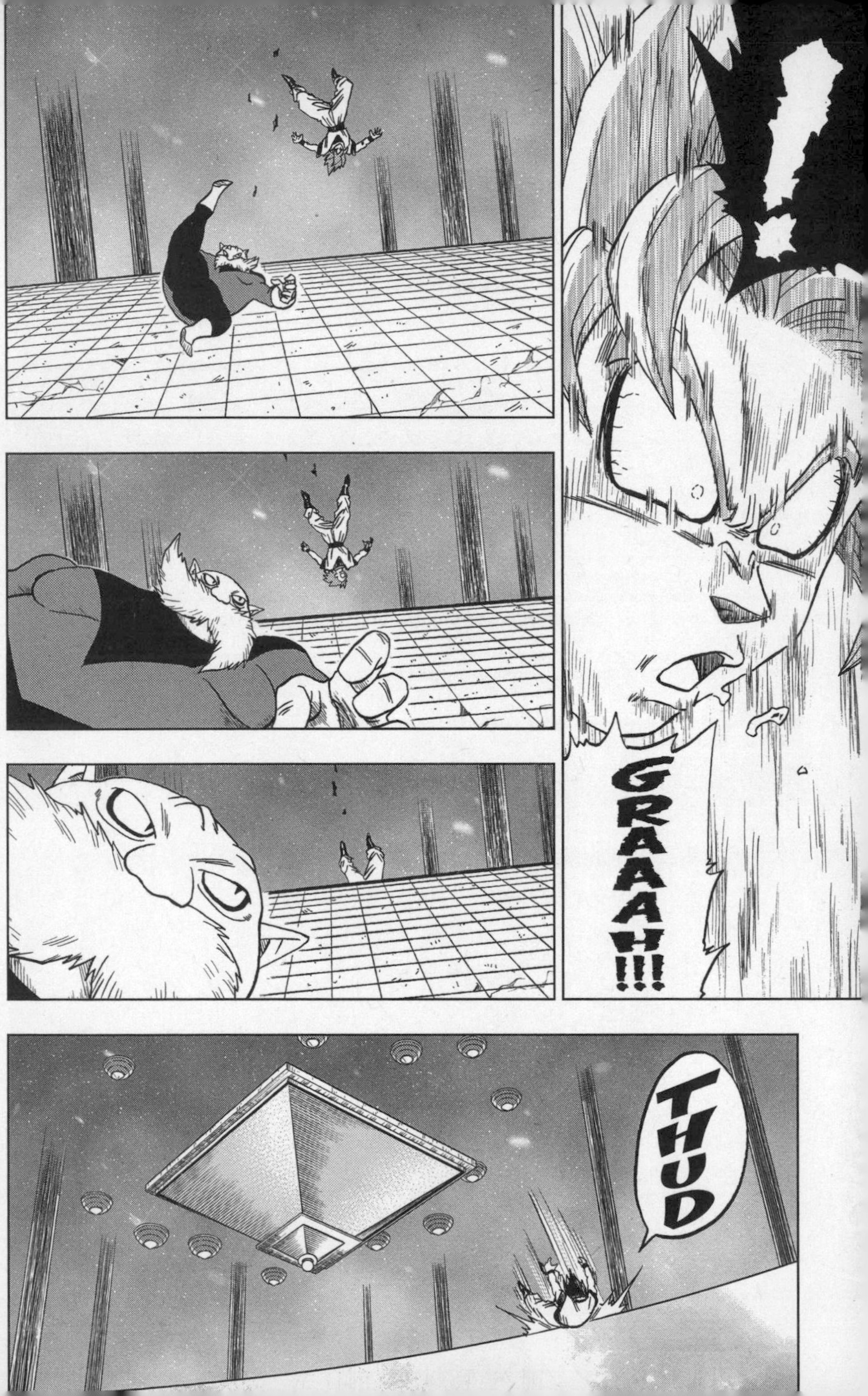
GRAAAH!!!
THUD

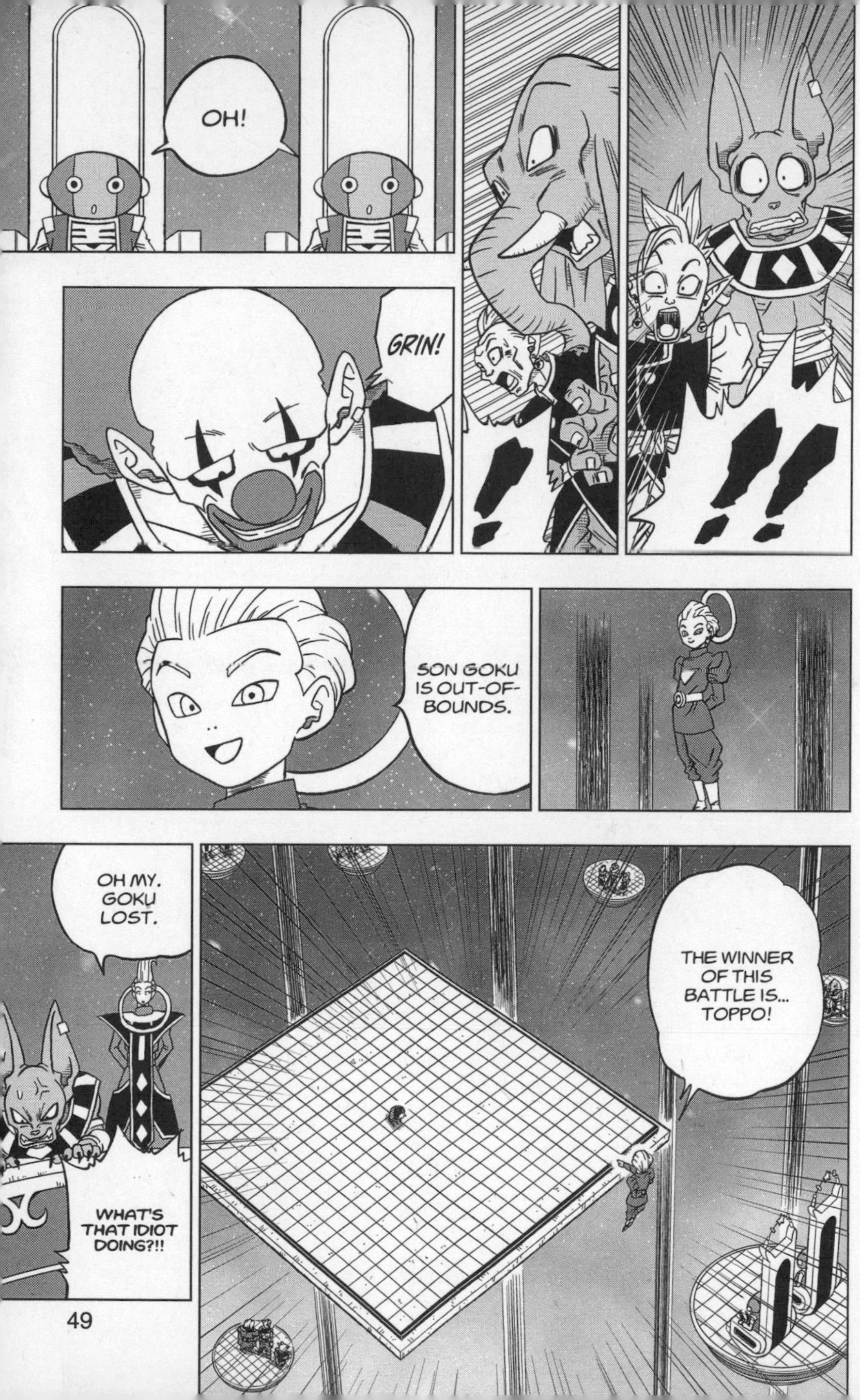
OH!
GRIN!
SON GOKU IS OUT-OF-BOUNDS.
THE WINNER OF THIS BATTLE IS... TOPPO!
OH MY. GOKU LOST.
WHAT'S THAT IDIOT DOING?!!

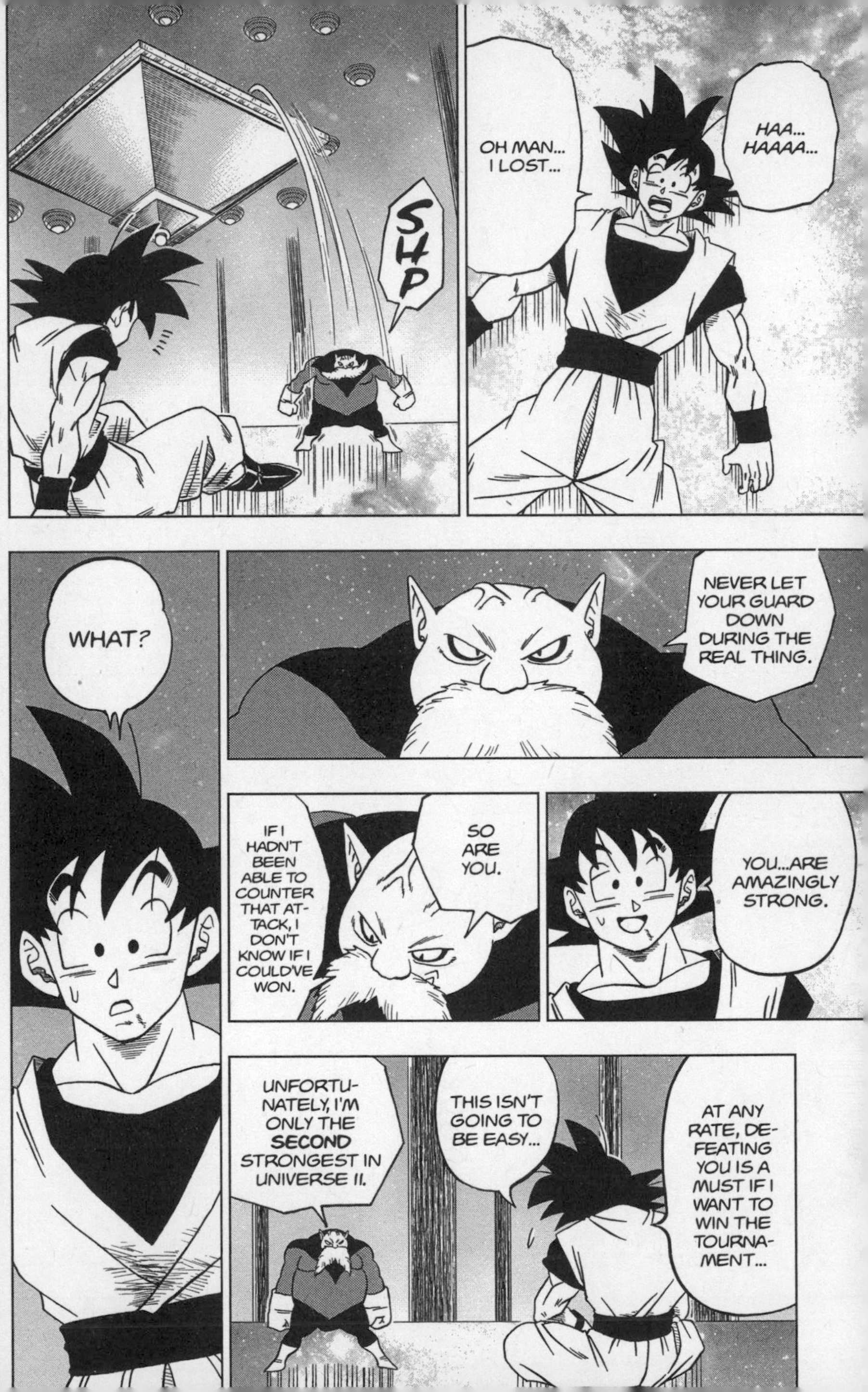
HAA... HAAAA...
OH MAN... I LOST...
SHP
NEVER LET YOUR GUARD DOWN DURING THE REAL THING.
YOU...ARE AMAZINGLY STRONG.
SO ARE YOU.
IF I HADN'T BEEN ABLE TO COUNTER THAT AT-TACK, I DON'T KNOW IF I COULD'VE WON.
AT ANY RATE, DE-FEATING YOU IS A MUST IF I WANT TO WIN THE TOURNA-MENT...
THIS ISN'T GOING TO BE EASY...
UNFORTU-NATELY, I'M ONLY THE **SECOND** STRONGEST IN UNIVERSE 11.
WHAT?

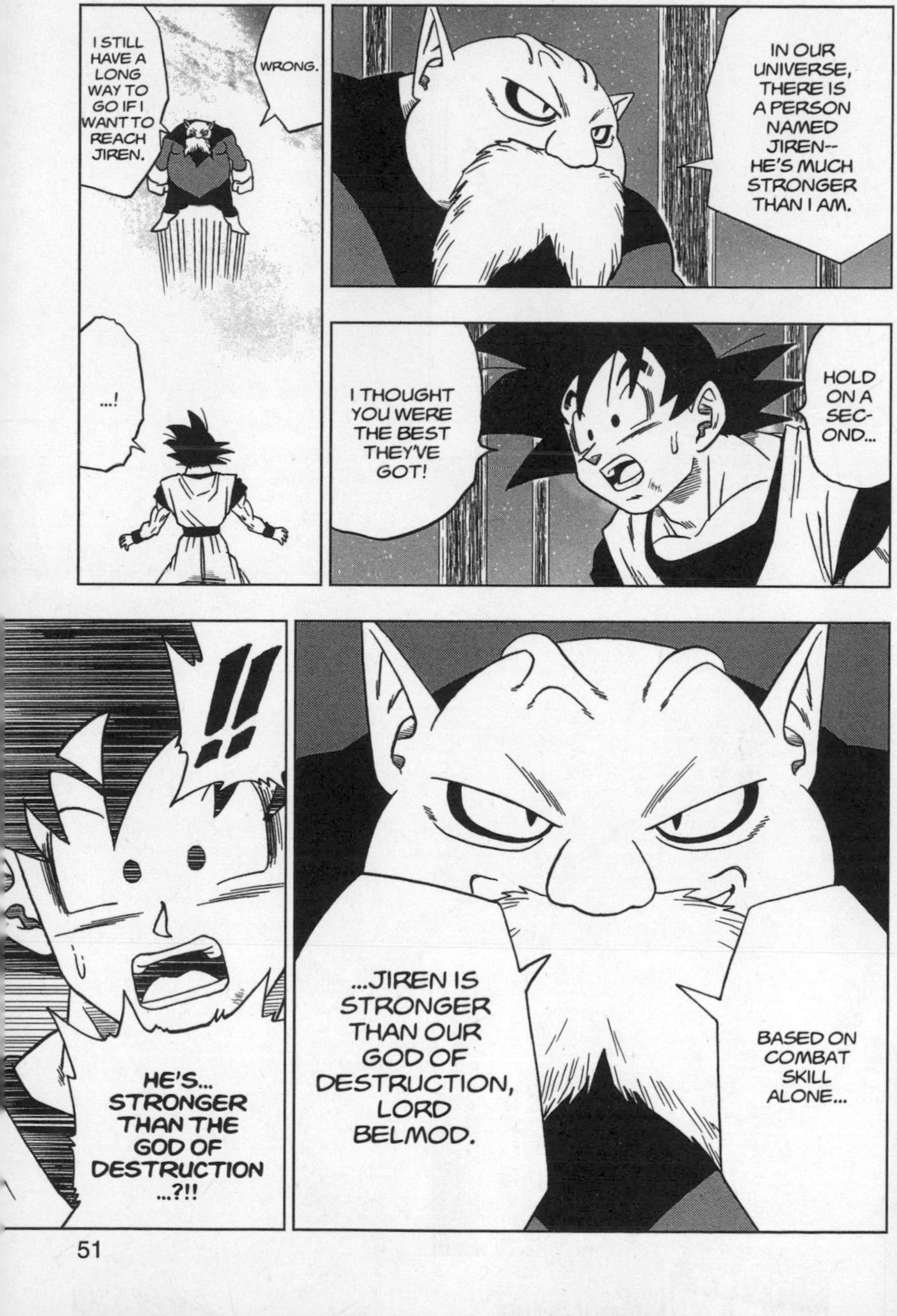
IN OUR UNIVERSE, THERE IS A PERSON NAMED JIREN-- HE'S MUCH STRONGER THAN I AM.
WRONG.
I STILL HAVE A LONG WAY TO GO IF I WANT TO REACH JIREN.
...!
HOLD ON A SEC-OND...
I THOUGHT YOU WERE THE BEST THEY'VE GOT!
BASED ON COMBAT SKILL ALONE...
...JIREN IS STRONGER THAN OUR GOD OF DESTRUCTION, LORD BELMOD.
!!
HE'S... STRONGER THAN THE GOD OF DESTRUCTION ...?!!

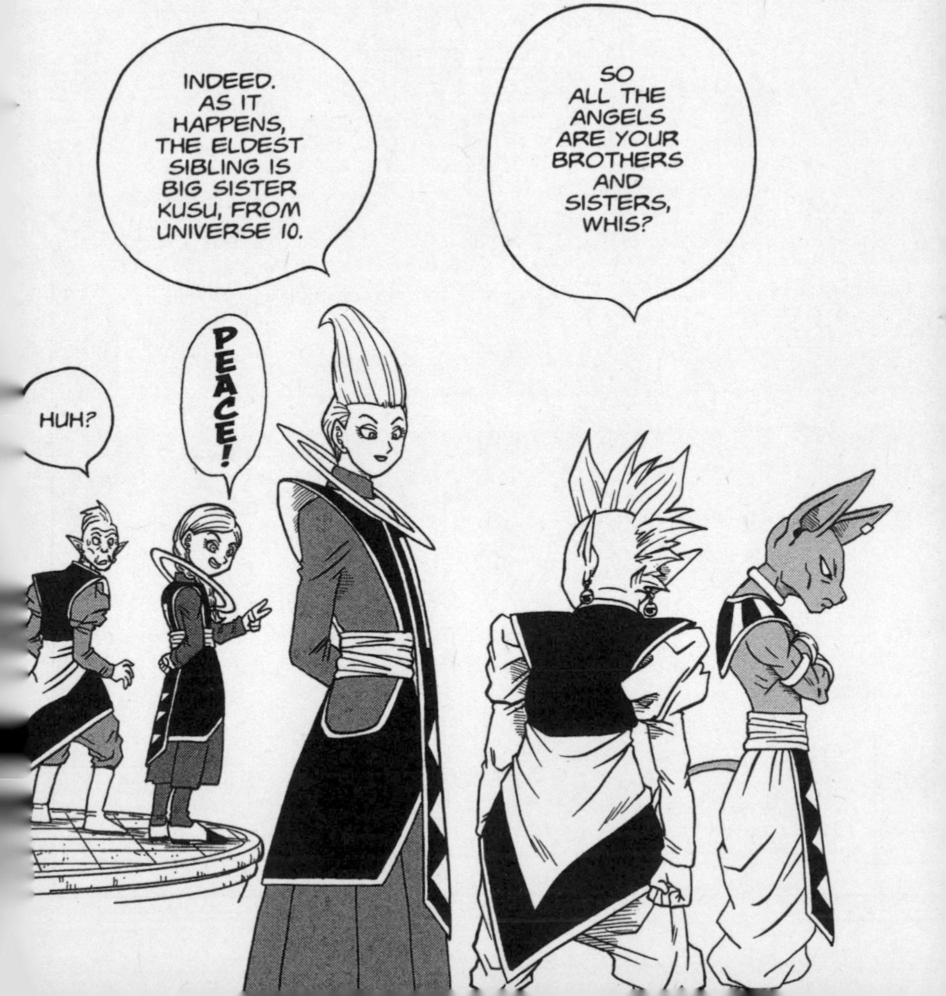
SO ALL THE ANGELS ARE YOUR BROTHERS AND SISTERS, WHIS?
INDEED. AS IT HAPPENS, THE ELDEST SIBLING IS BIG SISTER KUSU, FROM UNIVERSE 10.
PEACE!
HUH?

DRAGON BALL SUPER

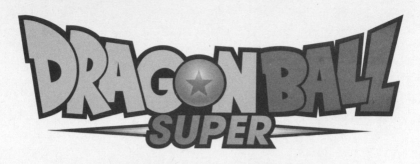

CHAPTER 30: THE MAN NAMED JIREN

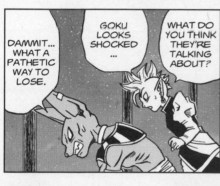

WHAT DO YOU THINK THEY'RE TALKING ABOUT?
GOKU LOOKS SHOCKED ...
DAMMIT... WHAT A PATHETIC WAY TO LOSE.
W-WAIT, SO YOU'RE SAYING THIS JIREN GUY IS STRONGER THAN THE GOD OF DESTRUCTION OF YOUR UNIVERSE?
THAT'S RIGHT.

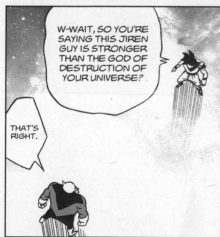

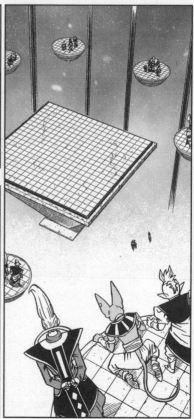

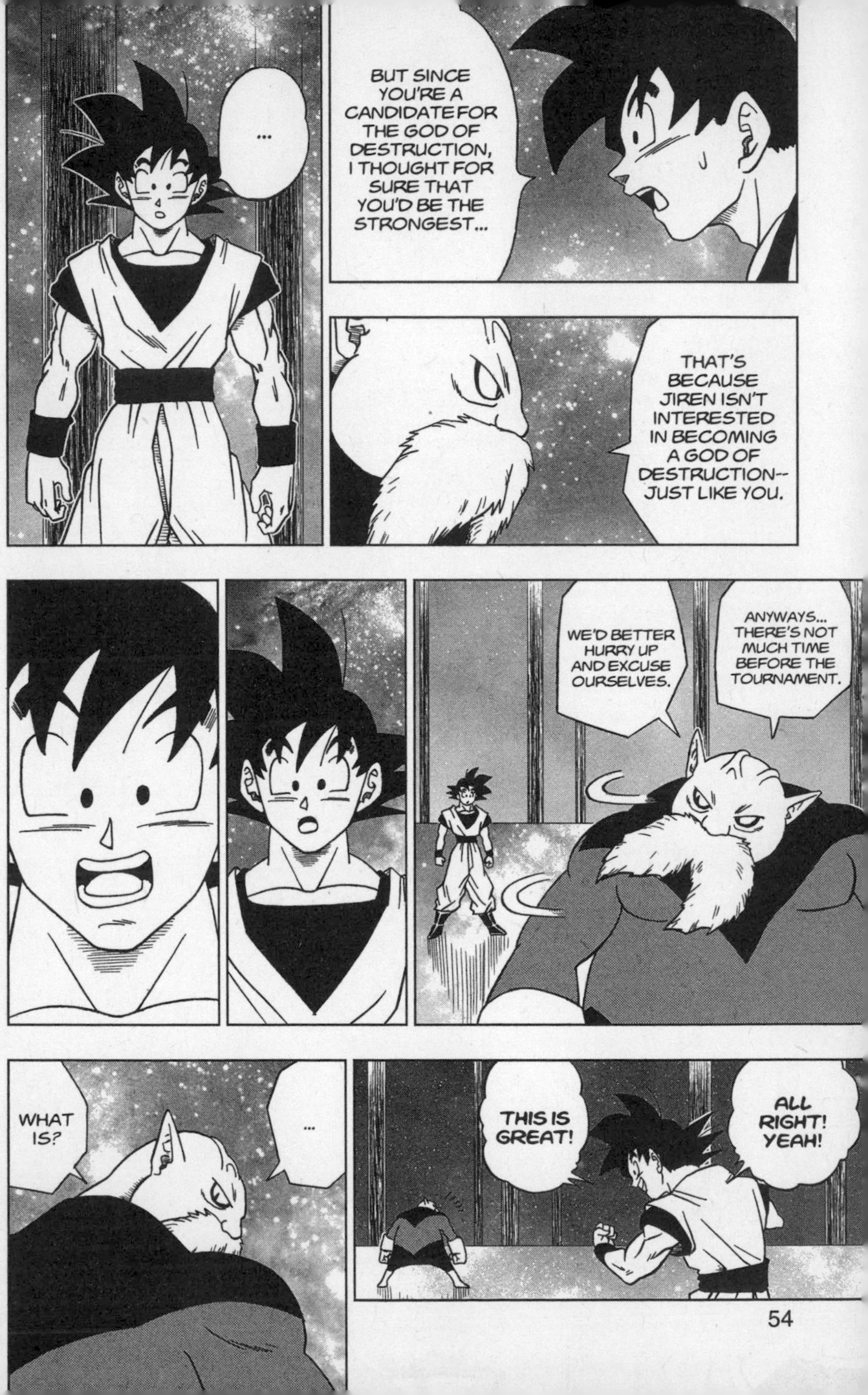
BUT SINCE YOU'RE A CANDIDATE FOR THE GOD OF DESTRUCTION, I THOUGHT FOR SURE THAT YOU'D BE THE STRONGEST...
THAT'S BECAUSE JIREN ISN'T INTERESTED IN BECOMING A GOD OF DESTRUCTION-- JUST LIKE YOU.
...
ANYWAYS... THERE'S NOT MUCH TIME BEFORE THE TOURNAMENT.
WE'D BETTER HURRY UP AND EXCUSE OURSELVES.
ALL RIGHT! YEAH!
THIS IS GREAT!
...
WHAT IS?

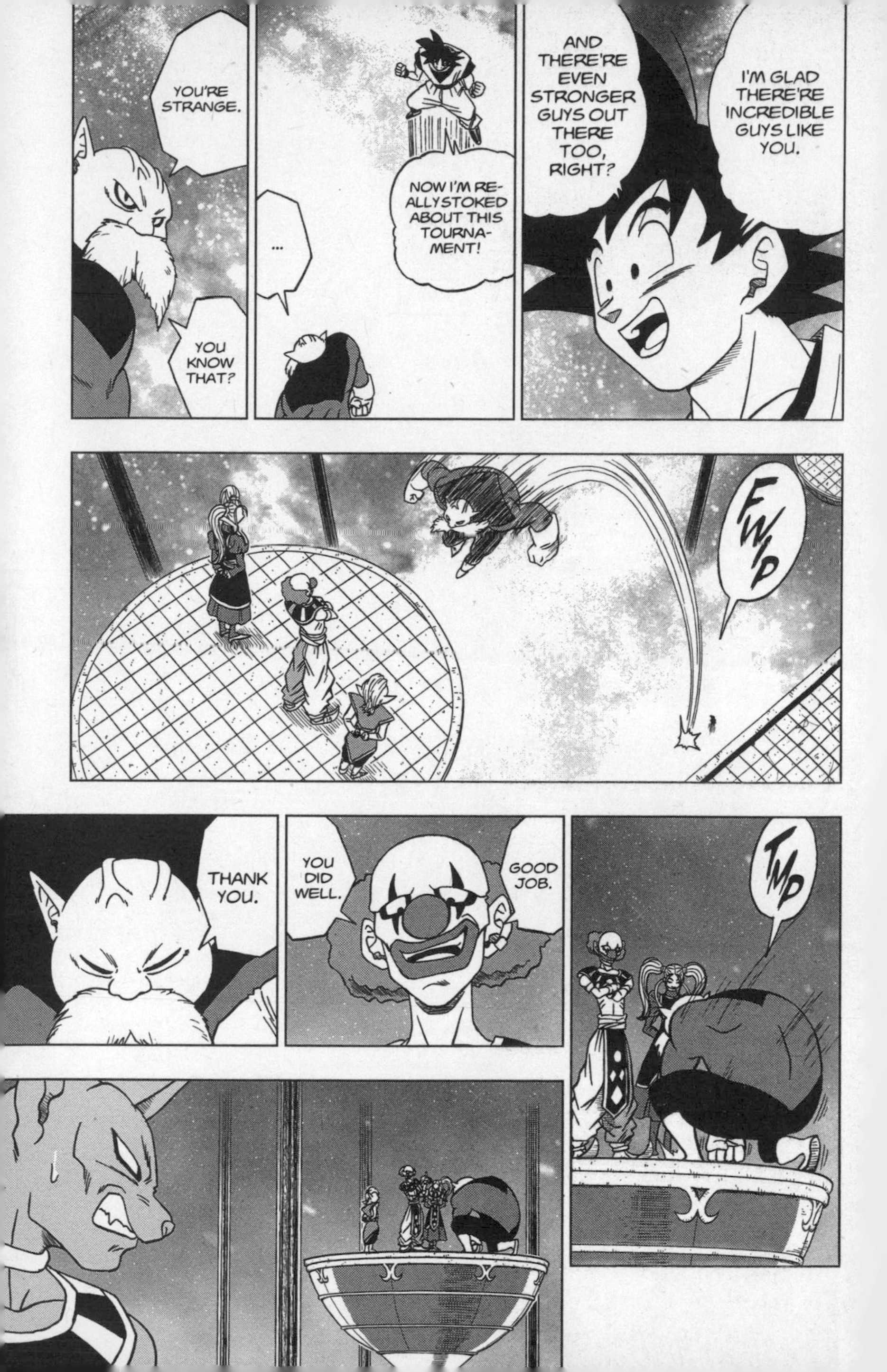
I'M GLAD THERE'RE INCREDIBLE GUYS LIKE YOU.
AND THERE'RE EVEN STRONGER GUYS OUT THERE TOO, RIGHT?
NOW I'M RE-ALLYSTOKED ABOUT THIS TOURNA-MENT!
...
YOU'RE STRANGE.
YOU KNOW THAT?
FWIP
TMP
GOOD JOB.
YOU DID WELL.
THANK YOU.

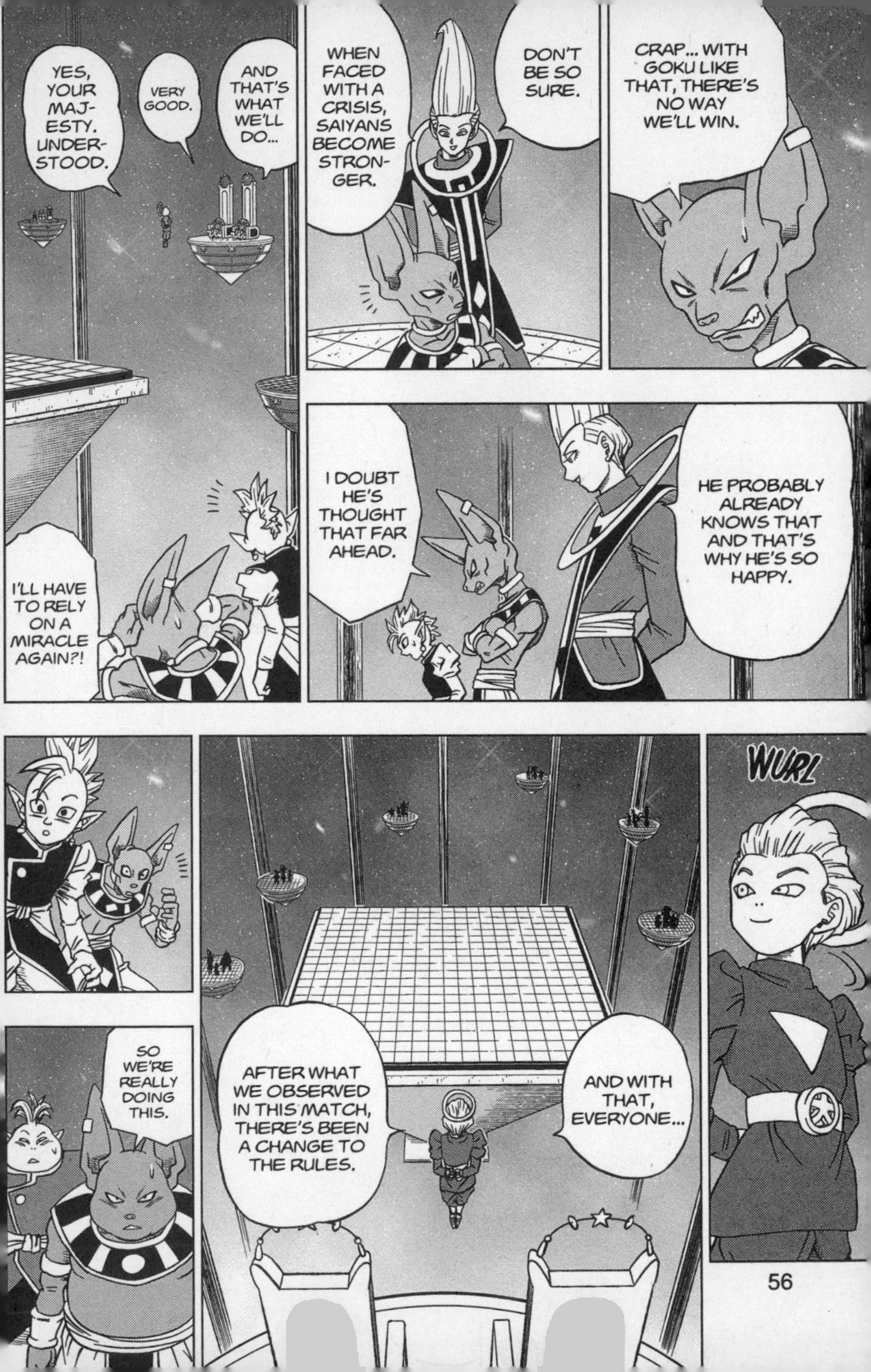
CRAP... WITH GOKU LIKE THAT, THERE'S NO WAY WE'LL WIN.
DON'T BE SO SURE.
WHEN FACED WITH A CRISIS, SAIYANS BECOME STRONGER.
HE PROBABLY ALREADY KNOWS THAT AND THAT'S WHY HE'S SO HAPPY.
I DOUBT HE'S THOUGHT THAT FAR AHEAD.
AND THAT'S WHAT WE'LL DO...
VERY GOOD.
YES, YOUR MAJESTY. UNDERSTOOD.
I'LL HAVE TO RELY ON A MIRACLE AGAIN?!
WURL
AND WITH THAT, EVERYONE...
AFTER WHAT WE OBSERVED IN THIS MATCH, THERE'S BEEN A CHANGE TO THE RULES.
SO WE'RE REALLY DOING THIS.

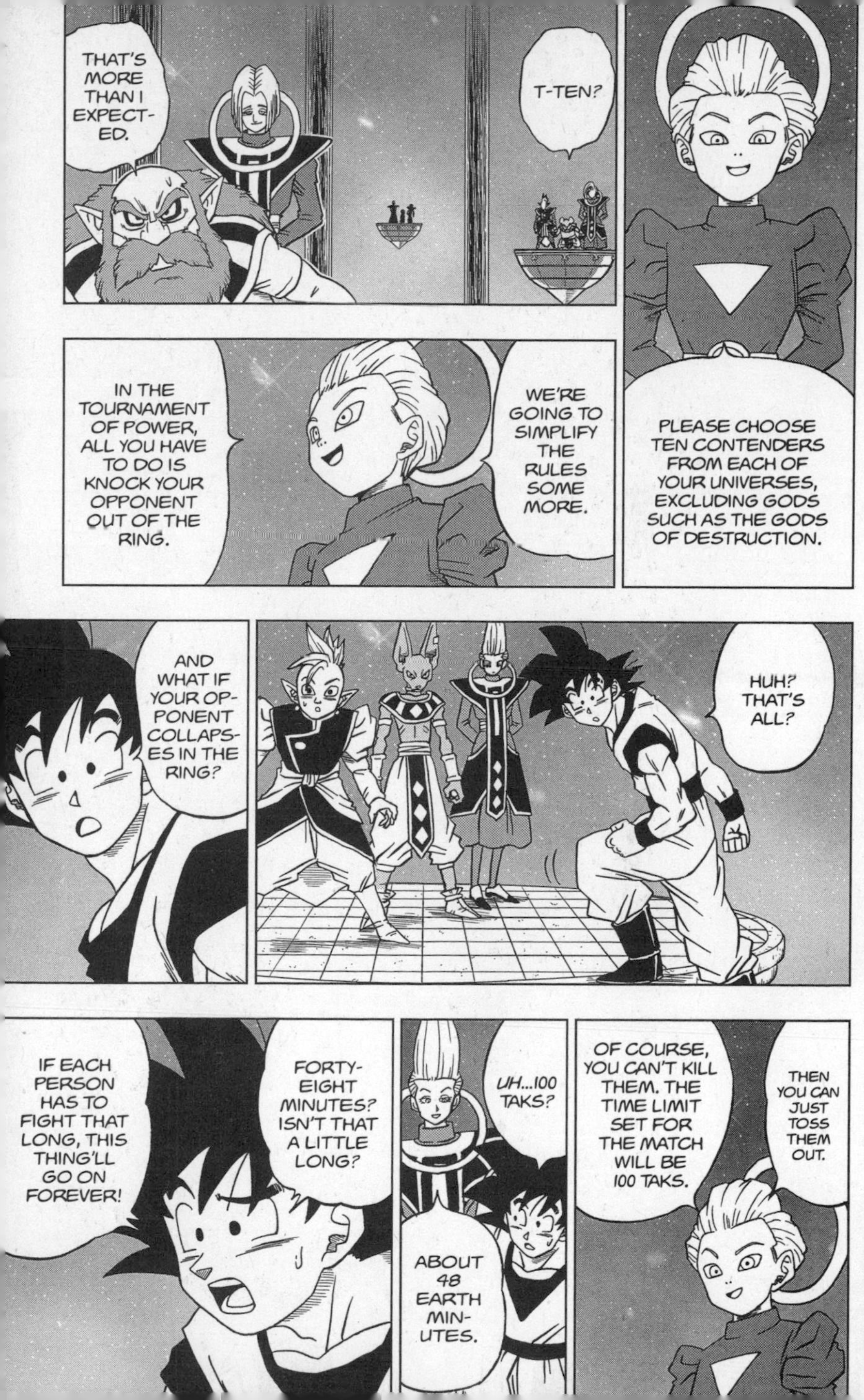
PLEASE CHOOSE TEN CONTENDERS FROM EACH OF YOUR UNIVERSES, EXCLUDING GODS SUCH AS THE GODS OF DESTRUCTION.
T-TEN?
THAT'S MORE THAN I EXPECT-ED.
WE'RE GOING TO SIMPLIFY THE RULES SOME MORE.
IN THE TOURNAMENT OF POWER, ALL YOU HAVE TO DO IS KNOCK YOUR OPPONENT OUT OF THE RING.
HUH? THAT'S ALL?
AND WHAT IF YOUR OP-PONENT COLLAPS-ES IN THE RING?
THEN YOU CAN JUST TOSS THEM OUT.
OF COURSE, YOU CAN'T KILL THEM. THE TIME LIMIT SET FOR THE MATCH WILL BE 100 TAKS.
UH...100 TAKS?
ABOUT 48 EARTH MIN-UTES.
FORTY-EIGHT MINUTES? ISN'T THAT A LITTLE LONG?
IF EACH PERSON HAS TO FIGHT THAT LONG, THIS THING'LL GO ON FOREVER!

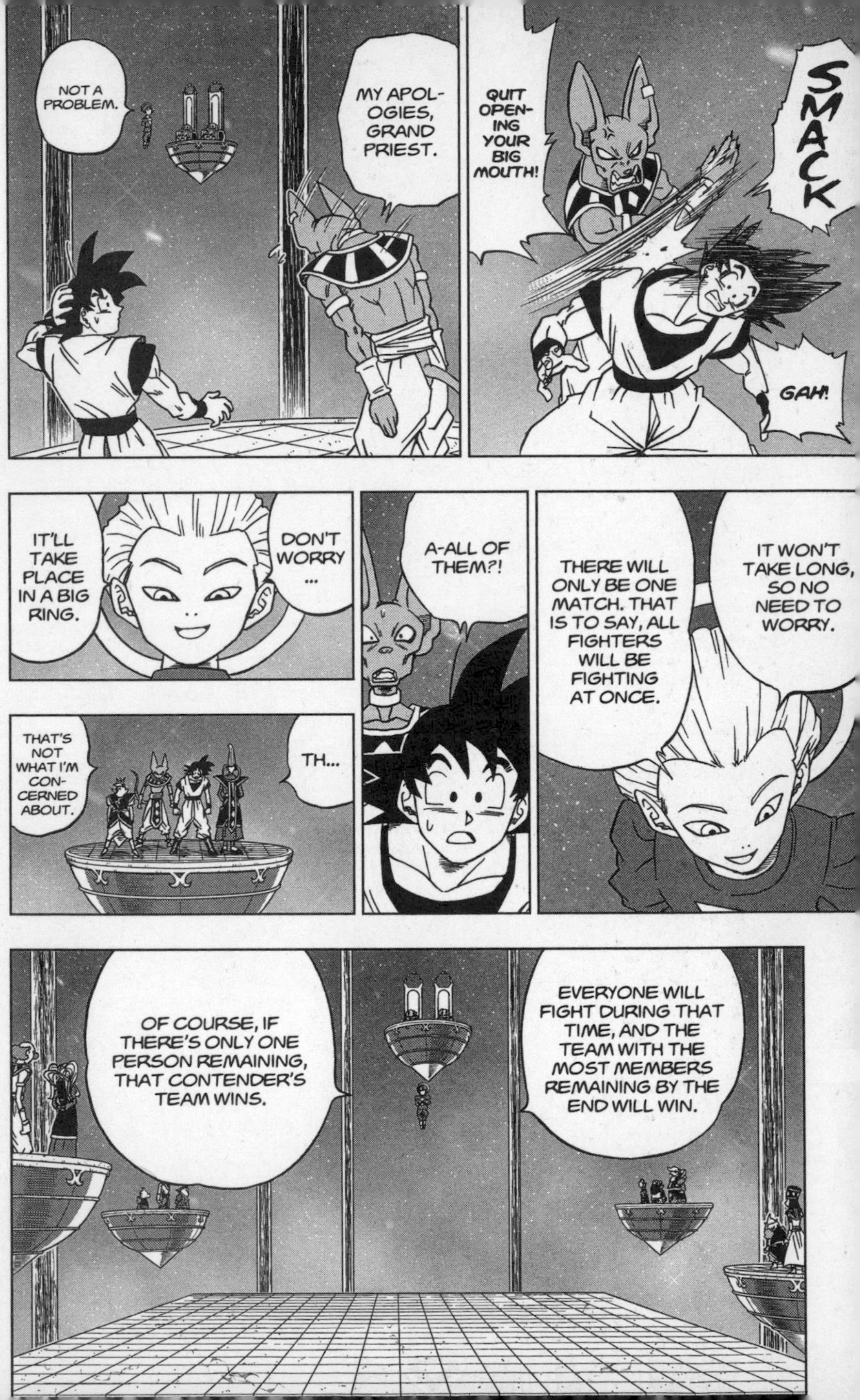

SMACK
QUIT OPENING YOUR BIG MOUTH!
GAH!
MY APOLOGIES, GRAND PRIEST.
NOT A PROBLEM.
IT WON'T TAKE LONG, SO NO NEED TO WORRY.
THERE WILL ONLY BE ONE MATCH. THAT IS TO SAY, ALL FIGHTERS WILL BE FIGHTING AT ONCE.
A-ALL OF THEM?!
DON'T WORRY...
IT'LL TAKE PLACE IN A BIG RING.
TH...
THAT'S NOT WHAT I'M CONCERNED ABOUT.
EVERYONE WILL FIGHT DURING THAT TIME, AND THE TEAM WITH THE MOST MEMBERS REMAINING BY THE END WILL WIN.
OF COURSE, IF THERE'S ONLY ONE PERSON REMAINING, THAT CONTENDER'S TEAM WINS.

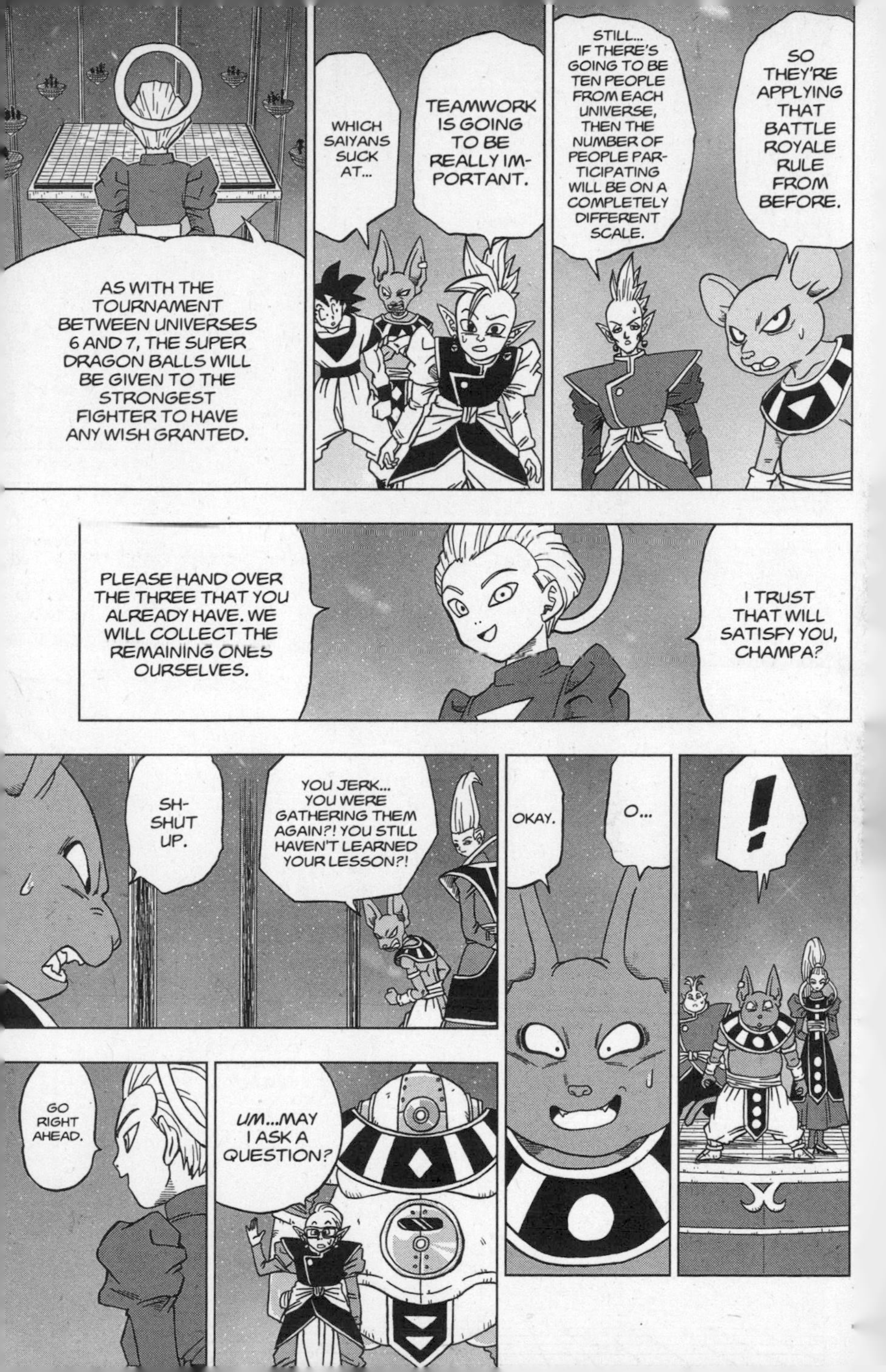
SO THEY'RE APPLYING THAT BATTLE ROYALE RULE FROM BEFORE.
STILL... IF THERE'S GOING TO BE TEN PEOPLE FROM EACH UNIVERSE, THEN THE NUMBER OF PEOPLE PARTICIPATING WILL BE ON A COMPLETELY DIFFERENT SCALE.
TEAMWORK IS GOING TO BE REALLY IMPORTANT.
WHICH SAIYANS SUCK AT...
AS WITH THE TOURNAMENT BETWEEN UNIVERSES 6 AND 7, THE SUPER DRAGON BALLS WILL BE GIVEN TO THE STRONGEST FIGHTER TO HAVE ANY WISH GRANTED.
I TRUST THAT WILL SATISFY YOU, CHAMPA?
PLEASE HAND OVER THE THREE THAT YOU ALREADY HAVE. WE WILL COLLECT THE REMAINING ONES OURSELVES.
!
O...
OKAY.
YOU JERK... YOU WERE GATHERING THEM AGAIN?! YOU STILL HAVEN'T LEARNED YOUR LESSON?!
SH-SHUT UP.
UM...MAY I ASK A QUESTION?
GO RIGHT AHEAD.

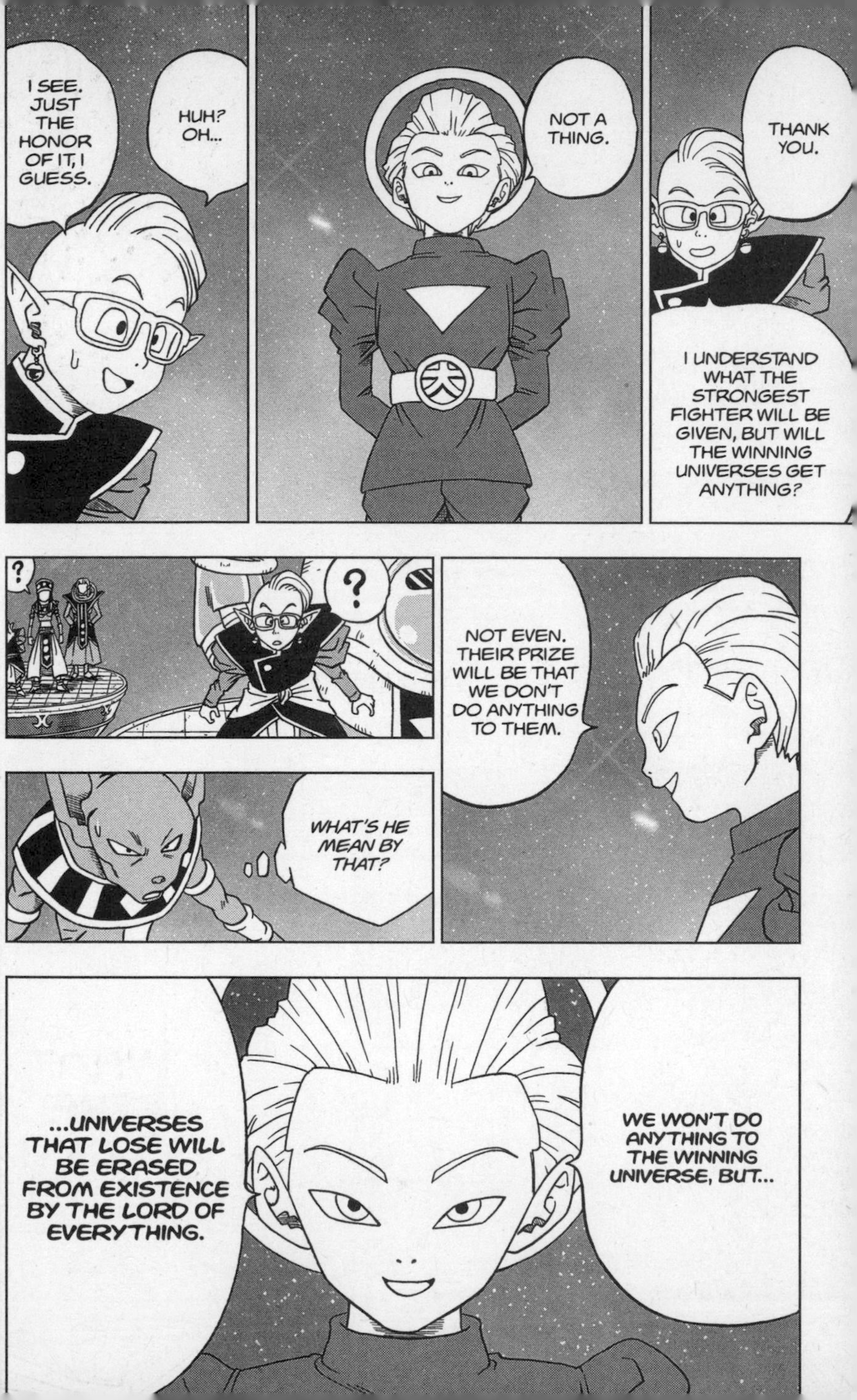
THANK YOU.
I UNDERSTAND WHAT THE STRONGEST FIGHTER WILL BE GIVEN, BUT WILL THE WINNING UNIVERSES GET ANYTHING?
NOT A THING.
HUH? OH...
I SEE. JUST THE HONOR OF IT, I GUESS.
NOT EVEN. THEIR PRIZE WILL BE THAT WE DON'T DO ANYTHING TO THEM.
?
?
WHAT'S HE MEAN BY THAT?
WE WON'T DO ANYTHING TO THE WINNING UNIVERSE, BUT...
...UNIVERSES THAT LOSE WILL BE ERASED FROM EXISTENCE BY THE LORD OF EVERYTHING.

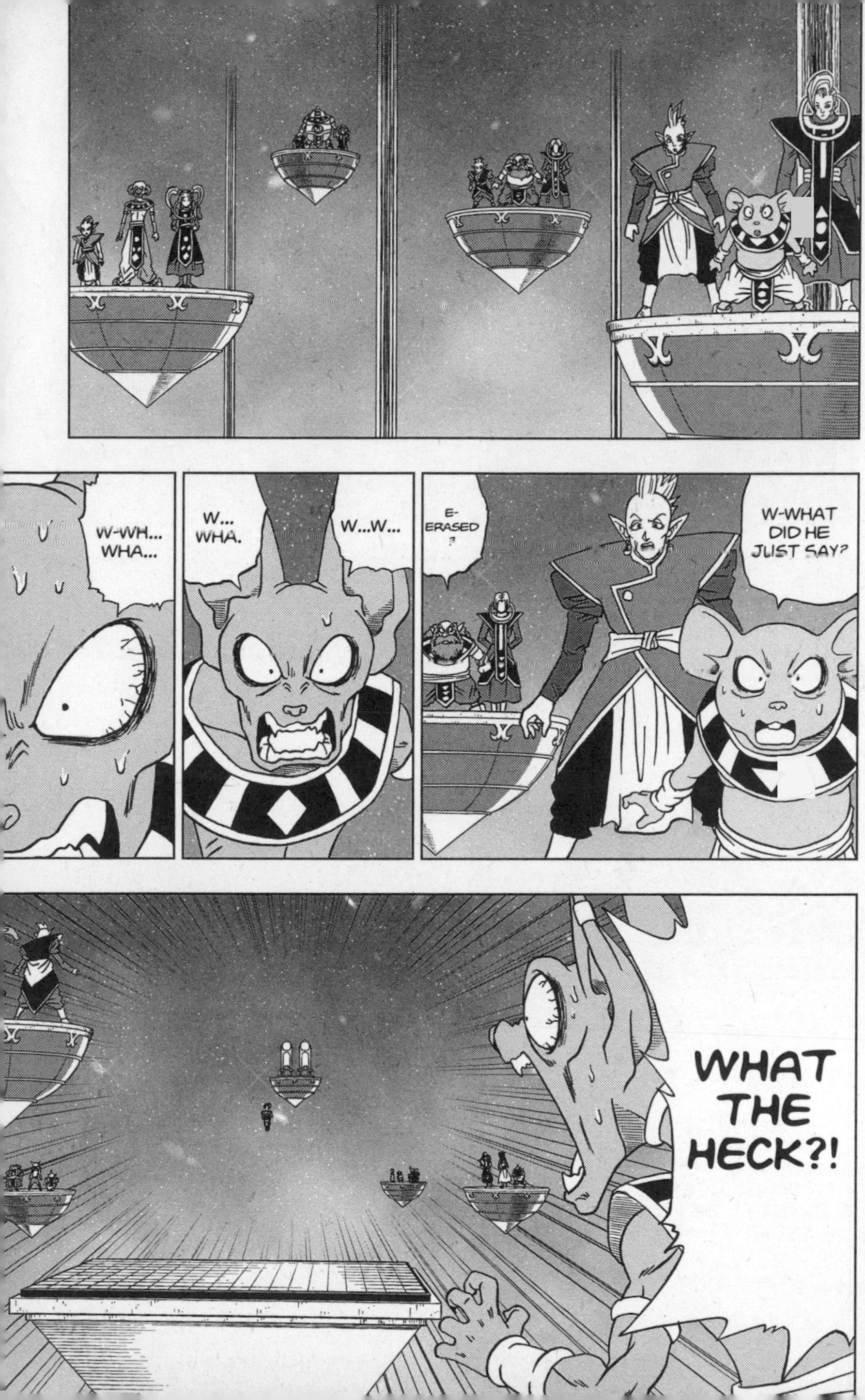
W-WHAT DID HE JUST SAY?
E-ERASED?!
W...W...
W... WHA.
W-WH... WHA...
WHAT THE HECK?!

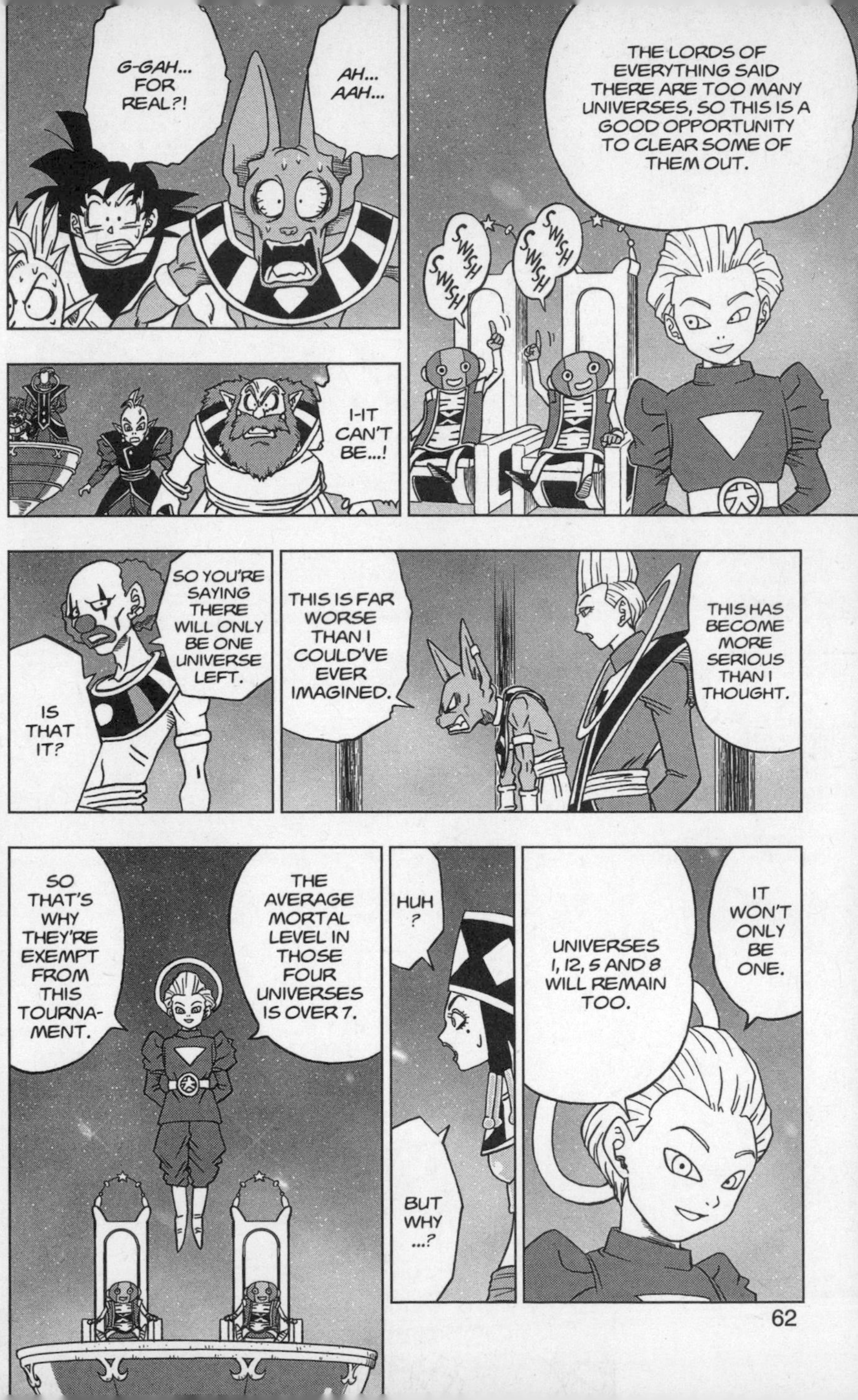
THE LORDS OF EVERYTHING SAID THERE ARE TOO MANY UNIVERSES, SO THIS IS A GOOD OPPORTUNITY TO CLEAR SOME OF THEM OUT.
SWISH SWISH
SWISH SWISH
AH... AAH...
G-GAH... FOR REAL?!
I-IT CAN'T BE...!
THIS HAS BECOME MORE SERIOUS THAN I THOUGHT.
THIS IS FAR WORSE THAN I COULD'VE EVER IMAGINED.
SO YOU'RE SAYING THERE WILL ONLY BE ONE UNIVERSE LEFT.
IS THAT IT?
IT WON'T ONLY BE ONE.
UNIVERSES 1, 12, 5 AND 8 WILL REMAIN TOO.
HUH?
BUT WHY...?
THE AVERAGE MORTAL LEVEL IN THOSE FOUR UNIVERSES IS OVER 7.
SO THAT'S WHY THEY'RE EXEMPT FROM THIS TOURNAMENT.

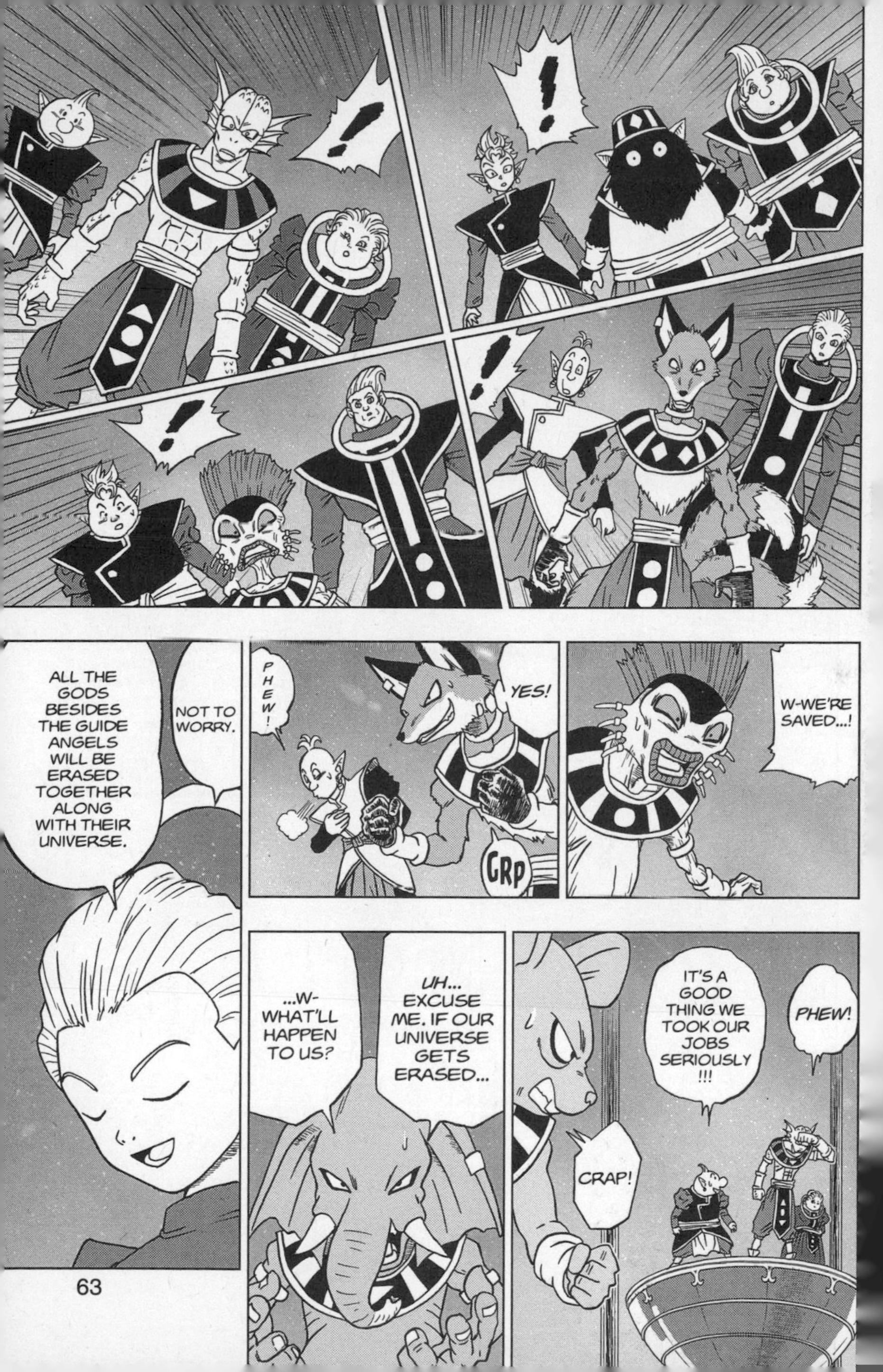
!
!
!
!
W-WE'RE SAVED...!
YES!
PHEW!
GRP
PHEW!
IT'S A GOOD THING WE TOOK OUR JOBS SERIOUSLY!!!
CRAP!
UH... EXCUSE ME. IF OUR UNIVERSE GETS ERASED...
...W-WHAT'LL HAPPEN TO US?
NOT TO WORRY.
ALL THE GODS BESIDES THE GUIDE ANGELS WILL BE ERASED TOGETHER ALONG WITH THEIR UNIVERSE.

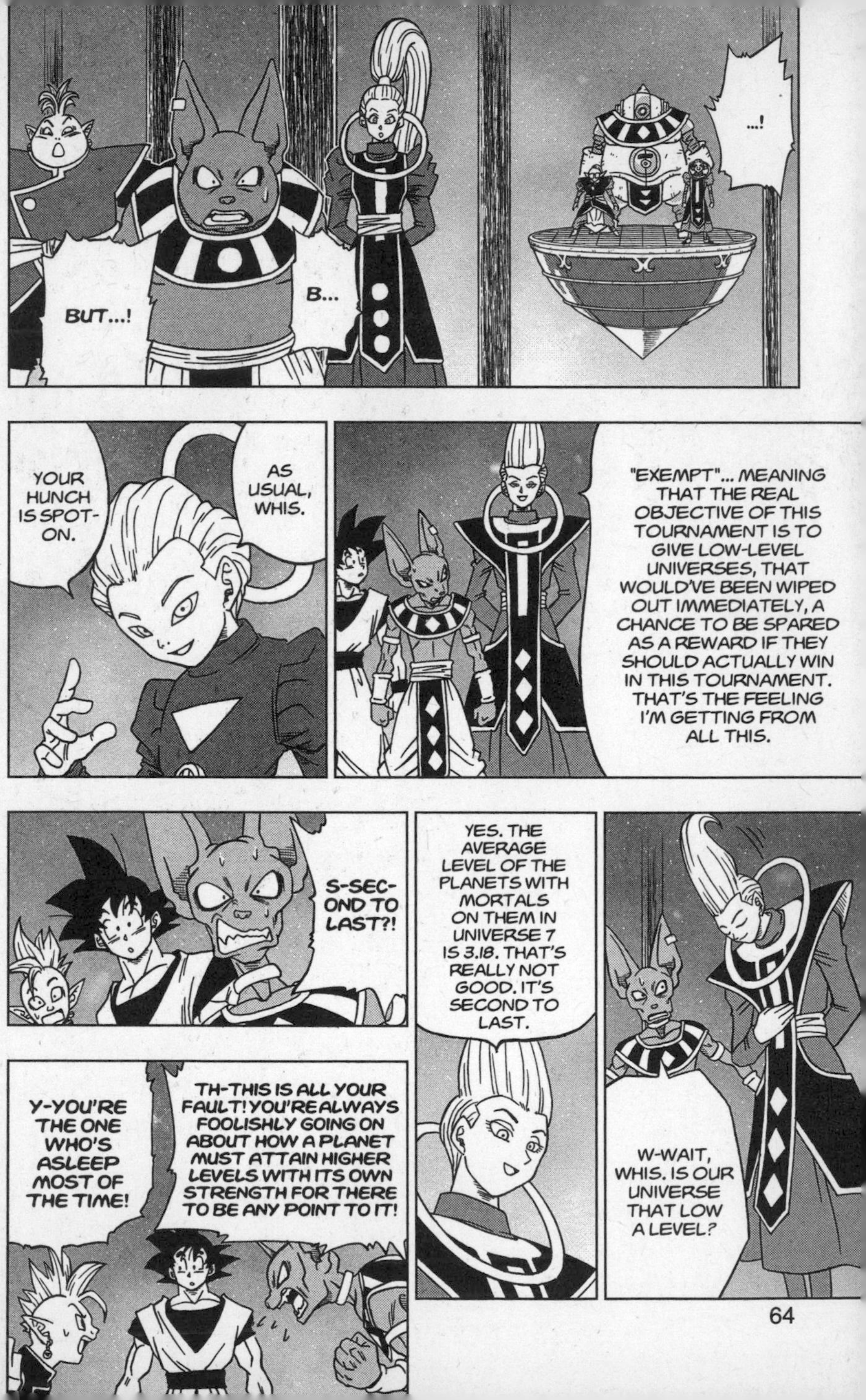
...!
B...
BUT...!
"EXEMPT"... MEANING THAT THE REAL OBJECTIVE OF THIS TOURNAMENT IS TO GIVE LOW-LEVEL UNIVERSES, THAT WOULD'VE BEEN WIPED OUT IMMEDIATELY, A CHANCE TO BE SPARED AS A REWARD IF THEY SHOULD ACTUALLY WIN IN THIS TOURNAMENT. THAT'S THE FEELING I'M GETTING FROM ALL THIS.
AS USUAL, WHIS.
YOUR HUNCH IS SPOT-ON.
W-WAIT, WHIS. IS OUR UNIVERSE THAT LOW A LEVEL?
YES. THE AVERAGE LEVEL OF THE PLANETS WITH MORTALS ON THEM IN UNIVERSE 7 IS 3.18. THAT'S REALLY NOT GOOD. IT'S SECOND TO LAST.
S-SEC-OND TO LAST?!
TH-THIS IS ALL YOUR FAULT! YOU'RE ALWAYS FOOLISHLY GOING ON ABOUT HOW A PLANET MUST ATTAIN HIGHER LEVELS WITH ITS OWN STRENGTH FOR THERE TO BE ANY POINT TO IT!
Y-YOU'RE THE ONE WHO'S ASLEEP MOST OF THE TIME!

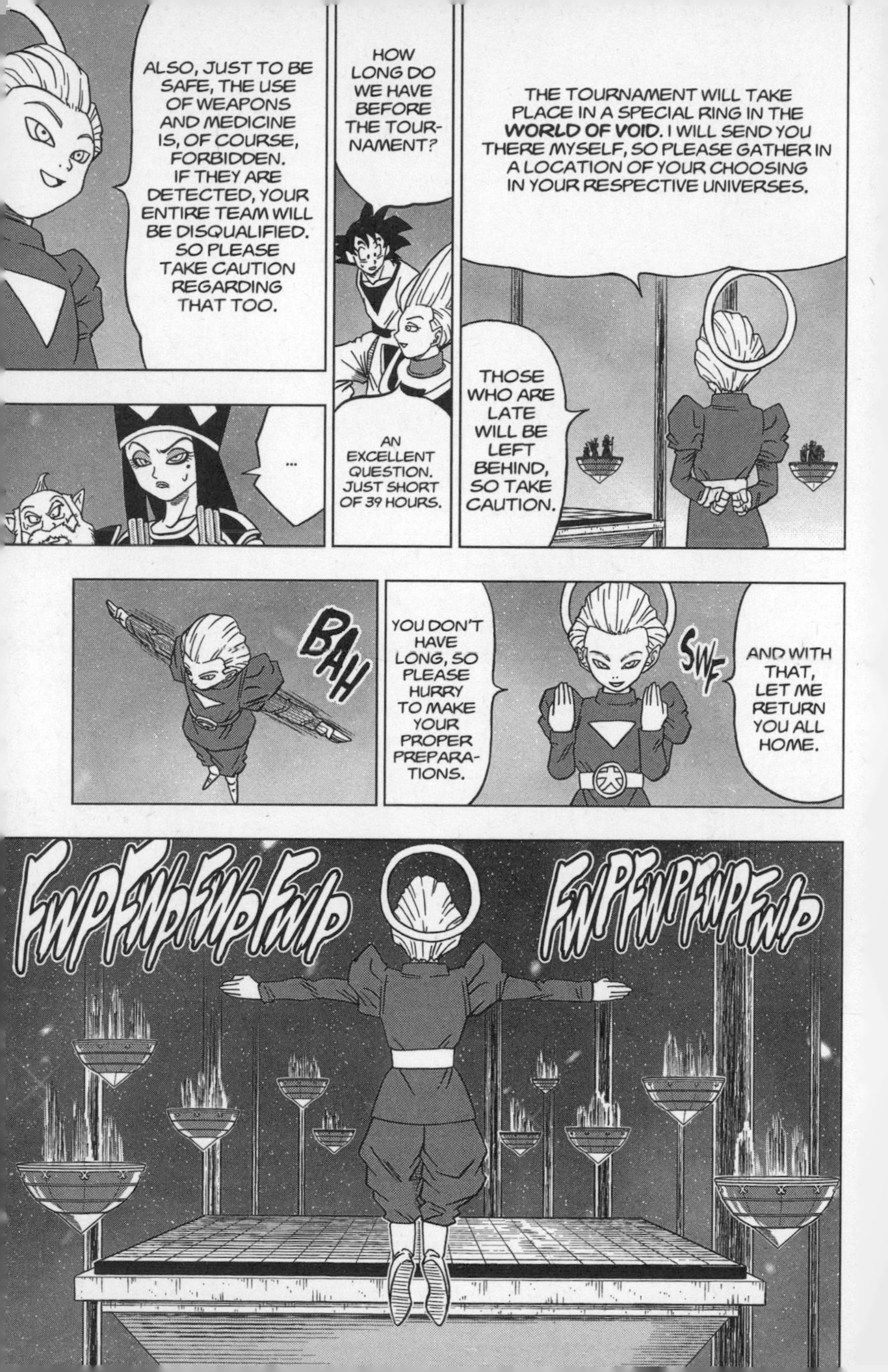
THE TOURNAMENT WILL TAKE PLACE IN A SPECIAL RING IN THE **WORLD OF VOID**. I WILL SEND YOU THERE MYSELF, SO PLEASE GATHER IN A LOCATION OF YOUR CHOOSING IN YOUR RESPECTIVE UNIVERSES.
THOSE WHO ARE LATE WILL BE LEFT BEHIND, SO TAKE CAUTION.
HOW LONG DO WE HAVE BEFORE THE TOURNAMENT?
AN EXCELLENT QUESTION. JUST SHORT OF 39 HOURS.
ALSO, JUST TO BE SAFE, THE USE OF WEAPONS AND MEDICINE IS, OF COURSE, FORBIDDEN. IF THEY ARE DETECTED, YOUR ENTIRE TEAM WILL BE DISQUALIFIED. SO PLEASE TAKE CAUTION REGARDING THAT TOO.
...
AND WITH THAT, LET ME RETURN YOU ALL HOME.
SWF
YOU DON'T HAVE LONG, SO PLEASE HURRY TO MAKE YOUR PROPER PREPARATIONS.
BAH
FWIP FWIP FWIP FWIP
FWIP FWIP FWIP FWIP

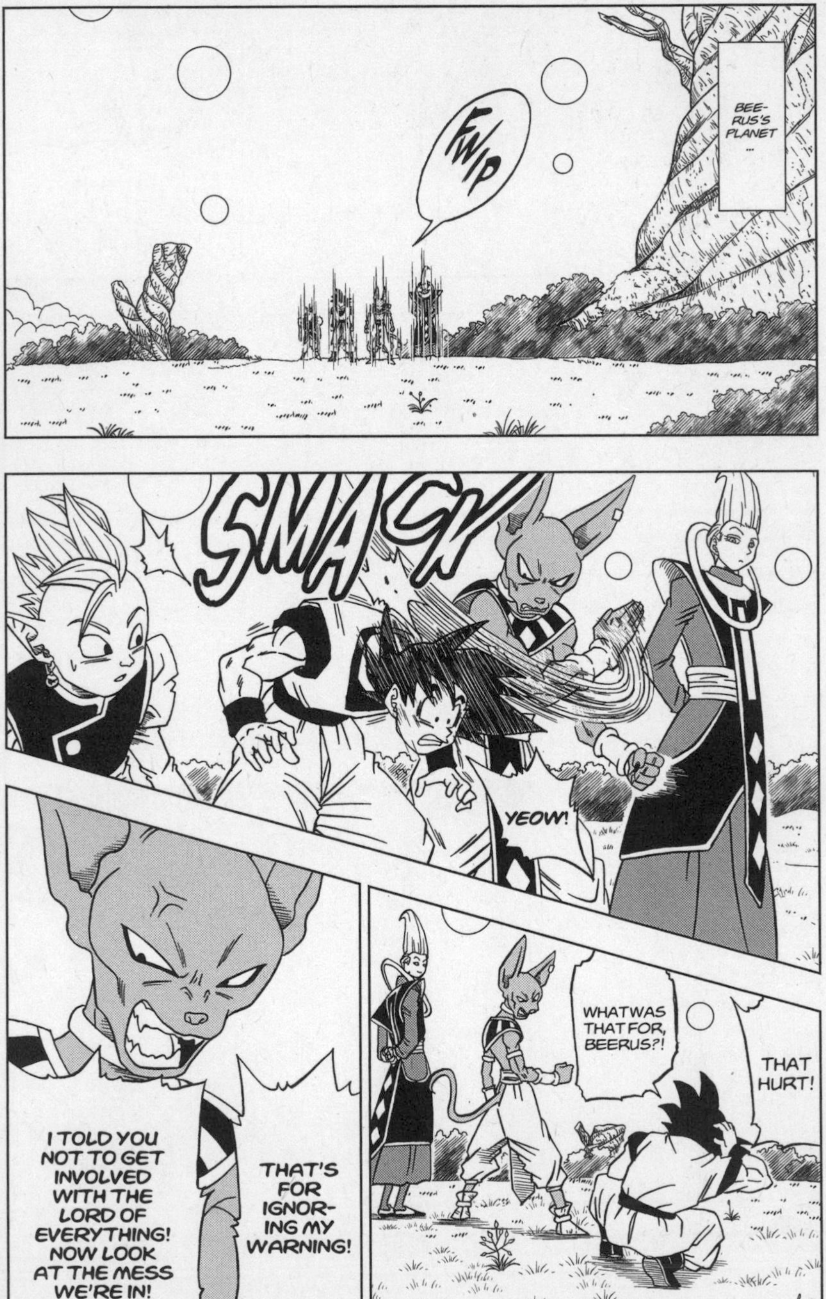
BEE-RUS'S PLANET ...
FWIP
SMACK
YEOW!
THAT HURT!
WHATWAS THAT FOR, BEERUS?!
THAT'S FOR IGNORING MY WARNING!
I TOLD YOU NOT TO GET INVOLVED WITH THE LORD OF EVERYTHING! NOW LOOK AT THE MESS WE'RE IN!

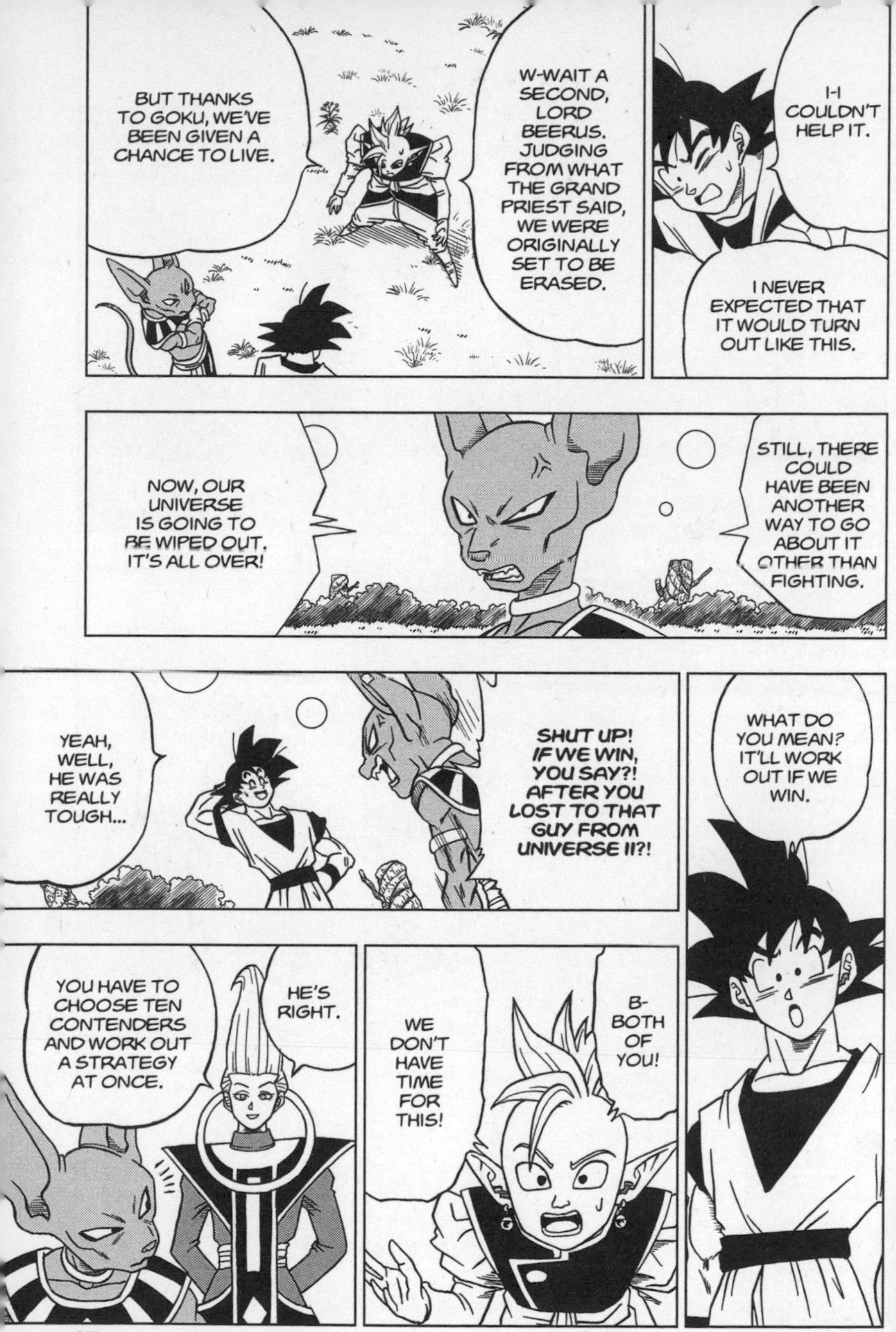
I-I COULDN'T HELP IT.
I NEVER EXPECTED THAT IT WOULD TURN OUT LIKE THIS.
W-WAIT A SECOND, LORD BEERUS. JUDGING FROM WHAT THE GRAND PRIEST SAID, WE WERE ORIGINALLY SET TO BE ERASED.
BUT THANKS TO GOKU, WE'VE BEEN GIVEN A CHANCE TO LIVE.
STILL, THERE COULD HAVE BEEN ANOTHER WAY TO GO ABOUT IT OTHER THAN FIGHTING.
NOW, OUR UNIVERSE IS GOING TO BE WIPED OUT. IT'S ALL OVER!
WHAT DO YOU MEAN? IT'LL WORK OUT IF WE WIN.
SHUT UP! IF WE WIN, YOU SAY?! AFTER YOU LOST TO THAT GUY FROM UNIVERSE 11?!
YEAH, WELL, HE WAS REALLY TOUGH...
B-BOTH OF YOU!
WE DON'T HAVE TIME FOR THIS!
HE'S RIGHT.
YOU HAVE TO CHOOSE TEN CONTENDERS AND WORK OUT A STRATEGY AT ONCE.

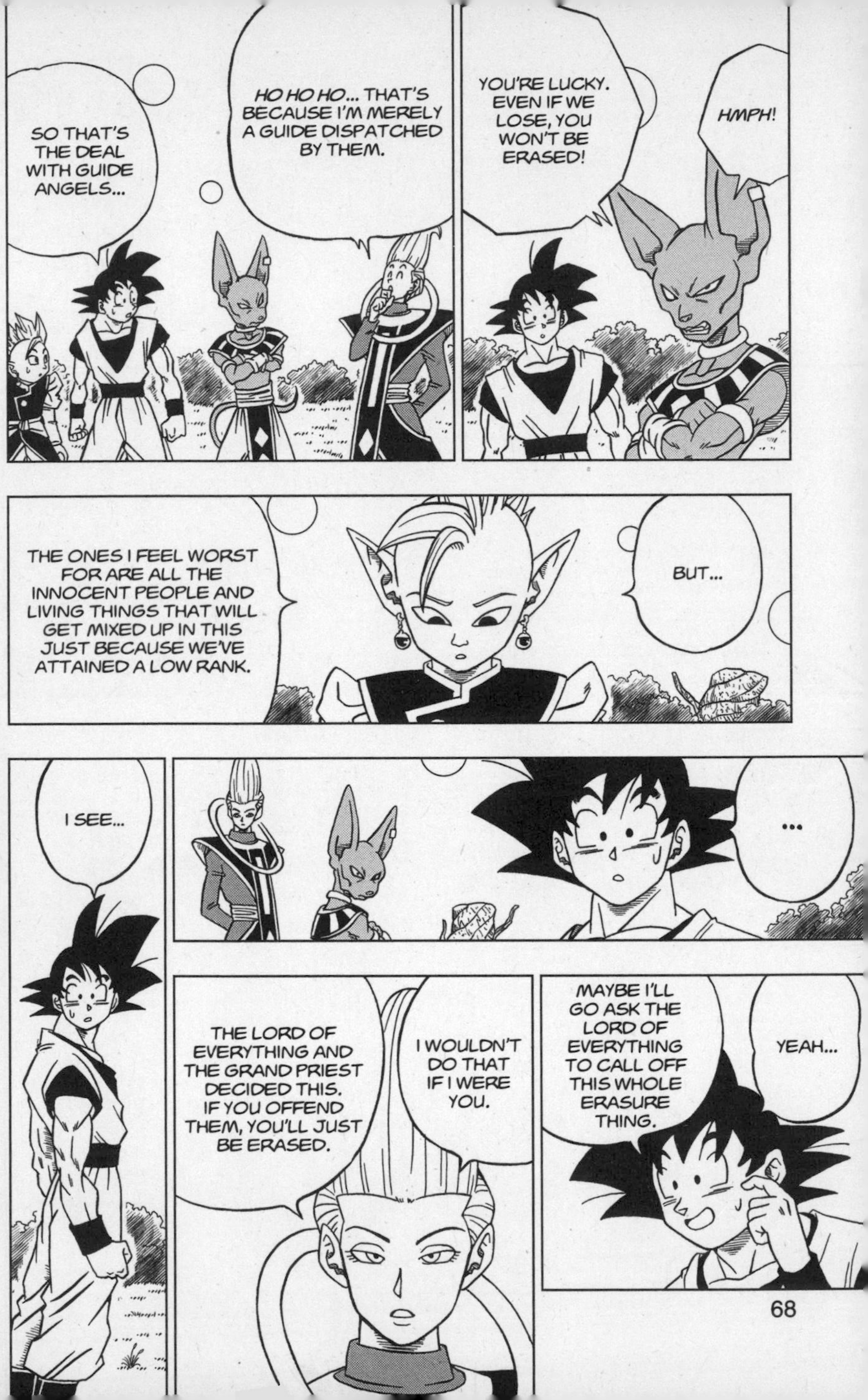

YOU'RE LUCKY. EVEN IF WE LOSE, YOU WON'T BE ERASED!
HMPH!
HO HO HO... THAT'S BECAUSE I'M MERELY A GUIDE DISPATCHED BY THEM.
SO THAT'S THE DEAL WITH GUIDE ANGELS...
BUT...
THE ONES I FEEL WORST FOR ARE ALL THE INNOCENT PEOPLE AND LIVING THINGS THAT WILL GET MIXED UP IN THIS JUST BECAUSE WE'VE ATTAINED A LOW RANK.
...
YEAH...
MAYBE I'LL GO ASK THE LORD OF EVERYTHING TO CALL OFF THIS WHOLE ERASURE THING.
I WOULDN'T DO THAT IF I WERE YOU.
THE LORD OF EVERYTHING AND THE GRAND PRIEST DECIDED THIS. IF YOU OFFEND THEM, YOU'LL JUST BE ERASED.
I SEE...

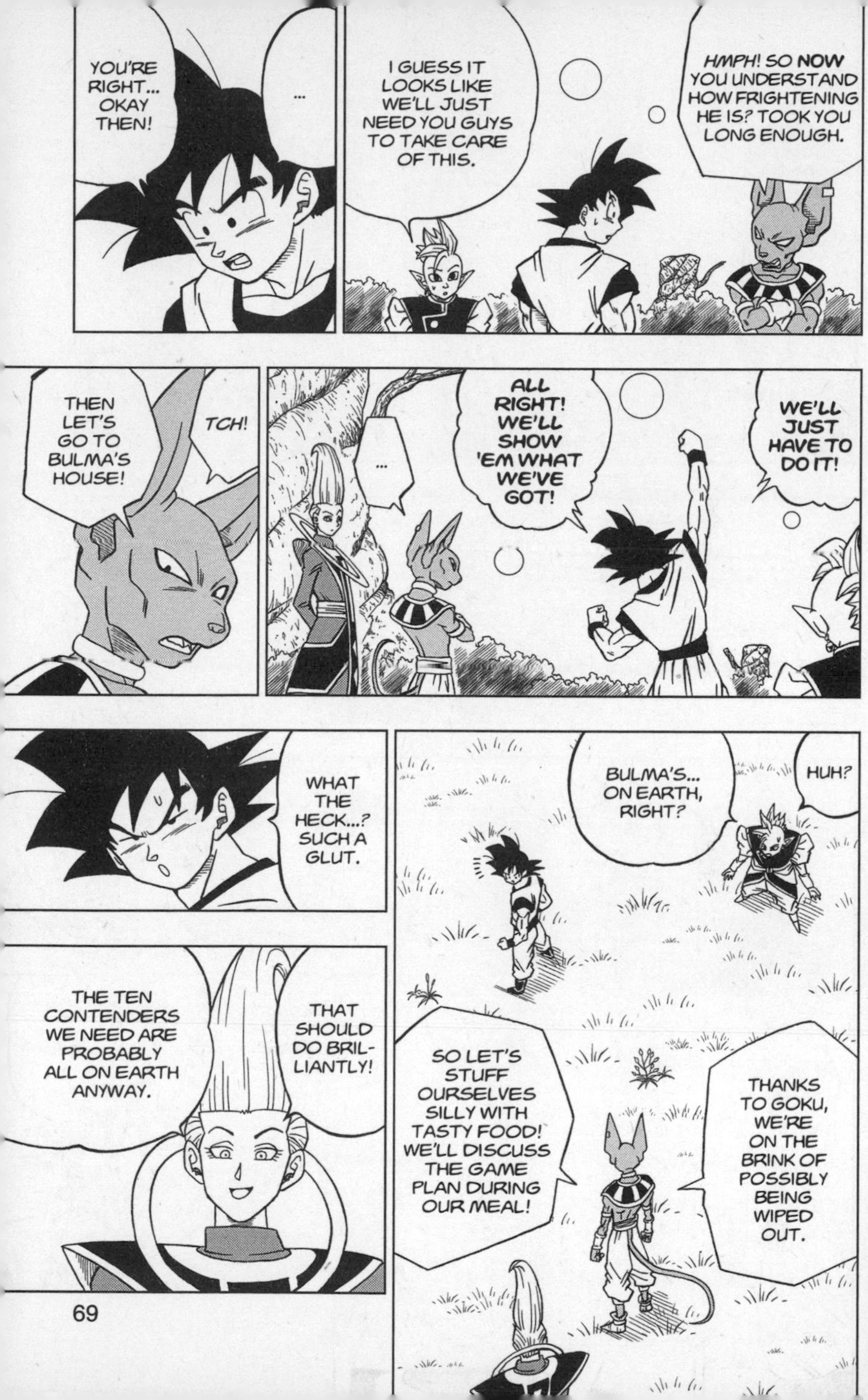
HMPH! SO NOW YOU UNDERSTAND HOW FRIGHTENING HE IS? TOOK YOU LONG ENOUGH.
I GUESS IT LOOKS LIKE WE'LL JUST NEED YOU GUYS TO TAKE CARE OF THIS.
...
YOU'RE RIGHT... OKAY THEN!
WE'LL JUST HAVE TO DO IT!
ALL RIGHT! WE'LL SHOW 'EM WHAT WE'VE GOT!
...
TCH!
THEN LET'S GO TO BULMA'S HOUSE!
HUH?
BULMA'S... ON EARTH, RIGHT?
THANKS TO GOKU, WE'RE ON THE BRINK OF POSSIBLY BEING WIPED OUT.
SO LET'S STUFF OURSELVES SILLY WITH TASTY FOOD! WE'LL DISCUSS THE GAME PLAN DURING OUR MEAL!
WHAT THE HECK...? SUCH A GLUT.
THAT SHOULD DO BRILLIANTLY!
THE TEN CONTENDERS WE NEED ARE PROBABLY ALL ON EARTH ANYWAY.

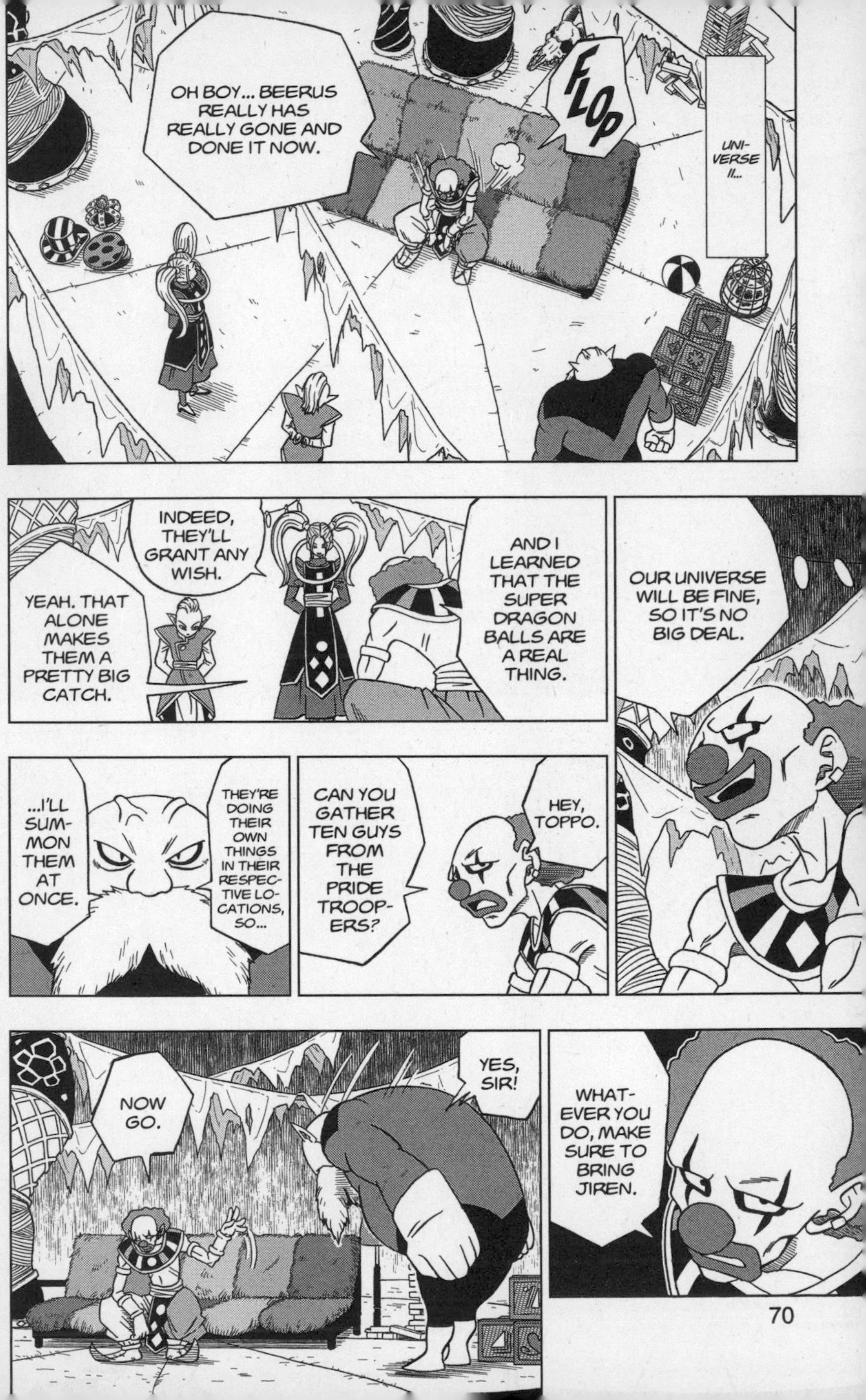
UNIVERSE 11...
FLOP
OH BOY... BEERUS REALLY HAS REALLY GONE AND DONE IT NOW.
OUR UNIVERSE WILL BE FINE, SO IT'S NO BIG DEAL.
AND I LEARNED THAT THE SUPER DRAGON BALLS ARE A REAL THING.
INDEED, THEY'LL GRANT ANY WISH.
YEAH. THAT ALONE MAKES THEM A PRETTY BIG CATCH.
HEY, TOPPO.
CAN YOU GATHER TEN GUYS FROM THE PRIDE TROOPERS?
THEY'RE DOING THEIR OWN THINGS IN THEIR RESPECTIVE LOCATIONS, SO...
...I'LL SUMMON THEM AT ONCE.
WHATEVER YOU DO, MAKE SURE TO BRING JIREN.
YES, SIR!
NOW GO.

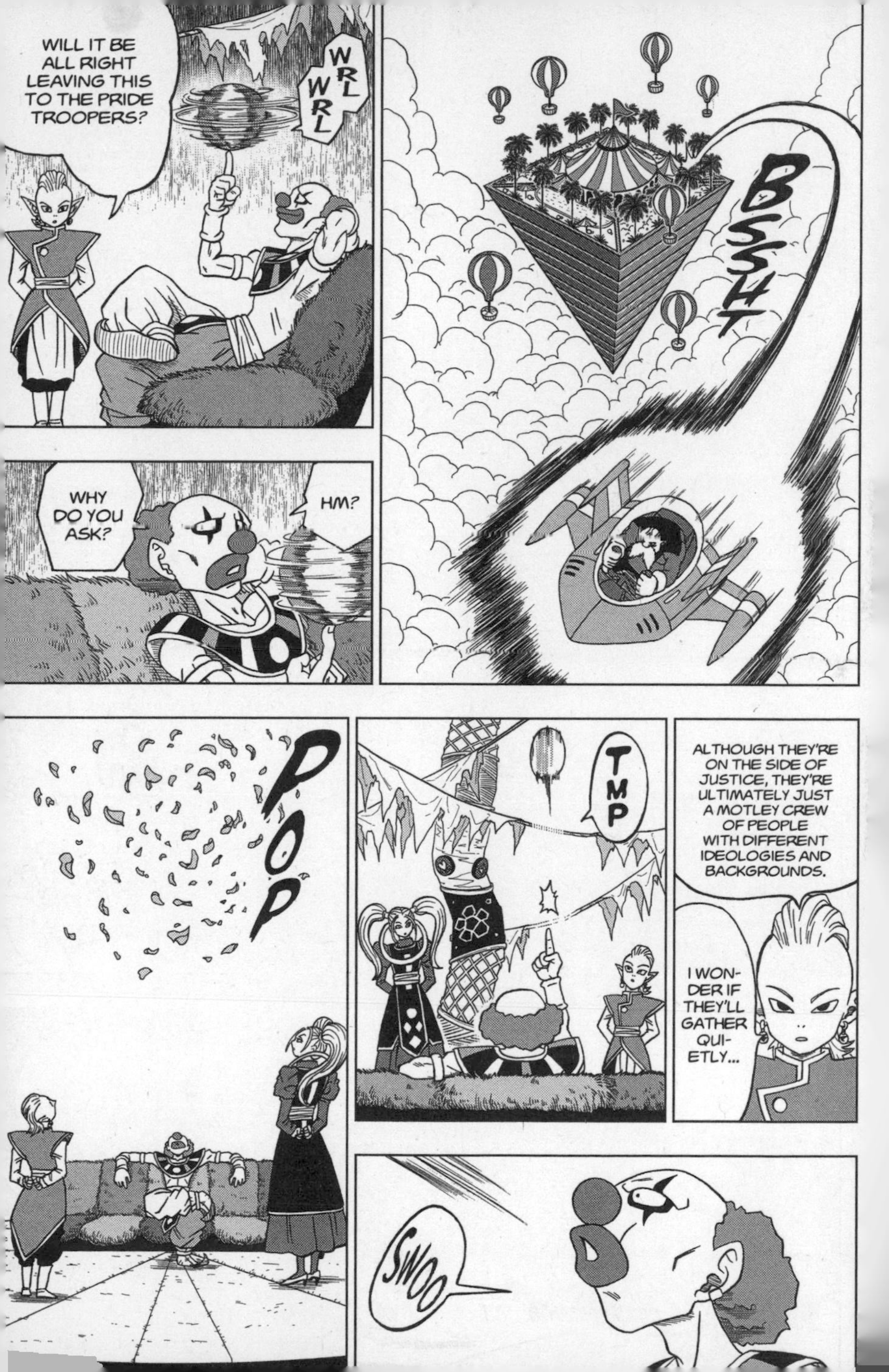
BSSHT
WRL WRL
WILL IT BE ALL RIGHT LEAVING THIS TO THE PRIDE TROOPERS?
HM?
WHY DO YOU ASK?
ALTHOUGH THEY'RE ON THE SIDE OF JUSTICE, THEY'RE ULTIMATELY JUST A MOTLEY CREW OF PEOPLE WITH DIFFERENT IDEOLOGIES AND BACKGROUNDS.
I WONDER IF THEY'LL GATHER QUIETLY...
TMP
SWOO
POP

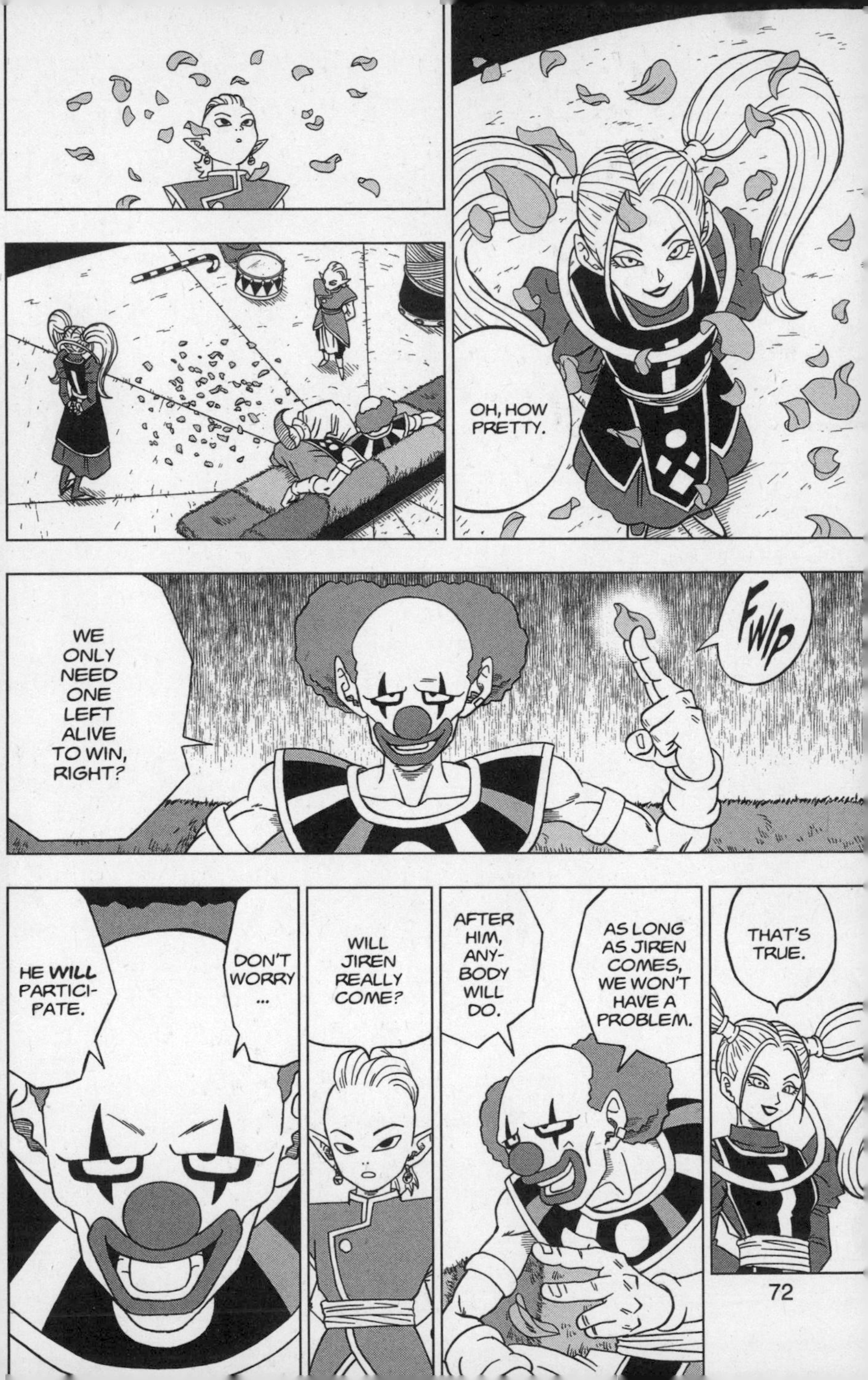
OH, HOW PRETTY.
FWIP
WE ONLY NEED ONE LEFT ALIVE TO WIN, RIGHT?
THAT'S TRUE.
AS LONG AS JIREN COMES, WE WON'T HAVE A PROBLEM.
AFTER HIM, ANYBODY WILL DO.
WILL JIREN REALLY COME?
DON'T WORRY...
HE **WILL** PARTICIPATE.

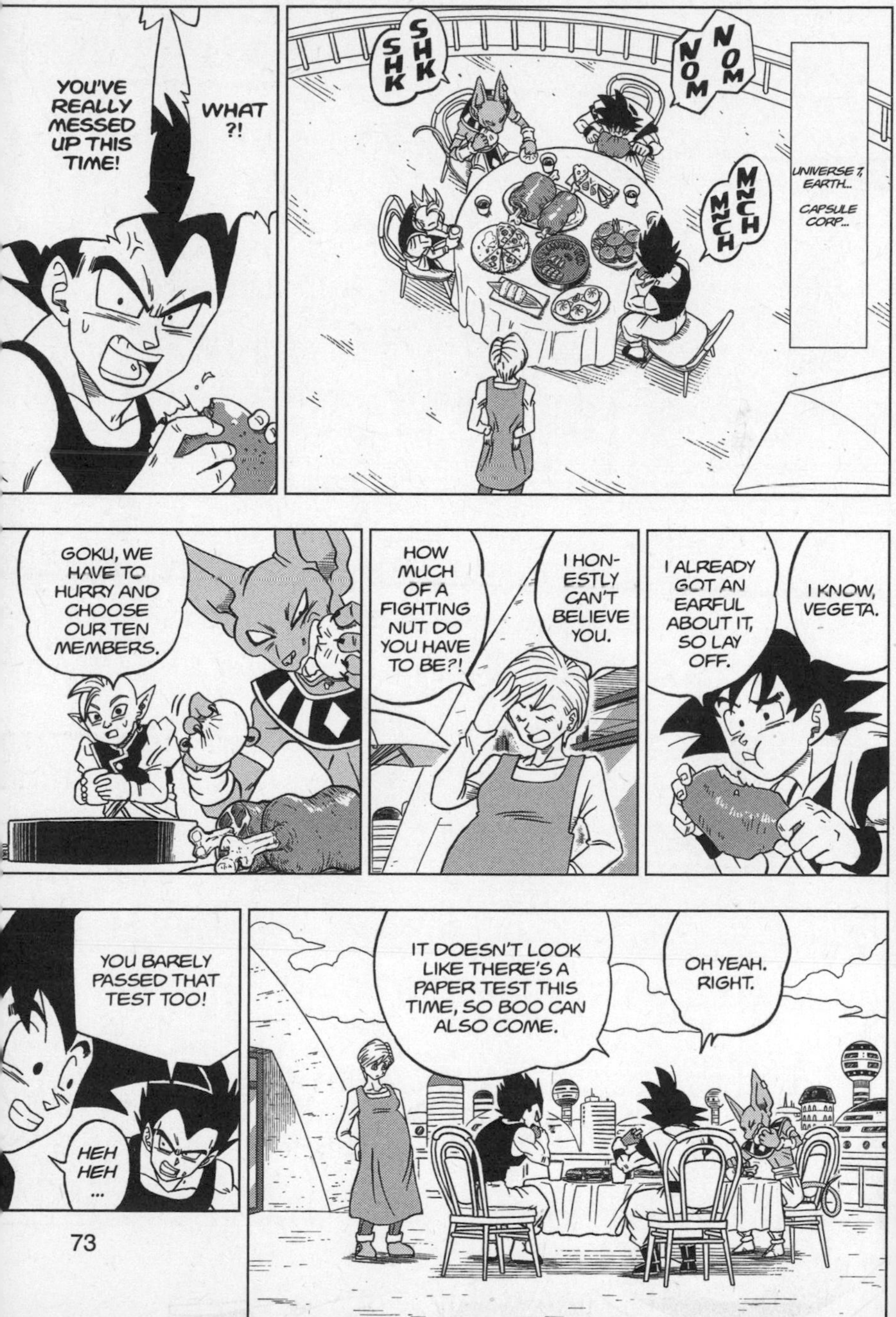
UNIVERSE 7, EARTH...
CAPSULE CORP...
NOM NOM
SHK SHK
MNCH MNCH
WHAT ?!
YOU'VE REALLY MESSED UP THIS TIME!
I KNOW, VEGETA.
I ALREADY GOT AN EARFUL ABOUT IT, SO LAY OFF.
I HON-ESTLY CAN'T BELIEVE YOU.
HOW MUCH OF A FIGHTING NUT DO YOU HAVE TO BE?!
GOKU, WE HAVE TO HURRY AND CHOOSE OUR TEN MEMBERS.
OH YEAH. RIGHT.
IT DOESN'T LOOK LIKE THERE'S A PAPER TEST THIS TIME, SO BOO CAN ALSO COME.
YOU BARELY PASSED THAT TEST TOO!
HEH HEH ...

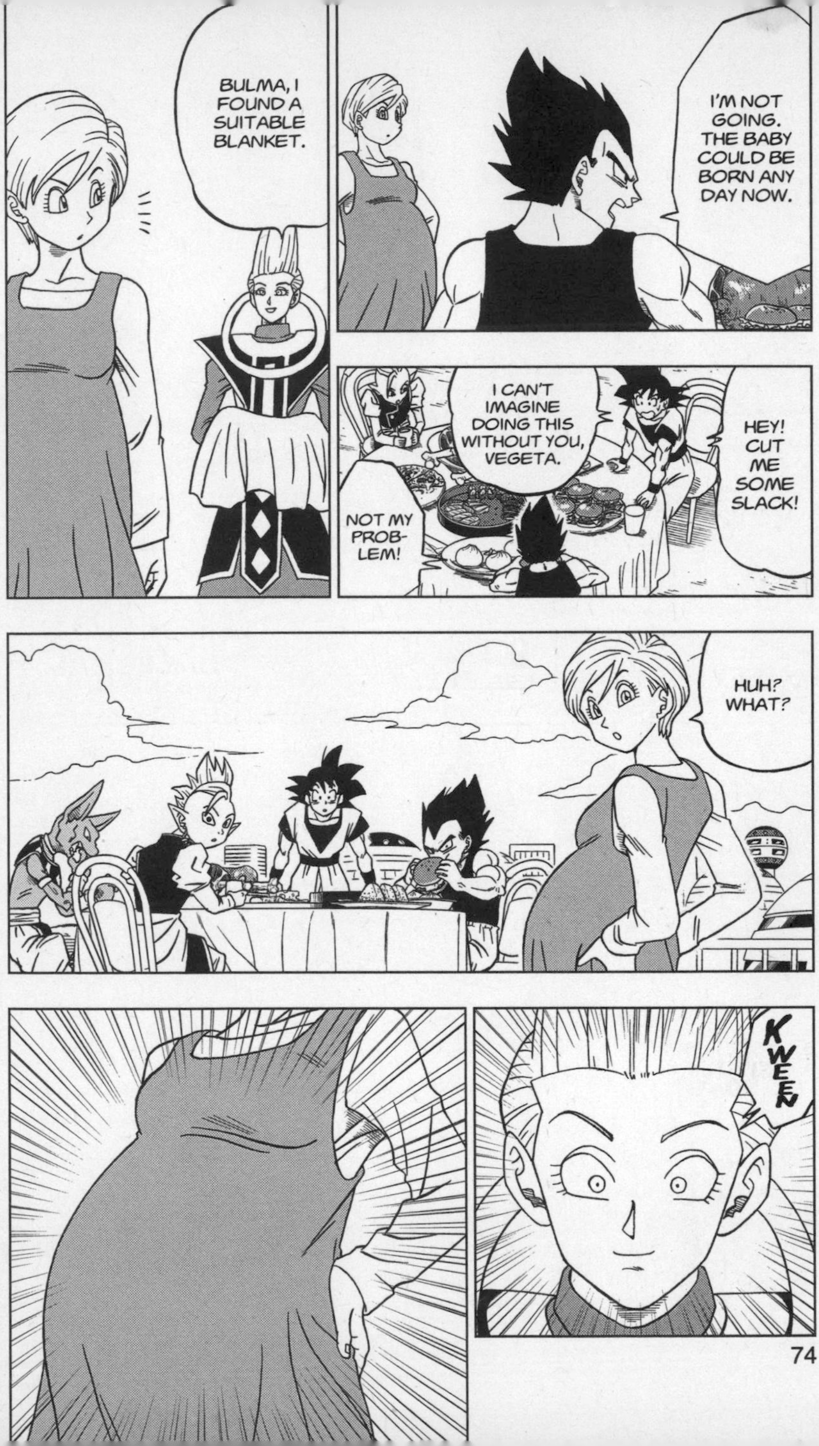

I'M NOT GOING. THE BABY COULD BE BORN ANY DAY NOW.
I CAN'T IMAGINE DOING THIS WITHOUT YOU, VEGETA.
NOT MY PROB-LEM!
HEY! CUT ME SOME SLACK!
BULMA, I FOUND A SUITABLE BLANKET.
HUH? WHAT?
KWEEN

THERE YOU GO, BULMA.

....!

!

NO WAY!

HUH?!

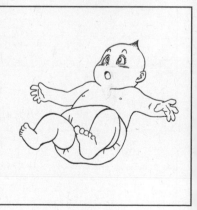

POOMF

75

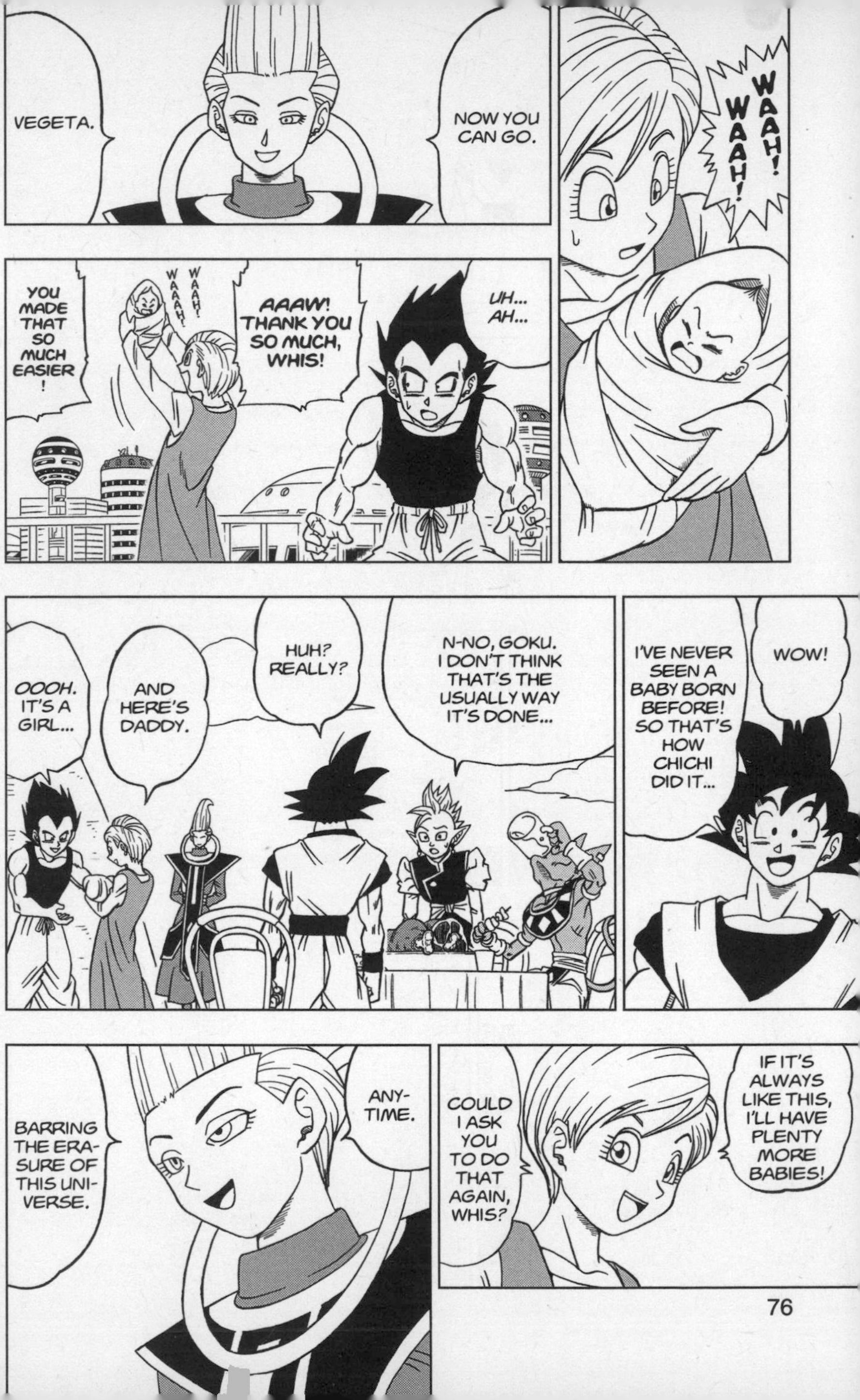
WAAH!
WAAH!
NOW YOU CAN GO.
VEGETA.
UH... AH...
AAAW! THANK YOU SO MUCH, WHIS!
WAAAH!
WAAH!
YOU MADE THAT SO MUCH EASIER!
WOW!
I'VE NEVER SEEN A BABY BORN BEFORE! SO THAT'S HOW CHICHI DID IT...
N-NO, GOKU. I DON'T THINK THAT'S THE USUALLY WAY IT'S DONE...
HUH? REALLY?
AND HERE'S DADDY.
OOOH. IT'S A GIRL...
IF IT'S ALWAYS LIKE THIS, I'LL HAVE PLENTY MORE BABIES!
COULD I ASK YOU TO DO THAT AGAIN, WHIS?
ANY-TIME.
BARRING THE ERA-SURE OF THIS UNI-VERSE.

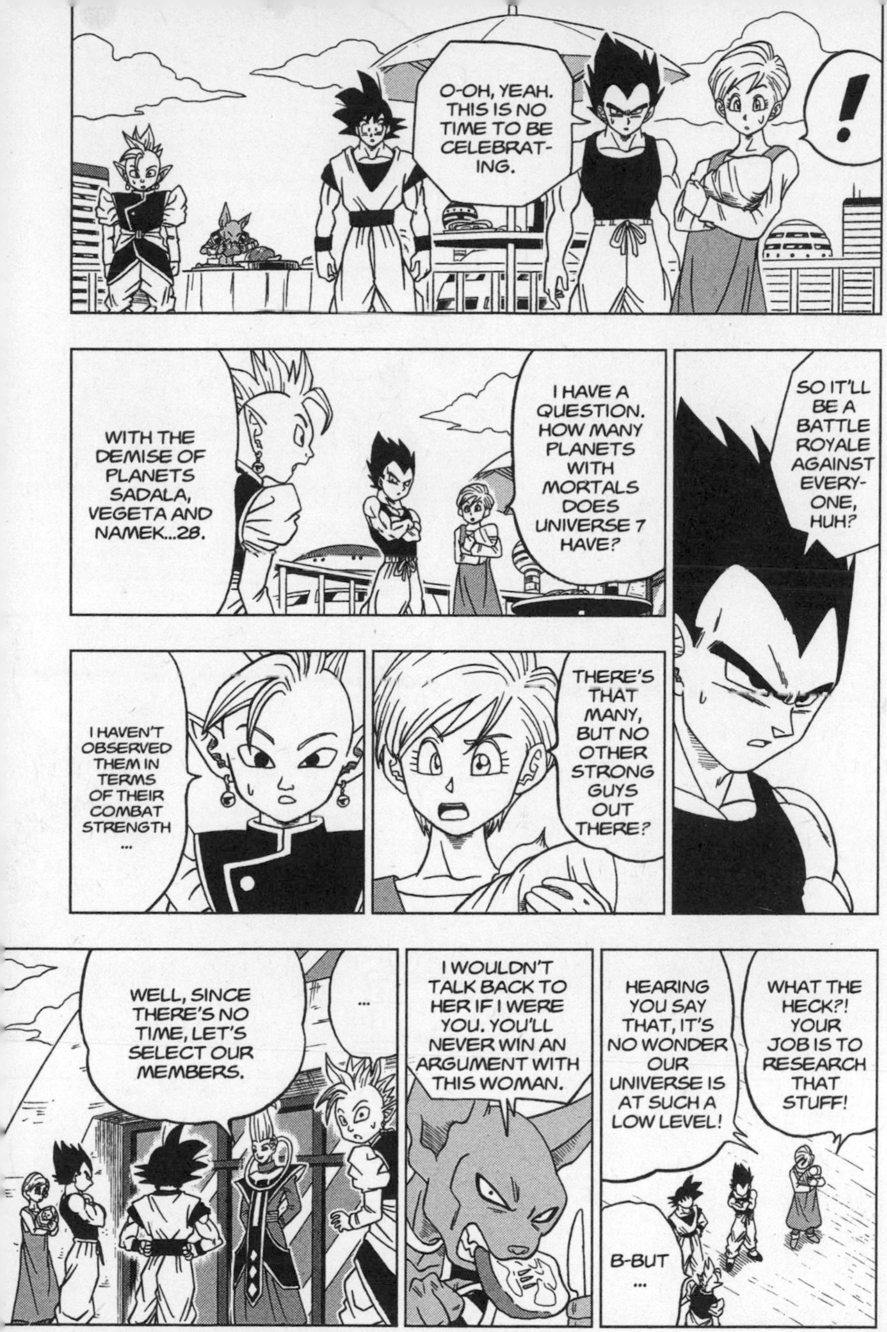
!
O-OH, YEAH. THIS IS NO TIME TO BE CELEBRAT-ING.
SO IT'LL BE A BATTLE ROYALE AGAINST EVERY-ONE, HUH?
I HAVE A QUESTION. HOW MANY PLANETS WITH MORTALS DOES UNIVERSE 7 HAVE?
WITH THE DEMISE OF PLANETS SADALA, VEGETA AND NAMEK...28.
THERE'S THAT MANY, BUT NO OTHER STRONG GUYS OUT THERE?
I HAVEN'T OBSERVED THEM IN TERMS OF THEIR COMBAT STRENGTH ...
WHAT THE HECK?! YOUR JOB IS TO RESEARCH THAT STUFF!
HEARING YOU SAY THAT, IT'S NO WONDER OUR UNIVERSE IS AT SUCH A LOW LEVEL!
B-BUT ...
I WOULDN'T TALK BACK TO HER IF I WERE YOU. YOU'LL NEVER WIN AN ARGUMENT WITH THIS WOMAN.
...
WELL, SINCE THERE'S NO TIME, LET'S SELECT OUR MEMBERS.

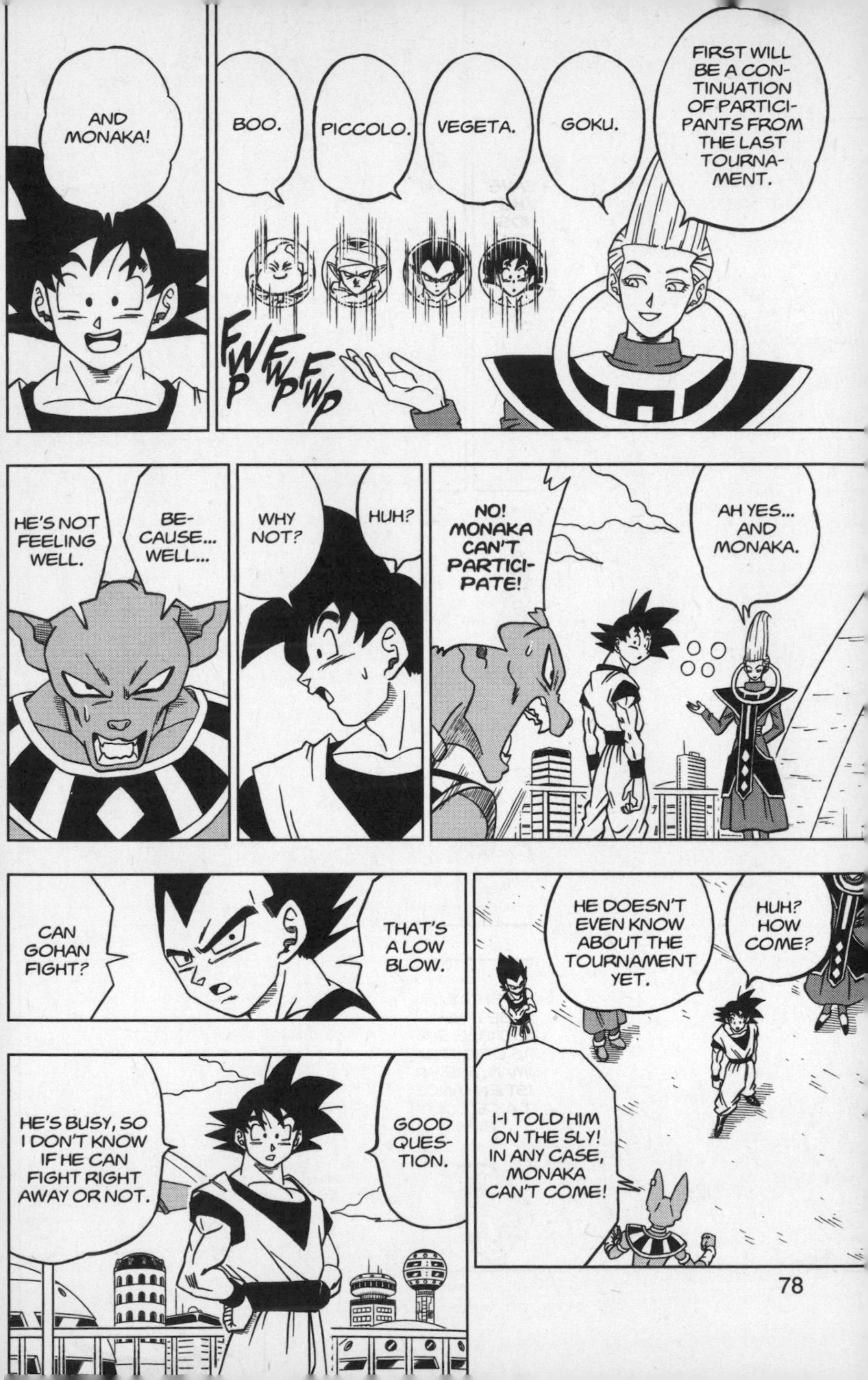
FIRST WILL BE A CONTINUATION OF PARTICIPANTS FROM THE LAST TOURNAMENT.
GOKU.
VEGETA.
PICCOLO.
BOO.
FWP FWP FWP FWP
AND MONAKA!
AH YES... AND MONAKA.
NO! MONAKA CAN'T PARTICIPATE!
HUH?
WHY NOT?
BECAUSE... WELL...
HE'S NOT FEELING WELL.
HUH? HOW COME?
HE DOESN'T EVEN KNOW ABOUT THE TOURNAMENT YET.
I-I TOLD HIM ON THE SLY! IN ANY CASE, MONAKA CAN'T COME!
THAT'S A LOW BLOW.
CAN GOHAN FIGHT?
GOOD QUESTION.
HE'S BUSY, SO I DON'T KNOW IF HE CAN FIGHT RIGHT AWAY OR NOT.

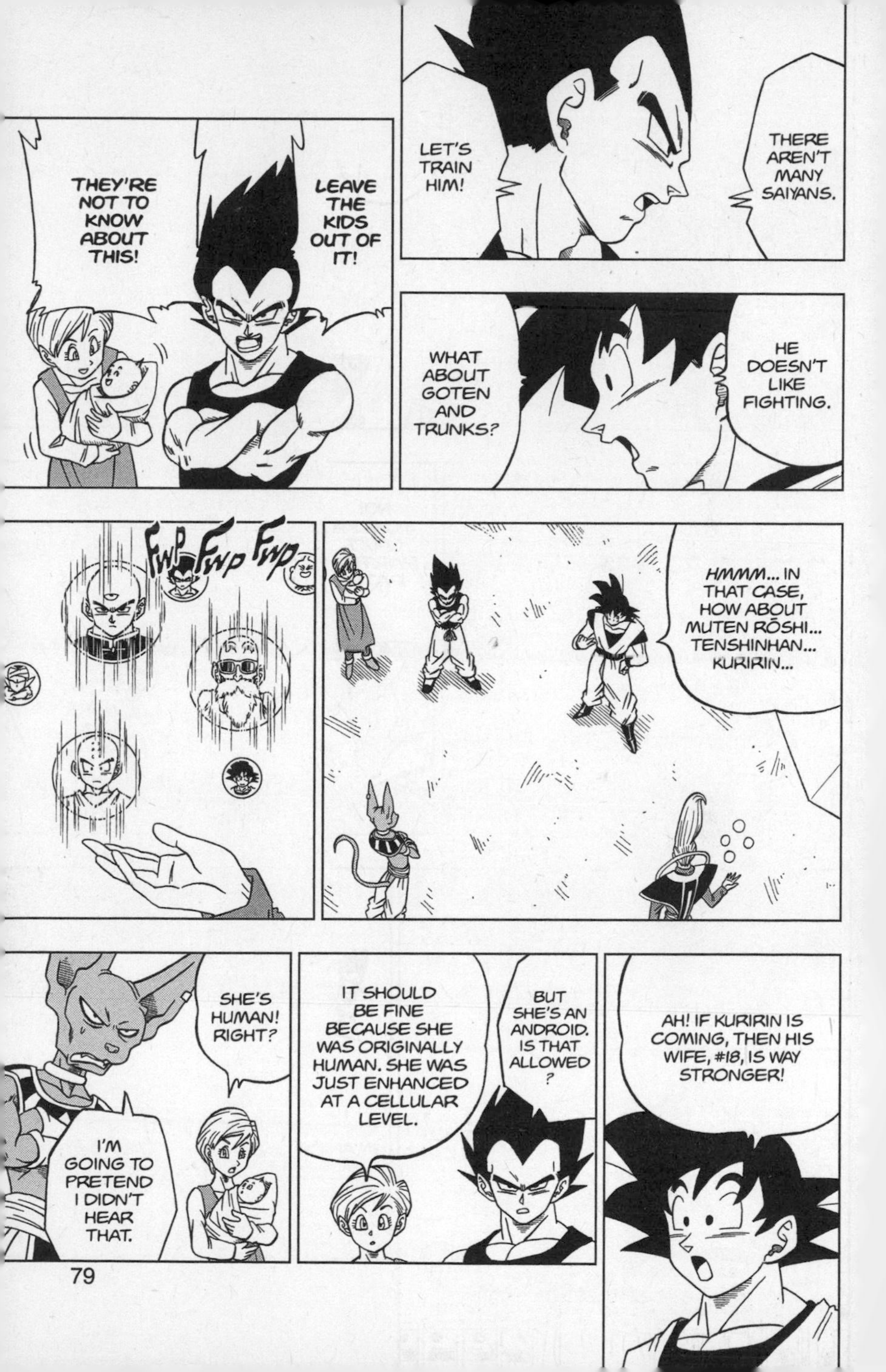
THERE AREN'T MANY SAIYANS.
LET'S TRAIN HIM!
HE DOESN'T LIKE FIGHTING.
WHAT ABOUT GOTEN AND TRUNKS?
LEAVE THE KIDS OUT OF IT!
THEY'RE NOT TO KNOW ABOUT THIS!
HMMM... IN THAT CASE, HOW ABOUT MUTEN RŌSHI... TENSHINHAN... KURIRIN...
FWP FWP FWP
AH! IF KURIRIN IS COMING, THEN HIS WIFE, #18, IS WAY STRONGER!
BUT SHE'S AN ANDROID. IS THAT ALLOWED?
IT SHOULD BE FINE BECAUSE SHE WAS ORIGINALLY HUMAN. SHE WAS JUST ENHANCED AT A CELLULAR LEVEL.
SHE'S HUMAN! RIGHT?
I'M GOING TO PRETEND I DIDN'T HEAR THAT.

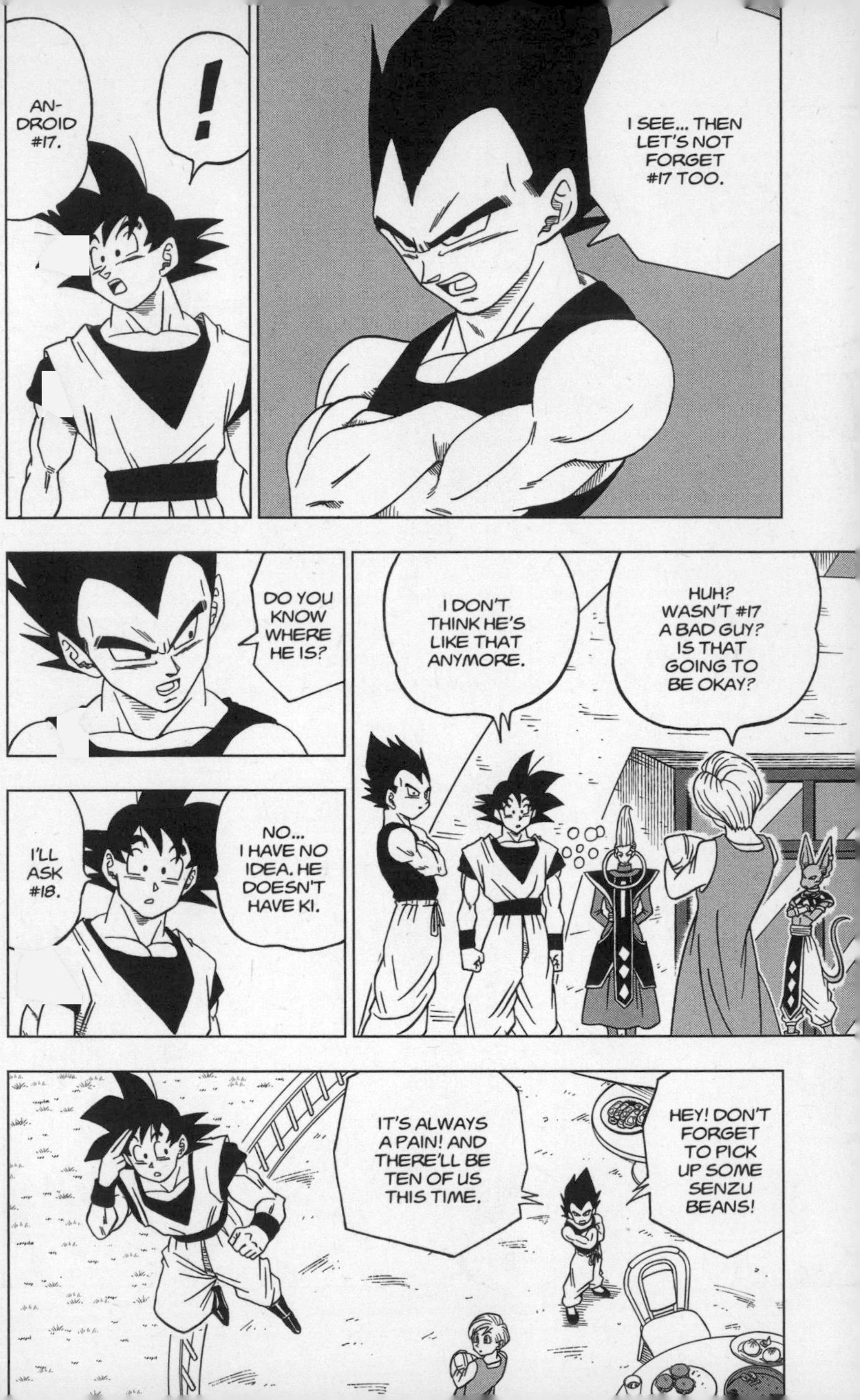

I SEE... THEN LET'S NOT FORGET #17 TOO.
!
AN-DROID #17.
HUH? WASN'T #17 A BAD GUY? IS THAT GOING TO BE OKAY?
I DON'T THINK HE'S LIKE THAT ANYMORE.
DO YOU KNOW WHERE HE IS?
NO... I HAVE NO IDEA. HE DOESN'T HAVE KI.
I'LL ASK #18.
HEY! DON'T FORGET TO PICK UP SOME SENZU BEANS!
IT'S ALWAYS A PAIN! AND THERE'LL BE TEN OF US THIS TIME.

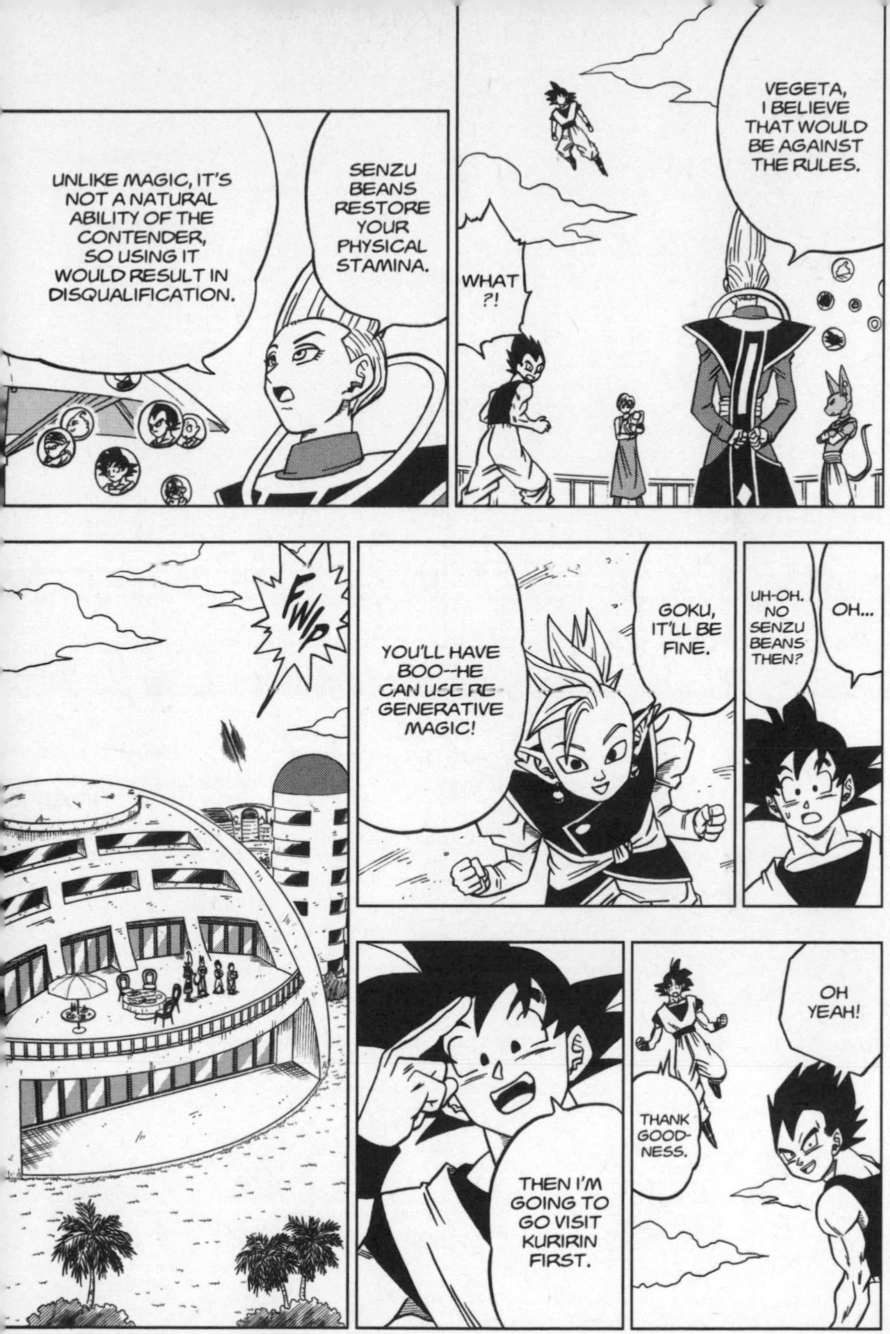
VEGETA, I BELIEVE THAT WOULD BE AGAINST THE RULES.
WHAT ?!
SENZU BEANS RESTORE YOUR PHYSICAL STAMINA.
UNLIKE MAGIC, IT'S NOT A NATURAL ABILITY OF THE CONTENDER, SO USING IT WOULD RESULT IN DISQUALIFICATION.
OH...
UH-OH. NO SENZU BEANS THEN?
GOKU, IT'LL BE FINE.
YOU'LL HAVE BOO--HE CAN USE RE-GENERATIVE MAGIC!
OH YEAH!
THANK GOOD-NESS.
THEN I'M GOING TO GO VISIT KURIRIN FIRST.
FWIP

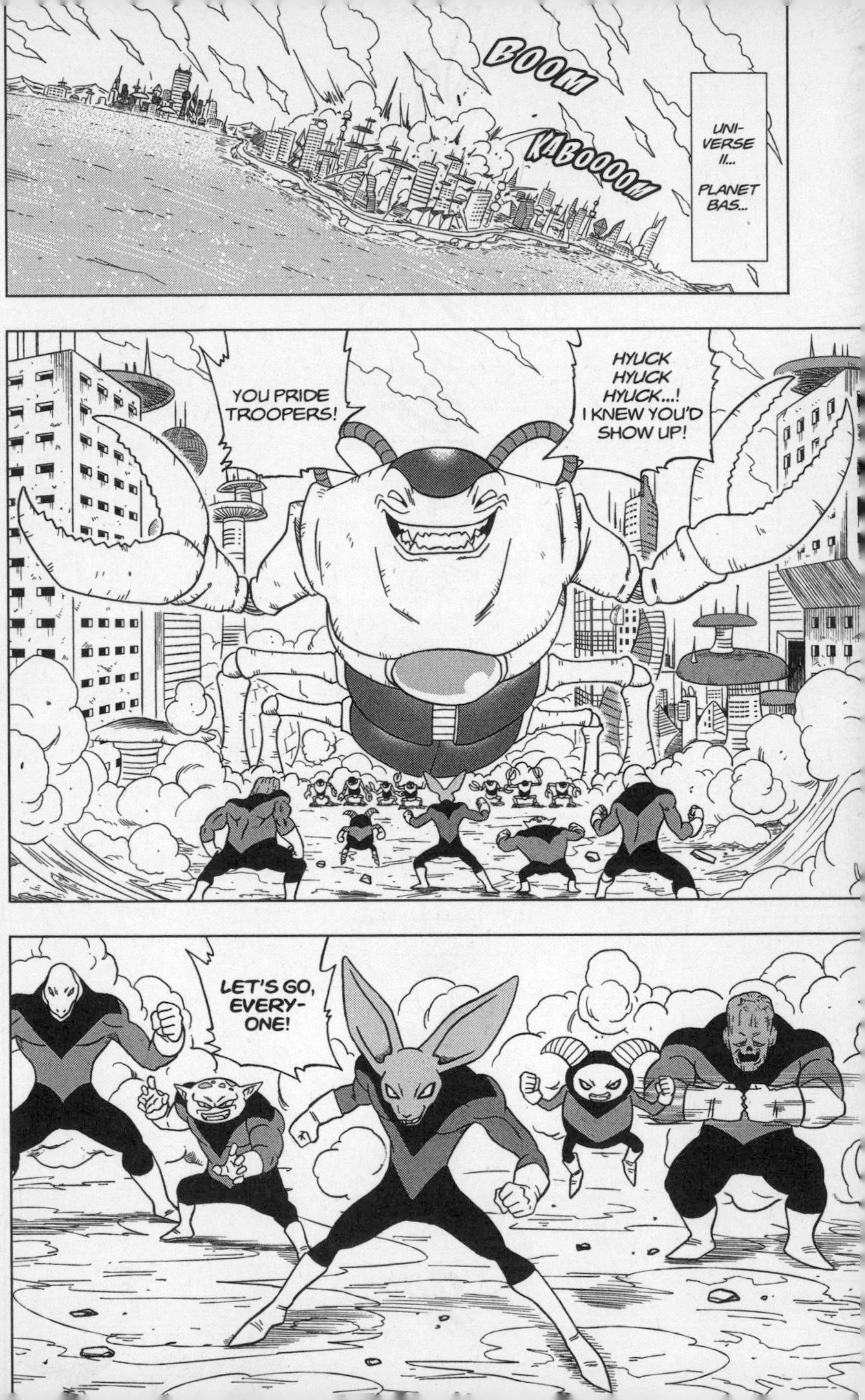
UNI-VERSE 11... PLANET BAS...
BOOM
KABOOOOM
HYUCK HYUCK HYUCK...! I KNEW YOU'D SHOW UP!
YOU PRIDE TROOPERS!
LET'S GO, EVERY-ONE!

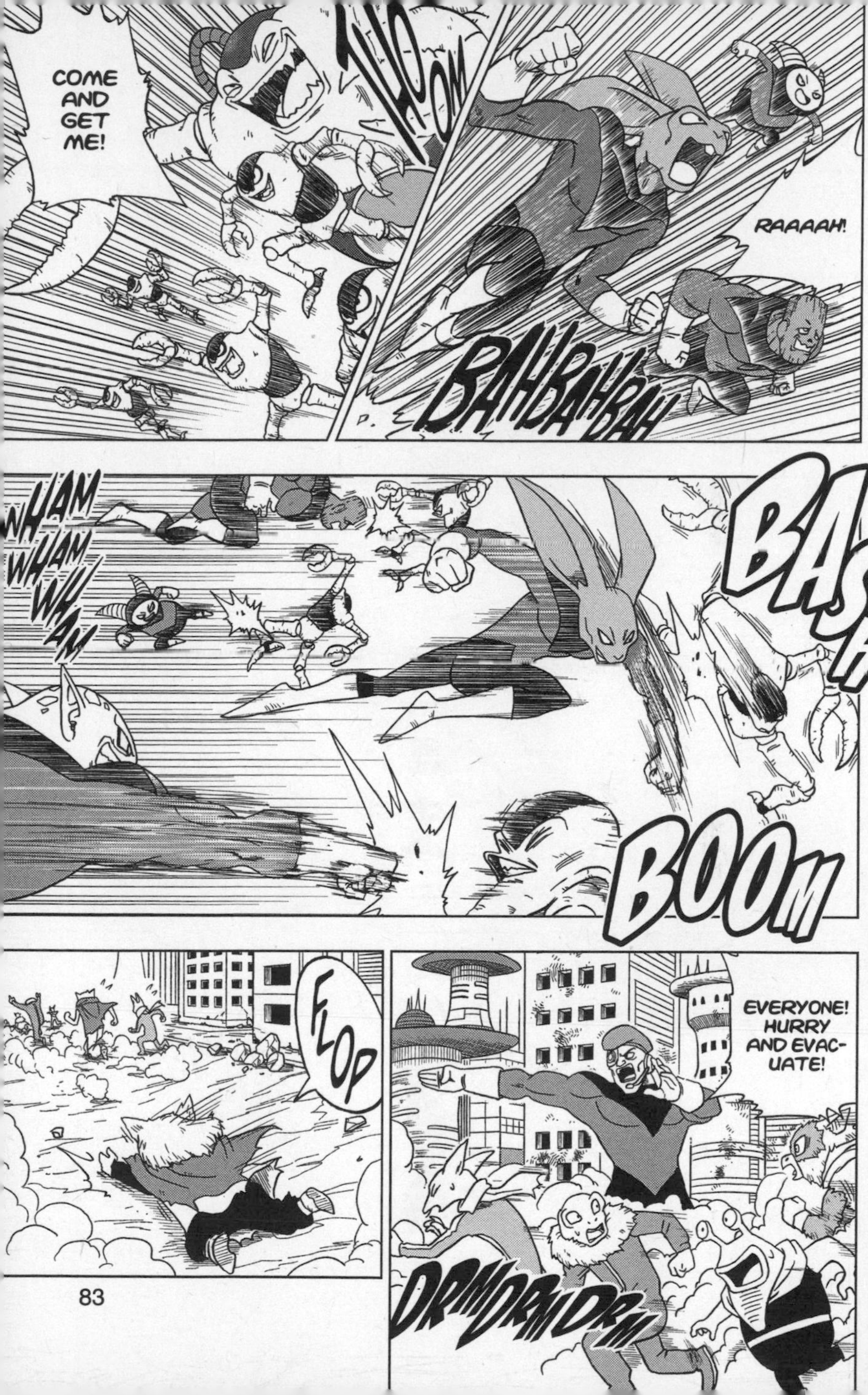
RAAAAH!
BAHBAHBAH
VROOM
COME AND GET ME!
BASH
BOOM
WHAM WHAM WHAM WHAM
EVERYONE! HURRY AND EVAC-UATE!
DRMDRMDRM
FLOP

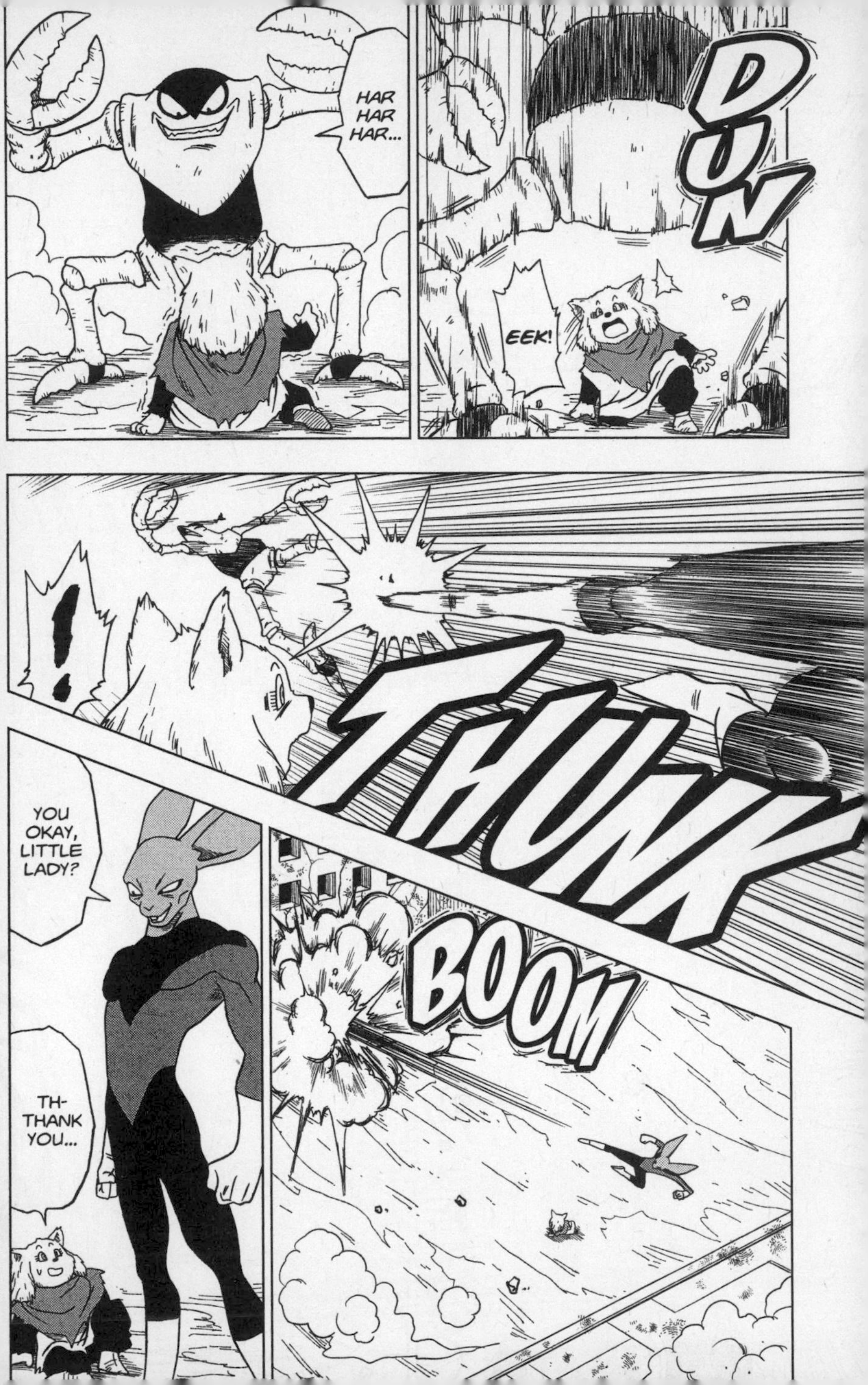
DON
EEK!
HAR HAR HAR...
!
THUNK
BOOM
YOU OKAY, LITTLE LADY?
TH- THANK YOU...

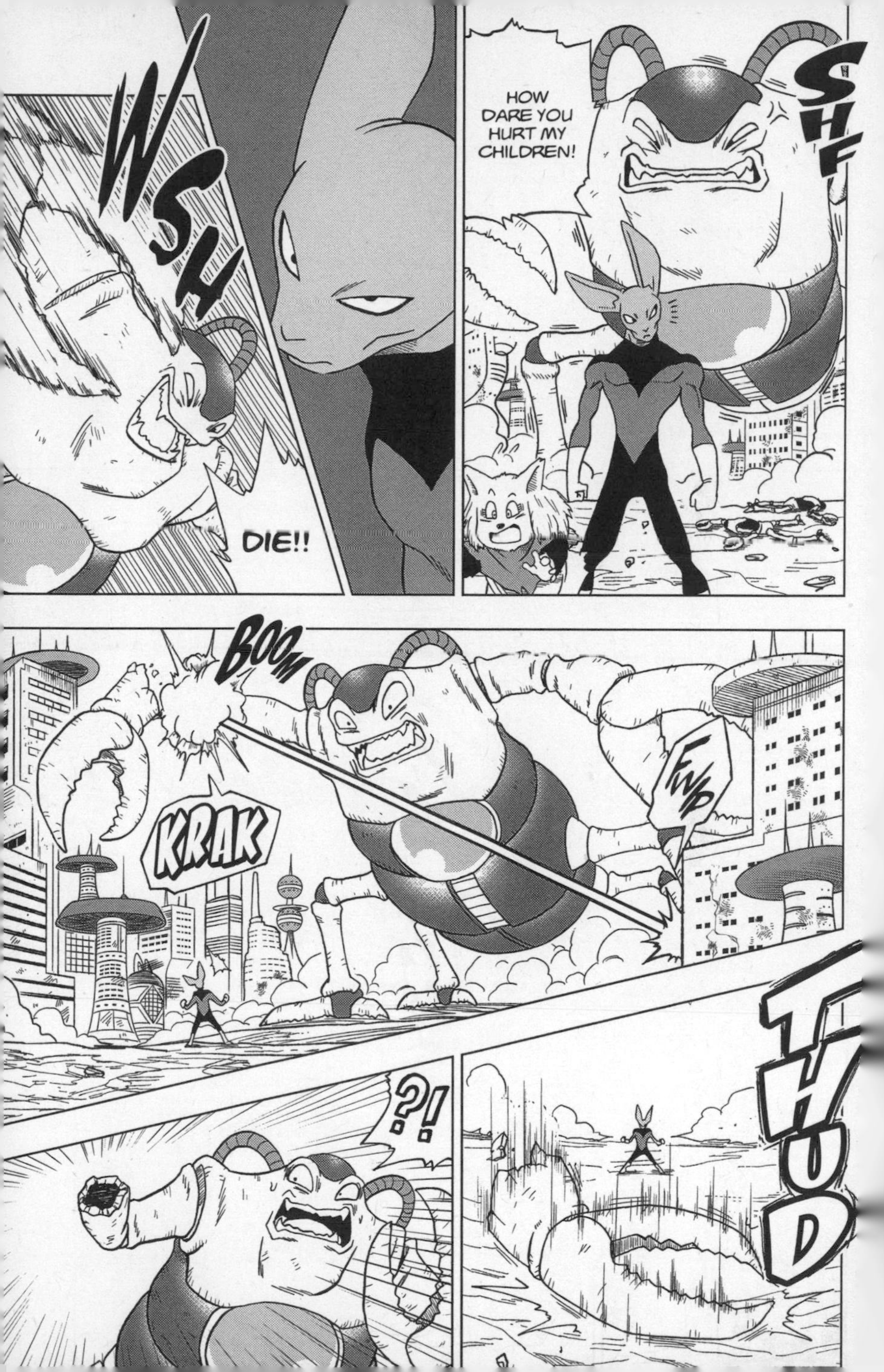
SHF
HOW DARE YOU HURT MY CHILDREN!
WSH
DIE!!
FWP
BOOM
KRAK
THUD
?!

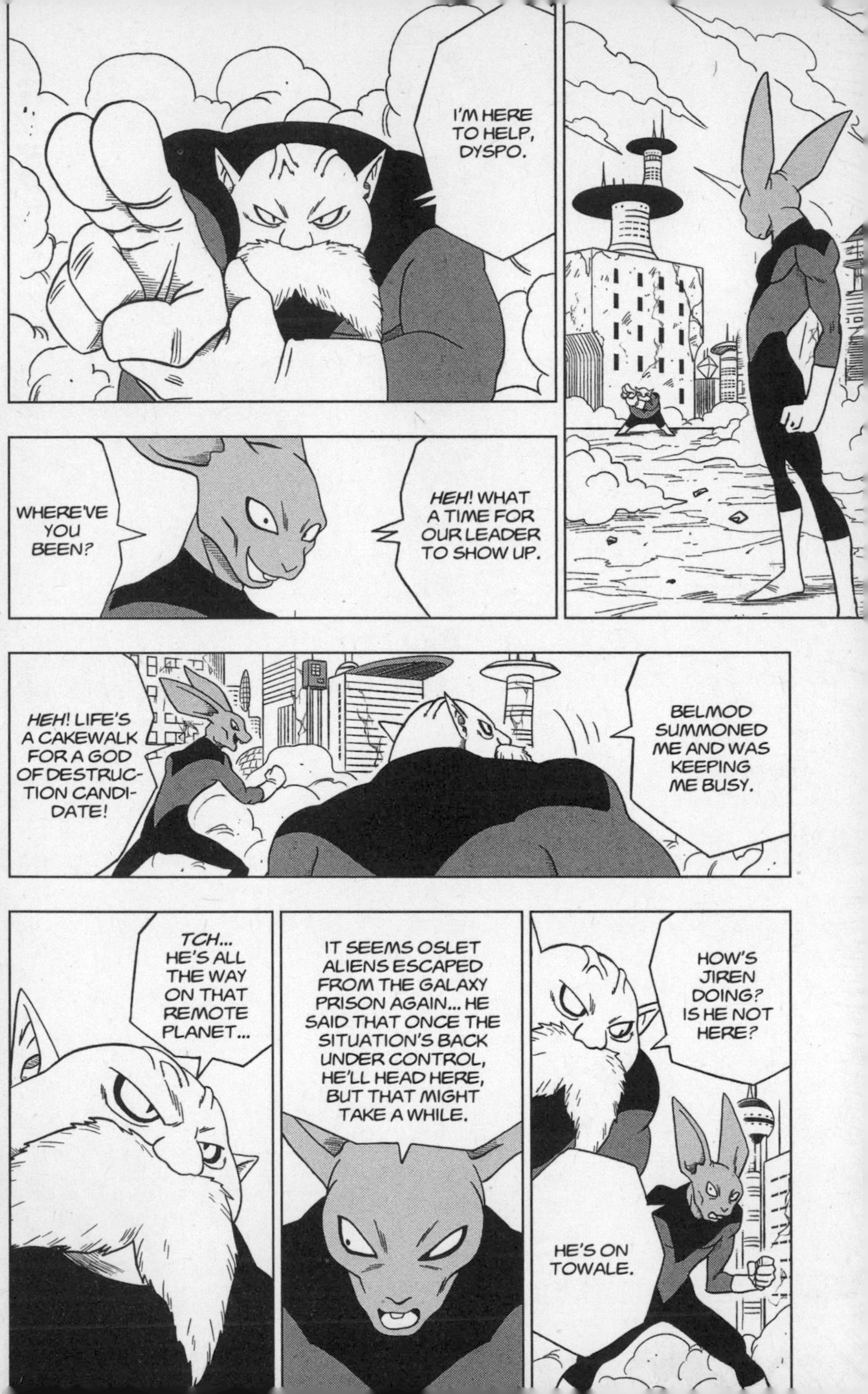
I'M HERE TO HELP, DYSPO.
HEH! WHAT A TIME FOR OUR LEADER TO SHOW UP.
WHERE'VE YOU BEEN?
BELMOD SUMMONED ME AND WAS KEEPING ME BUSY.
HEH! LIFE'S A CAKEWALK FOR A GOD OF DESTRUCTION CANDIDATE!
HOW'S JIREN DOING? IS HE NOT HERE?
HE'S ON TOWALE.
IT SEEMS OSLET ALIENS ESCAPED FROM THE GALAXY PRISON AGAIN... HE SAID THAT ONCE THE SITUATION'S BACK UNDER CONTROL, HE'LL HEAD HERE, BUT THAT MIGHT TAKE A WHILE.
TCH... HE'S ALL THE WAY ON THAT REMOTE PLANET...

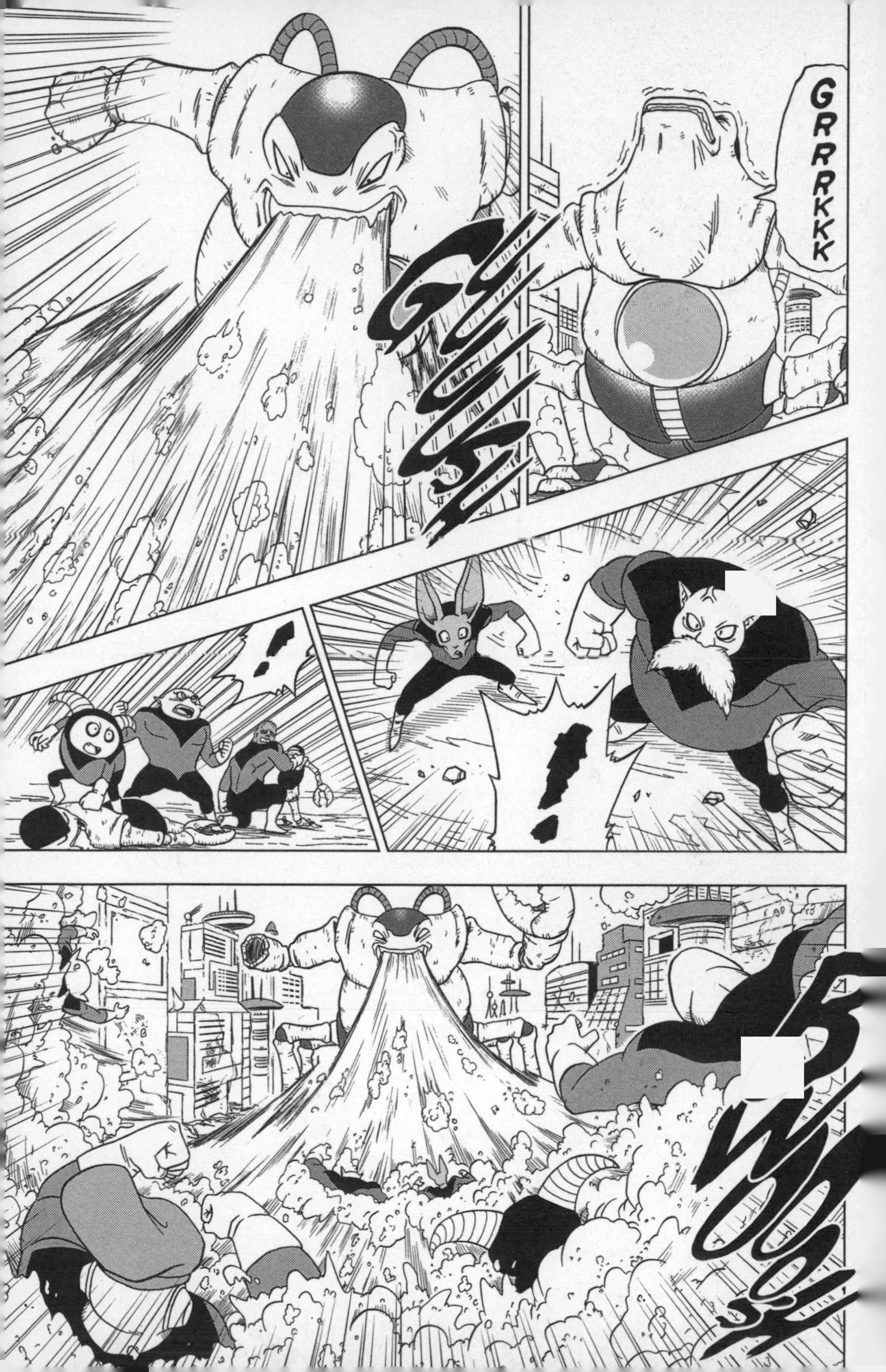
GRRRKKK
GYUUSH
!
!
SWOOSH

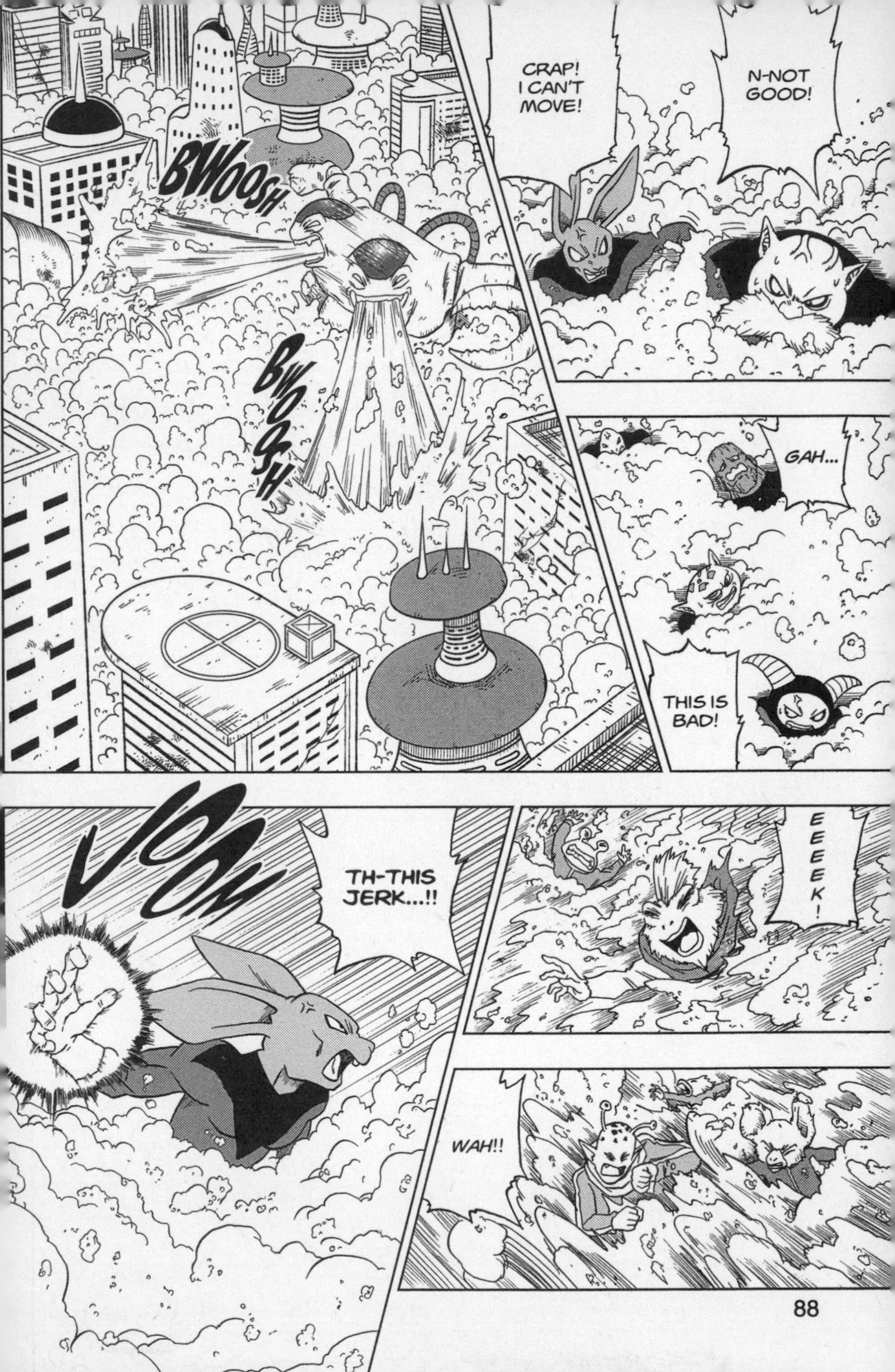
N-NOT GOOD!
CRAP! I CAN'T MOVE!
GAH...
THIS IS BAD!
BWOOSH
BWOOSH
EEEEK!
WAH!!
VOOM
TH-THIS JERK...!!

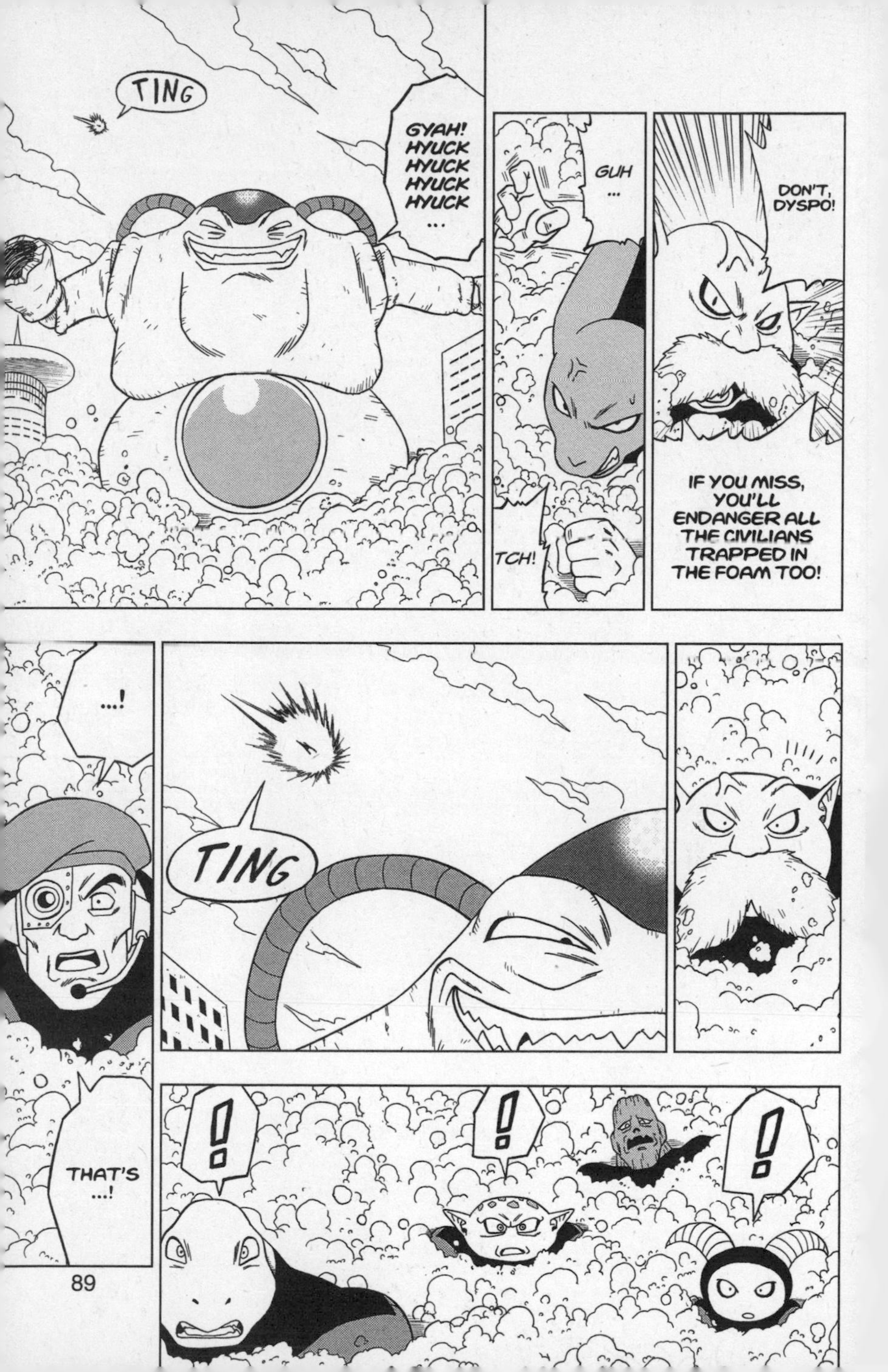
DON'T, DYSPO!
IF YOU MISS, YOU'LL ENDANGER ALL THE CIVILIANS TRAPPED IN THE FOAM TOO!
GUH ...
TCH!
TING
GYAH! HYUCK HYUCK HYUCK HYUCK ...
TING
!
!
!
...!
THAT'S ...!

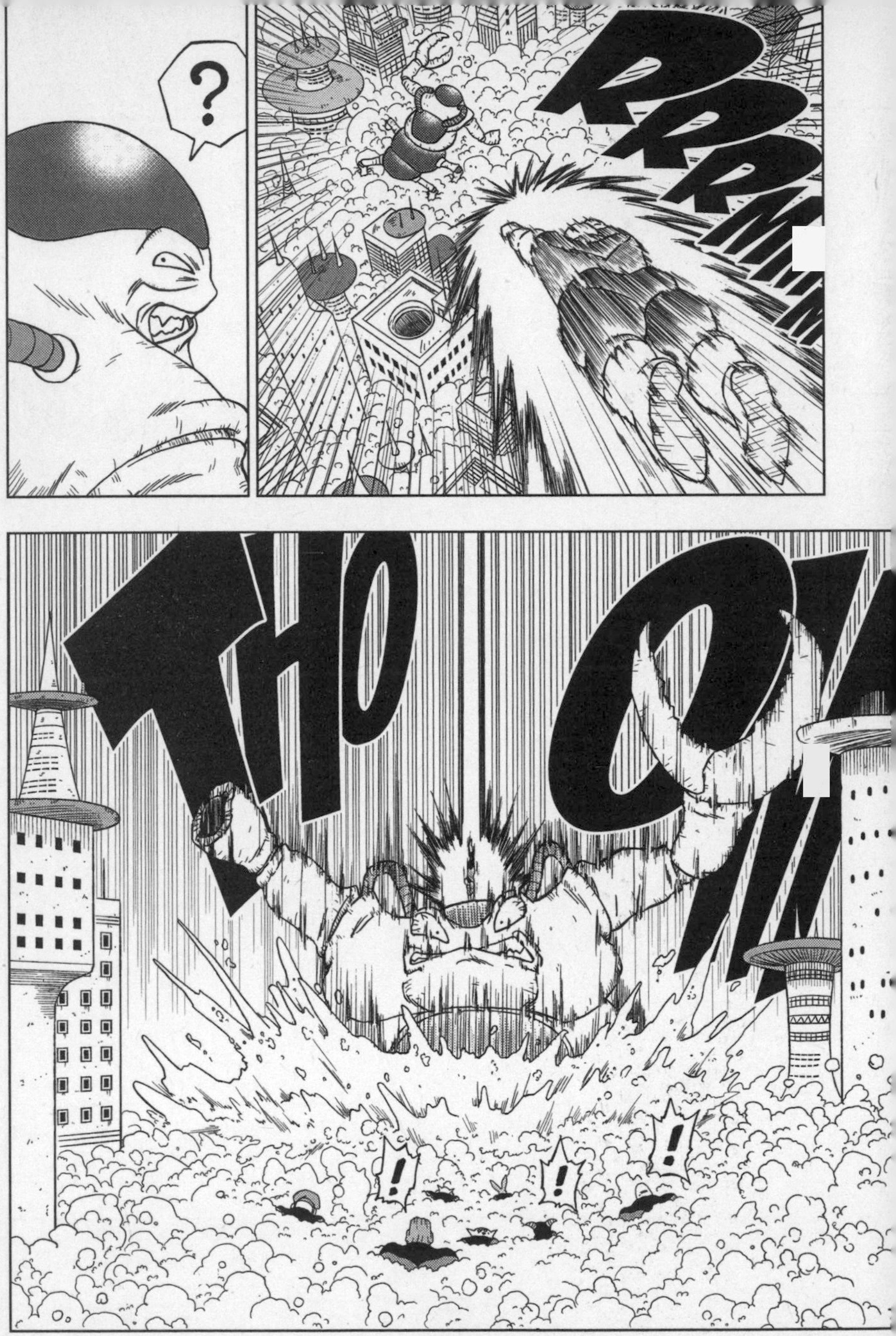
RRRMMM
?
THOOM
!
!
!

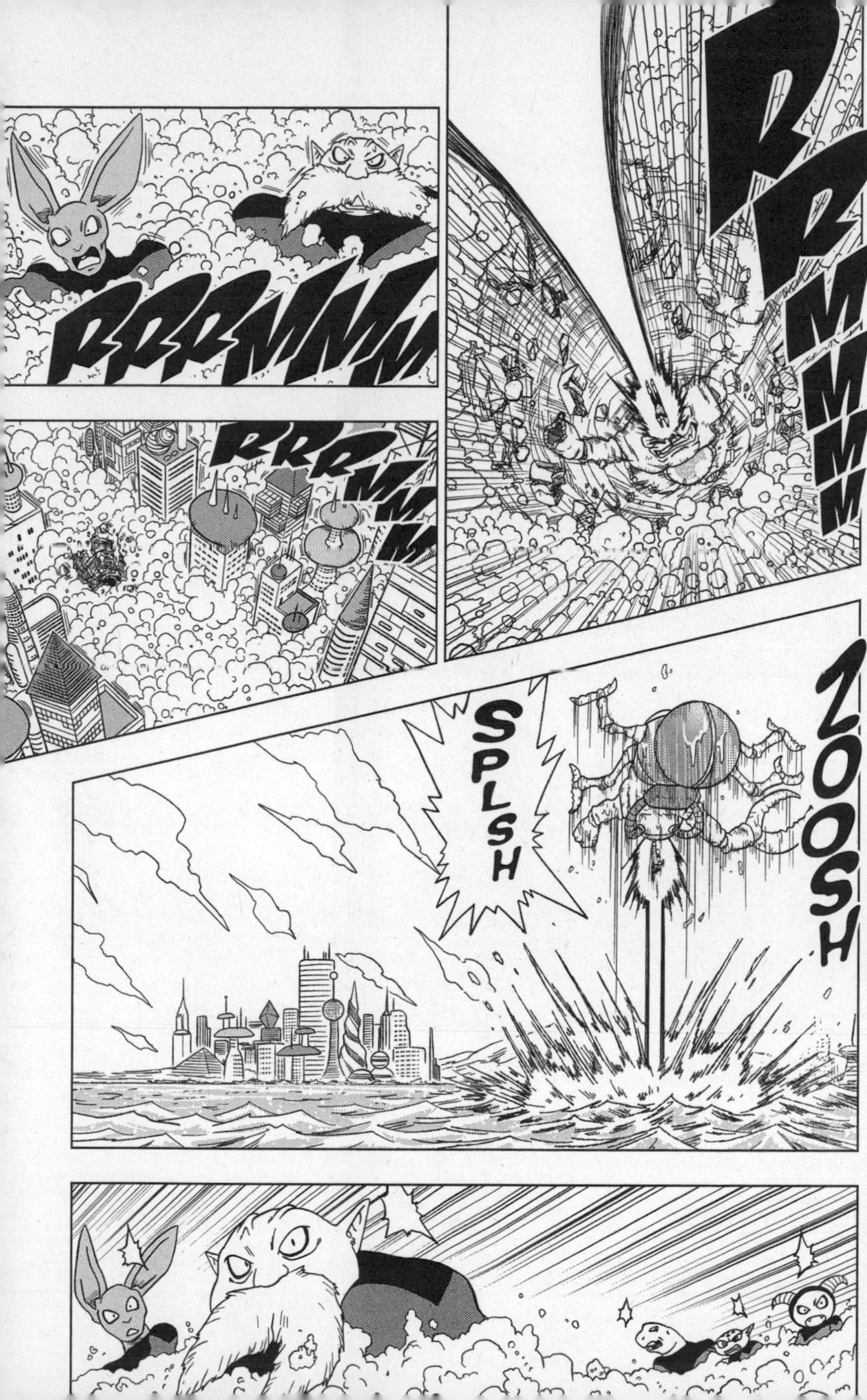
RRMMMMM
BRRMMM
BRRMMM
ZOOOSH
SPLSH

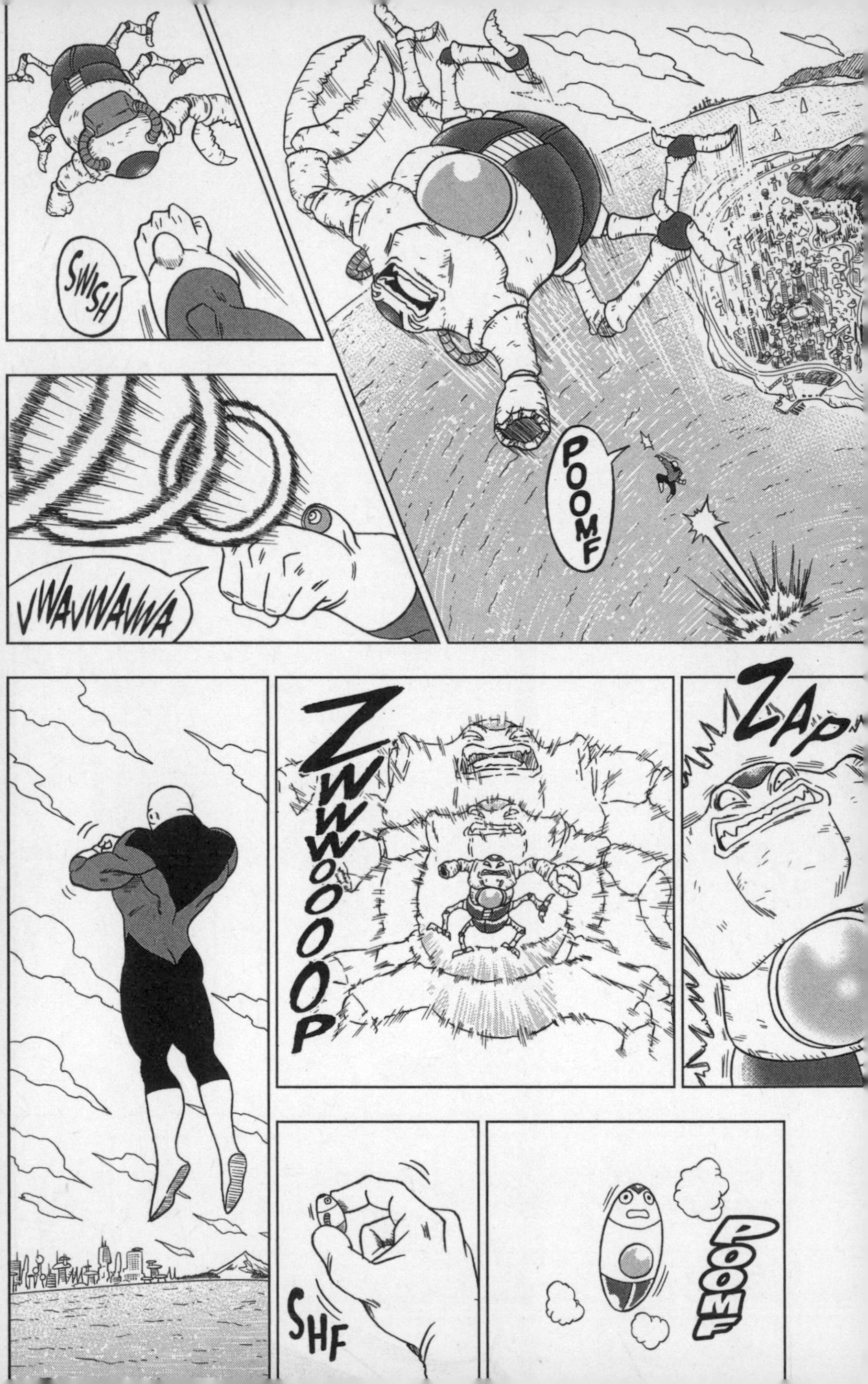
POOMF
SWISH
VWAVWAWA
ZAP
ZWWWOOOOP
POOMF
SHF

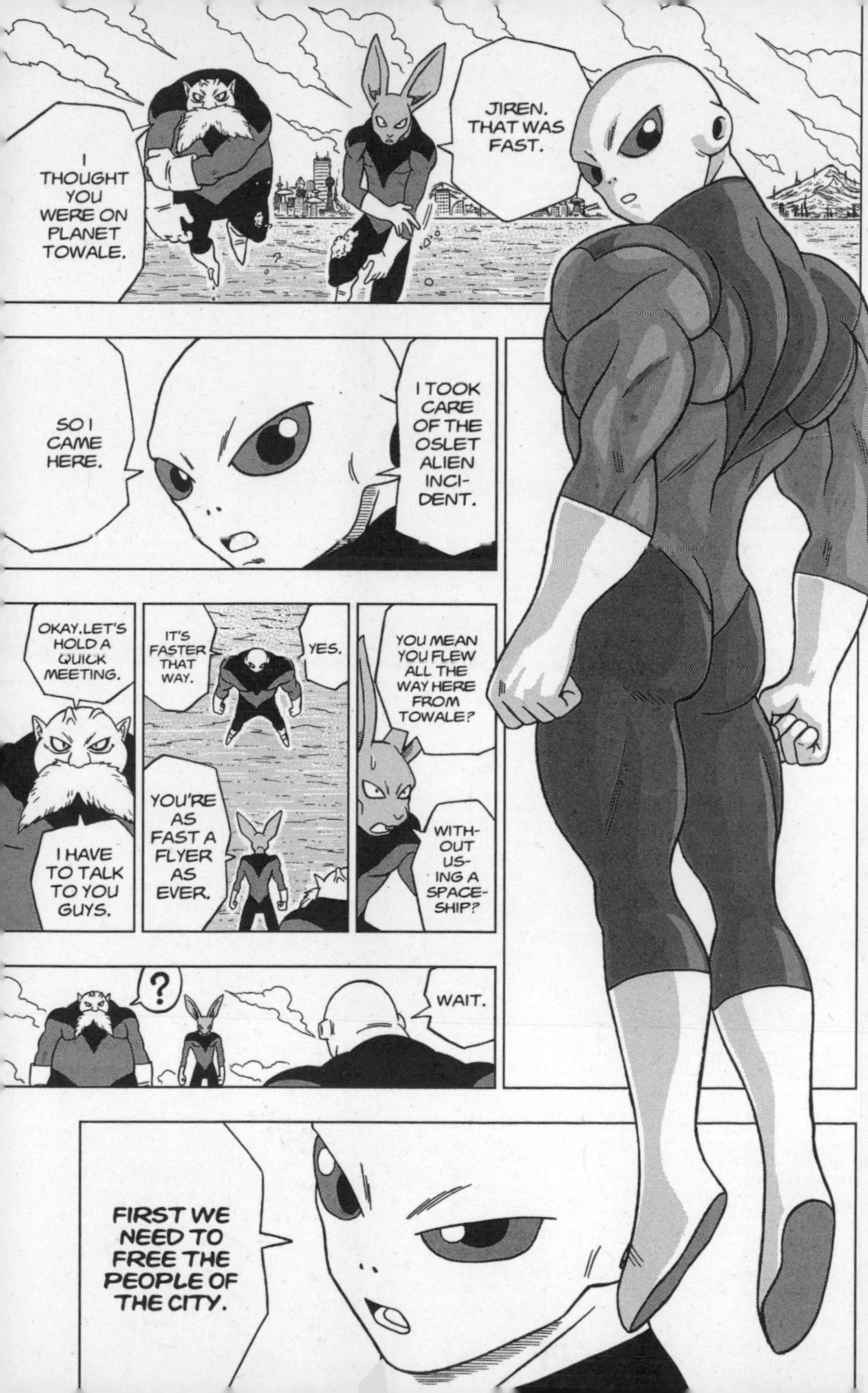
JIREN. THAT WAS FAST.
I THOUGHT YOU WERE ON PLANET TOWALE.
I TOOK CARE OF THE OSLET ALIEN INCIDENT.
SO I CAME HERE.
YOU MEAN YOU FLEW ALL THE WAY HERE FROM TOWALE?
WITHOUT USING A SPACESHIP?
YES.
IT'S FASTER THAT WAY.
YOU'RE AS FAST A FLYER AS EVER.
OKAY.LET'S HOLD A QUICK MEETING.
I HAVE TO TALK TO YOU GUYS.
WAIT.
?
FIRST WE NEED TO FREE THE PEOPLE OF THE CITY.

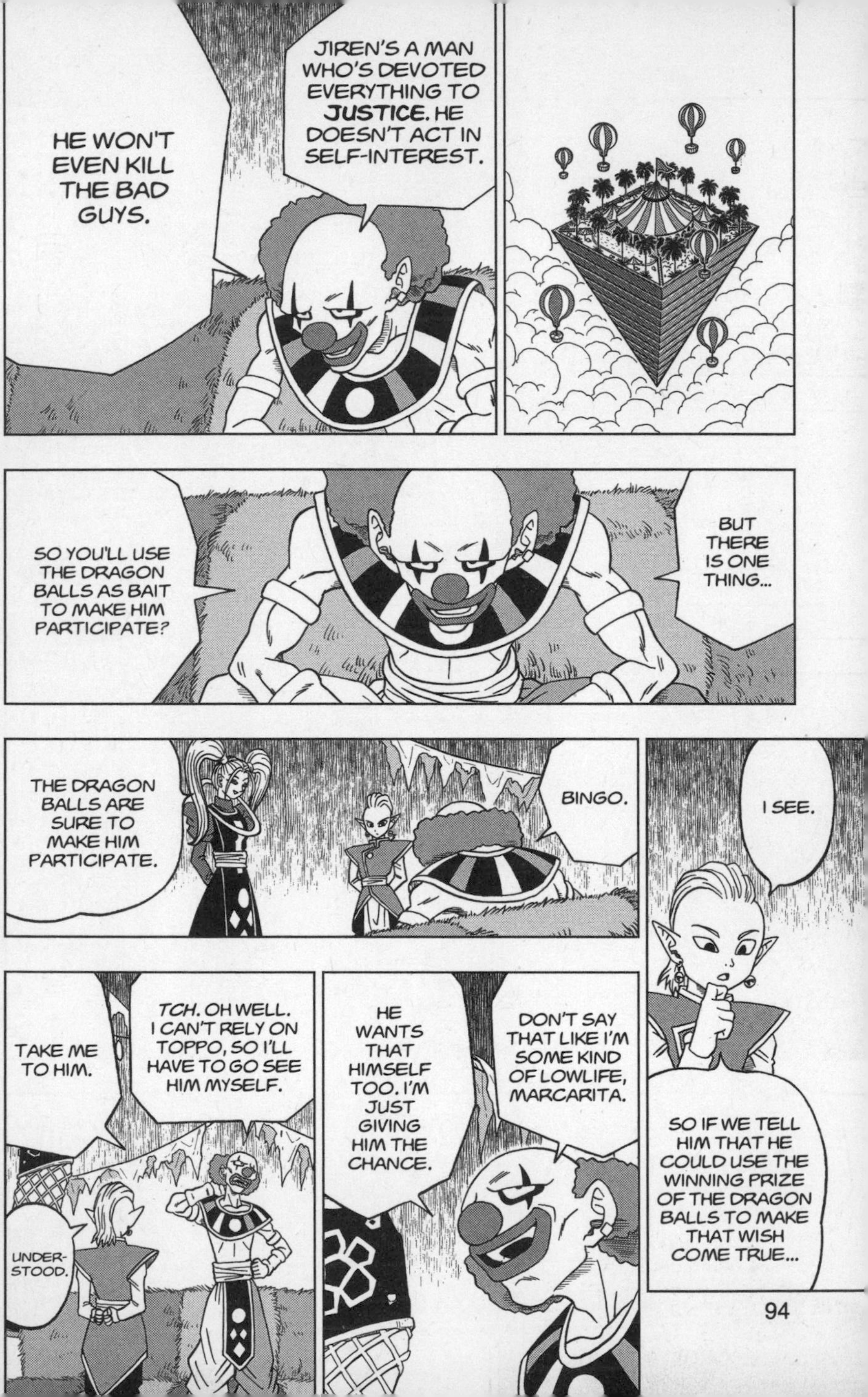
JIREN'S A MAN WHO'S DEVOTED EVERYTHING TO **JUSTICE**. HE DOESN'T ACT IN SELF-INTEREST.
HE WON'T EVEN KILL THE BAD GUYS.
BUT THERE IS ONE THING...
SO YOU'LL USE THE DRAGON BALLS AS BAIT TO MAKE HIM PARTICIPATE?
I SEE.
SO IF WE TELL HIM THAT HE COULD USE THE WINNING PRIZE OF THE DRAGON BALLS TO MAKE THAT WISH COME TRUE...
BINGO.
THE DRAGON BALLS ARE SURE TO MAKE HIM PARTICIPATE.
DON'T SAY THAT LIKE I'M SOME KIND OF LOWLIFE, MARCARITA.
HE WANTS THAT HIMSELF TOO. I'M JUST GIVING HIM THE CHANCE.
TCH. OH WELL. I CAN'T RELY ON TOPPO, SO I'LL HAVE TO GO SEE HIM MYSELF.
TAKE ME TO HIM.
UNDER-STOOD.

THANK YOU, MISTER!

I'M SURE YOU WERE SCARED, BUT IT'S OKAY NOW.

IF WE LOSE THIS MATCH, THERE WON'T BE A UNIVERSE LEFT TO DEFEND.

H-HOW CAN YOU SAY THAT, JIREN?

!

MY FIRST PRIORITY IS PROTECTING THE PEACE OF THE UNIVERSE.

I'M SORRY, BUT I'LL HAVE TO DECLINE.

THEN THAT IS THE FATE OF OUR UNIVERSE.

I'M NOT ABOUT TO SAVE OUR OWN UNIVERSE AT THE COST OF HAVING OTHERS BE ERASED.

...

IS THAT REALLY THE KIND OF JUSTICE YOU BELIEVE IN?!

YOU WOULD LOSE EVERYTHING YOU'VE WORKED SO HARD TO PROTECT.

ARE YOU REALLY OKAY WITH THAT?

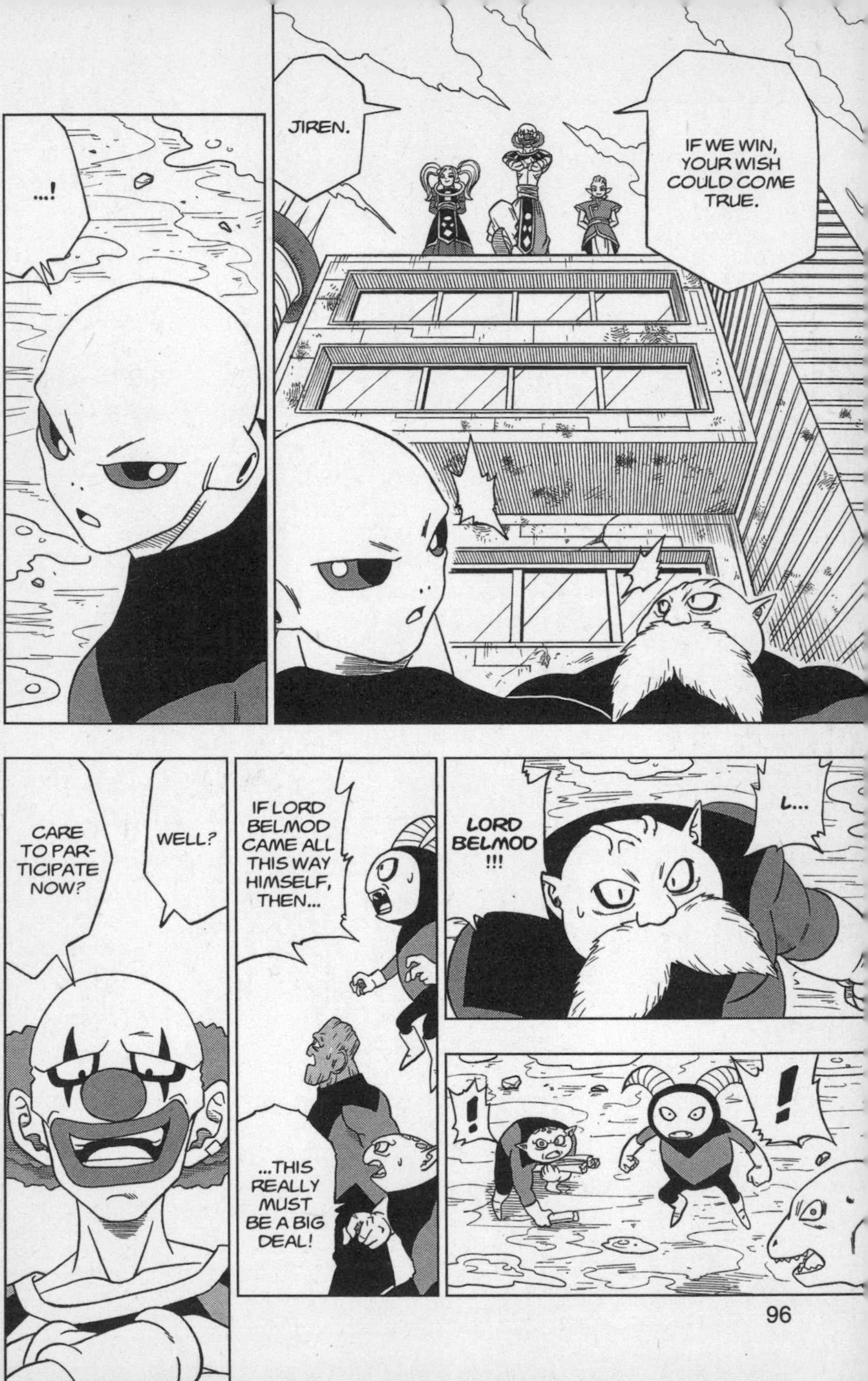

IF WE WIN, YOUR WISH COULD COME TRUE.
JIREN.
...!
L...
LORD BELMOD!!!
!
!
IF LORD BELMOD CAME ALL THIS WAY HIMSELF, THEN...
...THIS REALLY MUST BE A BIG DEAL!
WELL?
CARE TO PARTICIPATE NOW?

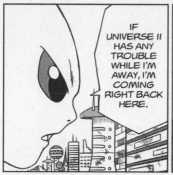

H-HEY, JIREN!
LORD BELMOD IS ASKING FOR YOU PERSONALLY!
...
IF UNIVERSE 11 HAS ANY TROUBLE WHILE I'M AWAY, I'M COMING RIGHT BACK HERE.
THOSE ARE MY CONDITIONS.
GOT IT.
THAT'S FINE.

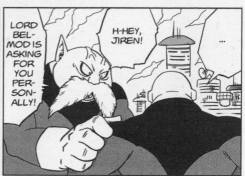

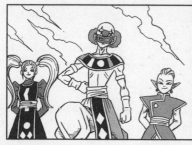

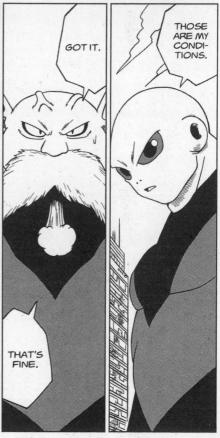

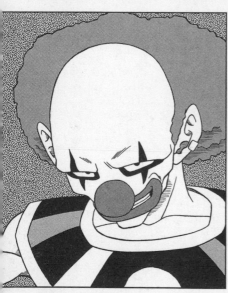

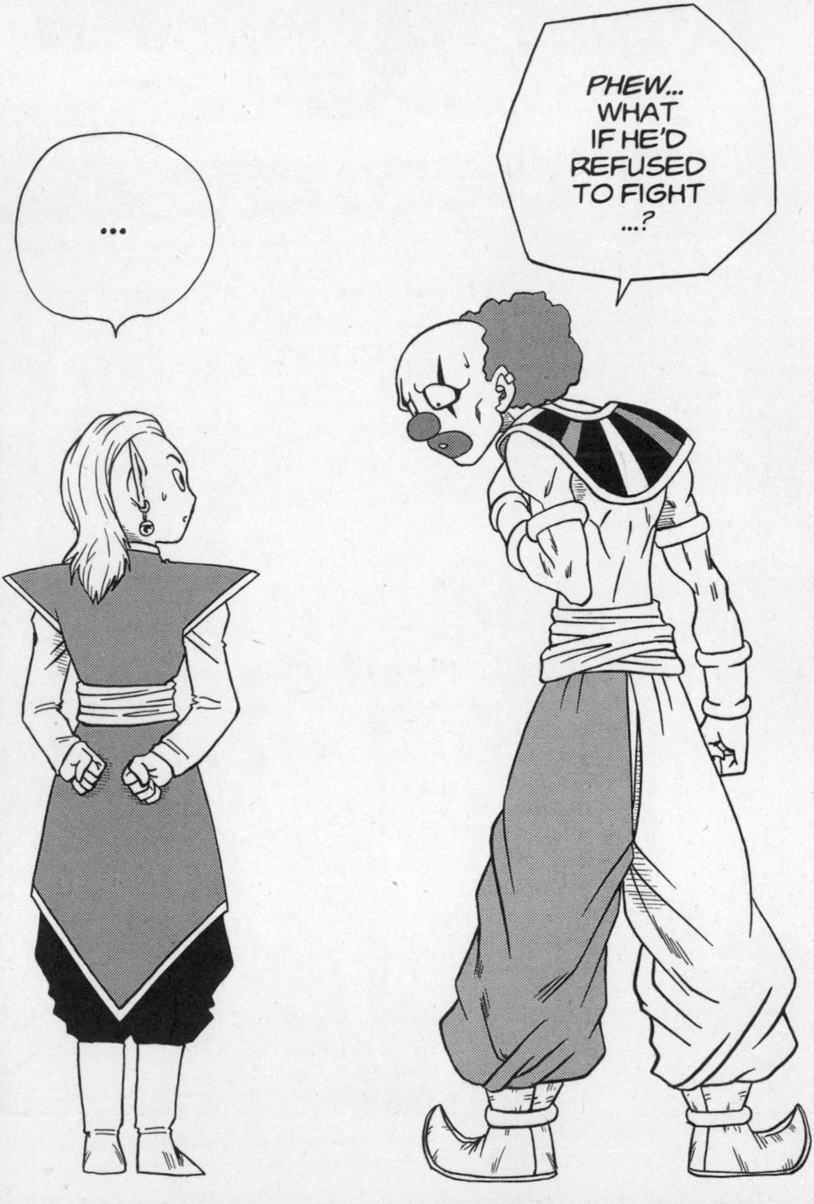
PHEW... WHAT IF HE'D REFUSED TO FIGHT ...?
...

DRAGON BALL SUPER

CHAPTER 31: THE SUPER WARRIORS GATHER!

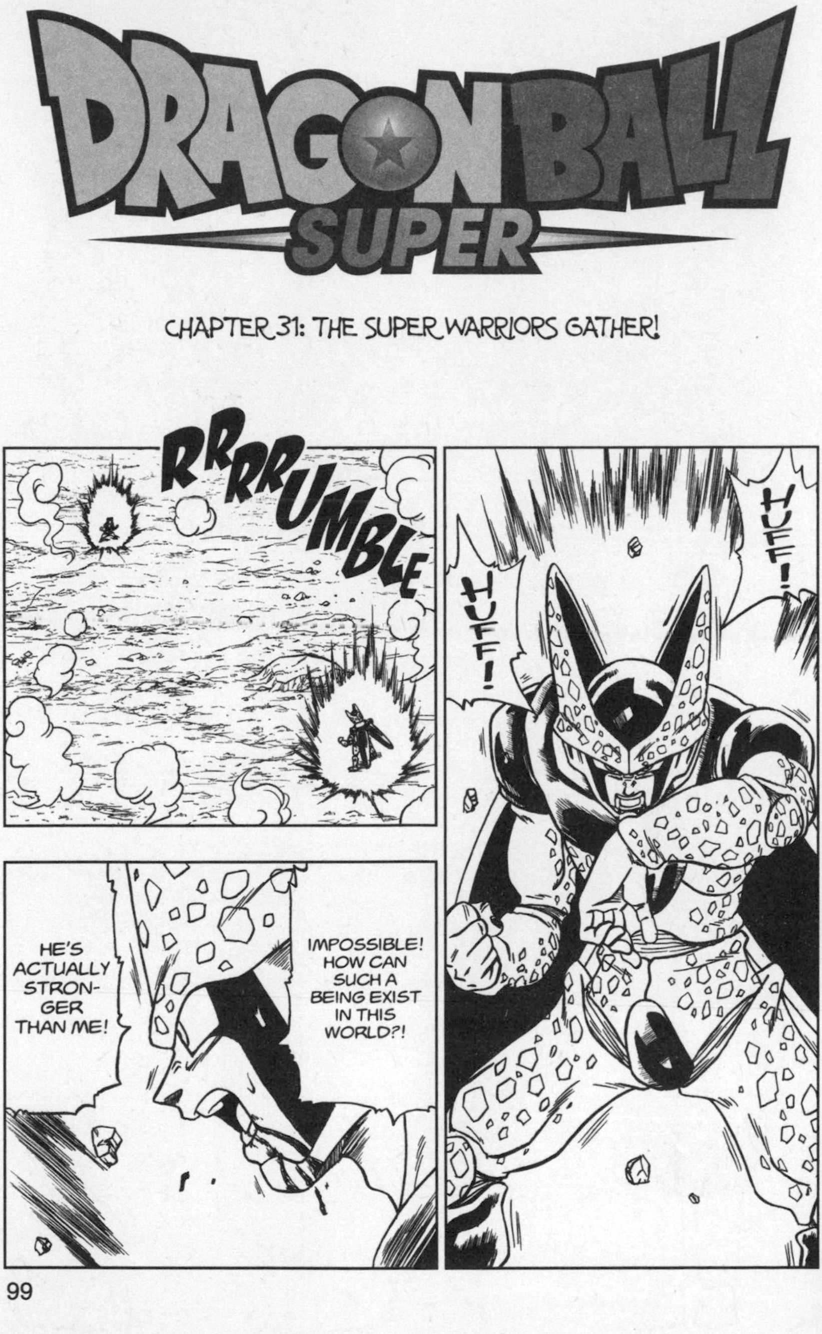
HUFF!
HUFF!
RRRRRUMBLE
IMPOSSIBLE! HOW CAN SUCH A BEING EXIST IN THIS WORLD?!
HE'S ACTUALLY STRONGER THAN ME!

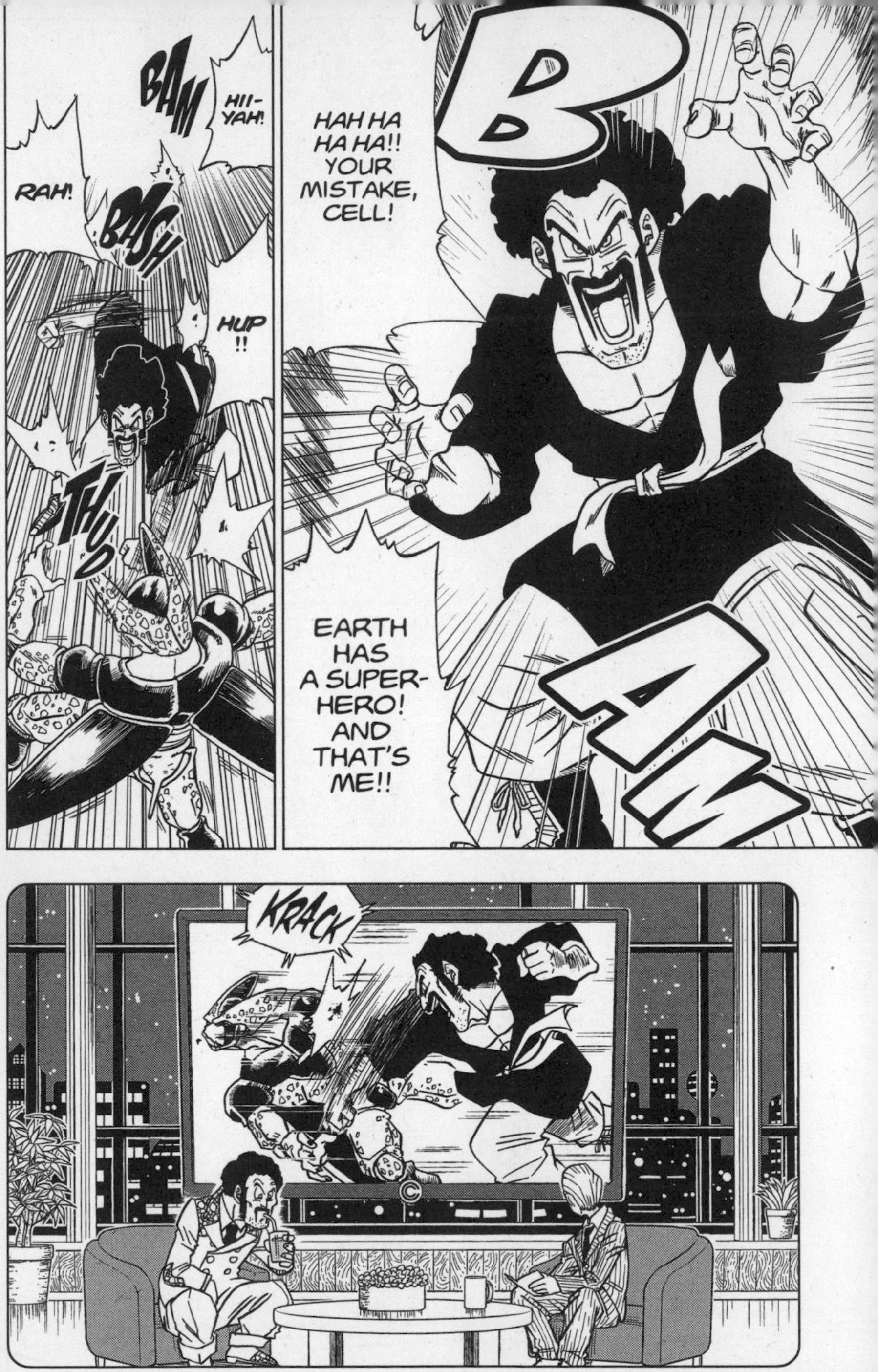
BAM
HAH HA HA HA!! YOUR MISTAKE, CELL!
EARTH HAS A SUPER-HERO! AND THAT'S ME!!
BAM
HII-YAH!
RAH!
BASH
HUP!!
THUD
KRACK

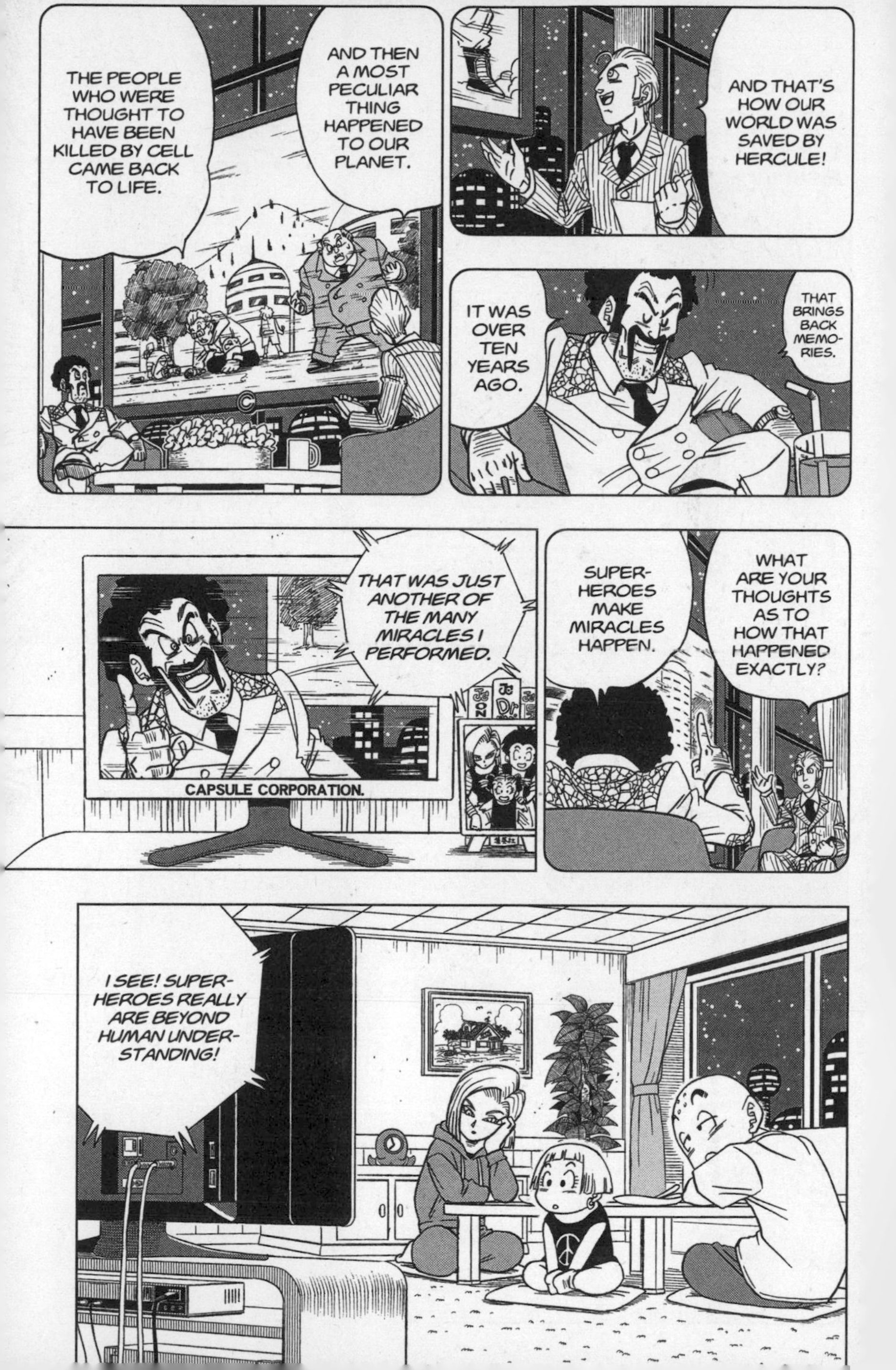
AND THAT'S HOW OUR WORLD WAS SAVED BY HERCULE!
THAT BRINGS BACK MEMO-RIES.
IT WAS OVER TEN YEARS AGO.
AND THEN A MOST PECULIAR THING HAPPENED TO OUR PLANET.
THE PEOPLE WHO WERE THOUGHT TO HAVE BEEN KILLED BY CELL CAME BACK TO LIFE.
WHAT ARE YOUR THOUGHTS AS TO HOW THAT HAPPENED EXACTLY?
SUPER-HEROES MAKE MIRACLES HAPPEN.
THAT WAS JUST ANOTHER OF THE MANY MIRACLES I PERFORMED.
CAPSULE CORPORATION.
I SEE! SUPER-HEROES REALLY ARE BEYOND HUMAN UNDER-STANDING!

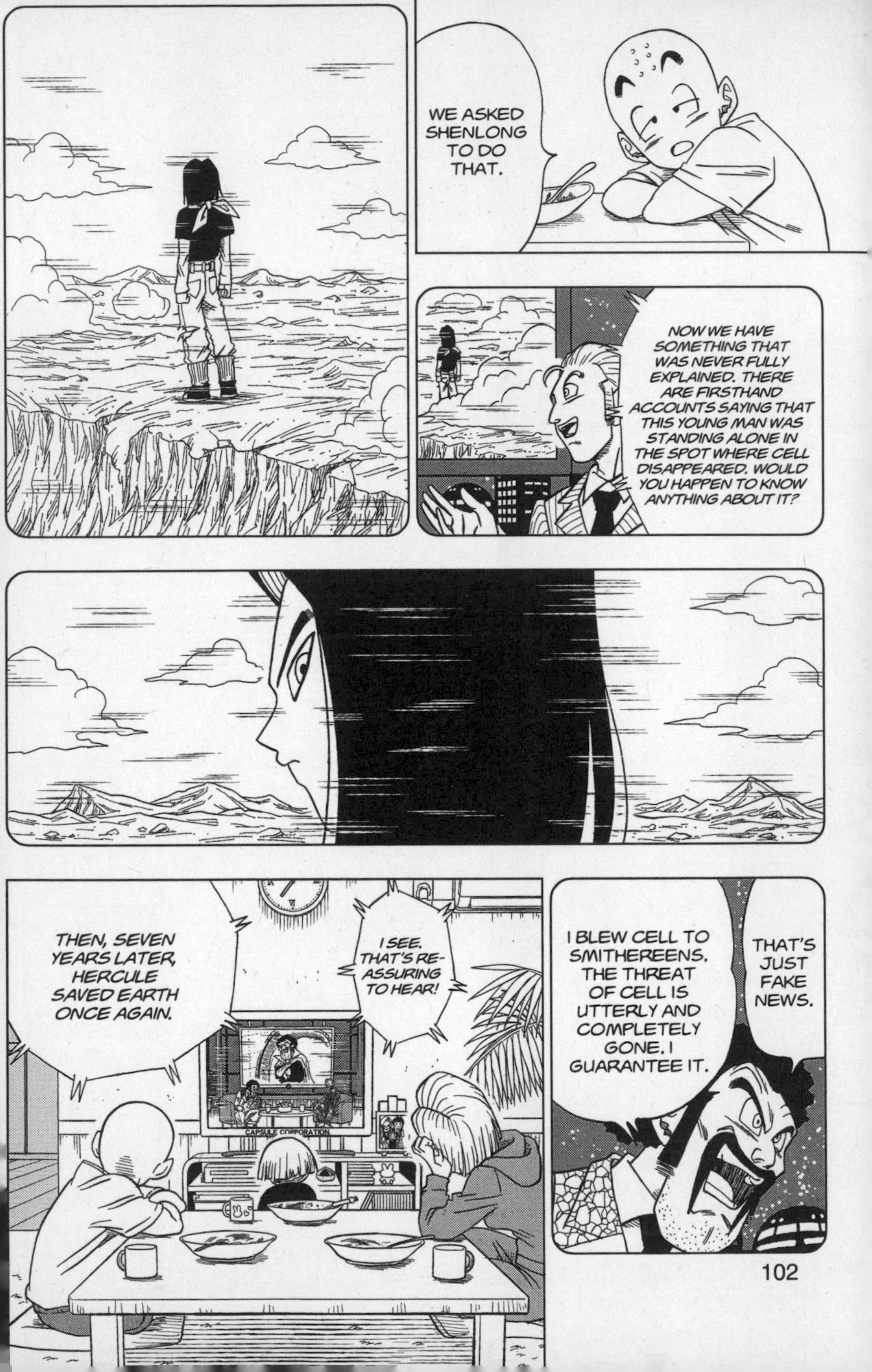
WE ASKED SHENLONG TO DO THAT.
NOW WE HAVE SOMETHING THAT WAS NEVER FULLY EXPLAINED. THERE ARE FIRSTHAND ACCOUNTS SAYING THAT THIS YOUNG MAN WAS STANDING ALONE IN THE SPOT WHERE CELL DISAPPEARED. WOULD YOU HAPPEN TO KNOW ANYTHING ABOUT IT?
THAT'S JUST FAKE NEWS.
I BLEW CELL TO SMITHEREENS. THE THREAT OF CELL IS UTTERLY AND COMPLETELY GONE. I GUARANTEE IT.
I SEE. THAT'S RE-ASSURING TO HEAR!
THEN, SEVEN YEARS LATER, HERCULE SAVED EARTH ONCE AGAIN.
CAPSULE CORPORATION

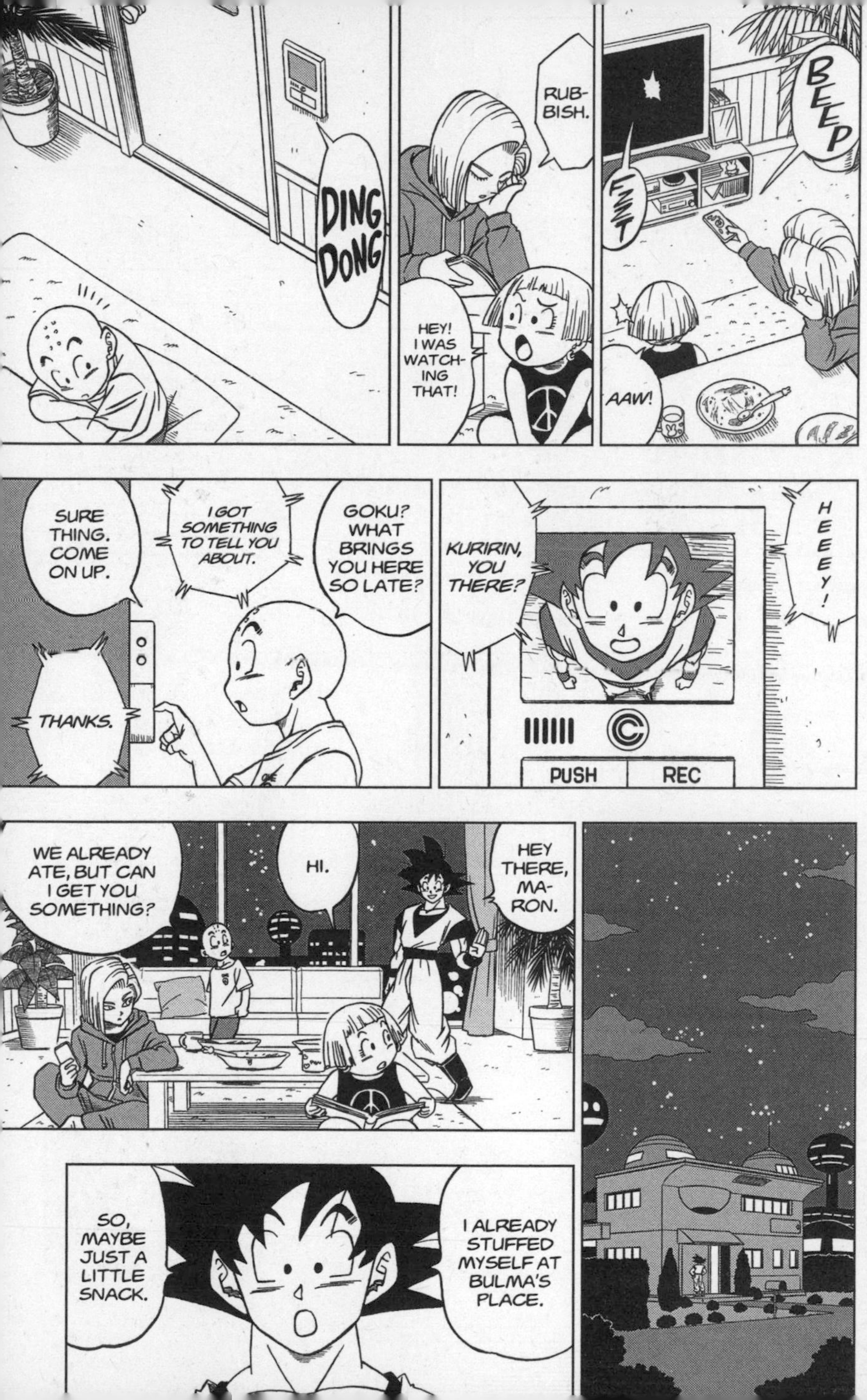
BEEP
FZZT
AAW!
RUB-BISH.
HEY! I WAS WATCHING THAT!
DING DONG
HEEEY!
KURIRIN, YOU THERE?
PUSH
REC
GOKU? WHAT BRINGS YOU HERE SO LATE?
I GOT SOMETHING TO TELL YOU ABOUT.
SURE THING. COME ON UP.
THANKS.
HEY THERE, MA-RON.
HI.
WE ALREADY ATE, BUT CAN I GET YOU SOMETHING?
I ALREADY STUFFED MYSELF AT BULMA'S PLACE.
SO, MAYBE JUST A LITTLE SNACK.

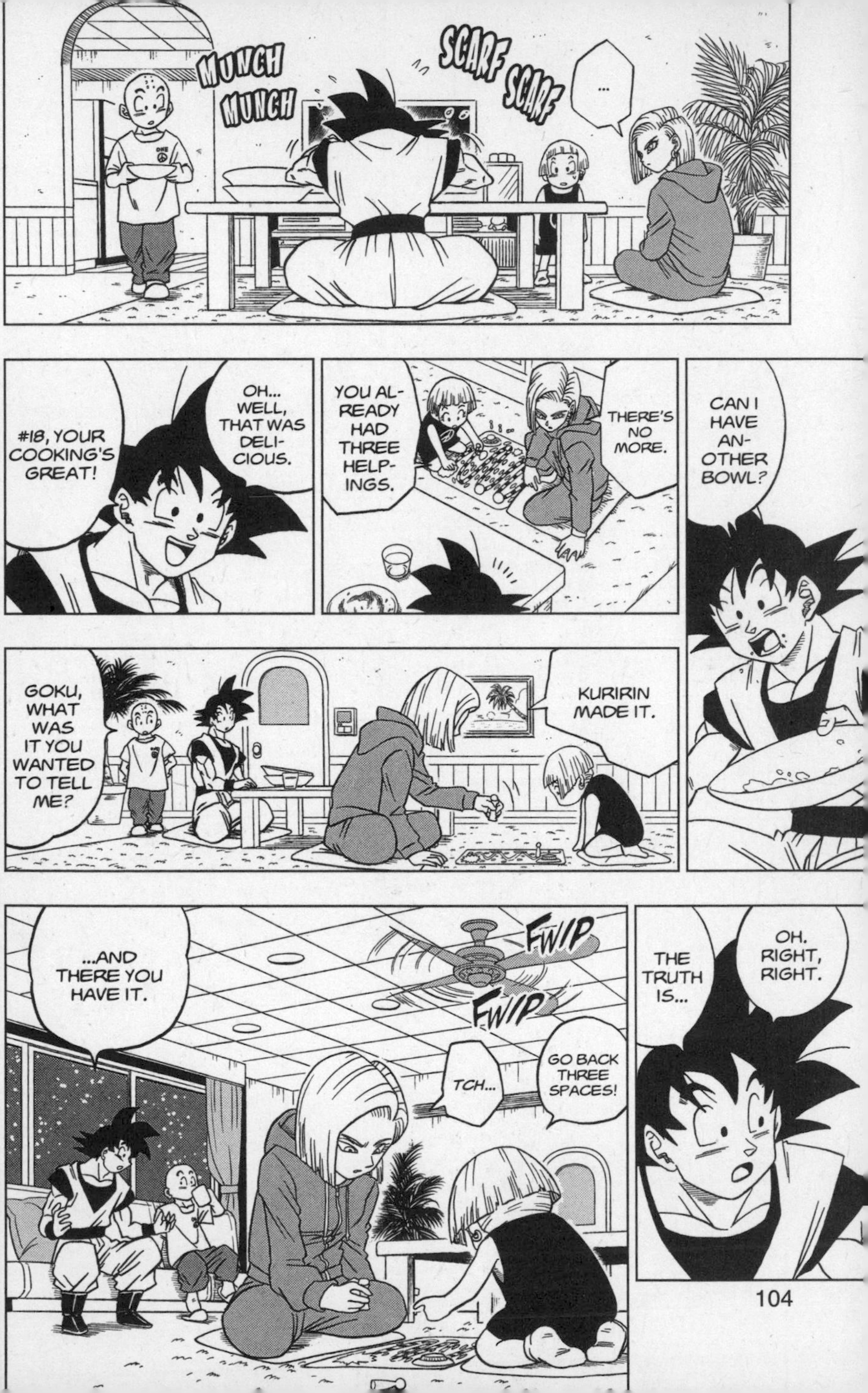
...
SCARF SCARF
MUNCH MUNCH
CAN I HAVE AN-OTHER BOWL?
THERE'S NO MORE.
YOU AL-READY HAD THREE HELP-INGS.
OH... WELL, THAT WAS DELI-CIOUS.
#18, YOUR COOKING'S GREAT!
...
KURIRIN MADE IT.
GOKU, WHAT WAS IT YOU WANTED TO TELL ME?
OH. RIGHT, RIGHT.
THE TRUTH IS...
FWIP
FWIP
GO BACK THREE SPACES!
TCH...
...AND THERE YOU HAVE IT.

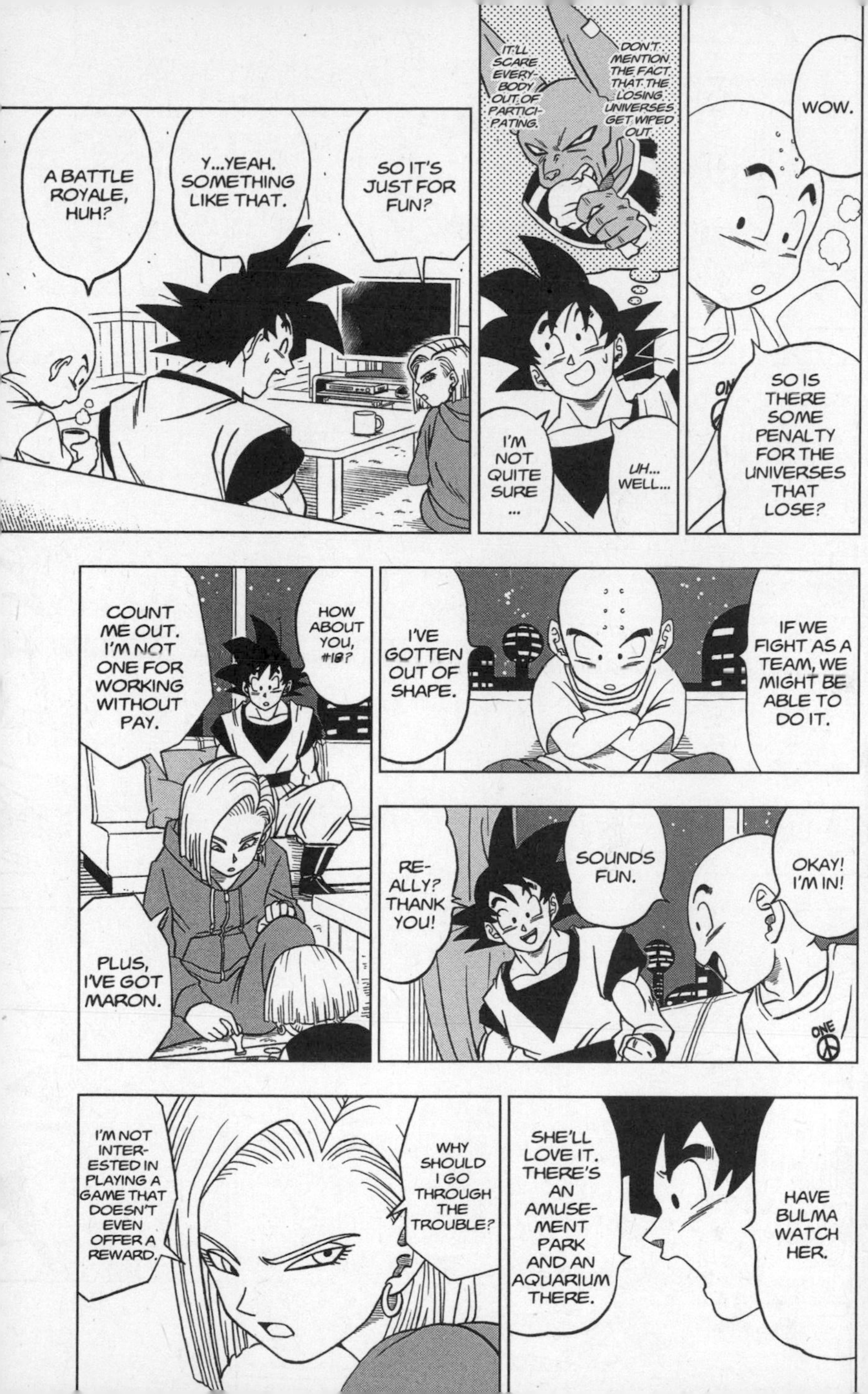
WOW.
SO IS THERE SOME PENALTY FOR THE UNIVERSES THAT LOSE?
DON'T MENTION THE FACT THAT THE LOSING UNIVERSES GET WIPED OUT.
IT'LL SCARE EVERYBODY OUT OF PARTICIPATING.
UH... WELL...
I'M NOT QUITE SURE...
SO IT'S JUST FOR FUN?
Y...YEAH. SOMETHING LIKE THAT.
A BATTLE ROYALE, HUH?
IF WE FIGHT AS A TEAM, WE MIGHT BE ABLE TO DO IT.
I'VE GOTTEN OUT OF SHAPE.
OKAY! I'M IN!
SOUNDS FUN.
REALLY? THANK YOU!
HOW ABOUT YOU, #18?
COUNT ME OUT. I'M NOT ONE FOR WORKING WITHOUT PAY.
PLUS, I'VE GOT MARON.
HAVE BULMA WATCH HER.
SHE'LL LOVE IT. THERE'S AN AMUSEMENT PARK AND AN AQUARIUM THERE.
WHY SHOULD I GO THROUGH THE TROUBLE?
I'M NOT INTERESTED IN PLAYING A GAME THAT DOESN'T EVEN OFFER A REWARD.

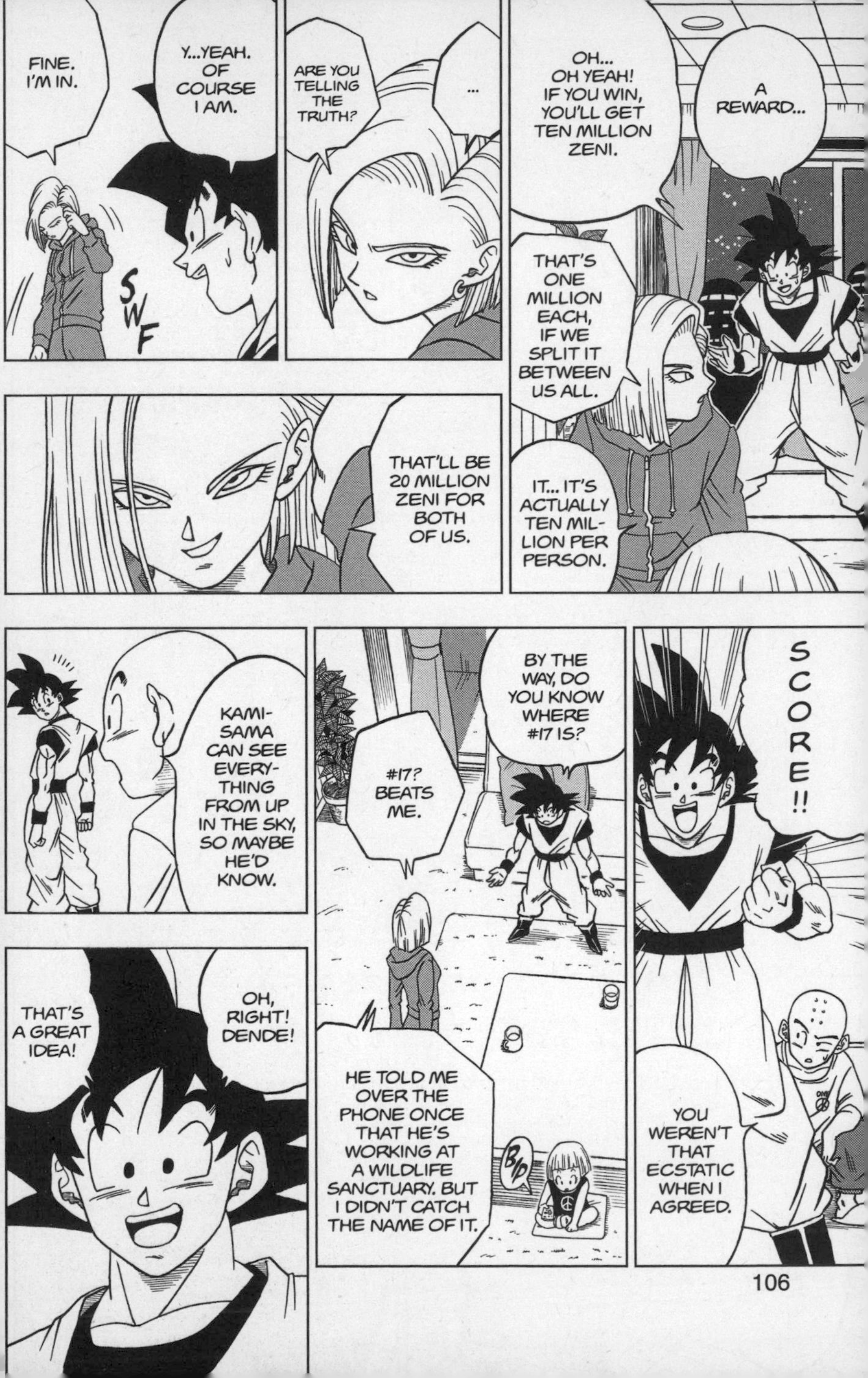
A REWARD...
OH... OH YEAH! IF YOU WIN, YOU'LL GET TEN MILLION ZENI.
THAT'S ONE MILLION EACH, IF WE SPLIT IT BETWEEN US ALL.
IT... IT'S ACTUALLY TEN MILLION PER PERSON.
...
ARE YOU TELLING THE TRUTH?
Y...YEAH. OF COURSE I AM.
FINE. I'M IN.
SWF
THAT'LL BE 20 MILLION ZENI FOR BOTH OF US.
SCORE!!
YOU WEREN'T THAT ECSTATIC WHEN I AGREED.
BY THE WAY, DO YOU KNOW WHERE #17 IS?
#17? BEATS ME.
HE TOLD ME OVER THE PHONE ONCE THAT HE'S WORKING AT A WILDLIFE SANCTUARY. BUT I DIDN'T CATCH THE NAME OF IT.
BIP
KAMI-SAMA CAN SEE EVERYTHING FROM UP IN THE SKY, SO MAYBE HE'D KNOW.
OH, RIGHT! DENDE!
THAT'S A GREAT IDEA!

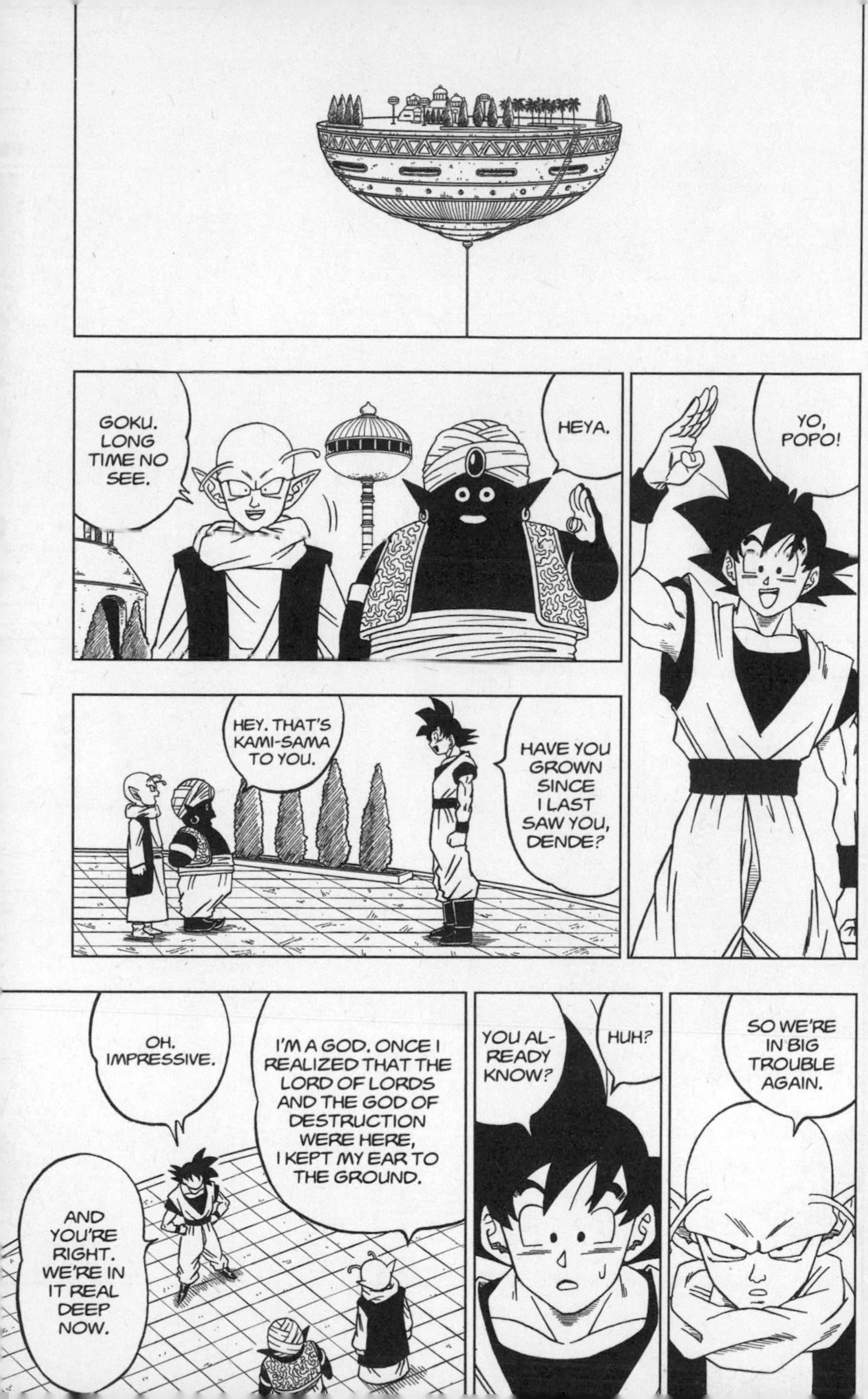
YO, POPO!
HEYA.
GOKU. LONG TIME NO SEE.
HAVE YOU GROWN SINCE I LAST SAW YOU, DENDE?
HEY. THAT'S KAMI-SAMA TO YOU.
SO WE'RE IN BIG TROUBLE AGAIN.
HUH?
YOU AL-READY KNOW?
I'M A GOD. ONCE I REALIZED THAT THE LORD OF LORDS AND THE GOD OF DESTRUCTION WERE HERE, I KEPT MY EAR TO THE GROUND.
OH. IMPRESSIVE.
AND YOU'RE RIGHT. WE'RE IN IT REAL DEEP NOW.

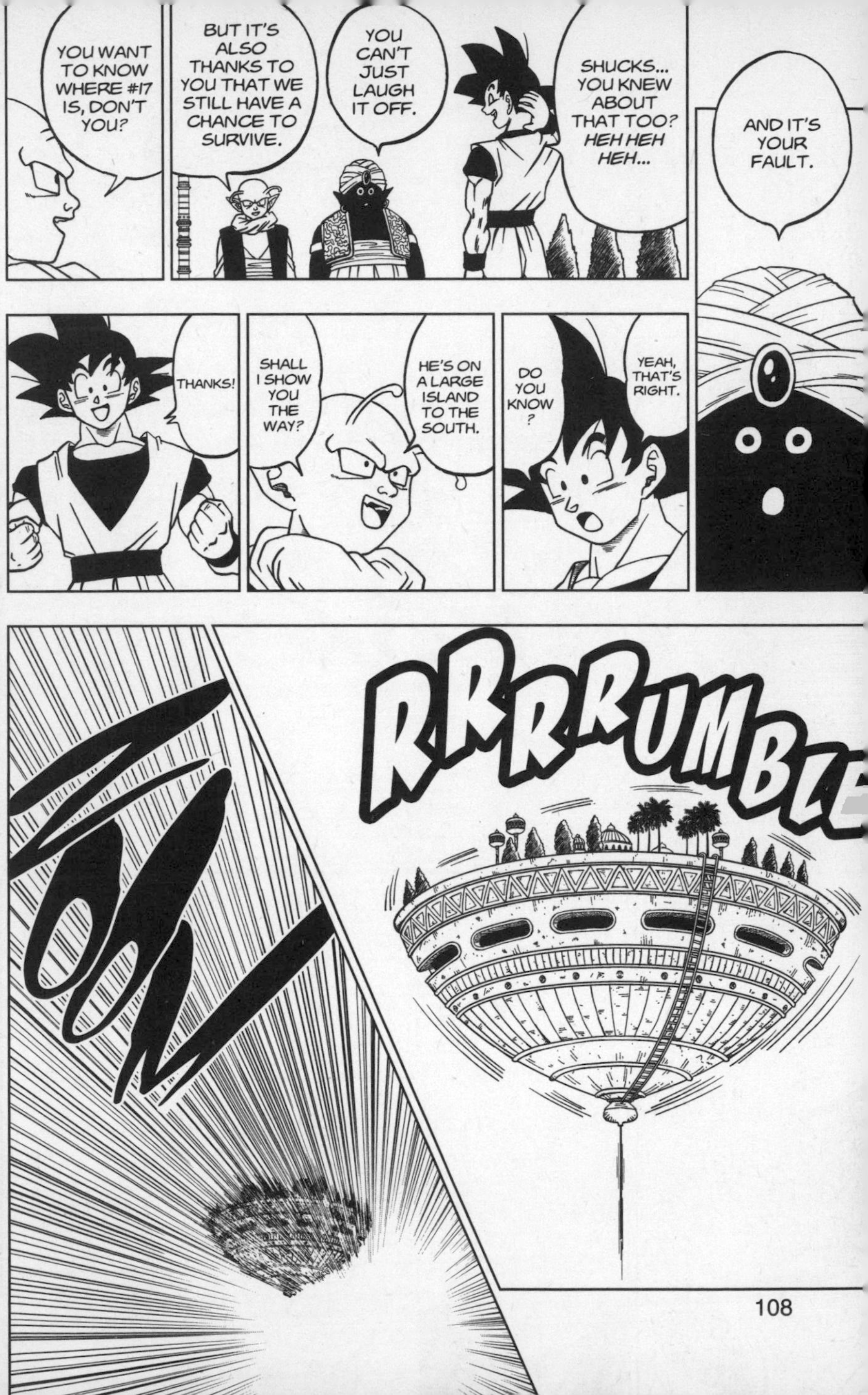
AND IT'S YOUR FAULT.
SHUCKS... YOU KNEW ABOUT THAT TOO? *HEH HEH HEH...*
YOU CAN'T JUST LAUGH IT OFF.
BUT IT'S ALSO THANKS TO YOU THAT WE STILL HAVE A CHANCE TO SURVIVE.
YOU WANT TO KNOW WHERE #17 IS, DON'T YOU?
YEAH, THAT'S RIGHT.
DO YOU KNOW?
HE'S ON A LARGE ISLAND TO THE SOUTH.
SHALL I SHOW YOU THE WAY?
THANKS!
RRRRUMBLE

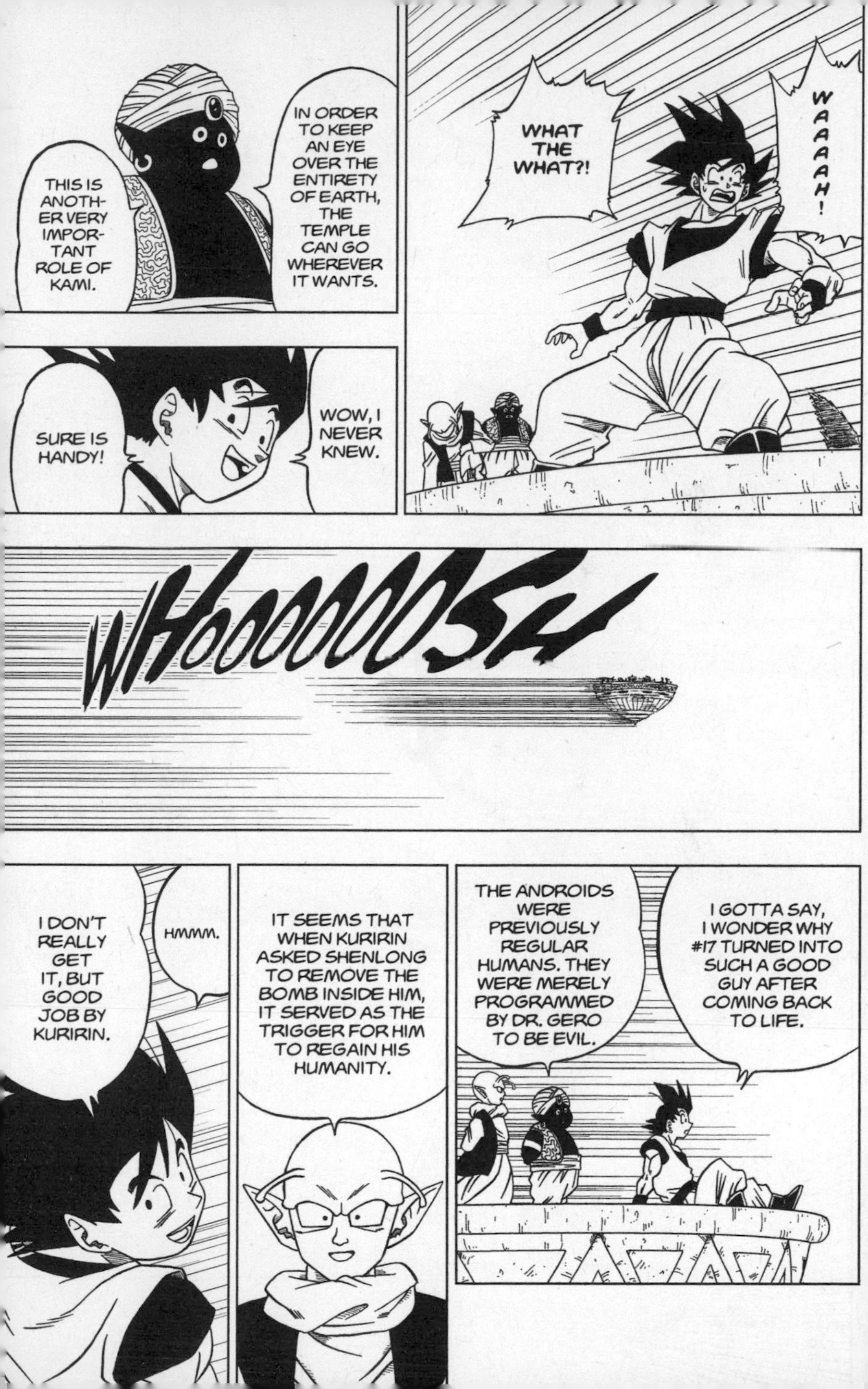

WAAAAH!
WHAT THE WHAT?!
IN ORDER TO KEEP AN EYE OVER THE ENTIRETY OF EARTH, THE TEMPLE CAN GO WHEREVER IT WANTS.
THIS IS ANOTHER VERY IMPORTANT ROLE OF KAMI.
WOW, I NEVER KNEW.
SURE IS HANDY!
WHOOOOOSH
I GOTTA SAY, I WONDER WHY #17 TURNED INTO SUCH A GOOD GUY AFTER COMING BACK TO LIFE.
THE ANDROIDS WERE PREVIOUSLY REGULAR HUMANS. THEY WERE MERELY PROGRAMMED BY DR. GERO TO BE EVIL.
IT SEEMS THAT WHEN KURIRIN ASKED SHENLONG TO REMOVE THE BOMB INSIDE HIM, IT SERVED AS THE TRIGGER FOR HIM TO REGAIN HIS HUMANITY.
HMMM.
I DON'T REALLY GET IT, BUT GOOD JOB BY KURIRIN.

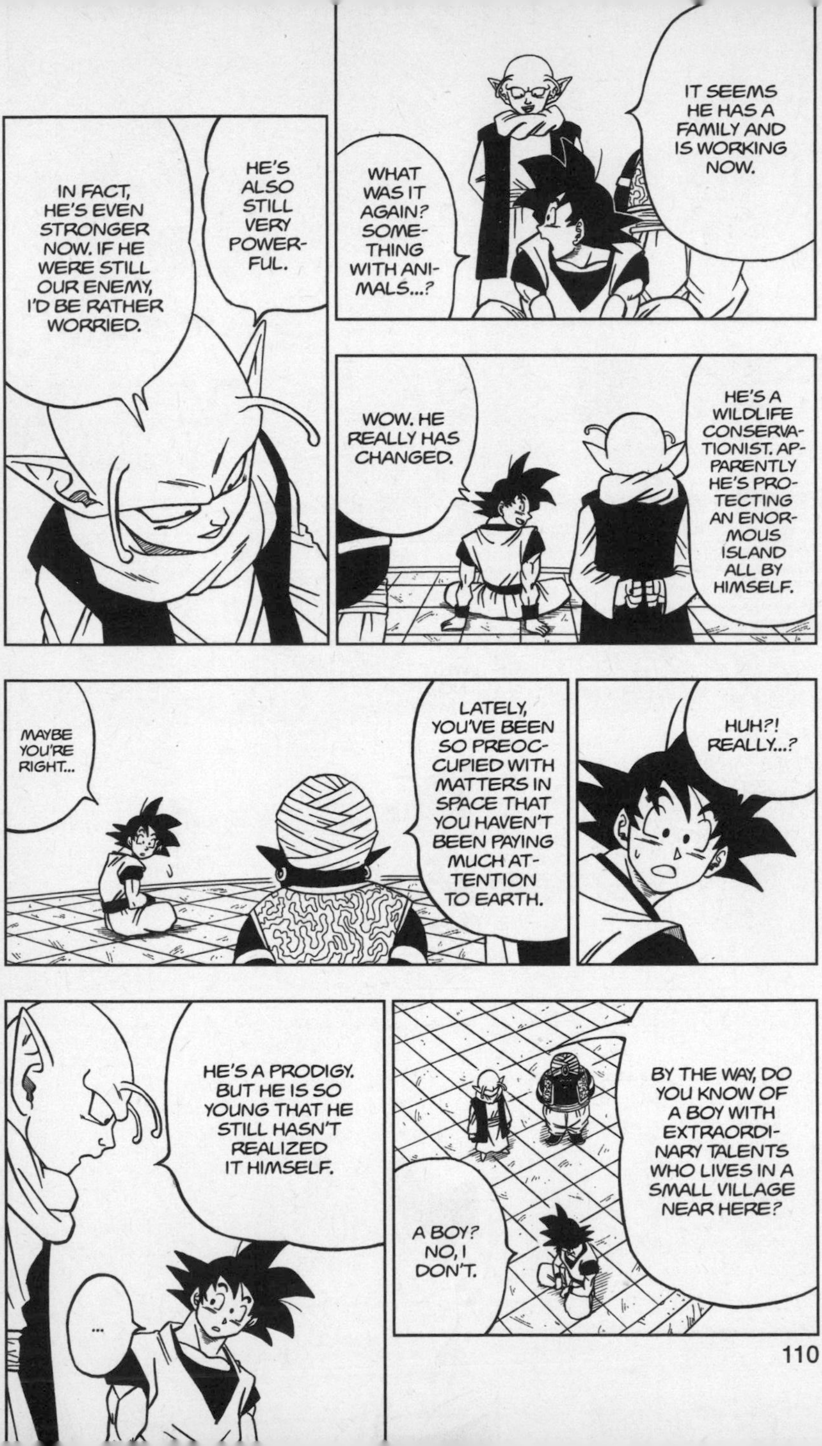
IT SEEMS HE HAS A FAMILY AND IS WORKING NOW.
WHAT WAS IT AGAIN? SOMETHING WITH ANIMALS...?
HE'S A WILDLIFE CONSERVATIONIST. APPARENTLY HE'S PROTECTING AN ENORMOUS ISLAND ALL BY HIMSELF.
WOW. HE REALLY HAS CHANGED.
HE'S ALSO STILL VERY POWERFUL.
IN FACT, HE'S EVEN STRONGER NOW. IF HE WERE STILL OUR ENEMY, I'D BE RATHER WORRIED.
HUH?! REALLY...?
LATELY, YOU'VE BEEN SO PREOCCUPIED WITH MATTERS IN SPACE THAT YOU HAVEN'T BEEN PAYING MUCH ATTENTION TO EARTH.
MAYBE YOU'RE RIGHT...
BY THE WAY, DO YOU KNOW OF A BOY WITH EXTRAORDINARY TALENTS WHO LIVES IN A SMALL VILLAGE NEAR HERE?
A BOY? NO, I DON'T.
HE'S A PRODIGY. BUT HE IS SO YOUNG THAT HE STILL HASN'T REALIZED IT HIMSELF.
...

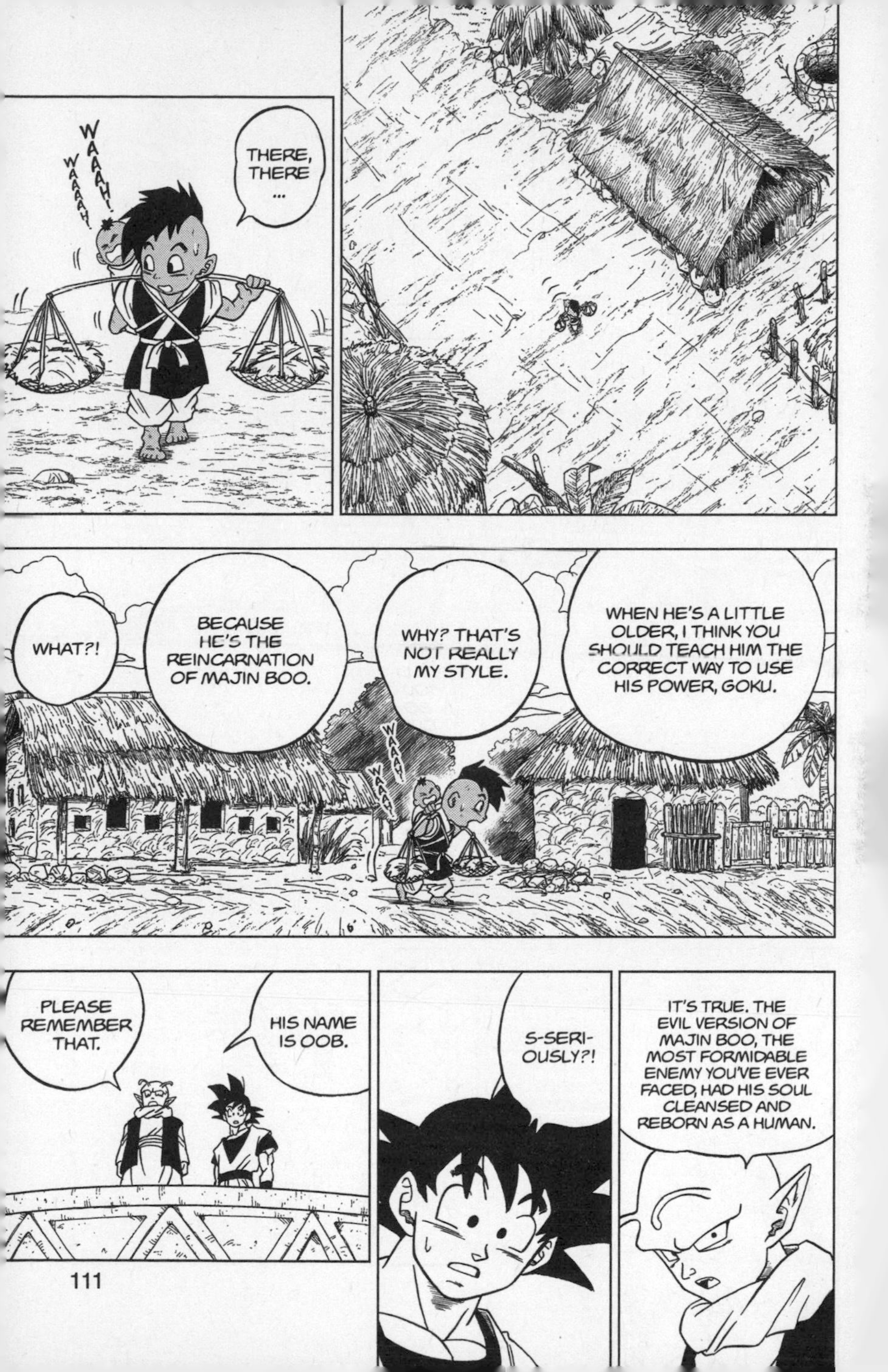

THERE, THERE ...
WAAAAH! WAAAAH!
WHEN HE'S A LITTLE OLDER, I THINK YOU SHOULD TEACH HIM THE CORRECT WAY TO USE HIS POWER, GOKU.
WHY? THAT'S NOT REALLY MY STYLE.
WAAAH! WAAAH!
BECAUSE HE'S THE REINCARNATION OF MAJIN BOO.
WHAT?!
IT'S TRUE. THE EVIL VERSION OF MAJIN BOO, THE MOST FORMIDABLE ENEMY YOU'VE EVER FACED, HAD HIS SOUL CLEANSED AND REBORN AS A HUMAN.
S-SERI-OUSLY?!
HIS NAME IS OOB.
PLEASE REMEMBER THAT.

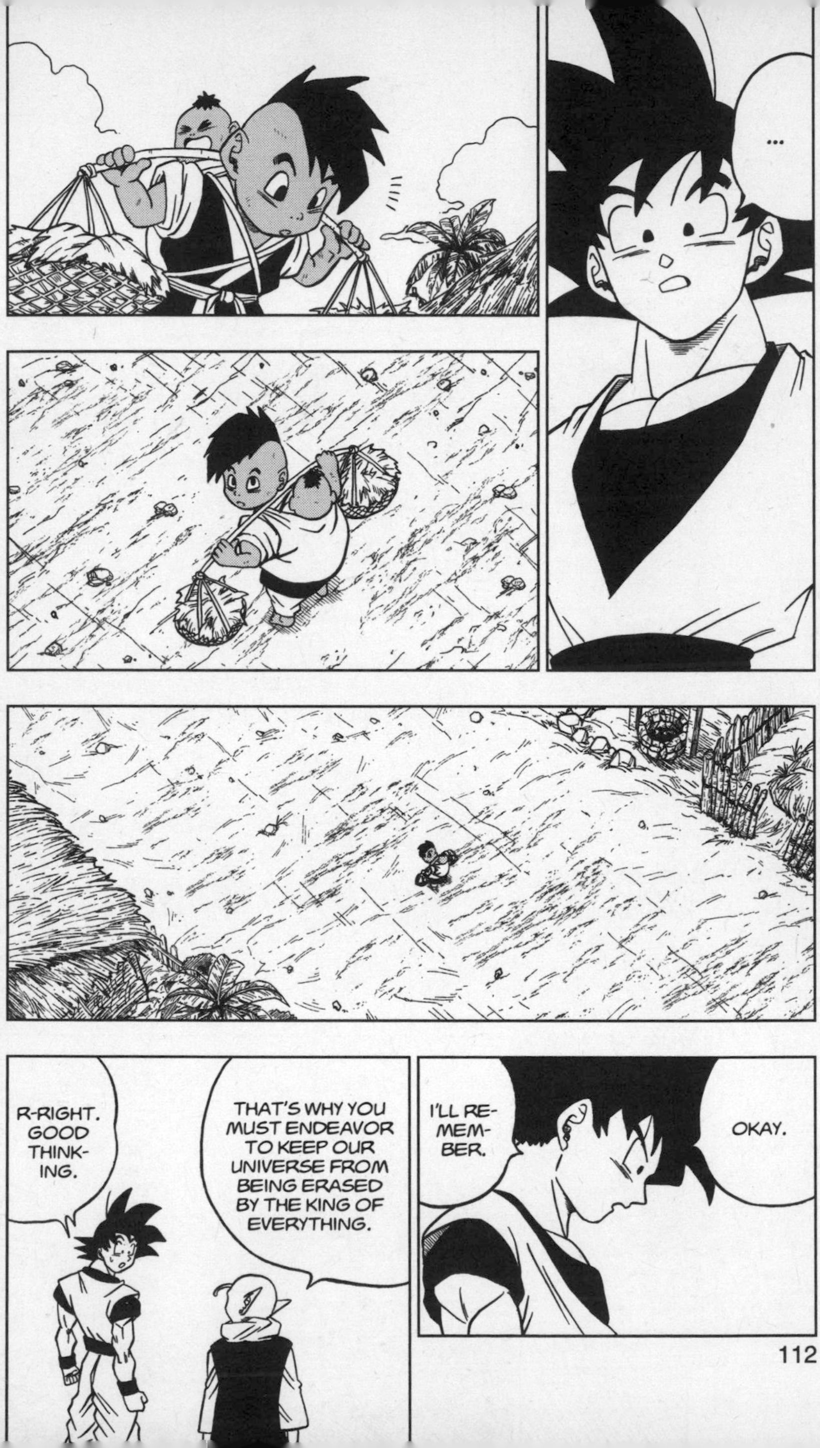
...
OKAY.
I'LL RE-MEM-BER.
THAT'S WHY YOU MUST ENDEAVOR TO KEEP OUR UNIVERSE FROM BEING ERASED BY THE KING OF EVERYTHING.
R-RIGHT. GOOD THINK-ING.

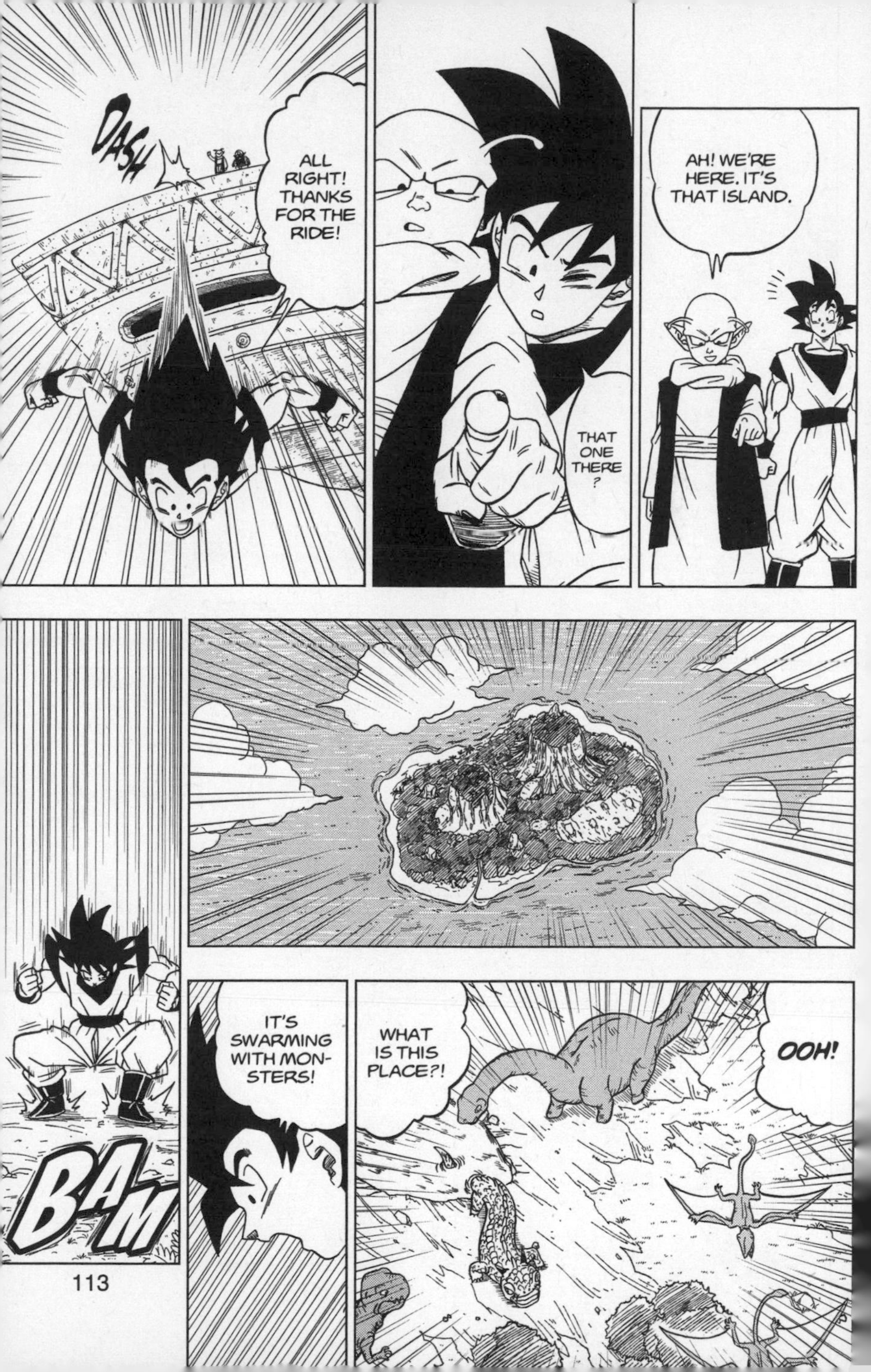
AH! WE'RE HERE. IT'S THAT ISLAND.
THAT ONE THERE?
ALL RIGHT! THANKS FOR THE RIDE!
DASH
OOH!
WHAT IS THIS PLACE?!
IT'S SWARMING WITH MON-STERS!
BAM

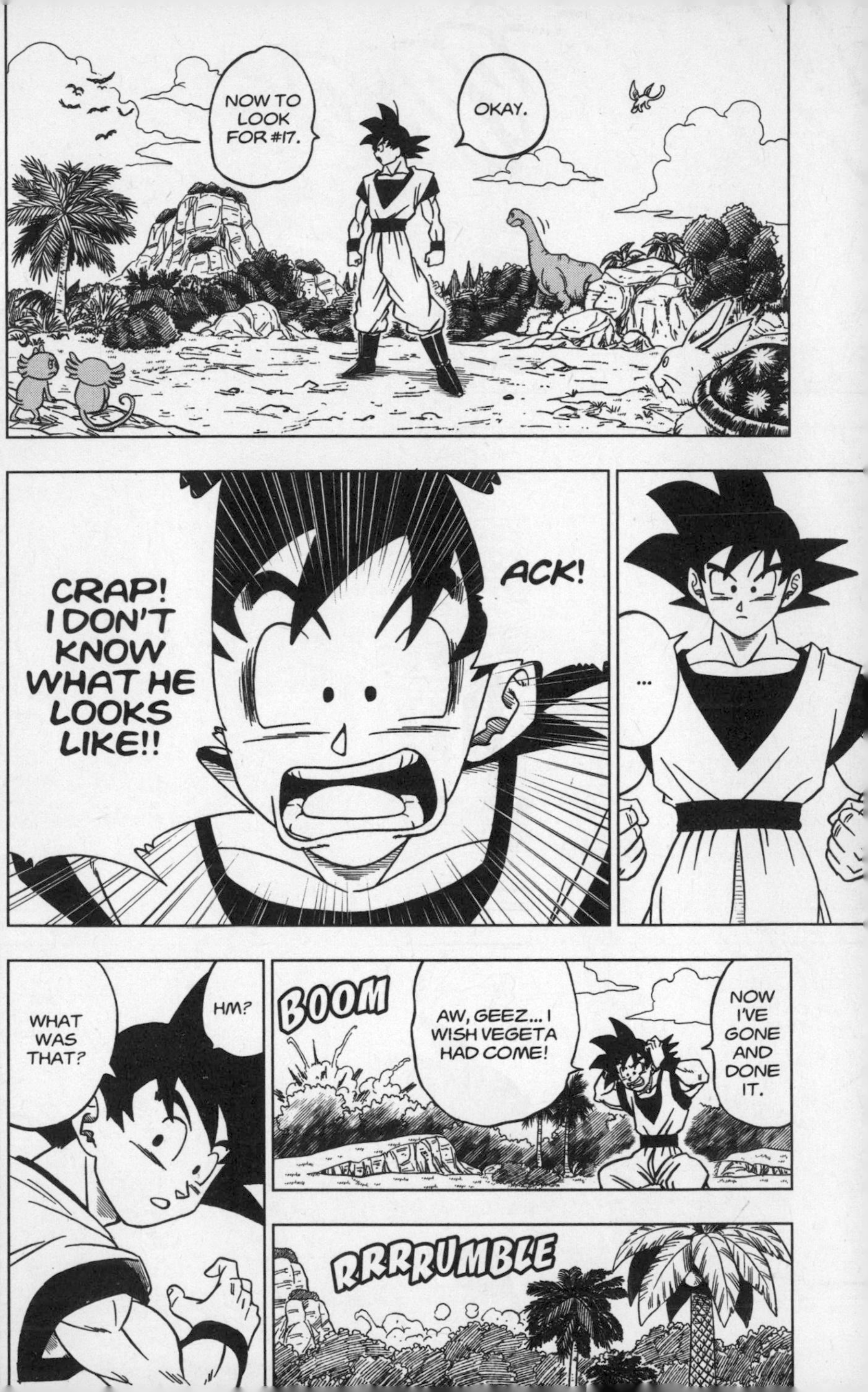
OKAY.
NOW TO LOOK FOR #17.
...
ACK!
CRAP! I DON'T KNOW WHAT HE LOOKS LIKE!!
NOW I'VE GONE AND DONE IT.
AW, GEEZ... I WISH VEGETA HAD COME!
BOOM
RRRRUMBLE
HM?
WHAT WAS THAT?

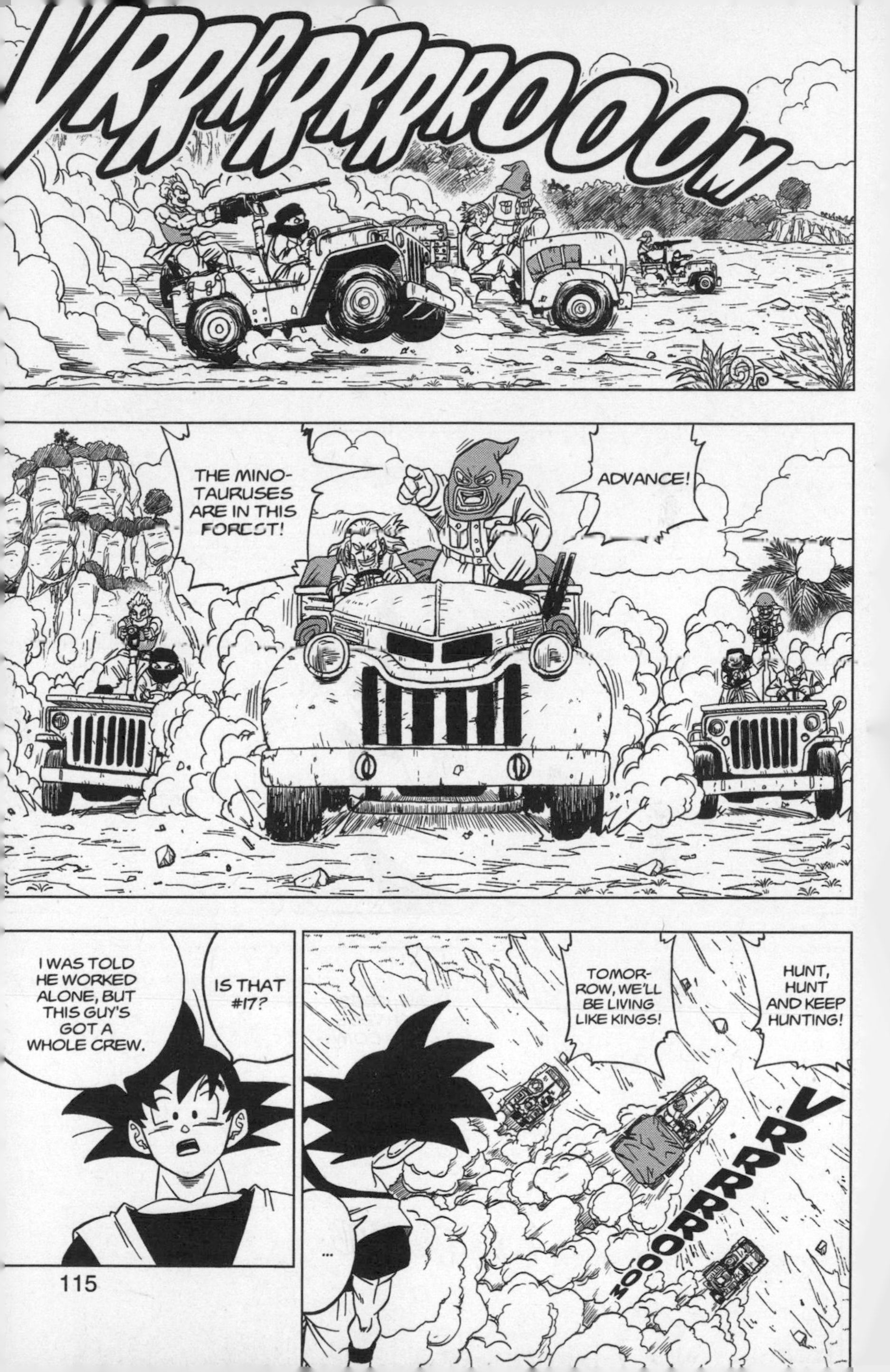
VRRRRRROOOOM
ADVANCE!
THE MINO-TAURUSES ARE IN THIS FOREST!
HUNT, HUNT AND KEEP HUNTING!
TOMOR-ROW, WE'LL BE LIVING LIKE KINGS!
...
VRRRRROOOOM
IS THAT #17?
I WAS TOLD HE WORKED ALONE, BUT THIS GUY'S GOT A WHOLE CREW.

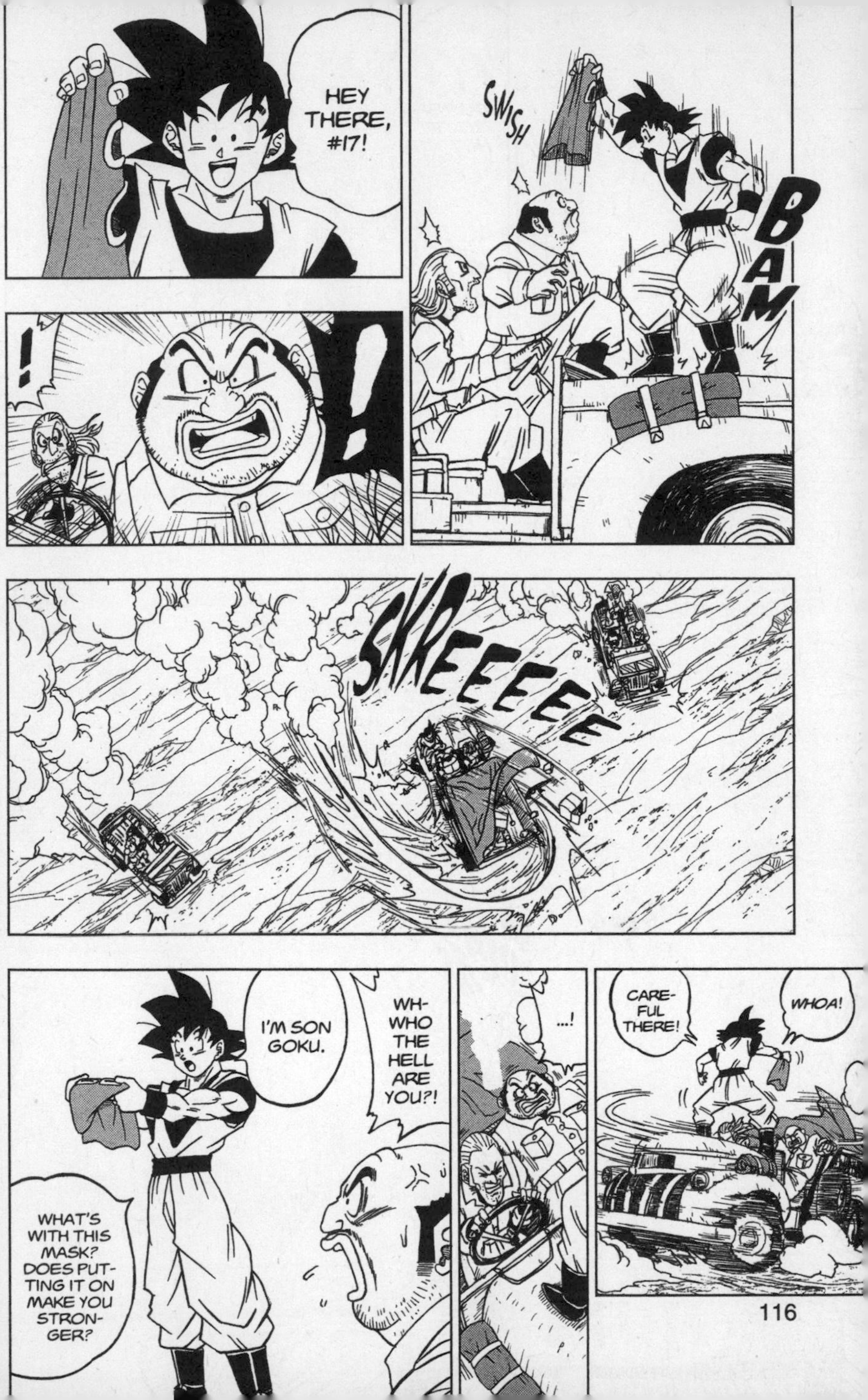
SWISH
BAM
HEY THERE, #17!
!
!
SKREEEEEE
WHOA!
CARE-FUL THERE!
...!
WH-WHO THE HELL ARE YOU?!
I'M SON GOKU.
WHAT'S WITH THIS MASK? DOES PUTTING IT ON MAKE YOU STRONGER?

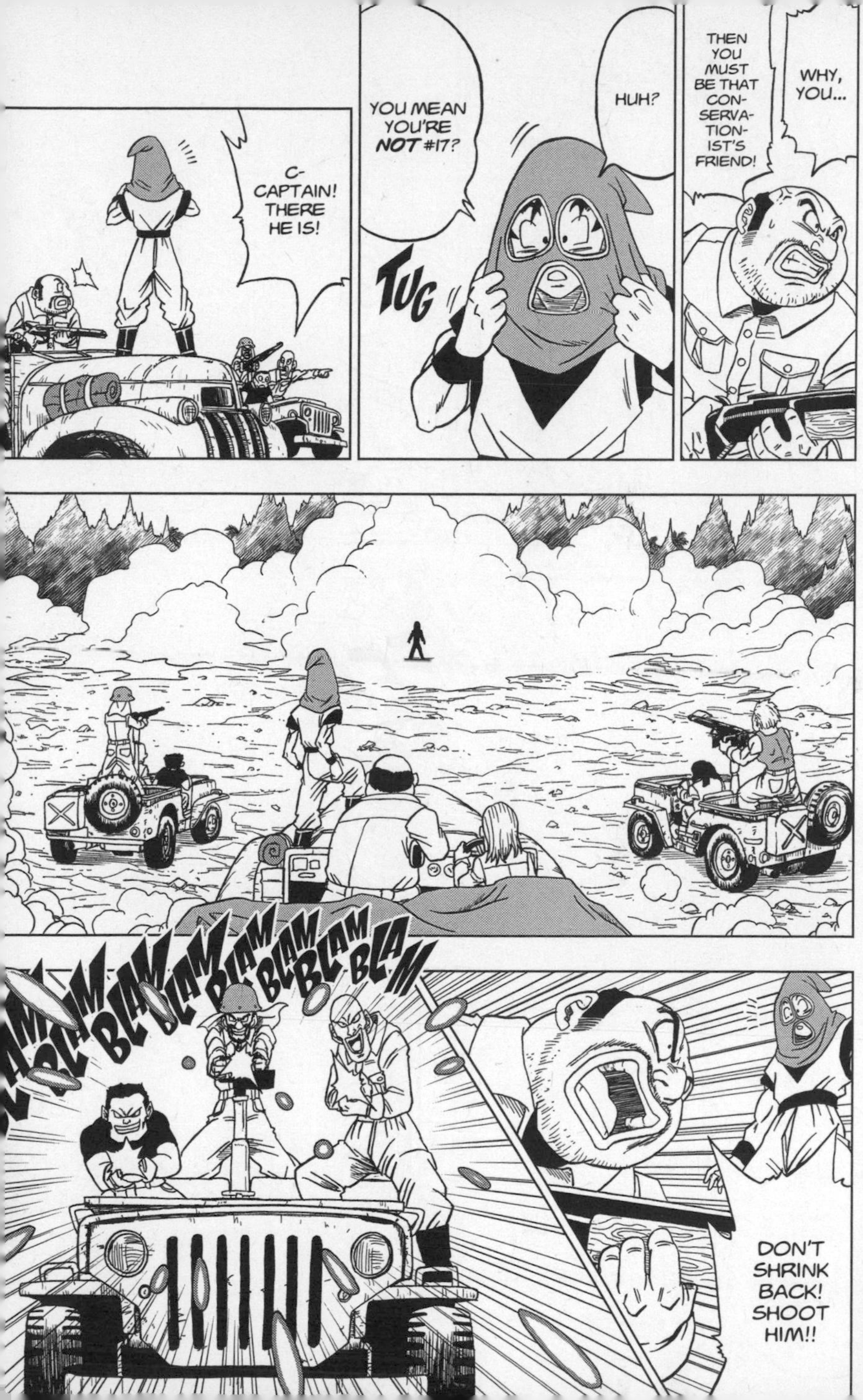
WHY, YOU...
THEN YOU MUST BE THAT CONSERVATIONIST'S FRIEND!
HUH?
YOU MEAN YOU'RE NOT #17?
TUG
C-CAPTAIN! THERE HE IS!
DON'T SHRINK BACK! SHOOT HIM!!
BLAM BLAM BLAM BLAM BLAM BLAM BLAM BLAM

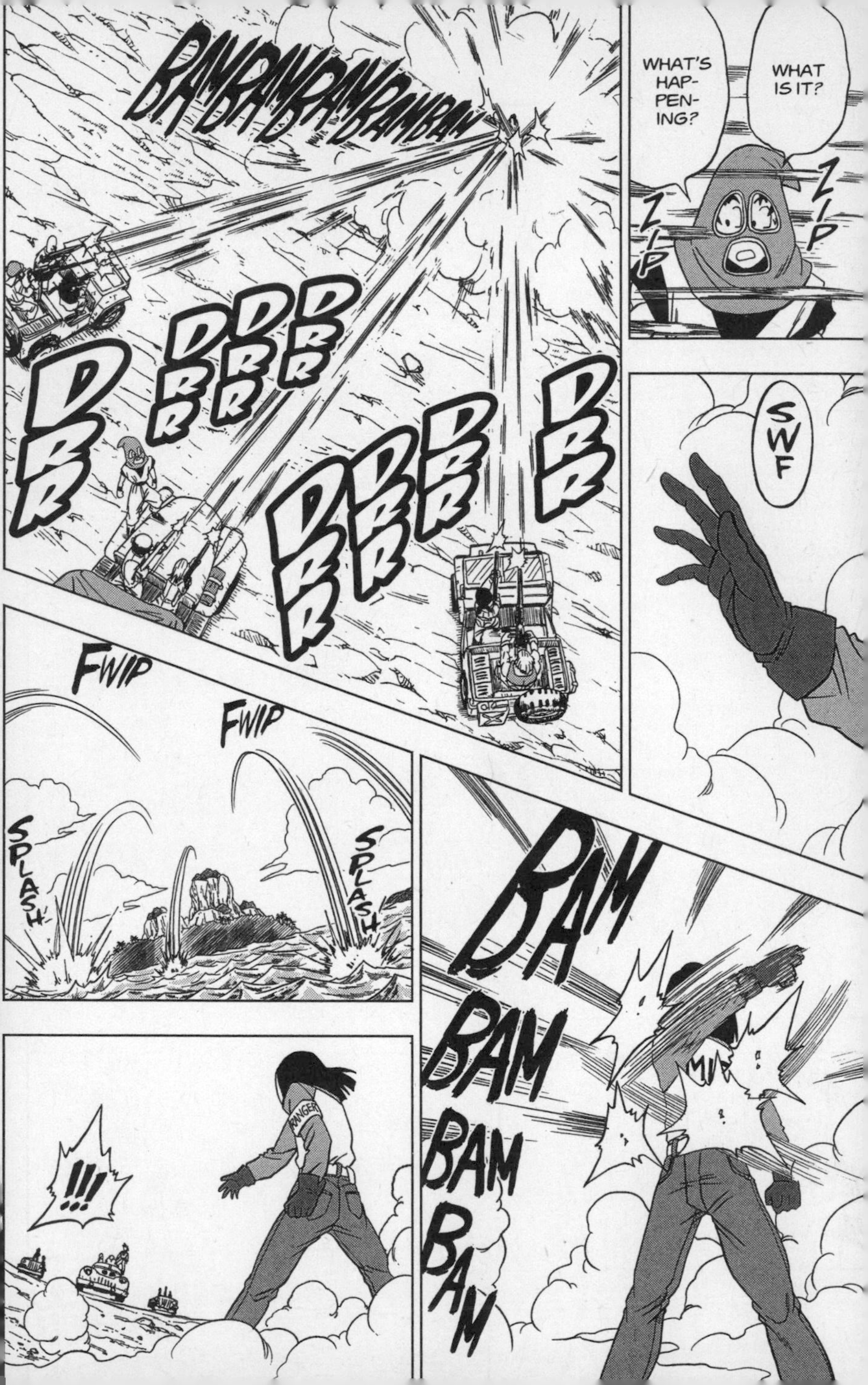
WHAT IS IT?
WHAT'S HAP-PEN-ING?
ZIP
ZIP
SWF
BAMBAMBAMBAMBAM
DRR
DRRR
DRRR
DRRR
DRRR
DRRR
DRRR
DRR
BAM BAM BAM BAM BAM
FWIP
FWIP
SPLASH
SPLASH
!!!

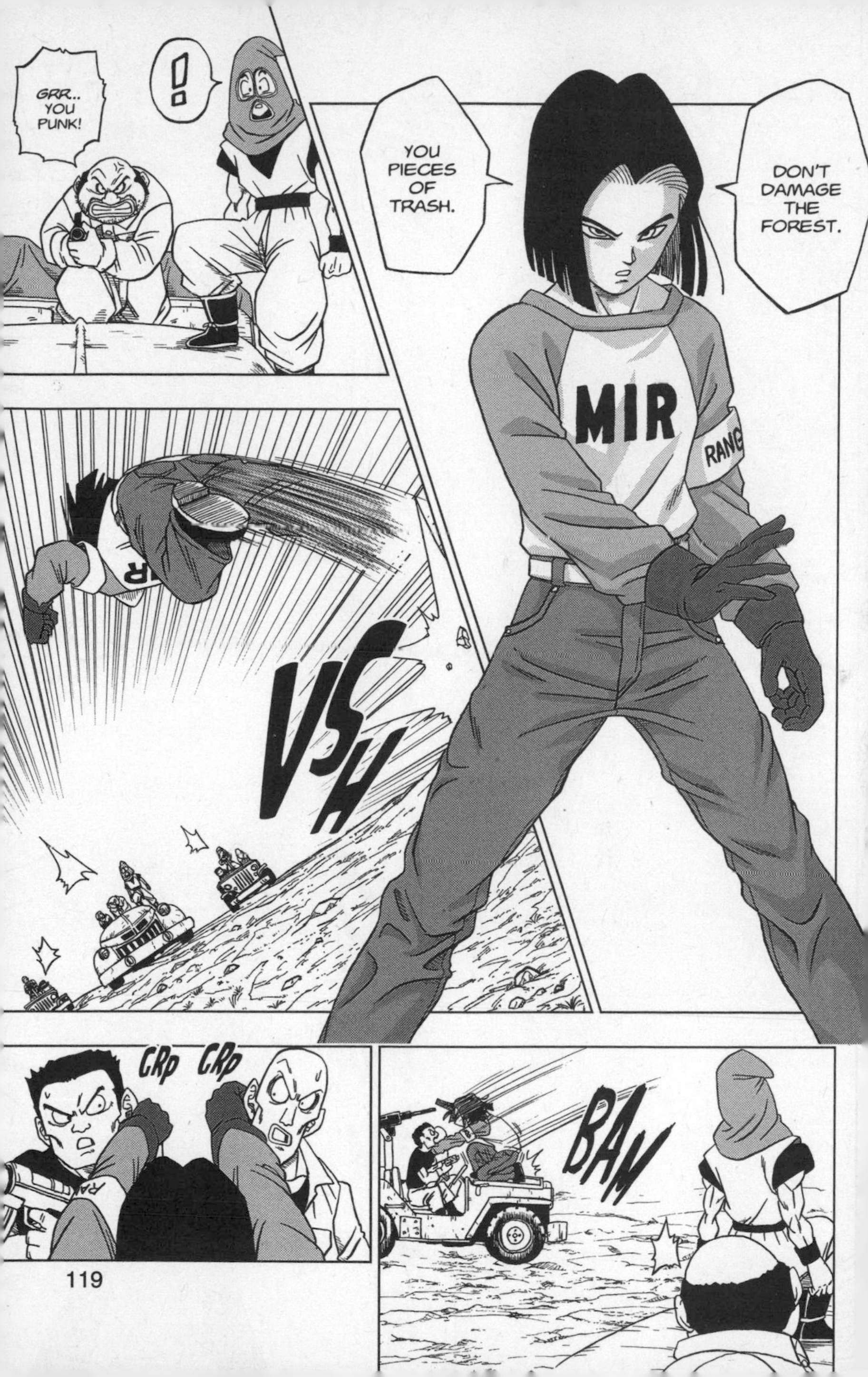
DON'T DAMAGE THE FOREST.
YOU PIECES OF TRASH.
MIR
RANG
!
GRR.. YOU PUNK!
VSH
BAM
CRp CRp

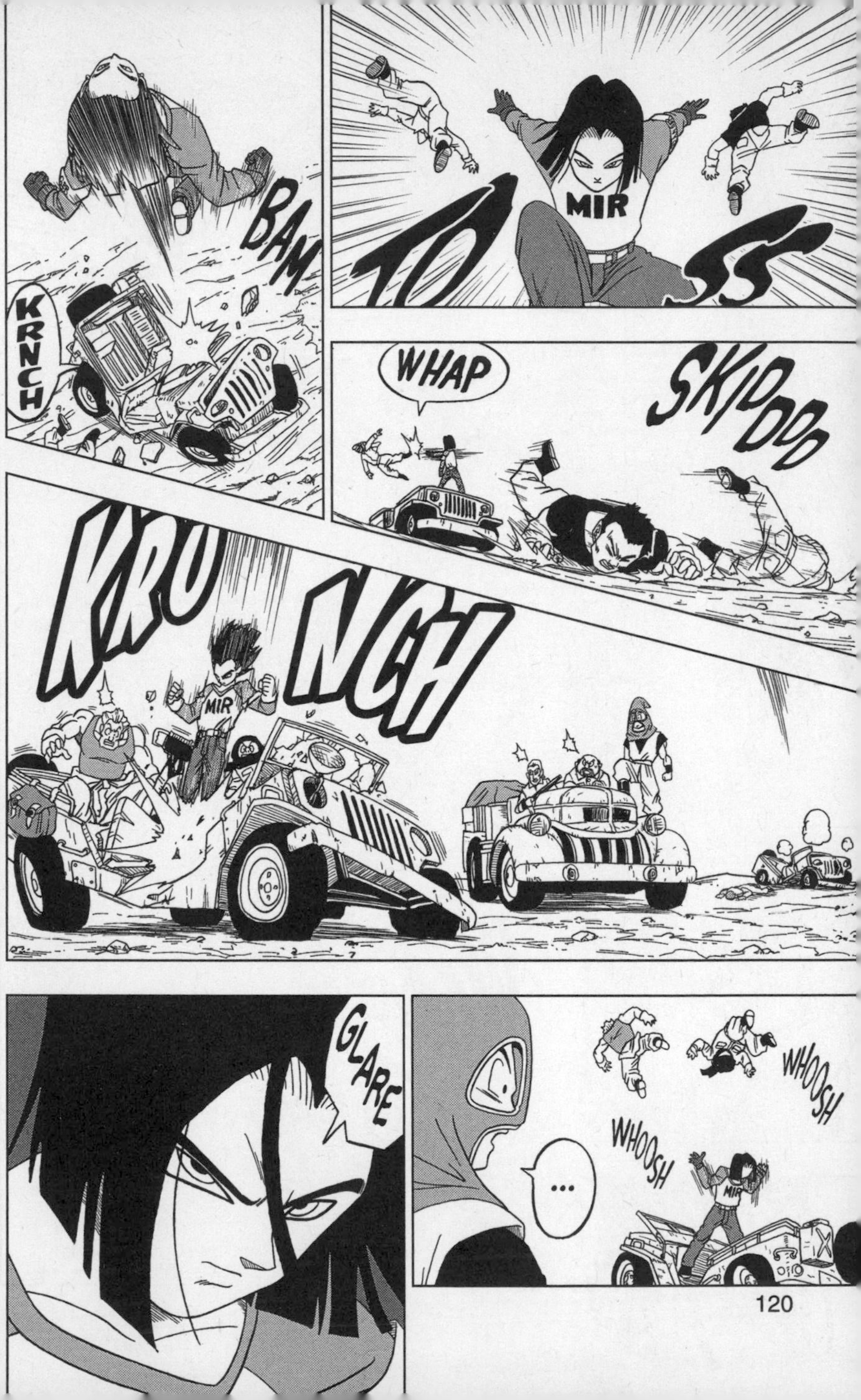
TOSS
WHAP
SKIDDD
BAM
KRNCH
KRUNCH
WHOOSH
WHOOSH
...
GLARE

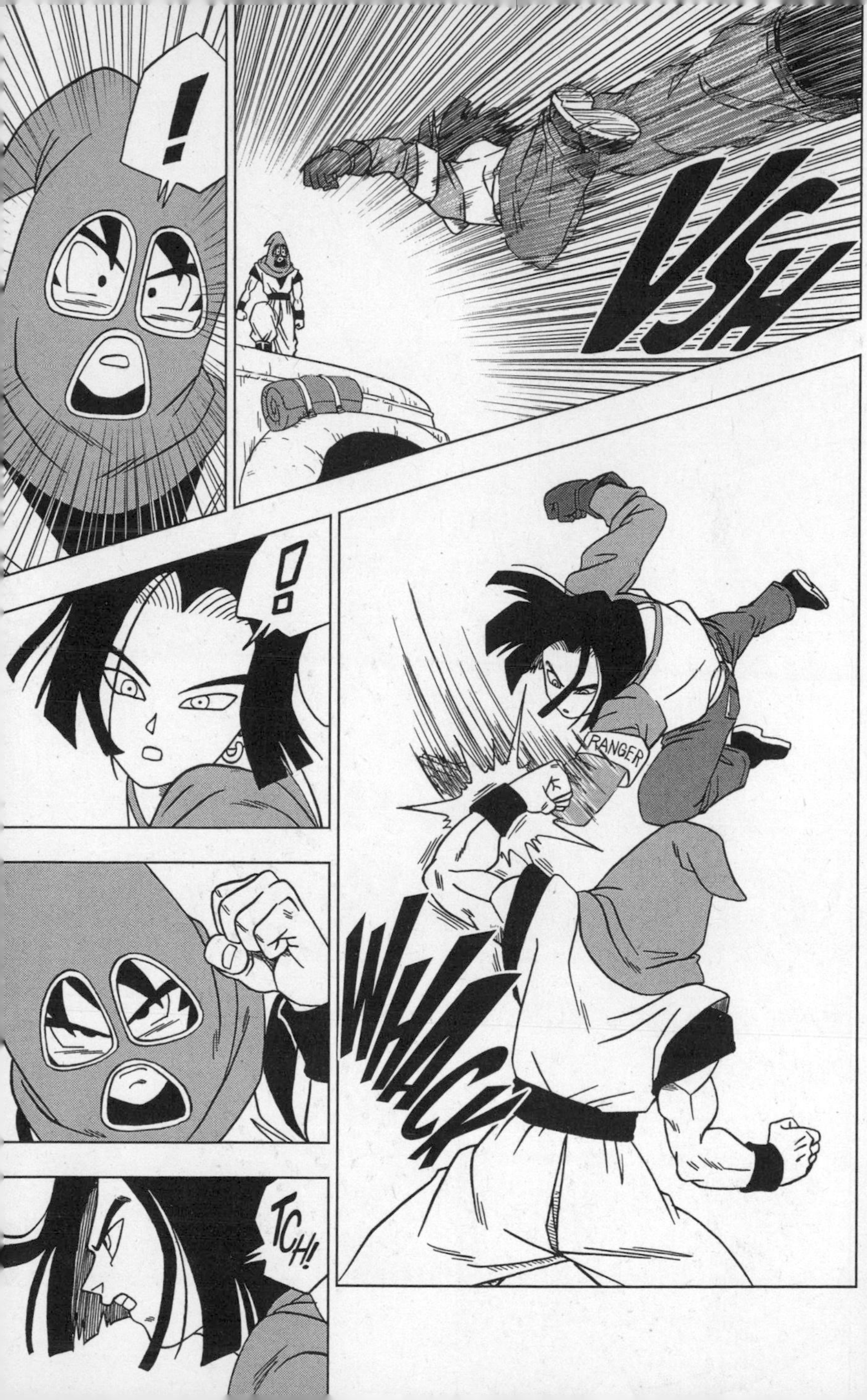
VSH
!
RANGER
WHACK
!
TCH!

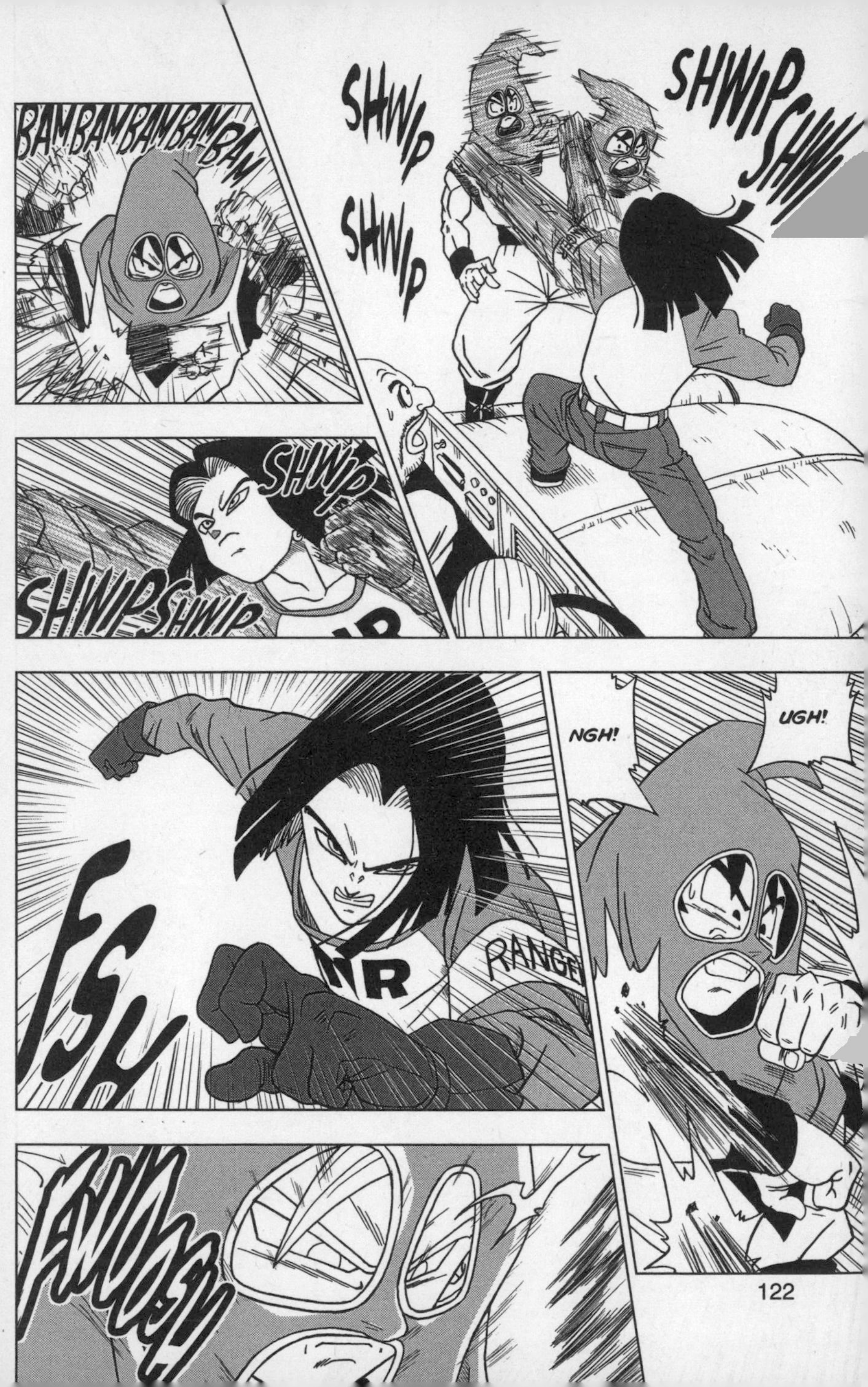
SHWIP SHWI
SHWIP
SHWIP
BAMBAMBAMBAMBAM
SHWIP
SHWIPSHWIP
UGH!
NGH!
RANGE
FSH

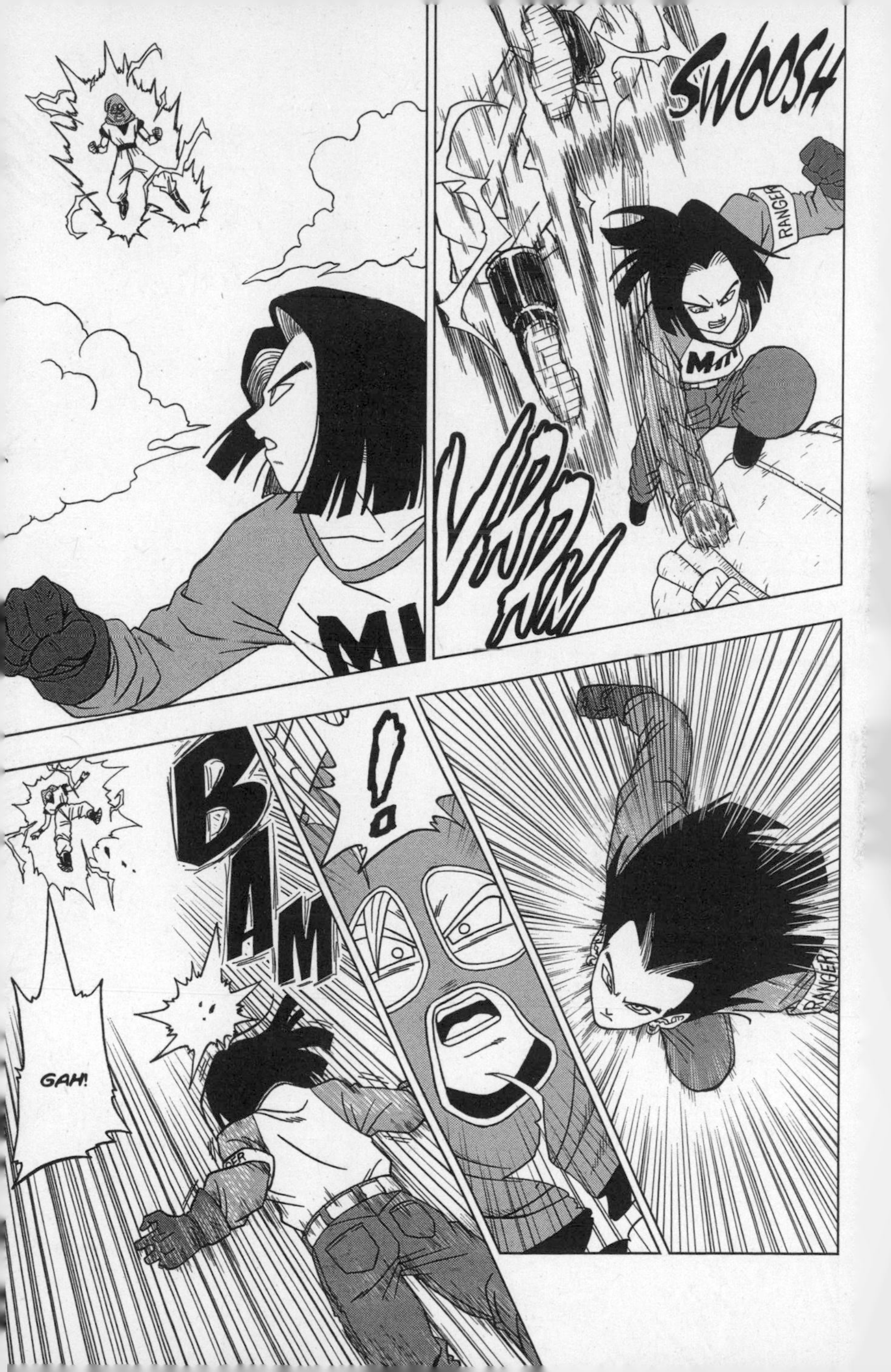
SWOOSH
RANGER
RANGER
!
BAM
GAH!

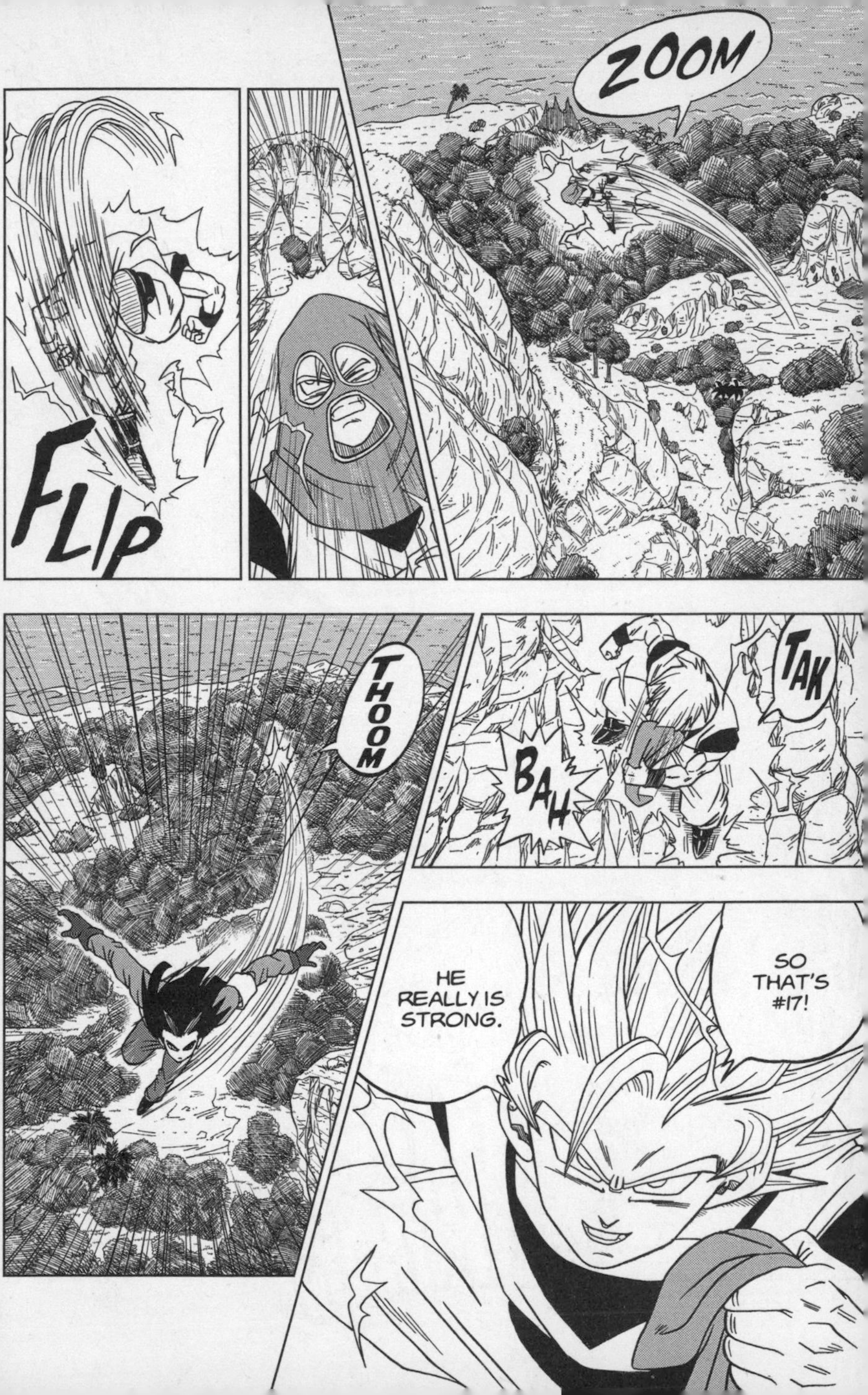
ZOOM
FLIP
TAK
BAH
SO THAT'S #17!
HE REALLY IS STRONG.
THOOM

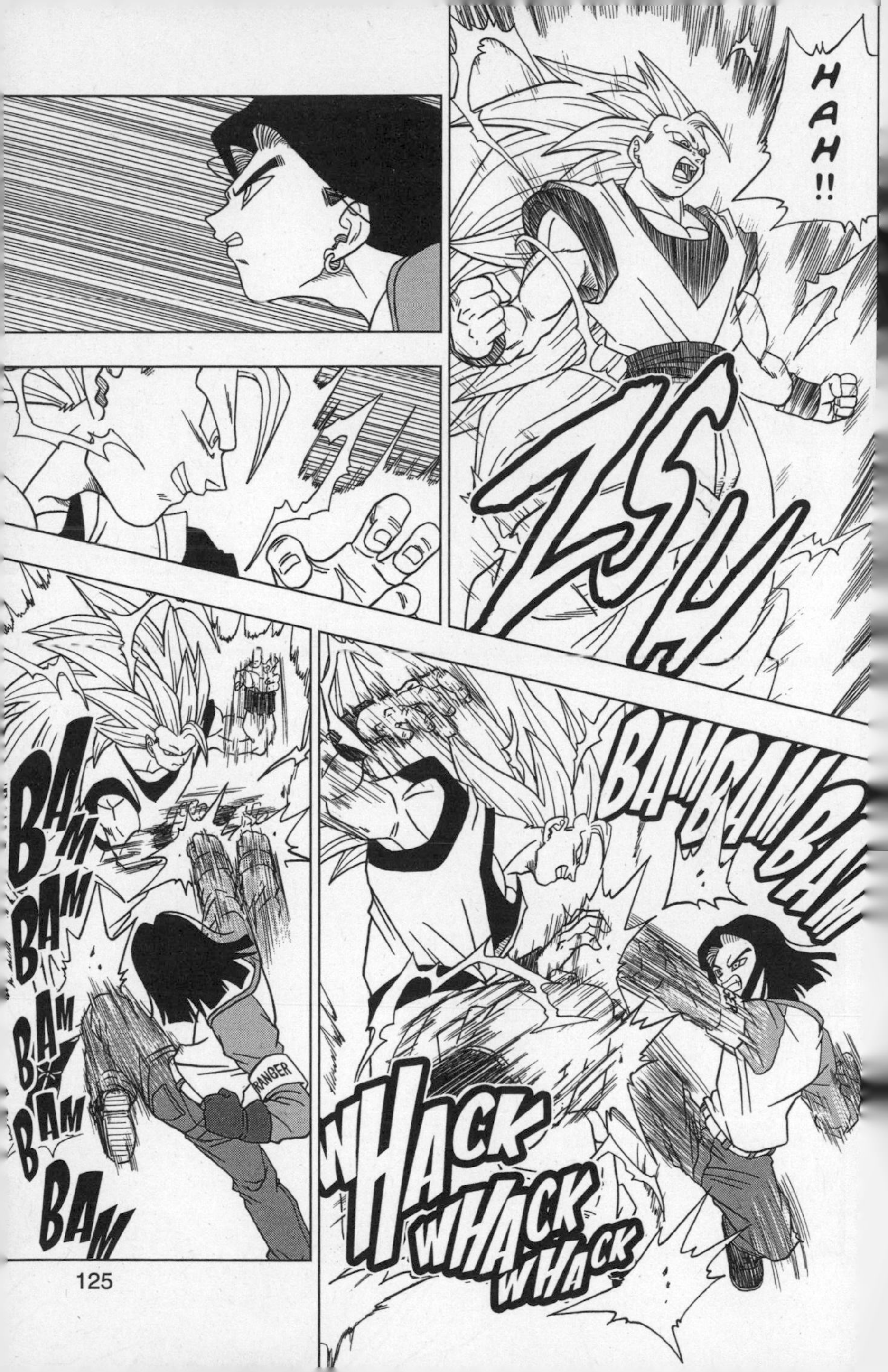
HAH!!
ZSH
BAMBAMBAMBAM
WHACK WHACK WHACK
BAM BAM BAM BAM BAM BAM
RANGER

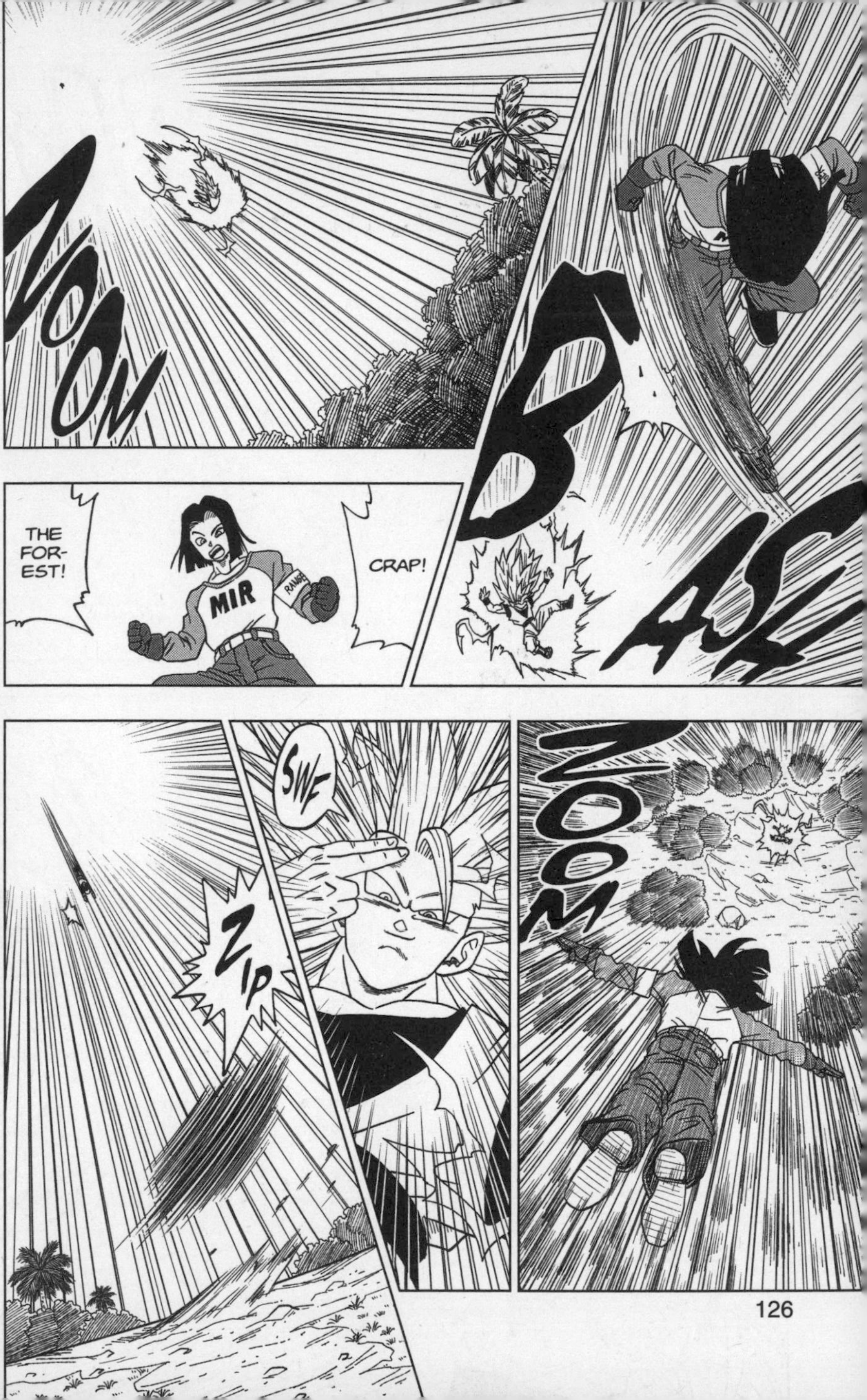
BASH
VOOM
CRAP!
THE FOR-EST!
MIR
VOOM
SWE
ZIP

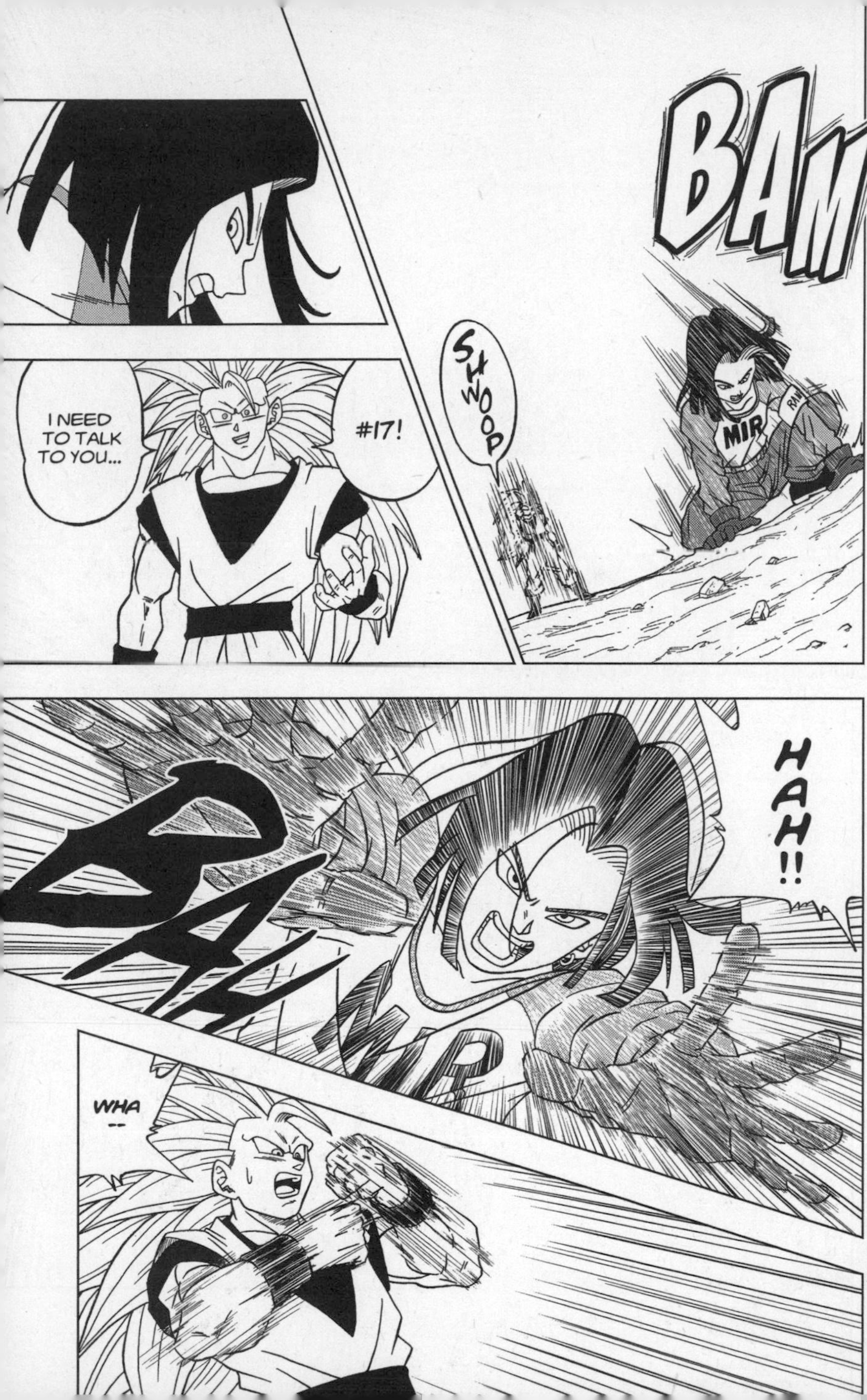
BAM
SHWOOP
#17!
I NEED TO TALK TO YOU...
HAH!!
WHA --

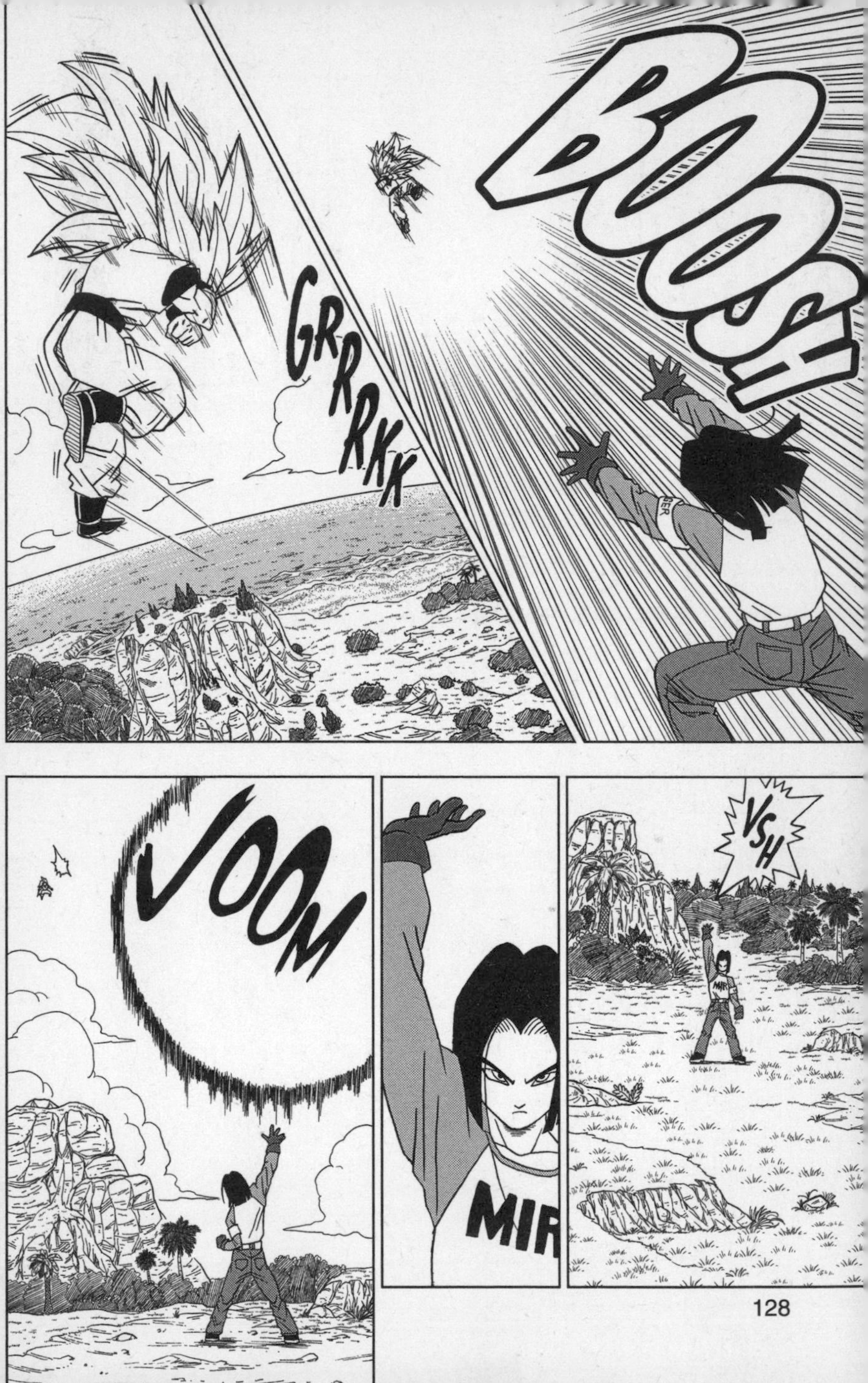
BOOSH!
GRRRKK
VSH
MIR
VOOM

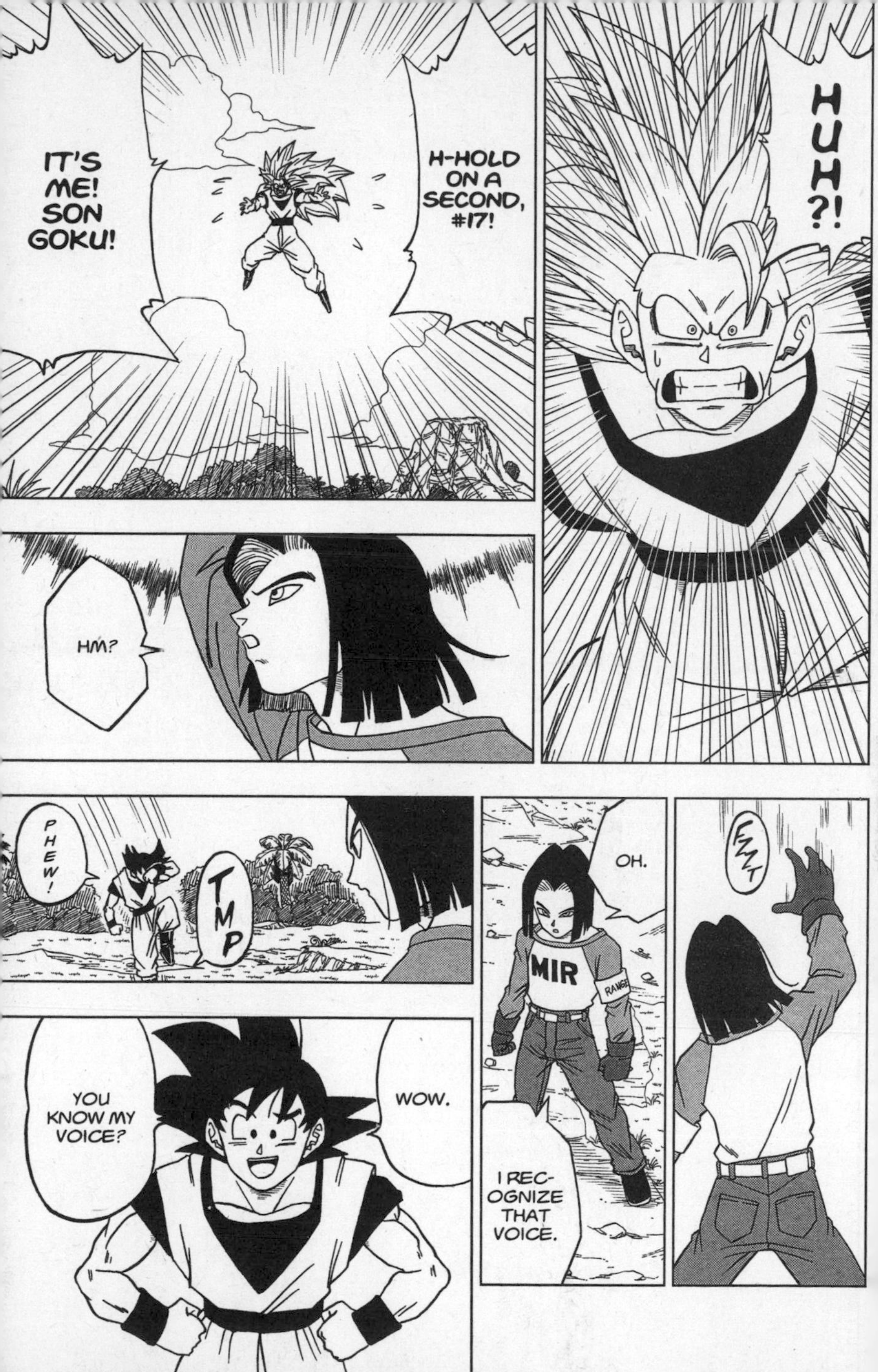
HUH?!
H-HOLD ON A SECOND, #17!
IT'S ME! SON GOKU!
HM?
FZZT
OH.
I RECOGNIZE THAT VOICE.
TMP
PHEW!
WOW.
YOU KNOW MY VOICE?

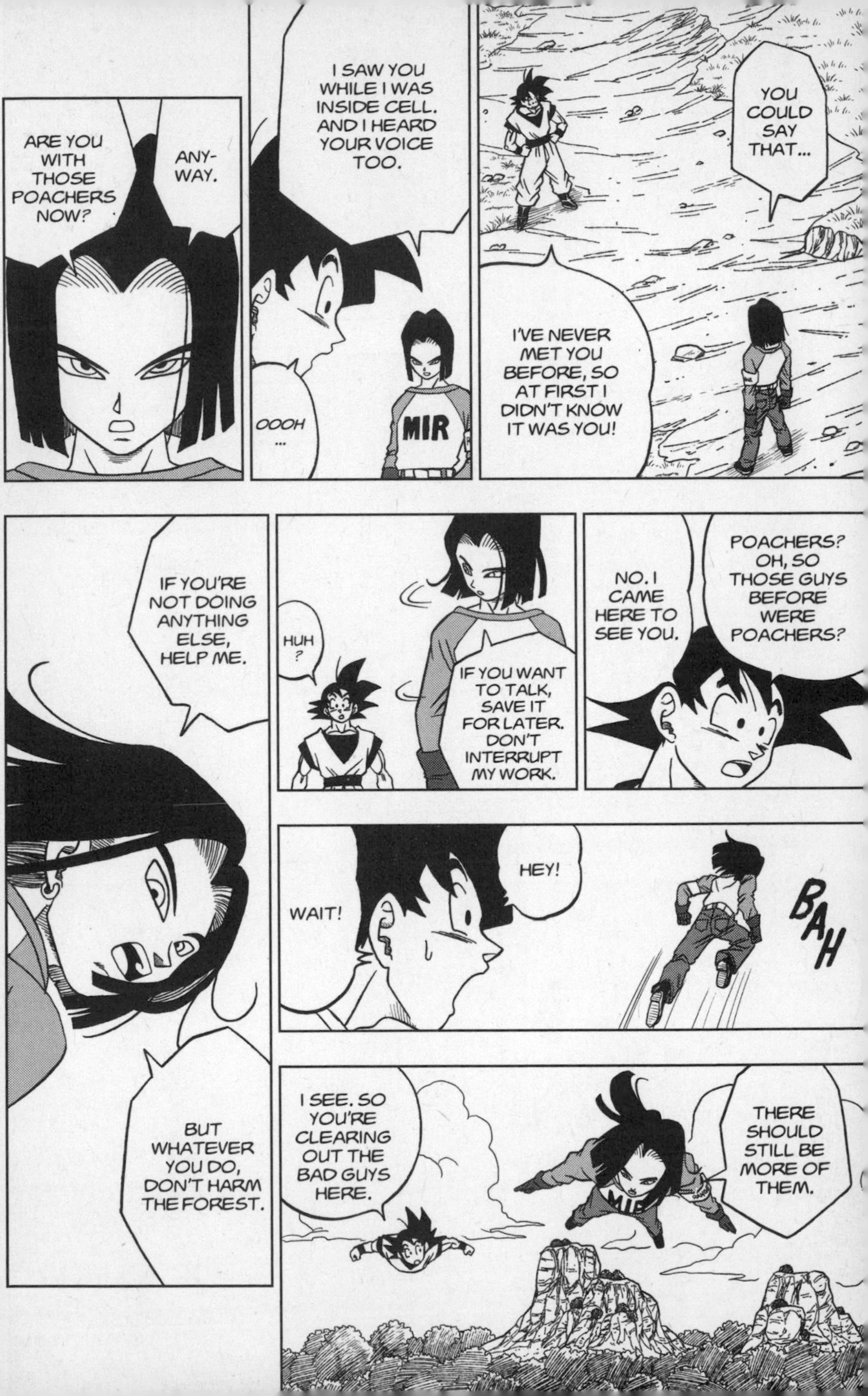
YOU COULD SAY THAT...
I'VE NEVER MET YOU BEFORE, SO AT FIRST I DIDN'T KNOW IT WAS YOU!
I SAW YOU WHILE I WAS INSIDE CELL. AND I HEARD YOUR VOICE TOO.
OOOH ...
ANY-WAY.
ARE YOU WITH THOSE POACHERS NOW?
POACHERS? OH, SO THOSE GUYS BEFORE WERE POACHERS?
NO. I CAME HERE TO SEE YOU.
IF YOU WANT TO TALK, SAVE IT FOR LATER. DON'T INTERRUPT MY WORK.
HUH ?
BAH
HEY!
WAIT!
THERE SHOULD STILL BE MORE OF THEM.
I SEE. SO YOU'RE CLEARING OUT THE BAD GUYS HERE.
IF YOU'RE NOT DOING ANYTHING ELSE, HELP ME.
BUT WHATEVER YOU DO, DON'T HARM THE FOREST.

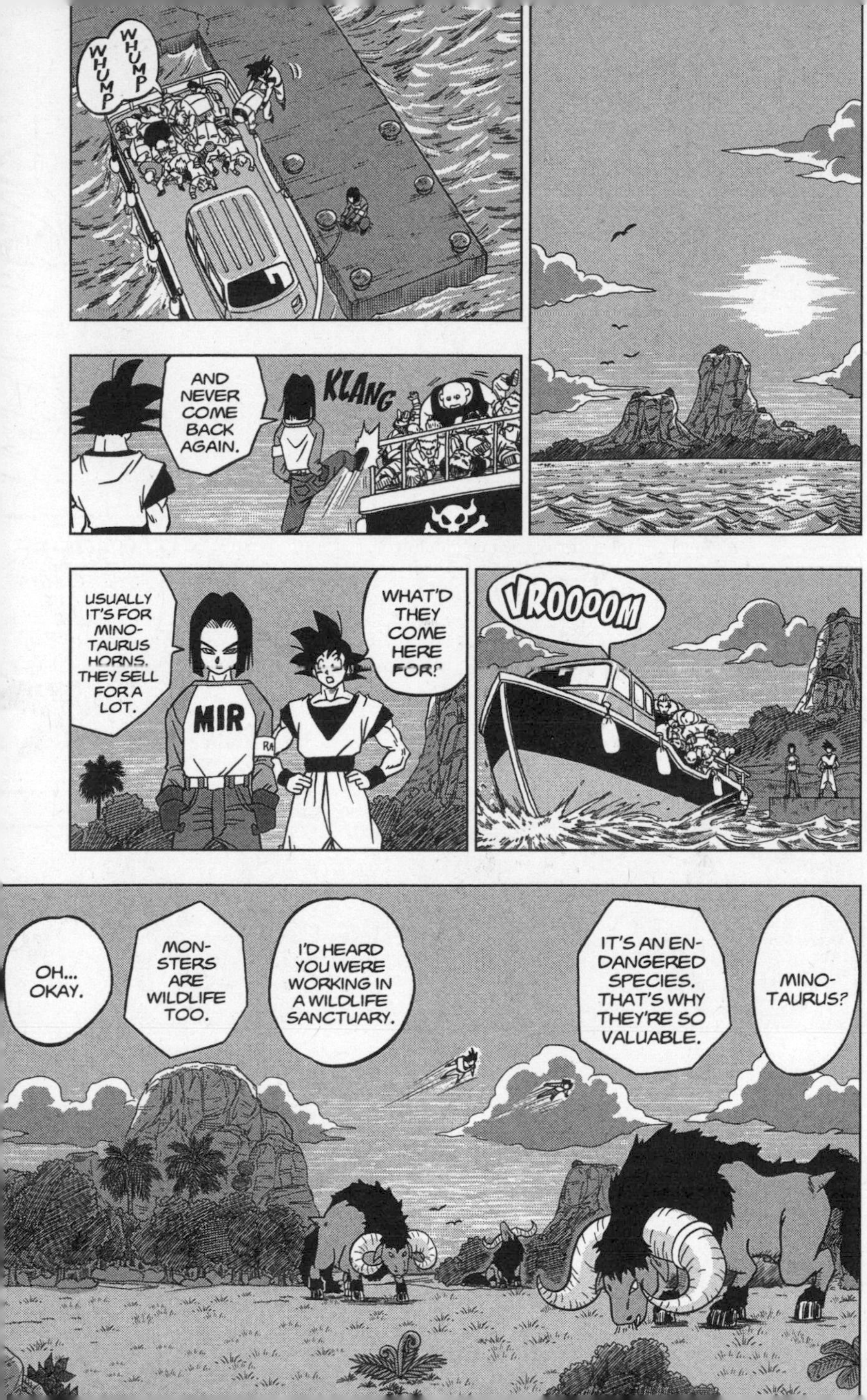
WHUMP WHUMP
AND NEVER COME BACK AGAIN.
KLANG
VROOOOM
WHAT'D THEY COME HERE FOR?
USUALLY IT'S FOR MINO-TAURUS HORNS. THEY SELL FOR A LOT.
MIR
MINO-TAURUS?
IT'S AN EN-DANGERED SPECIES. THAT'S WHY THEY'RE SO VALUABLE.
I'D HEARD YOU WERE WORKING IN A WILDLIFE SANCTUARY.
MON-STERS ARE WILDLIFE TOO.
OH... OKAY.

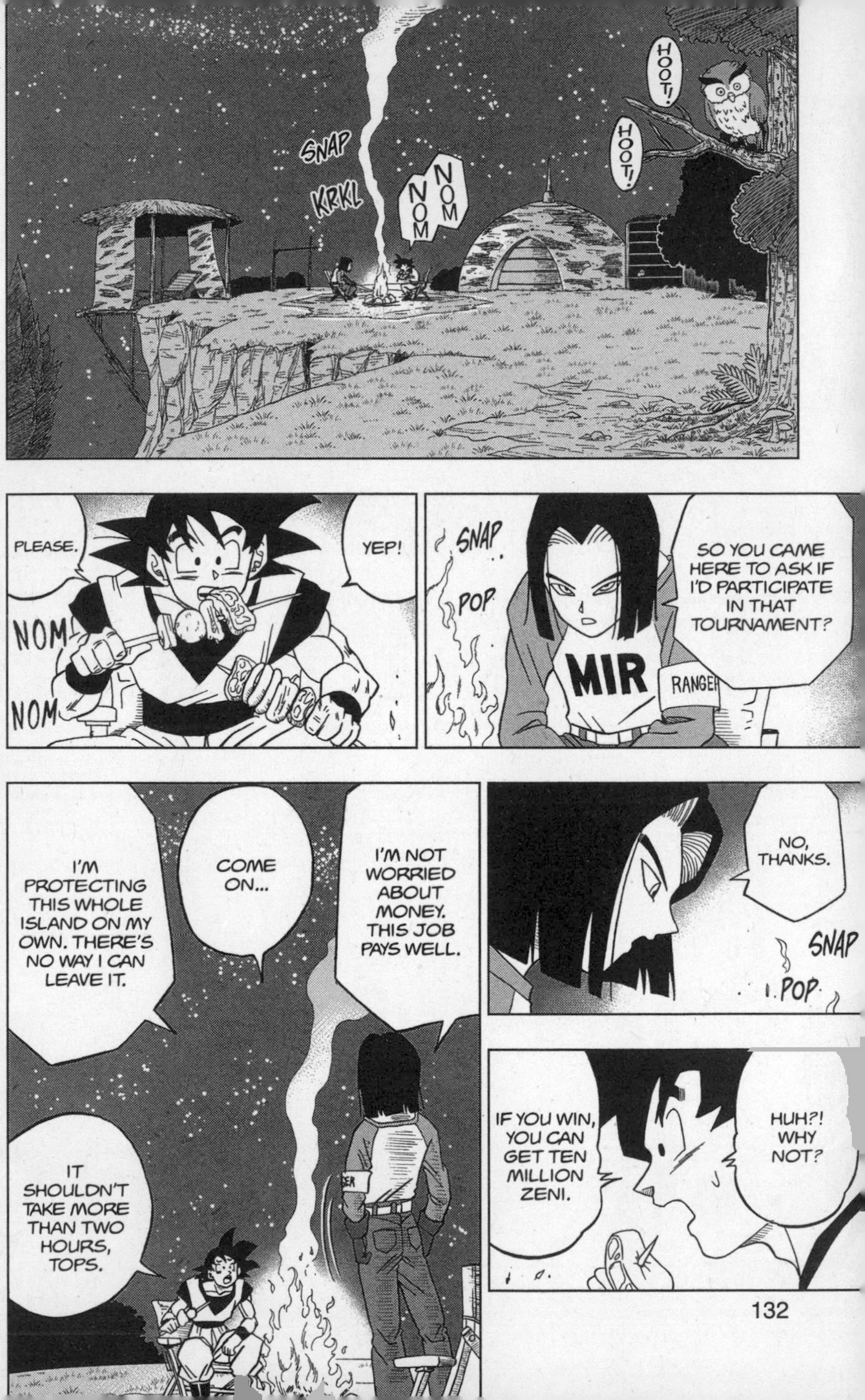
HOOT!
HOOT!
NOM NOM
SNAP
KRKL
SNAP
POP
SO YOU CAME HERE TO ASK IF I'D PARTICIPATE IN THAT TOURNAMENT?
MIR
RANGER
YEP!
PLEASE.
NOM
NOM
NO, THANKS.
SNAP
POP
HUH?! WHY NOT?
IF YOU WIN, YOU CAN GET TEN MILLION ZENI.
I'M NOT WORRIED ABOUT MONEY. THIS JOB PAYS WELL.
COME ON...
I'M PROTECTING THIS WHOLE ISLAND ON MY OWN. THERE'S NO WAY I CAN LEAVE IT.
IT SHOULDN'T TAKE MORE THAN TWO HOURS, TOPS.

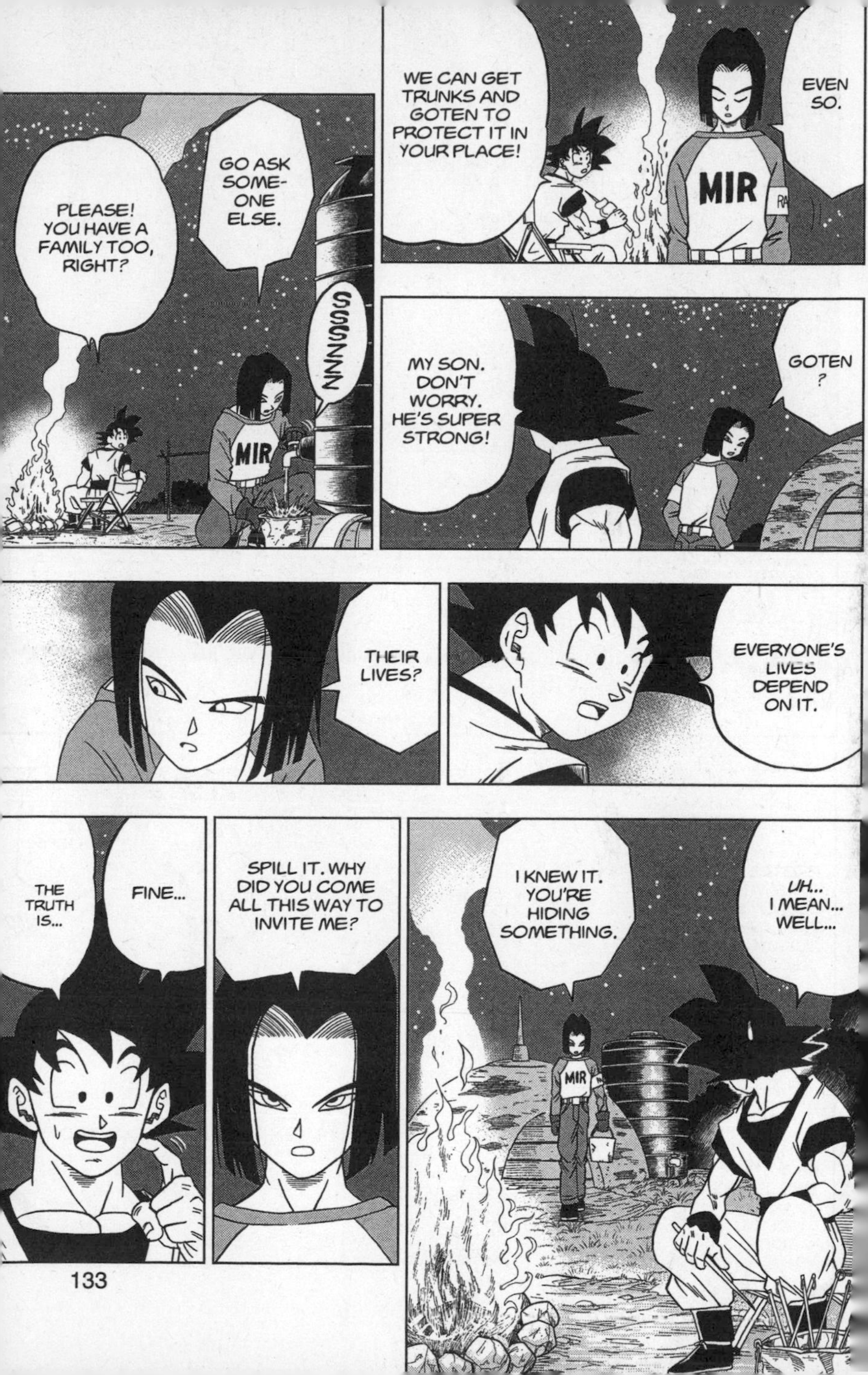
WE CAN GET TRUNKS AND GOTEN TO PROTECT IT IN YOUR PLACE!
EVEN SO.
MIR
GOTEN?
MY SON. DON'T WORRY. HE'S SUPER STRONG!
SSSSNNNN
GO ASK SOME-ONE ELSE.
PLEASE! YOU HAVE A FAMILY TOO, RIGHT?
MIR
EVERYONE'S LIVES DEPEND ON IT.
THEIR LIVES?
UH... I MEAN... WELL...
I KNEW IT. YOU'RE HIDING SOMETHING.
MIR
SPILL IT. WHY DID YOU COME ALL THIS WAY TO INVITE ME?
FINE...
THE TRUTH IS...

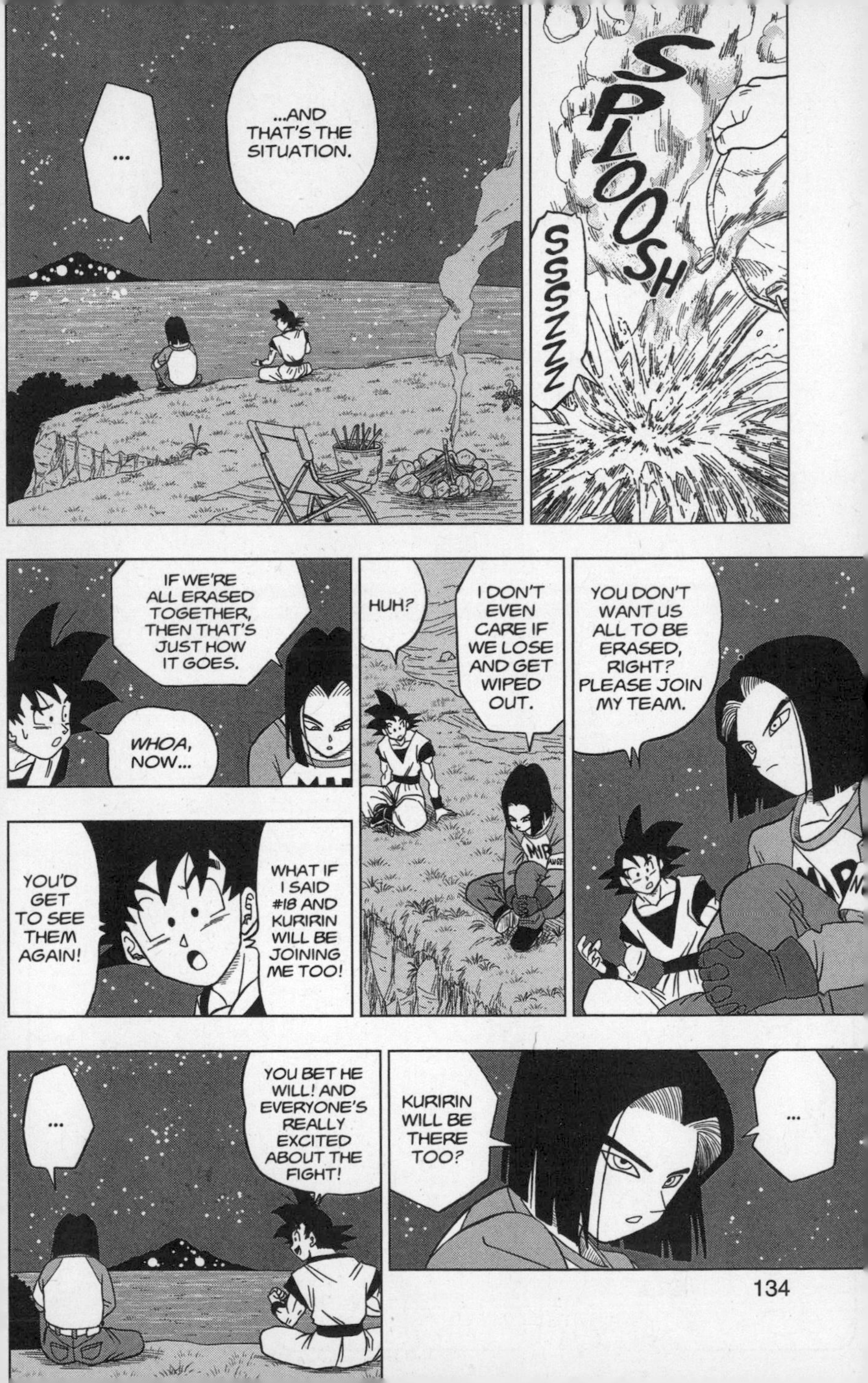
SPLOOSH
SSSZZZZ
...AND THAT'S THE SITUATION.
...
YOU DON'T WANT US ALL TO BE ERASED, RIGHT? PLEASE JOIN MY TEAM.
I DON'T EVEN CARE IF WE LOSE AND GET WIPED OUT.
HUH?
IF WE'RE ALL ERASED TOGETHER, THEN THAT'S JUST HOW IT GOES.
WHOA, NOW...
WHAT IF I SAID #18 AND KURIRIN WILL BE JOINING ME TOO!
YOU'D GET TO SEE THEM AGAIN!
...
KURIRIN WILL BE THERE TOO?
YOU BET HE WILL! AND EVERYONE'S REALLY EXCITED ABOUT THE FIGHT!
...

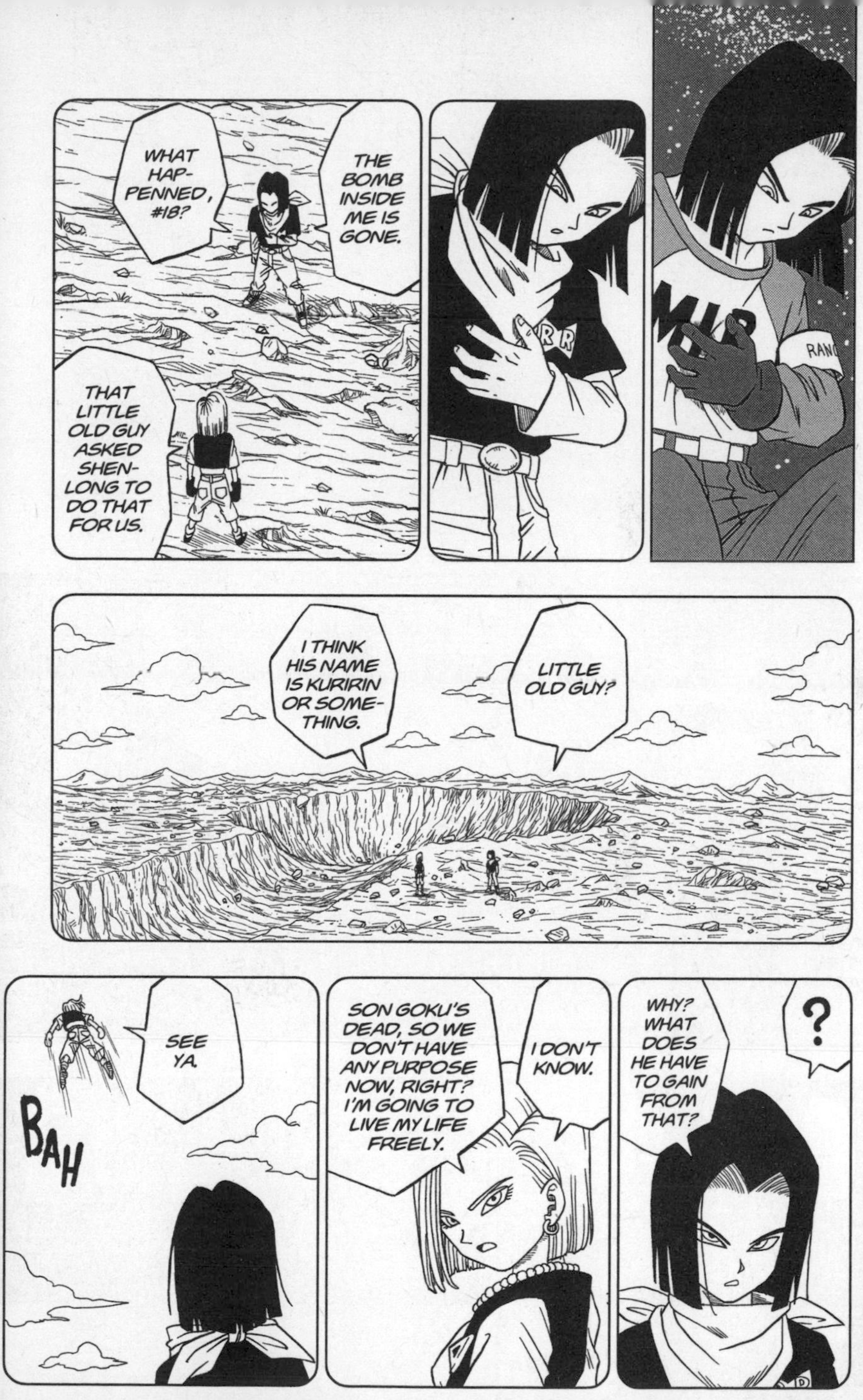
THE BOMB INSIDE ME IS GONE.
WHAT HAP-PENNED, #18?
THAT LITTLE OLD GUY ASKED SHEN-LONG TO DO THAT FOR US.
LITTLE OLD GUY?
I THINK HIS NAME IS KURIRIN OR SOME-THING.
?
WHY? WHAT DOES HE HAVE TO GAIN FROM THAT?
I DON'T KNOW.
SON GOKU'S DEAD, SO WE DON'T HAVE ANY PURPOSE NOW, RIGHT? I'M GOING TO LIVE MY LIFE FREELY.
SEE YA.
BAH

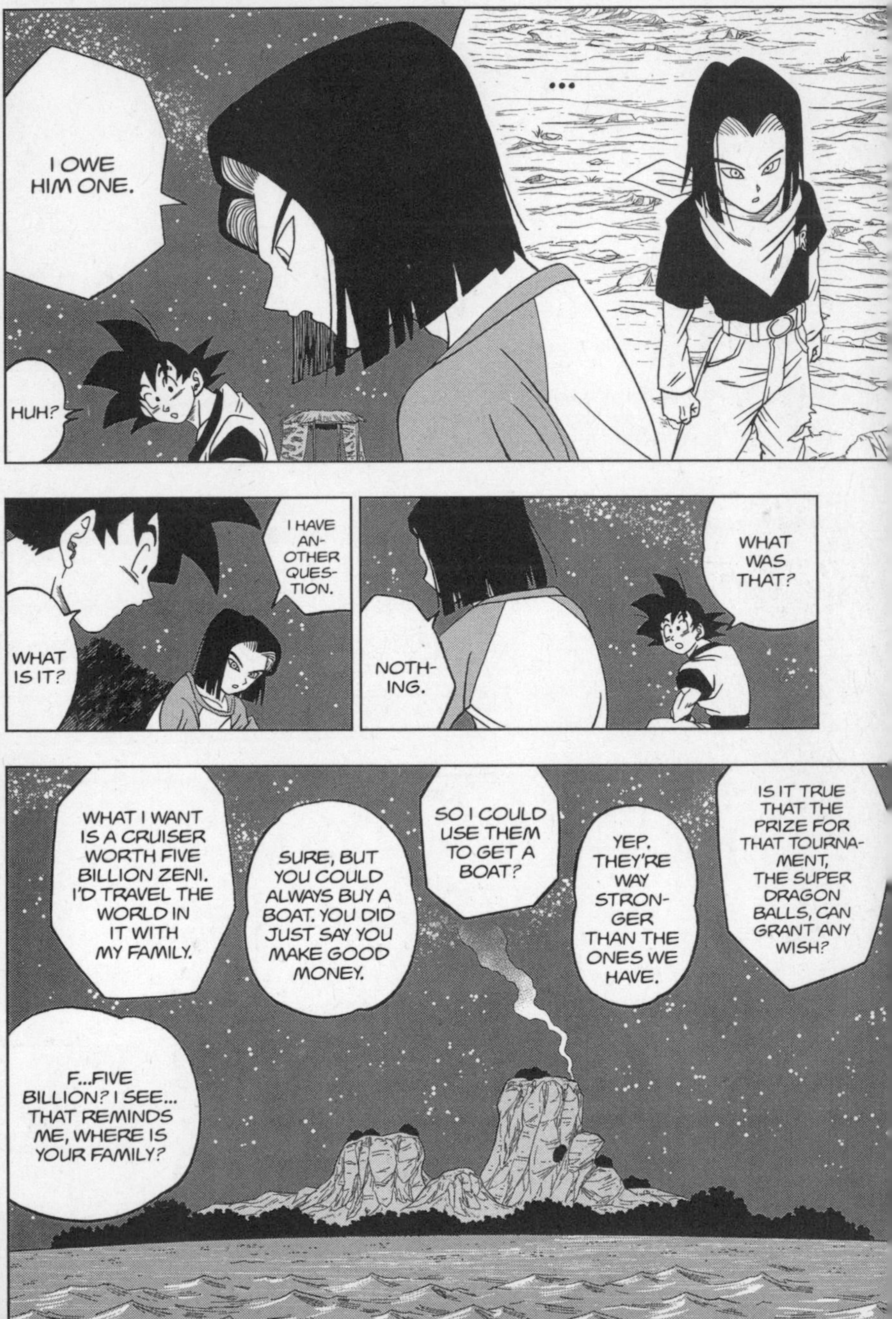
...
I OWE HIM ONE.
HUH?
WHAT WAS THAT?
NOTHING.
I HAVE ANOTHER QUESTION.
WHAT IS IT?
IS IT TRUE THAT THE PRIZE FOR THAT TOURNAMENT, THE SUPER DRAGON BALLS, CAN GRANT ANY WISH?
YEP. THEY'RE WAY STRONGER THAN THE ONES WE HAVE.
SO I COULD USE THEM TO GET A BOAT?
SURE, BUT YOU COULD ALWAYS BUY A BOAT. YOU DID JUST SAY YOU MAKE GOOD MONEY.
WHAT I WANT IS A CRUISER WORTH FIVE BILLION ZENI. I'D TRAVEL THE WORLD IN IT WITH MY FAMILY.
F...FIVE BILLION? I SEE... THAT REMINDS ME, WHERE IS YOUR FAMILY?

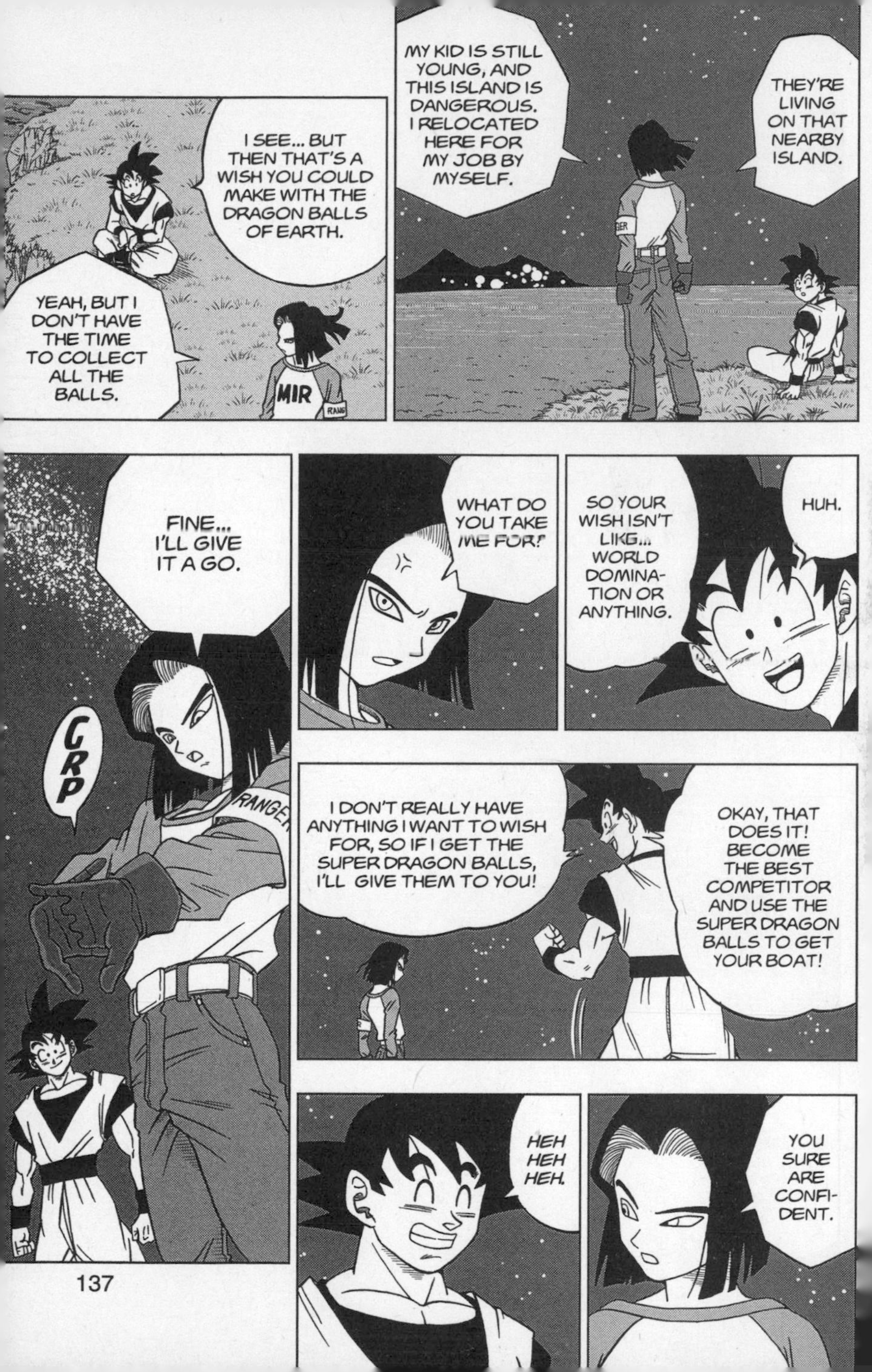
THEY'RE LIVING ON THAT NEARBY ISLAND.
MY KID IS STILL YOUNG, AND THIS ISLAND IS DANGEROUS. I RELOCATED HERE FOR MY JOB BY MYSELF.
I SEE... BUT THEN THAT'S A WISH YOU COULD MAKE WITH THE DRAGON BALLS OF EARTH.
YEAH, BUT I DON'T HAVE THE TIME TO COLLECT ALL THE BALLS.
HUH.
SO YOUR WISH ISN'T LIKE... WORLD DOMINATION OR ANYTHING.
WHAT DO YOU TAKE ME FOR?
OKAY, THAT DOES IT! BECOME THE BEST COMPETITOR AND USE THE SUPER DRAGON BALLS TO GET YOUR BOAT!
I DON'T REALLY HAVE ANYTHING I WANT TO WISH FOR, SO IF I GET THE SUPER DRAGON BALLS, I'LL GIVE THEM TO YOU!
YOU SURE ARE CONFIDENT.
HEH HEH HEH.
FINE... I'LL GIVE IT A GO.
GRP

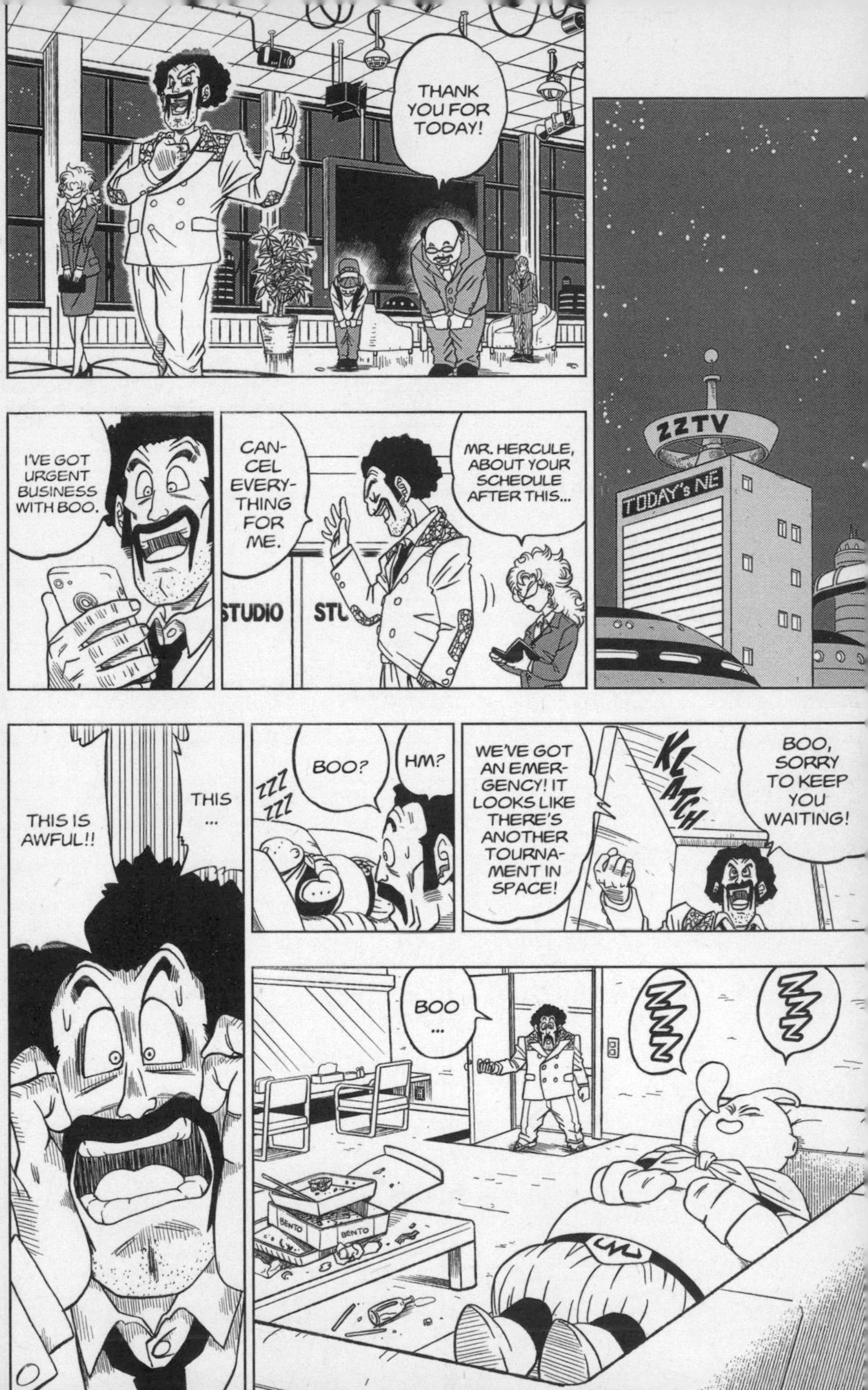
ZZTV
TODAY's NE
THANK YOU FOR TODAY!
MR. HERCULE, ABOUT YOUR SCHEDULE AFTER THIS...
CAN-CEL EVERY-THING FOR ME.
STUDIO
STU
I'VE GOT URGENT BUSINESS WITH BOO.
BOO, SORRY TO KEEP YOU WAITING!
KLATCH
WE'VE GOT AN EMER-GENCY! IT LOOKS LIKE THERE'S ANOTHER TOURNA-MENT IN SPACE!
HM?
BOO?
ZZZ ZZZ
ZZZ
ZZZ
BOO ...
BENTO
BENTO
THIS ...
THIS IS AWFUL!!

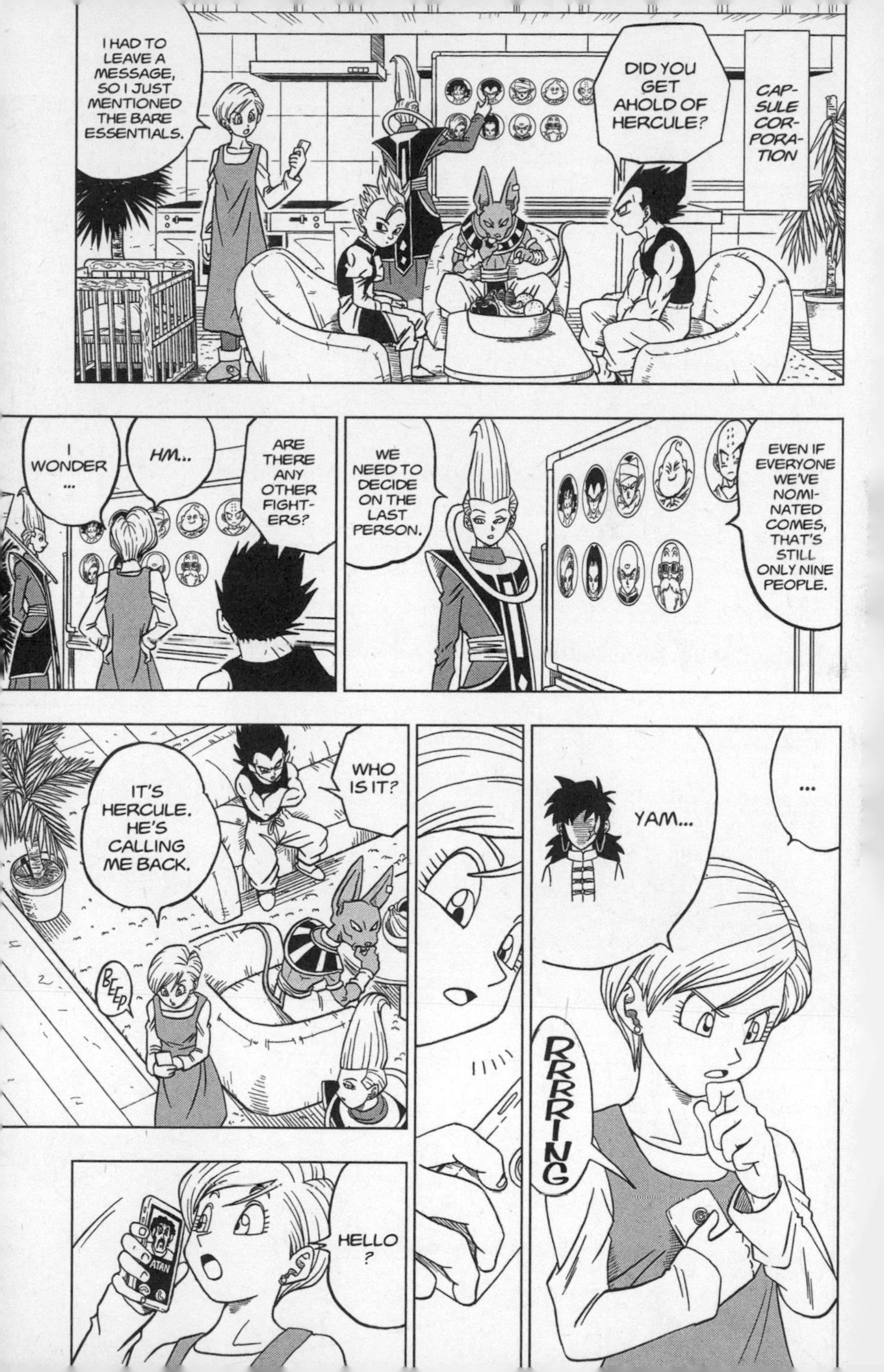
CAPSULE CORPORATION
DID YOU GET AHOLD OF HERCULE?
I HAD TO LEAVE A MESSAGE, SO I JUST MENTIONED THE BARE ESSENTIALS.
EVEN IF EVERYONE WE'VE NOMINATED COMES, THAT'S STILL ONLY NINE PEOPLE.
WE NEED TO DECIDE ON THE LAST PERSON.
ARE THERE ANY OTHER FIGHTERS?
HM...
I WONDER...
...
YAM...
RRRRING
WHO IS IT?
BEEP
IT'S HERCULE. HE'S CALLING ME BACK.
HELLO?

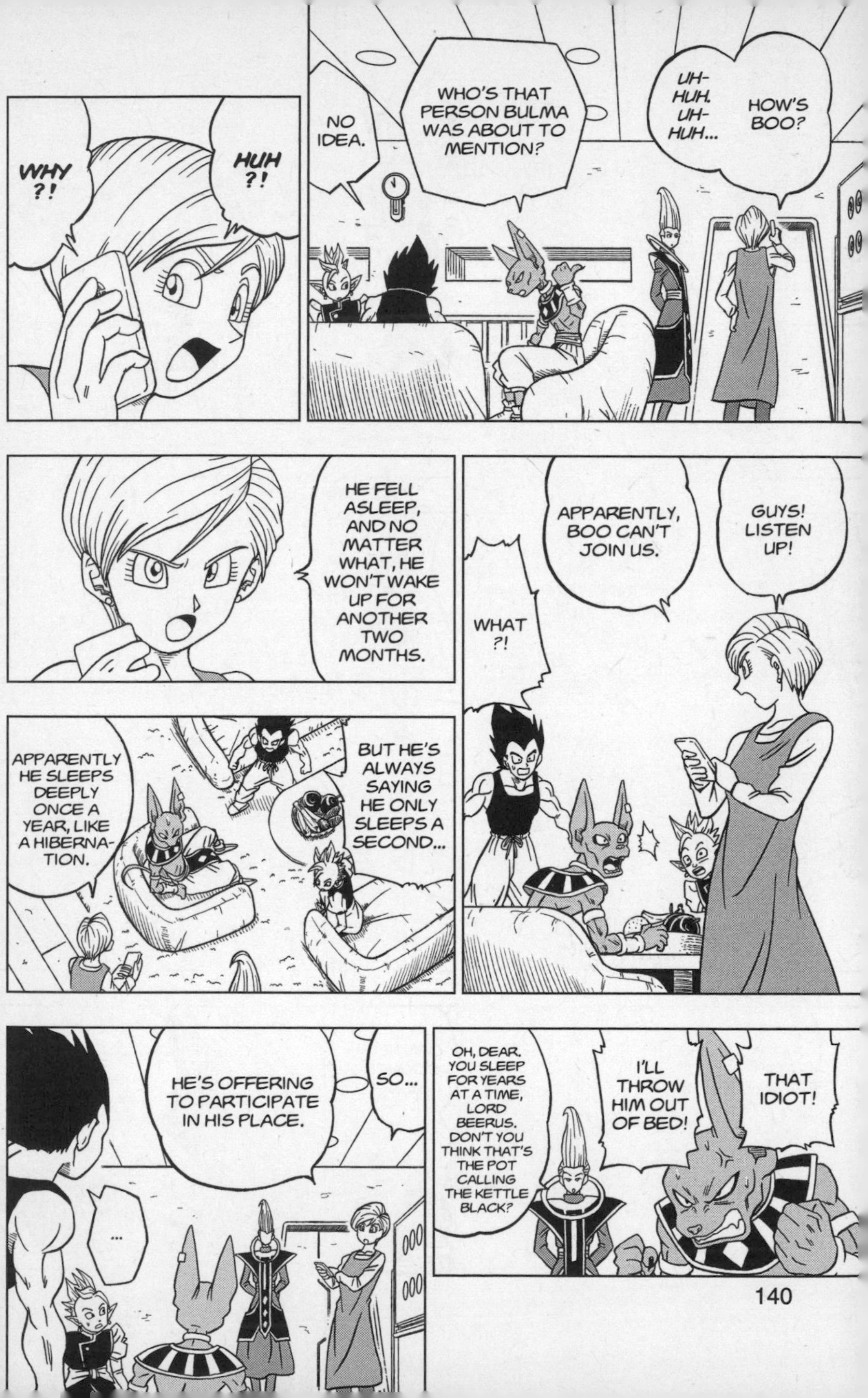
HOW'S BOO?
UH-HUH. UH-HUH...
WHO'S THAT PERSON BULMA WAS ABOUT TO MENTION?
NO IDEA.
HUH?!
WHY?!
GUYS! LISTEN UP!
APPARENTLY, BOO CAN'T JOIN US.
WHAT?!
HE FELL ASLEEP, AND NO MATTER WHAT, HE WON'T WAKE UP FOR ANOTHER TWO MONTHS.
BUT HE'S ALWAYS SAYING HE ONLY SLEEPS A SECOND...
APPARENTLY HE SLEEPS DEEPLY ONCE A YEAR, LIKE A HIBERNATION.
THAT IDIOT!
I'LL THROW HIM OUT OF BED!
OH, DEAR. YOU SLEEP FOR YEARS AT A TIME, LORD BEERUS. DON'T YOU THINK THAT'S THE POT CALLING THE KETTLE BLACK?
SO...
HE'S OFFERING TO PARTICIPATE IN HIS PLACE.
...

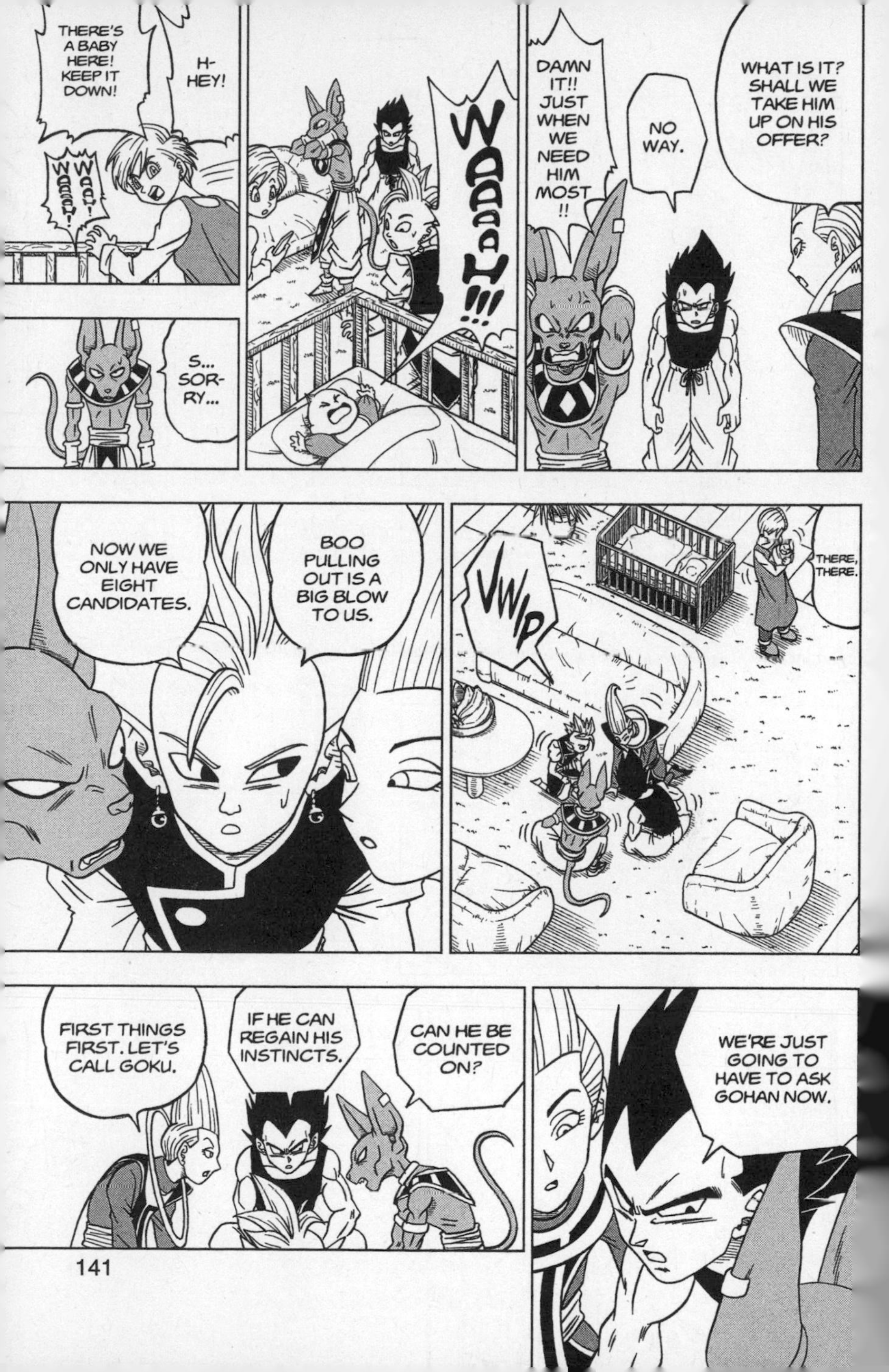
WHAT IS IT? SHALL WE TAKE HIM UP ON HIS OFFER?
NO WAY.
DAMN IT!! JUST WHEN WE NEED HIM MOST!!
WAAAAAH!!!
H- HEY!
THERE'S A BABY HERE! KEEP IT DOWN!
WAAAH! WAAAH!
S... SORRY...
THERE, THERE.
VWIP
BOO PULLING OUT IS A BIG BLOW TO US.
NOW WE ONLY HAVE EIGHT CANDIDATES.
WE'RE JUST GOING TO HAVE TO ASK GOHAN NOW.
CAN HE BE COUNTED ON?
IF HE CAN REGAIN HIS INSTINCTS.
FIRST THINGS FIRST. LET'S CALL GOKU.

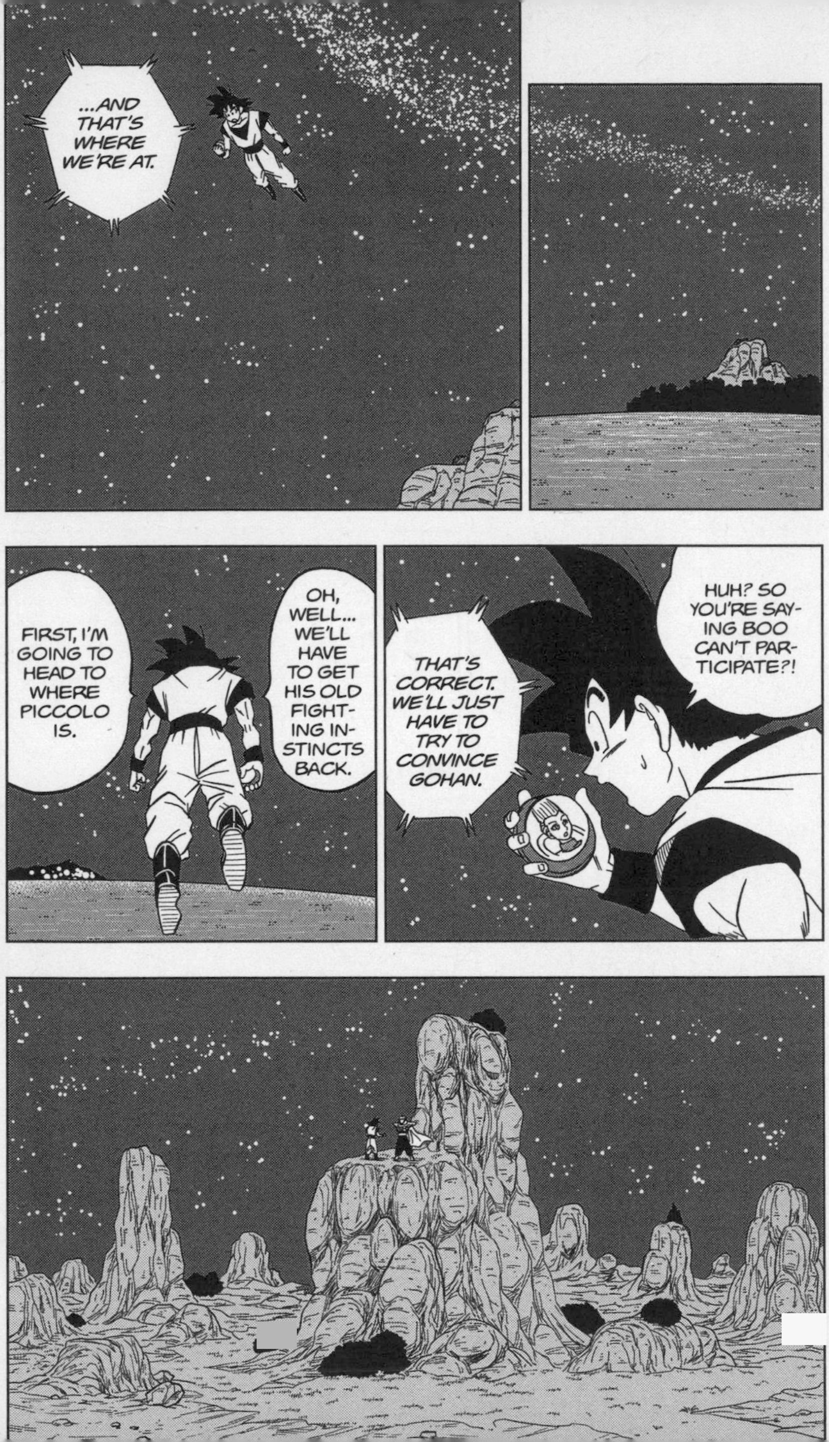
...AND THAT'S WHERE WE'RE AT.
HUH? SO YOU'RE SAYING BOO CAN'T PARTICIPATE?!
THAT'S CORRECT. WE'LL JUST HAVE TO TRY TO CONVINCE GOHAN.
OH, WELL... WE'LL HAVE TO GET HIS OLD FIGHTING INSTINCTS BACK.
FIRST, I'M GOING TO HEAD TO WHERE PICCOLO IS.

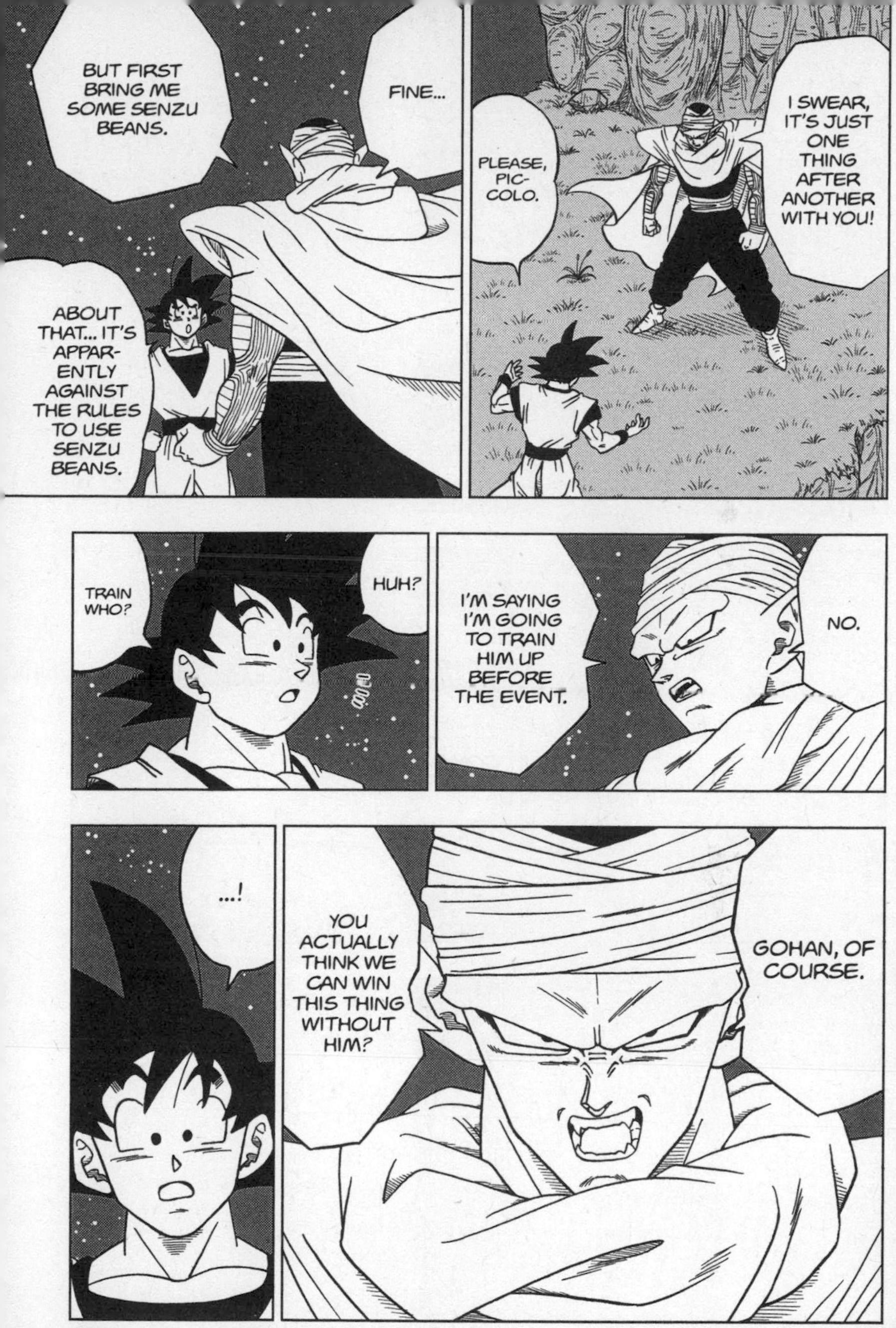
I SWEAR, IT'S JUST ONE THING AFTER ANOTHER WITH YOU!
PLEASE, PICCOLO.
FINE...
BUT FIRST BRING ME SOME SENZU BEANS.
ABOUT THAT... IT'S APPARENTLY AGAINST THE RULES TO USE SENZU BEANS.
NO.
I'M SAYING I'M GOING TO TRAIN HIM UP BEFORE THE EVENT.
HUH?
TRAIN WHO?
GOHAN, OF COURSE.
YOU ACTUALLY THINK WE CAN WIN THIS THING WITHOUT HIM?
...!

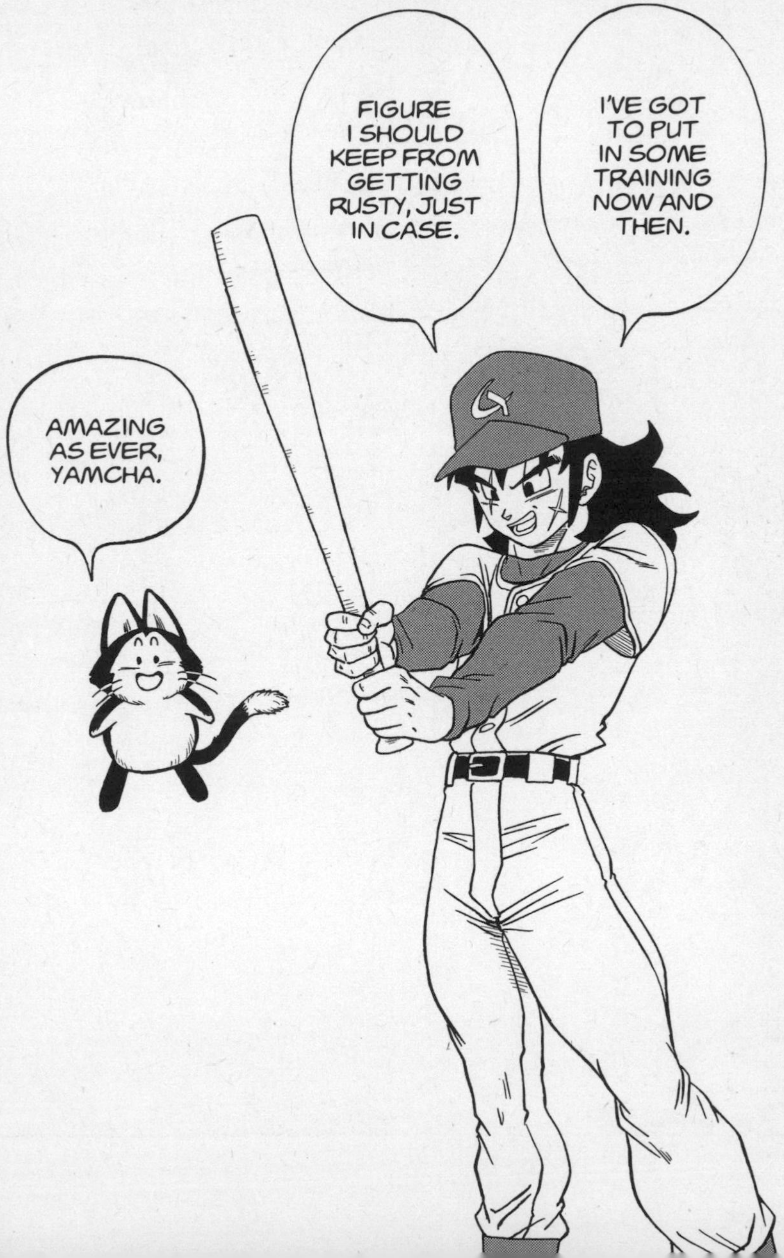
I'VE GOT TO PUT IN SOME TRAINING NOW AND THEN.
FIGURE I SHOULD KEEP FROM GETTING RUSTY, JUST IN CASE.
AMAZING AS EVER, YAMCHA.

DRAGON BALL SUPER

CHAPTER 32: THE SUPER WARRIORS GATHER! PART 2

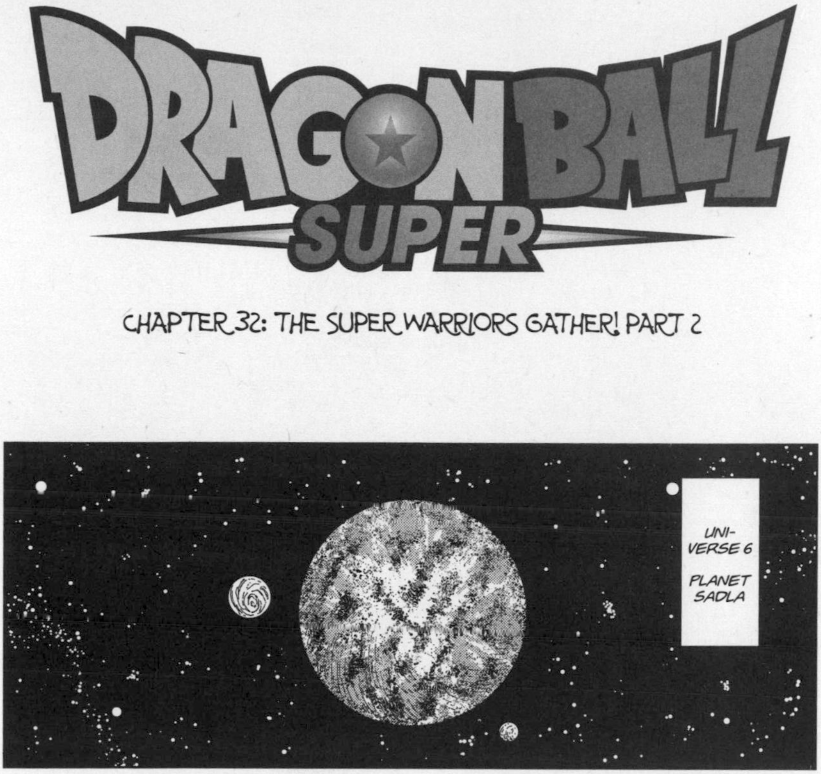
UNI-
VERSE 6
PLANET
SADLA

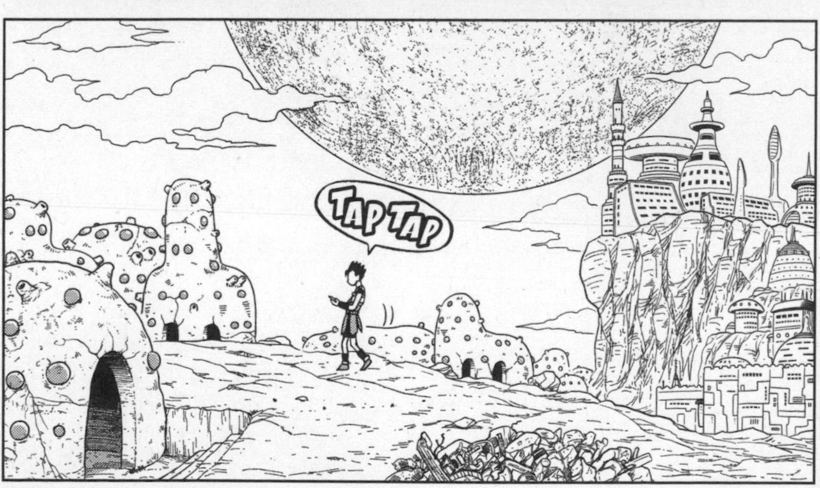
TAP TAP

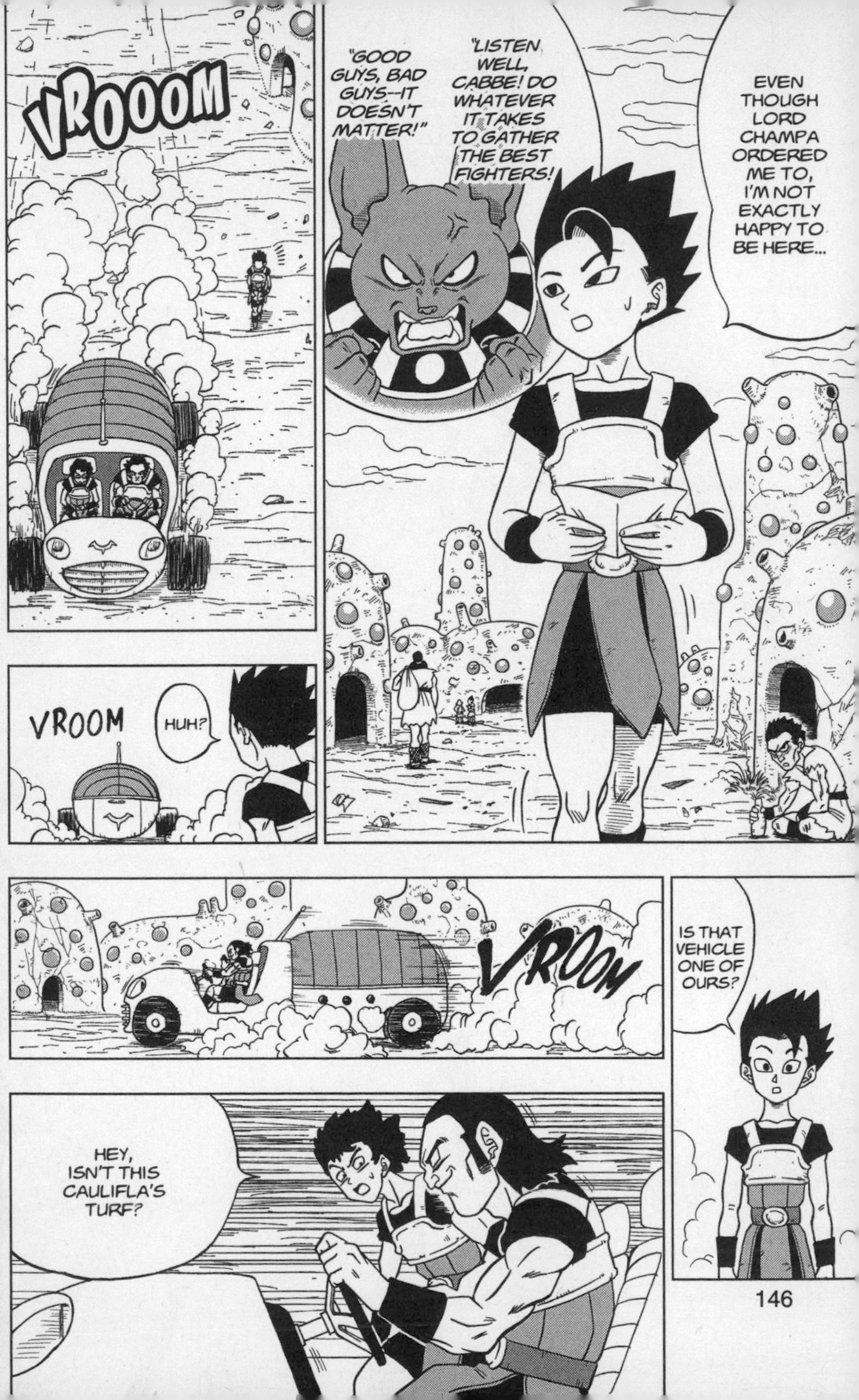
EVEN THOUGH LORD CHAMPA ORDERED ME TO, I'M NOT EXACTLY HAPPY TO BE HERE...
"LISTEN WELL, CABBE! DO WHATEVER IT TAKES TO GATHER THE BEST FIGHTERS!
"GOOD GUYS, BAD GUYS--IT DOESN'T MATTER!"
VROOOM
VROOM
HUH?
IS THAT VEHICLE ONE OF OURS?
VROOM
HEY, ISN'T THIS CAULIFLA'S TURF?

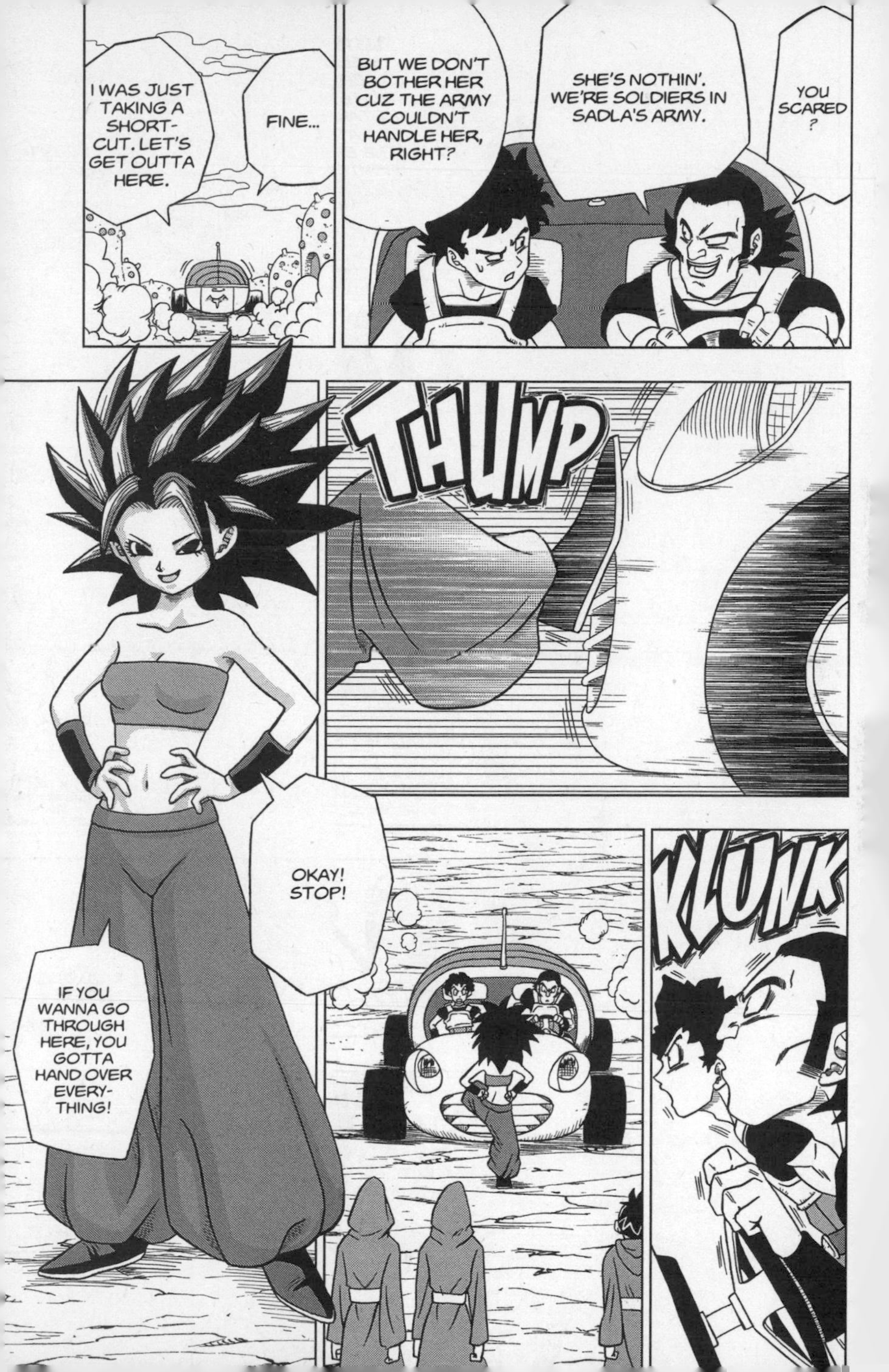
YOU SCARED?
SHE'S NOTHIN'. WE'RE SOLDIERS IN SADLA'S ARMY.
BUT WE DON'T BOTHER HER CUZ THE ARMY COULDN'T HANDLE HER, RIGHT?
FINE...
I WAS JUST TAKING A SHORT-CUT. LET'S GET OUTTA HERE.
THUMP
KLUNK
OKAY! STOP!
IF YOU WANNA GO THROUGH HERE, YOU GOTTA HAND OVER EVERY-THING!

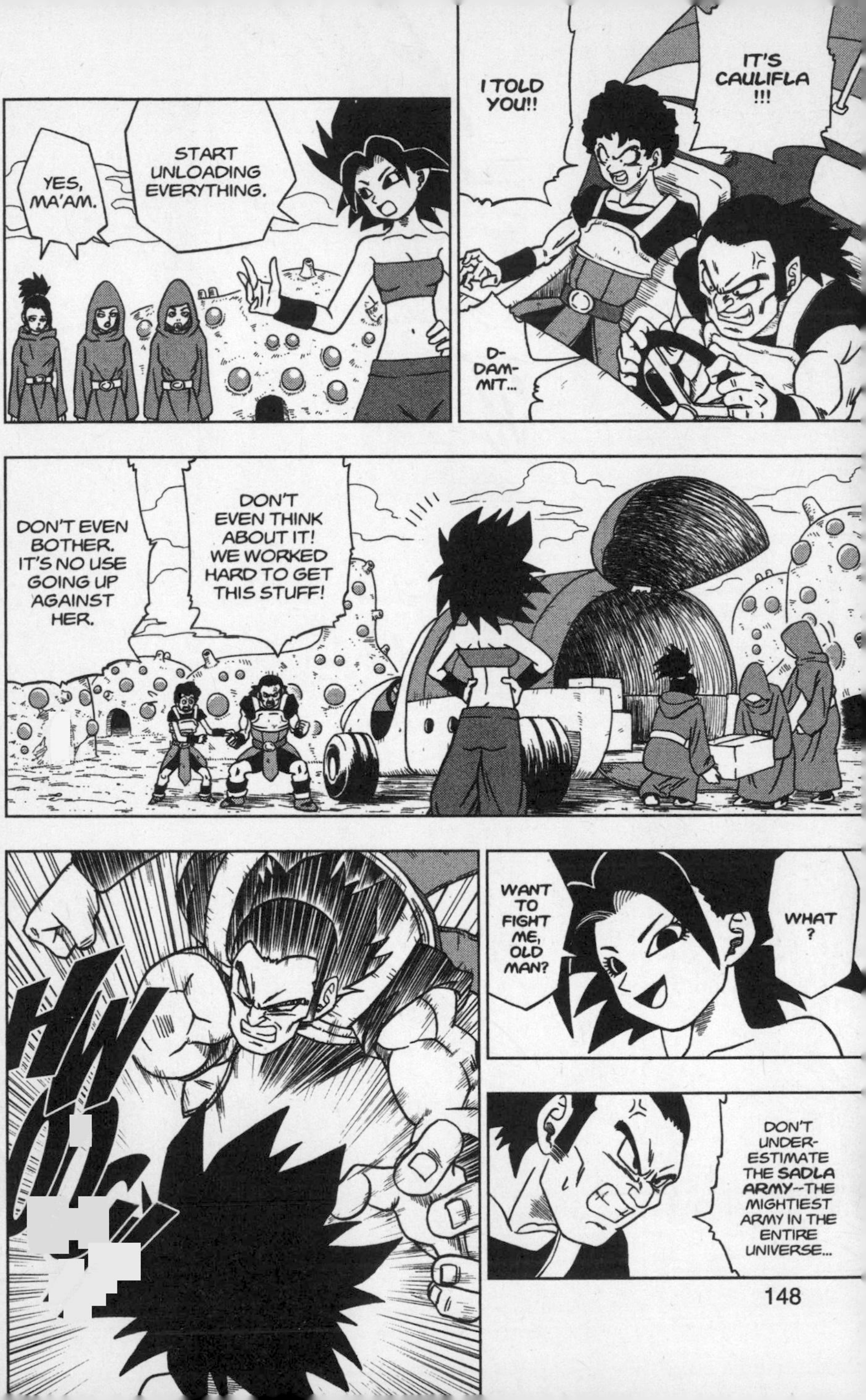
IT'S CAULIFLA!!!
I TOLD YOU!!
D-DAMMIT...
START UNLOADING EVERYTHING.
YES, MA'AM.
DON'T EVEN THINK ABOUT IT! WE WORKED HARD TO GET THIS STUFF!
DON'T EVEN BOTHER. IT'S NO USE GOING UP AGAINST HER.
WHAT?
WANT TO FIGHT ME, OLD MAN?
DON'T UNDER-ESTIMATE THE SADLA ARMY--THE MIGHTIEST ARMY IN THE ENTIRE UNIVERSE...

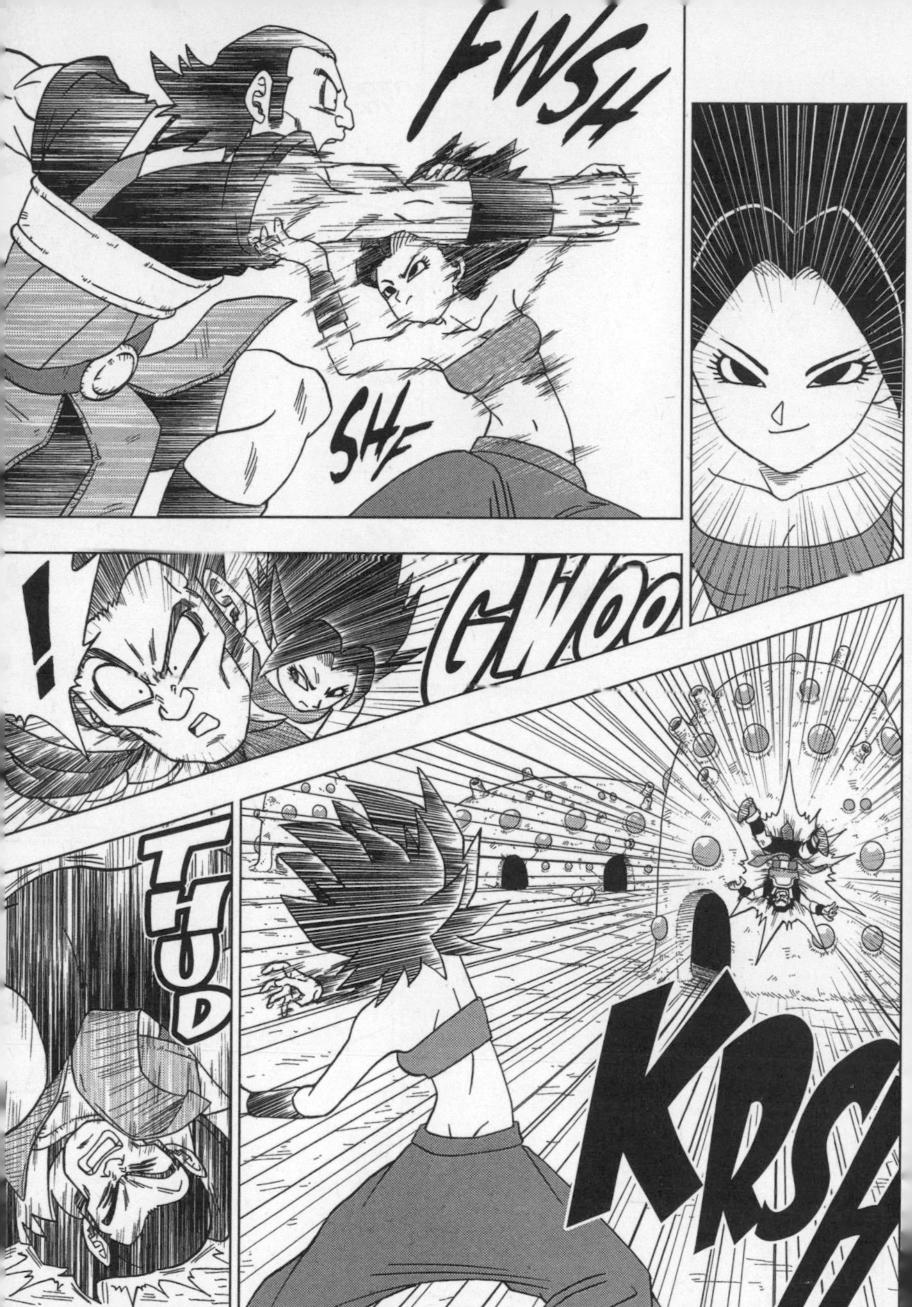
FWSH
SHF
GWOO
!
KRSH
THUD

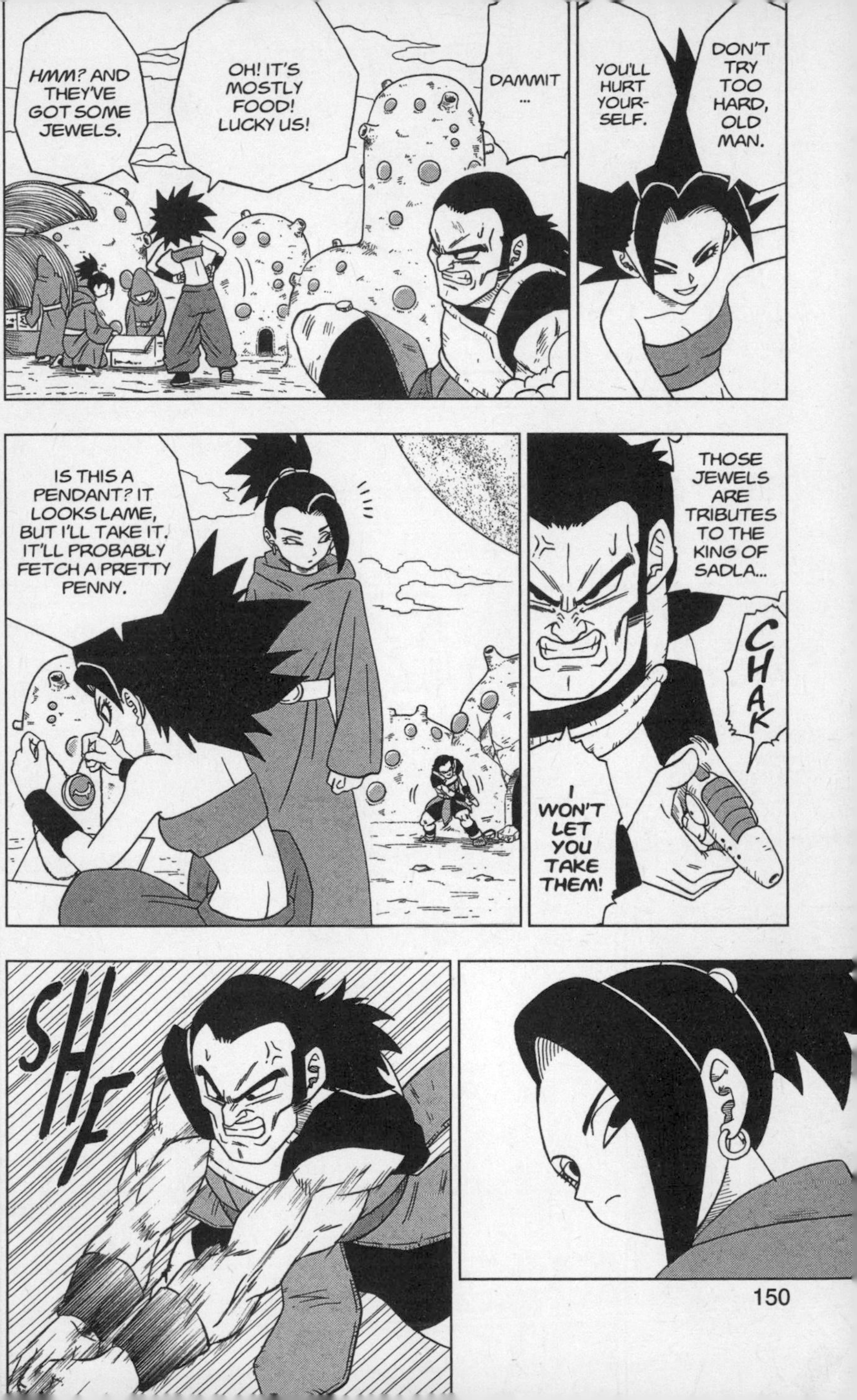
DON'T TRY TOO HARD, OLD MAN.
YOU'LL HURT YOURSELF.
DAMMIT ...
OH! IT'S MOSTLY FOOD! LUCKY US!
HMM? AND THEY'VE GOT SOME JEWELS.
THOSE JEWELS ARE TRIBUTES TO THE KING OF SADLA...
CHAK
I WON'T LET YOU TAKE THEM!
IS THIS A PENDANT? IT LOOKS LAME, BUT I'LL TAKE IT. IT'LL PROBABLY FETCH A PRETTY PENNY.
SHF

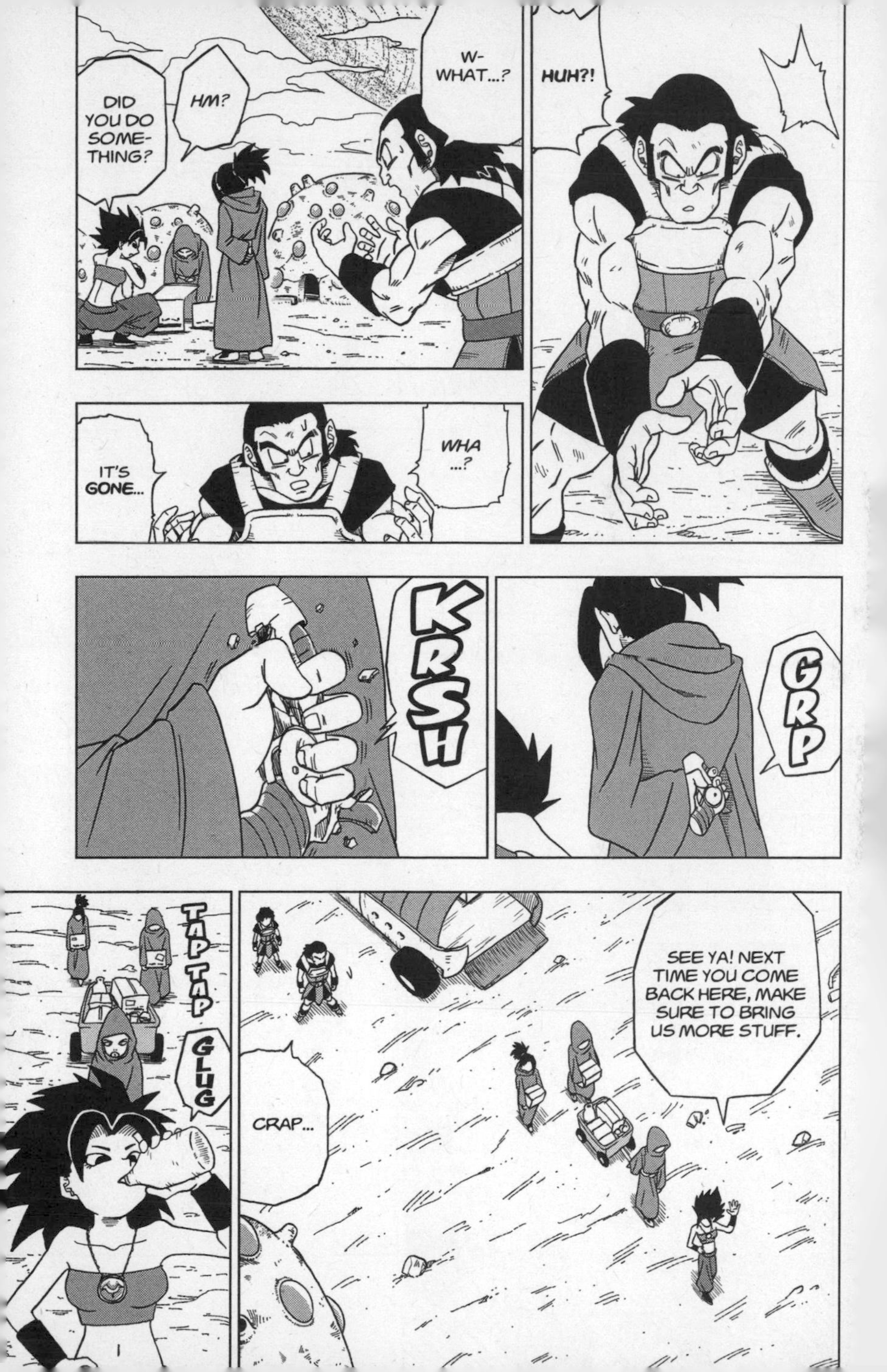
HUH?!
W-WHAT...?
HM?
DID YOU DO SOMETHING?
WHA ...?
IT'S GONE...
GRP
KRSH
SEE YA! NEXT TIME YOU COME BACK HERE, MAKE SURE TO BRING US MORE STUFF.
CRAP...
TAP TAP
GLUG

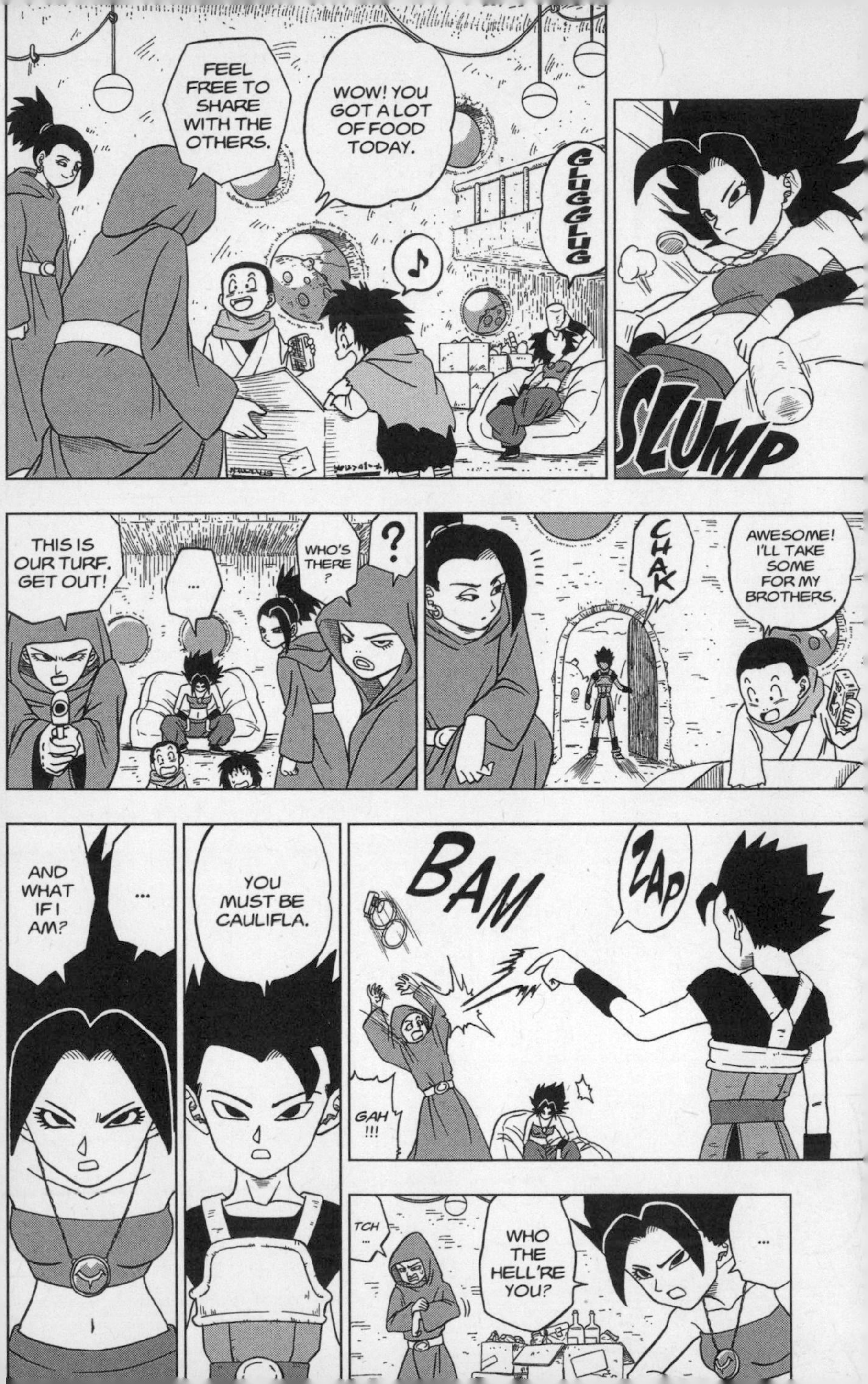
SLUMP
GLUGGLUG
♪
WOW! YOU GOT A LOT OF FOOD TODAY.
FEEL FREE TO SHARE WITH THE OTHERS.
AWESOME! I'LL TAKE SOME FOR MY BROTHERS.
CHAK
?
WHO'S THERE?
...
THIS IS OUR TURF. GET OUT!
ZAP
BAM
GAH!!!
...
WHO THE HELL'RE YOU?
TCH...
YOU MUST BE CAULIFLA.
...
AND WHAT IF I AM?

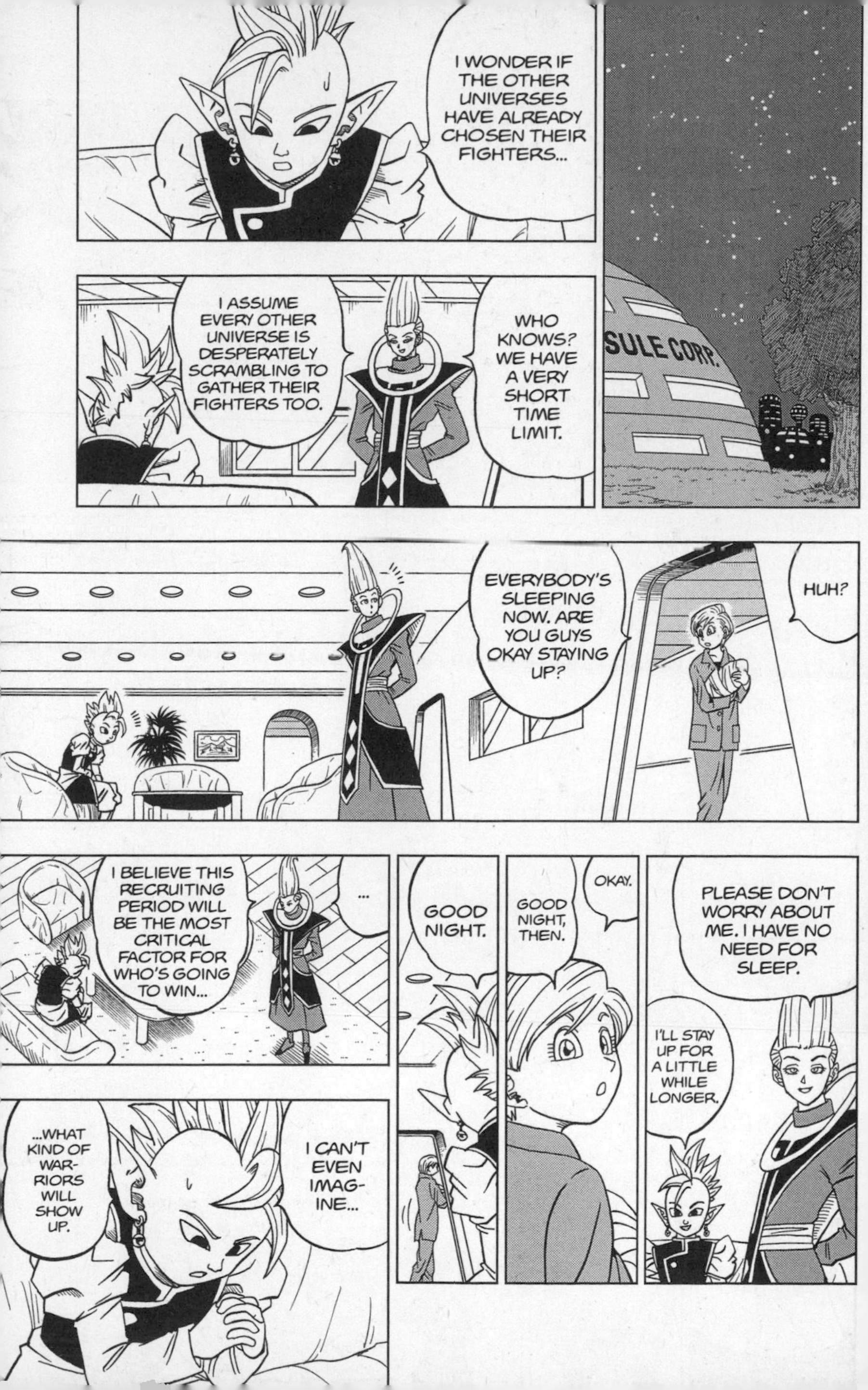
SULE CORP.
I WONDER IF THE OTHER UNIVERSES HAVE ALREADY CHOSEN THEIR FIGHTERS...
WHO KNOWS? WE HAVE A VERY SHORT TIME LIMIT.
I ASSUME EVERY OTHER UNIVERSE IS DESPERATELY SCRAMBLING TO GATHER THEIR FIGHTERS TOO.
HUH?
EVERYBODY'S SLEEPING NOW. ARE YOU GUYS OKAY STAYING UP?
PLEASE DON'T WORRY ABOUT ME. I HAVE NO NEED FOR SLEEP.
I'LL STAY UP FOR A LITTLE WHILE LONGER.
OKAY.
GOOD NIGHT, THEN.
GOOD NIGHT.
...
I BELIEVE THIS RECRUITING PERIOD WILL BE THE MOST CRITICAL FACTOR FOR WHO'S GOING TO WIN...
I CAN'T EVEN IMAGINE...
...WHAT KIND OF WARRIORS WILL SHOW UP.

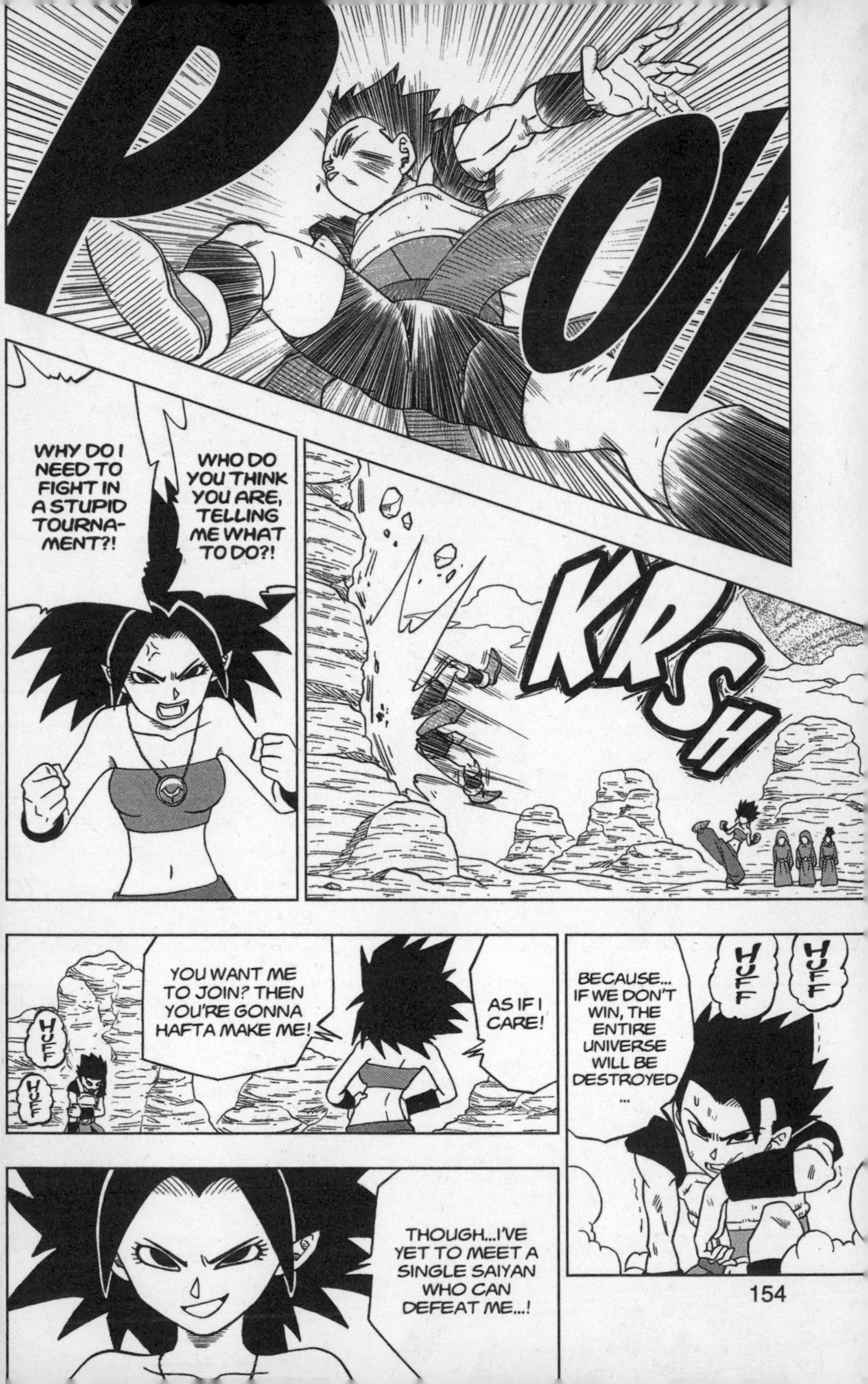
POW
KRSH
WHO DO YOU THINK YOU ARE, TELLING ME WHAT TO DO?!
WHY DO I NEED TO FIGHT IN A STUPID TOURNAMENT?!
HUFF
HUFF
BECAUSE... IF WE DON'T WIN, THE ENTIRE UNIVERSE WILL BE DESTROYED...
AS IF I CARE!
YOU WANT ME TO JOIN? THEN YOU'RE GONNA HAFTA MAKE ME!
HUFF
HUFF
THOUGH...I'VE YET TO MEET A SINGLE SAIYAN WHO CAN DEFEAT ME...!

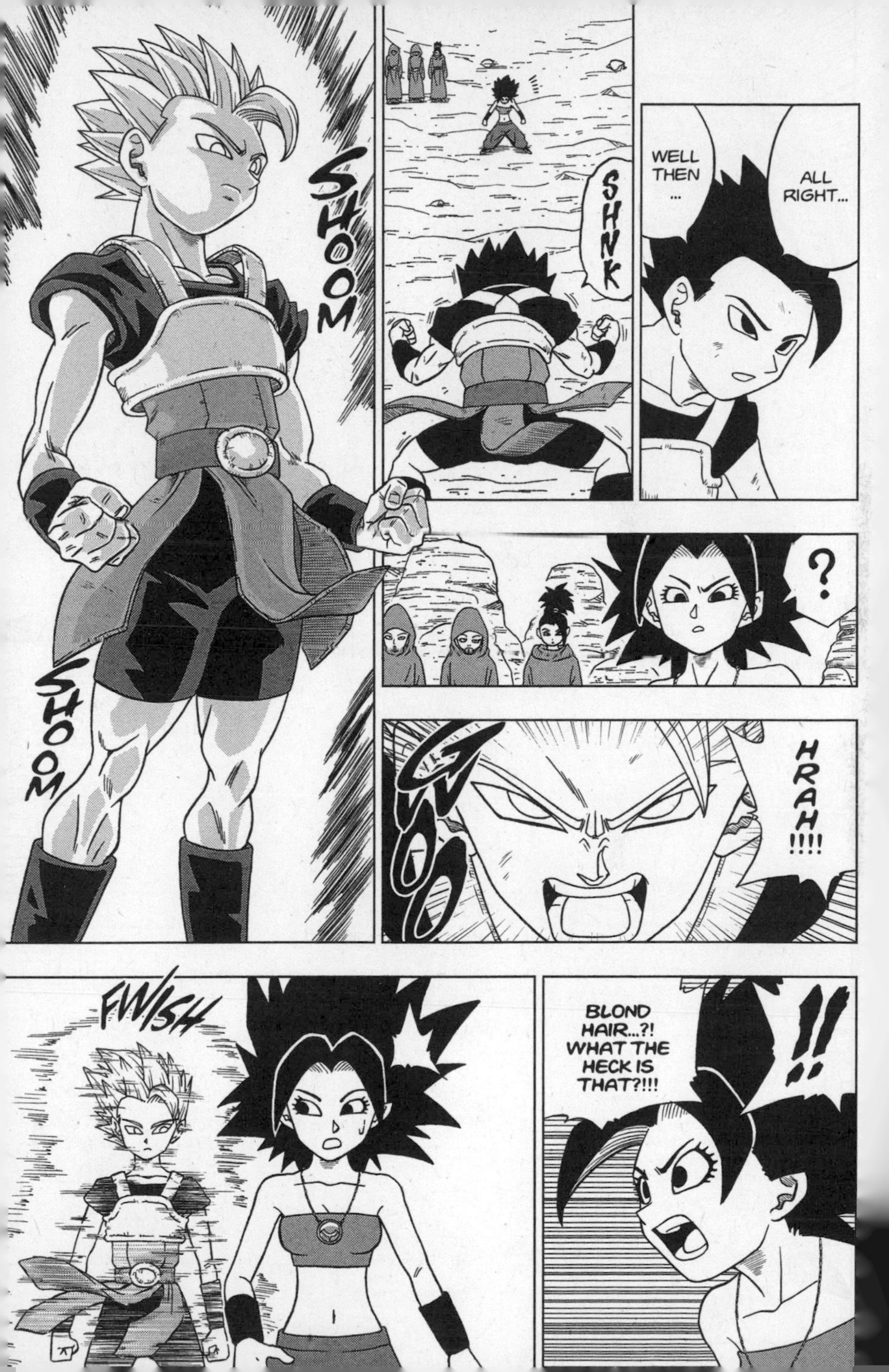
ALL RIGHT...
WELL THEN ...
SHNK
?
HRAH!!!!
SHOOM
SHOOM
!!
BLOND HAIR...?! WHAT THE HECK IS THAT?!!!
FWISH

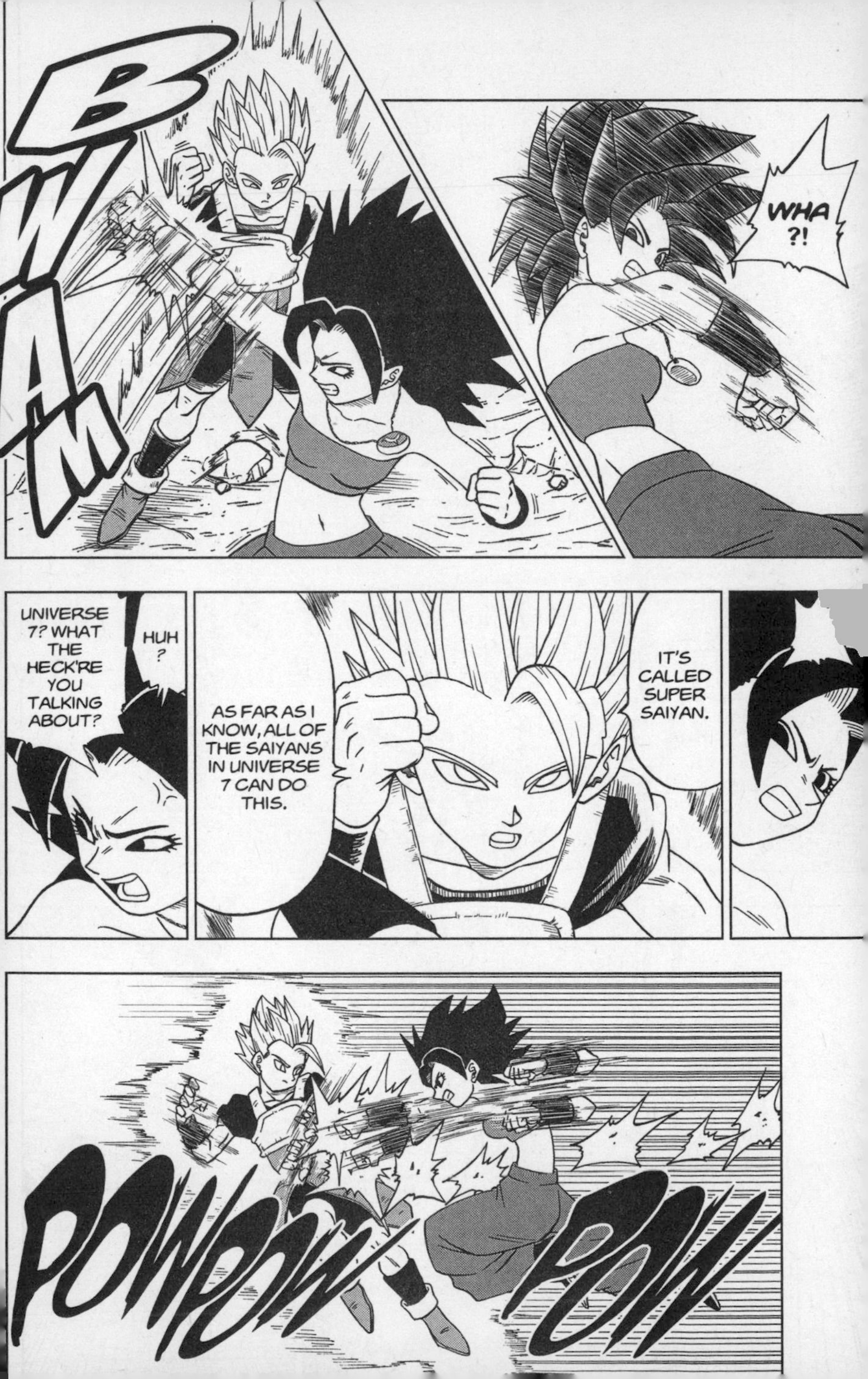
WHA ?!
BWAM
IT'S CALLED SUPER SAIYAN.
AS FAR AS I KNOW, ALL OF THE SAIYANS IN UNIVERSE 7 CAN DO THIS.
HUH ?
UNIVERSE 7? WHAT THE HECK'RE YOU TALKING ABOUT?
POW
POWPOW

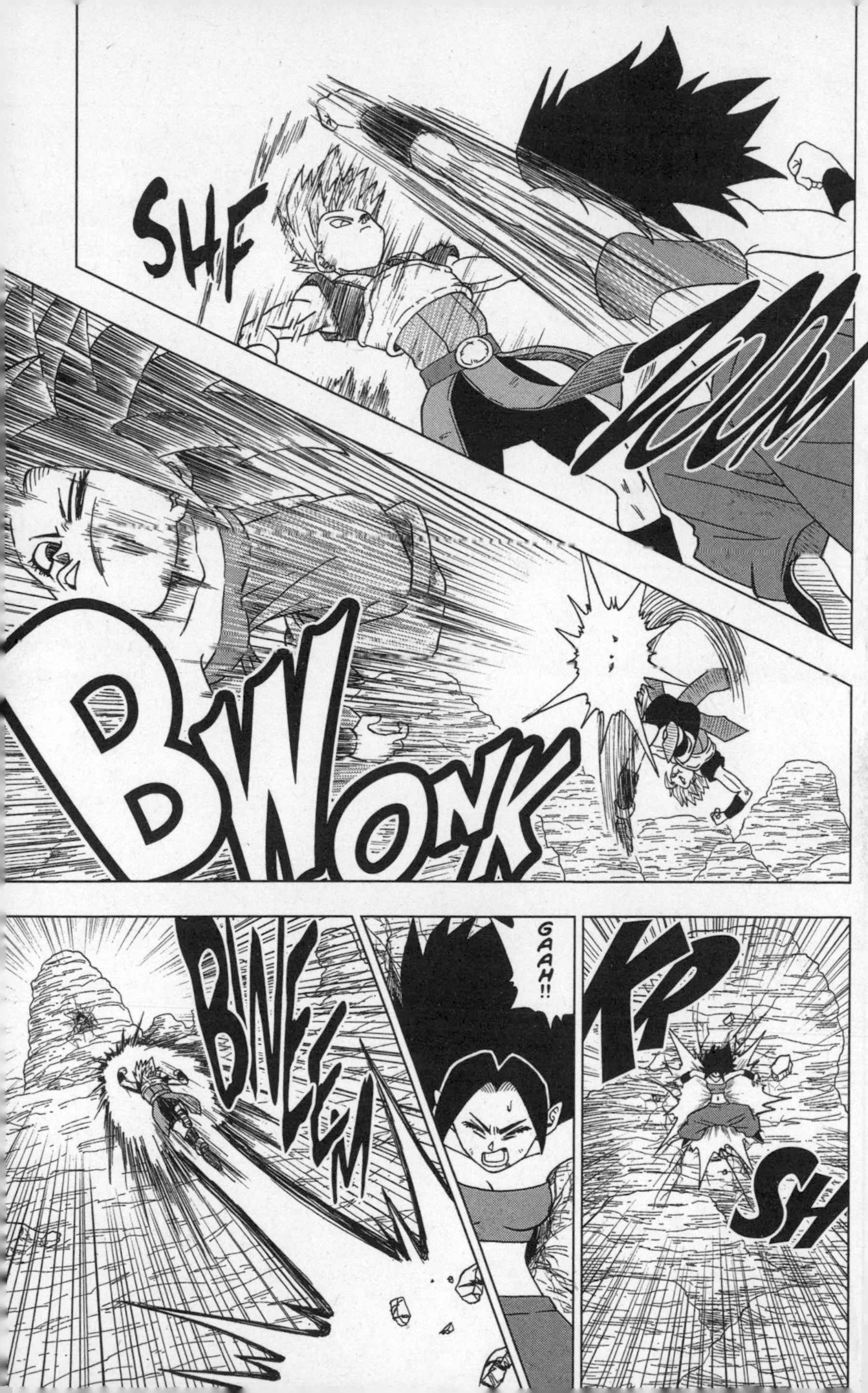
ZOOM
SHF
BWONK
KRSH
GAAH!!
BWEEEM

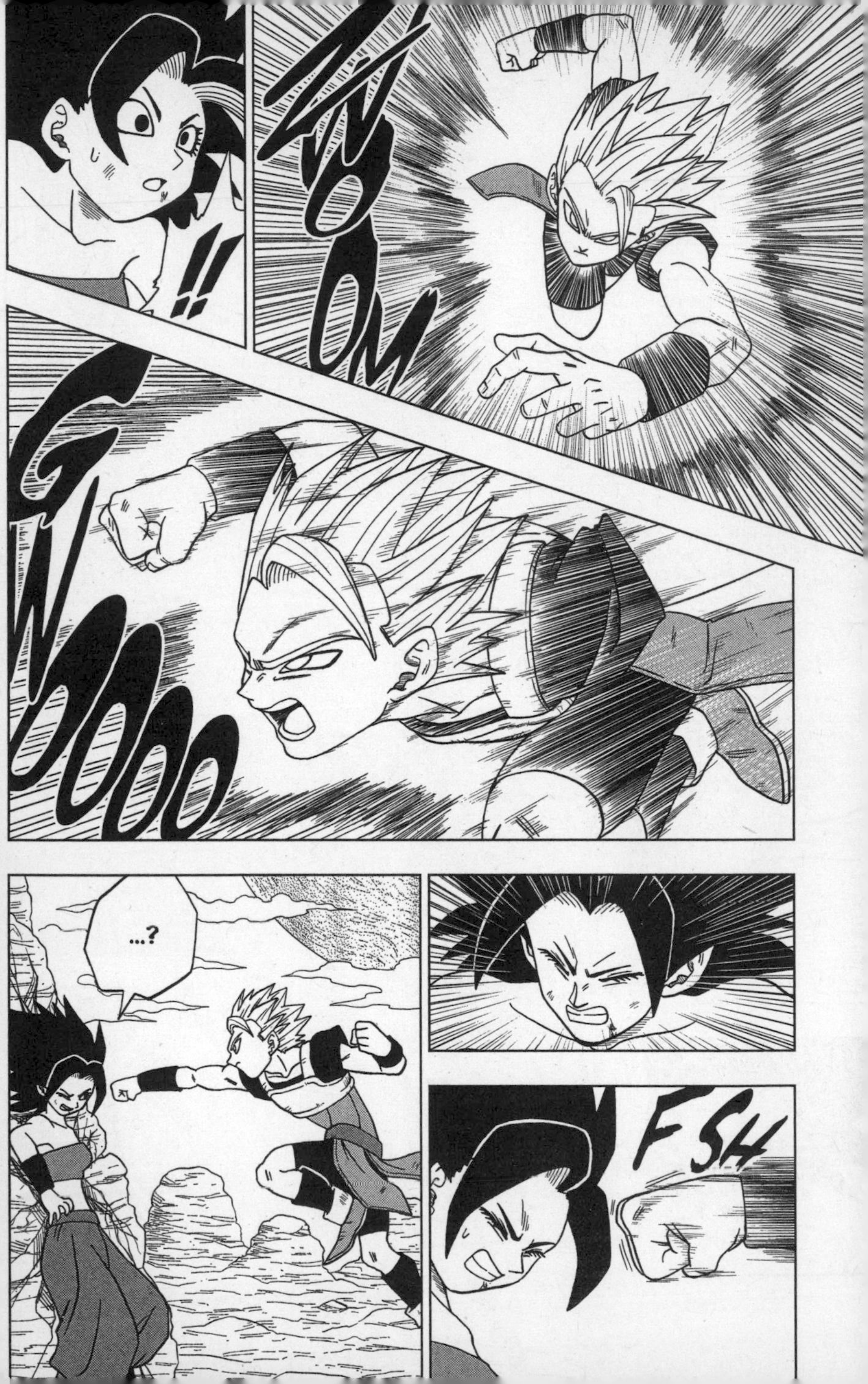
WHOOM
!!
GWOOOO
FSH
...?

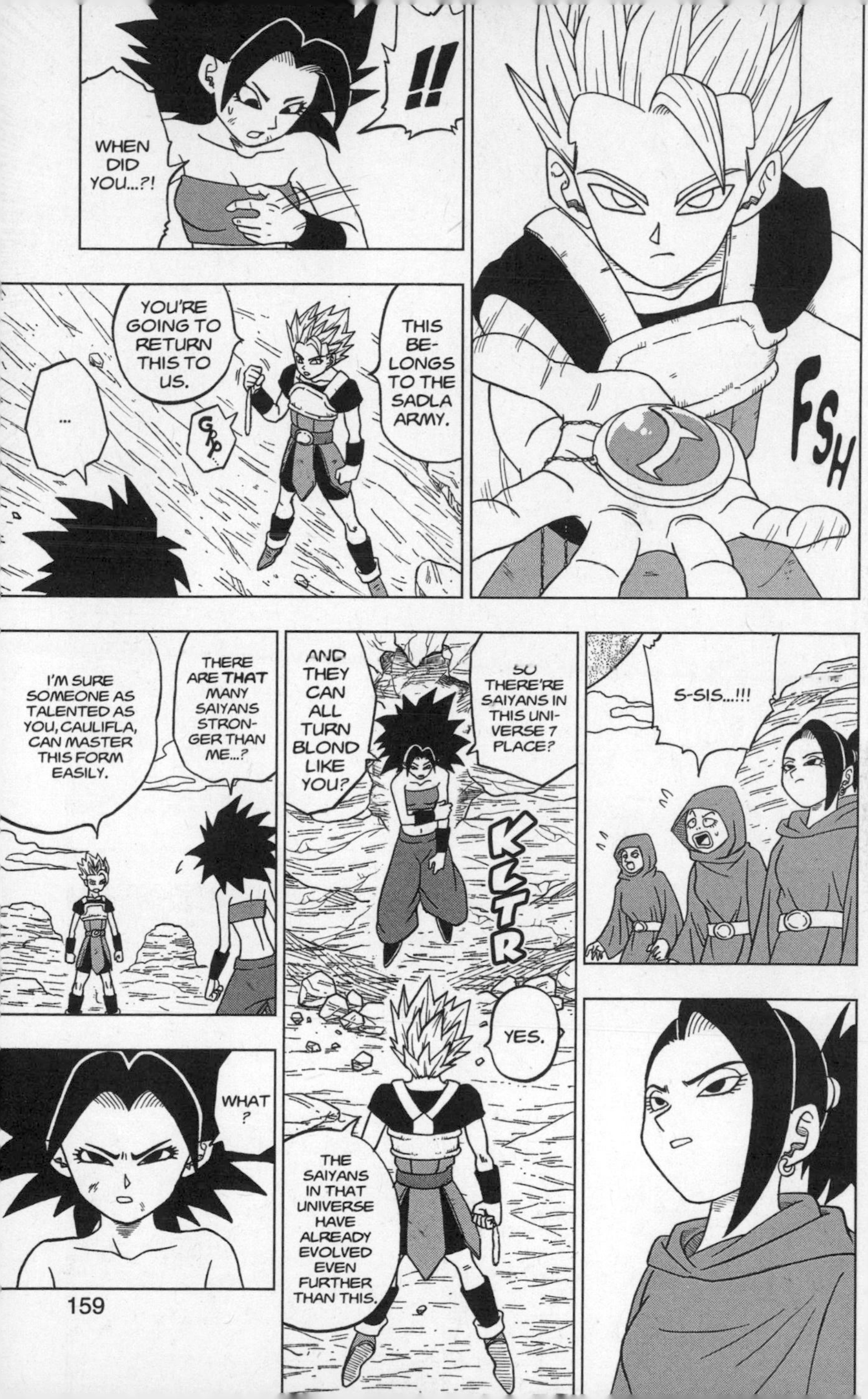
FSH
!!
WHEN DID YOU...?!
THIS BE-LONGS TO THE SADLA ARMY.
YOU'RE GOING TO RETURN THIS TO US.
GRR...
...
S-SIS...!!!
SO THERE'RE SAIYANS IN THIS UNI-VERSE 7 PLACE?
AND THEY CAN ALL TURN BLOND LIKE YOU?
KLTR
YES.
THE SAIYANS IN THAT UNIVERSE HAVE ALREADY EVOLVED EVEN FURTHER THAN THIS.
THERE ARE THAT MANY SAIYANS STRON-GER THAN ME...?
I'M SURE SOMEONE AS TALENTED AS YOU, CAULIFLA, CAN MASTER THIS FORM EASILY.
WHAT?

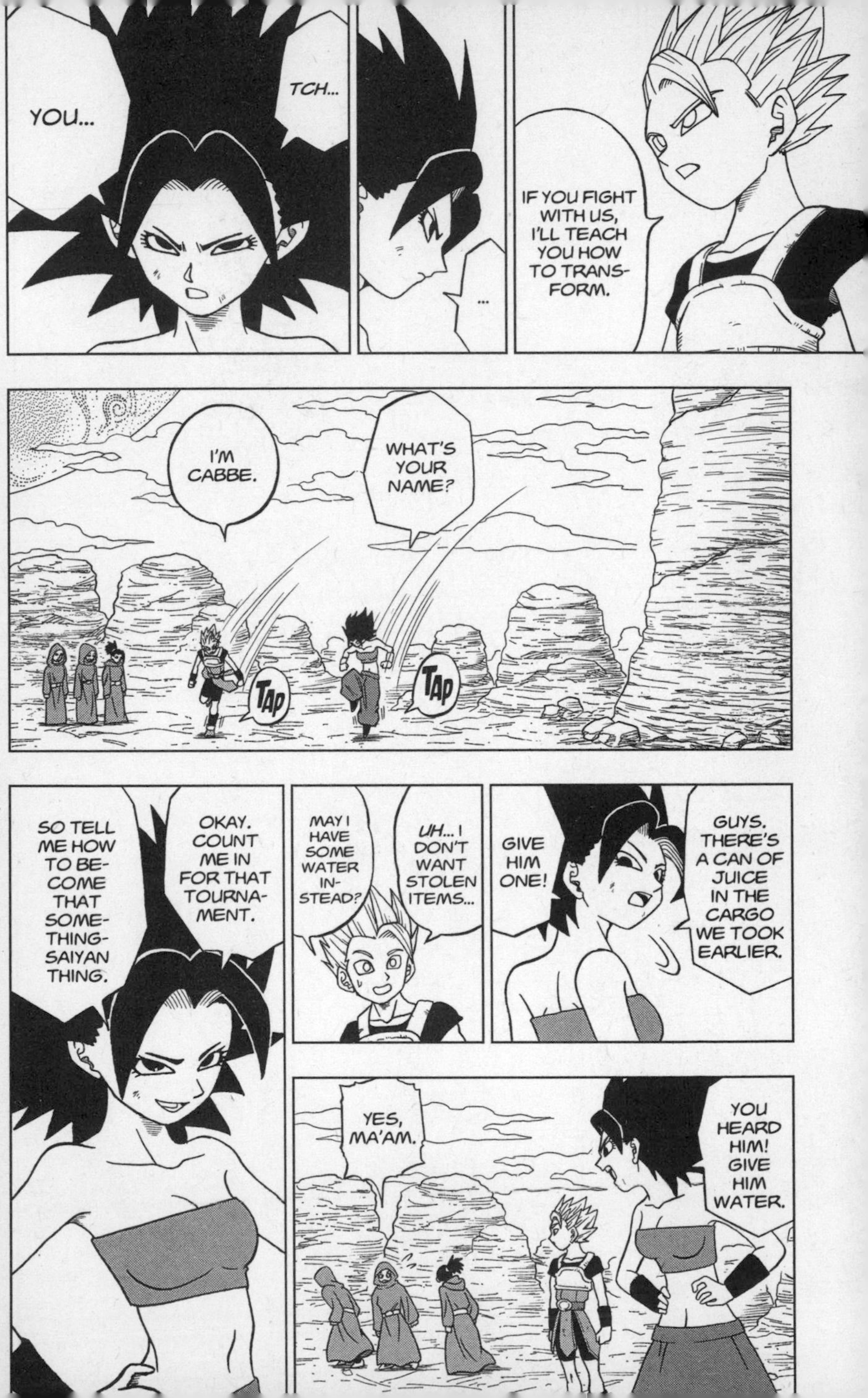
IF YOU FIGHT WITH US, I'LL TEACH YOU HOW TO TRANS-FORM.
TCH...
...
YOU...
WHAT'S YOUR NAME?
I'M CABBE.
TAP
TAP
GUYS. THERE'S A CAN OF JUICE IN THE CARGO WE TOOK EARLIER.
GIVE HIM ONE!
UH... I DON'T WANT STOLEN ITEMS...
MAY I HAVE SOME WATER IN-STEAD?
YOU HEARD HIM! GIVE HIM WATER.
YES, MA'AM.
OKAY. COUNT ME IN FOR THAT TOURNA-MENT.
SO TELL ME HOW TO BE-COME THAT SOME-THING-SAIYAN THING.

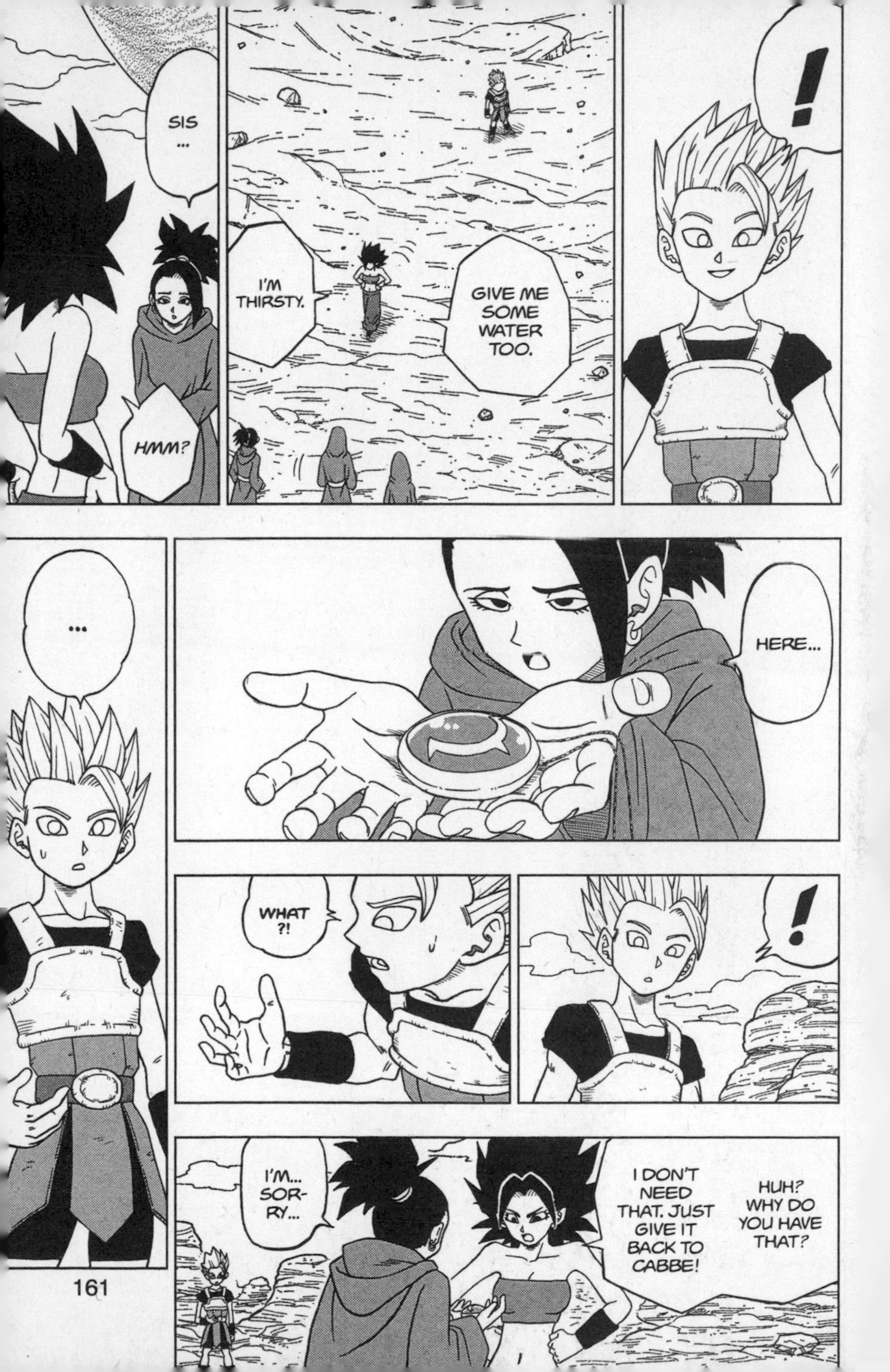
!
GIVE ME SOME WATER TOO.
I'M THIRSTY.
SIS ...
HMM?
HERE...
!
WHAT ?!
...
HUH? WHY DO YOU HAVE THAT?
I DON'T NEED THAT. JUST GIVE IT BACK TO CABBE!
I'M... SOR-RY...

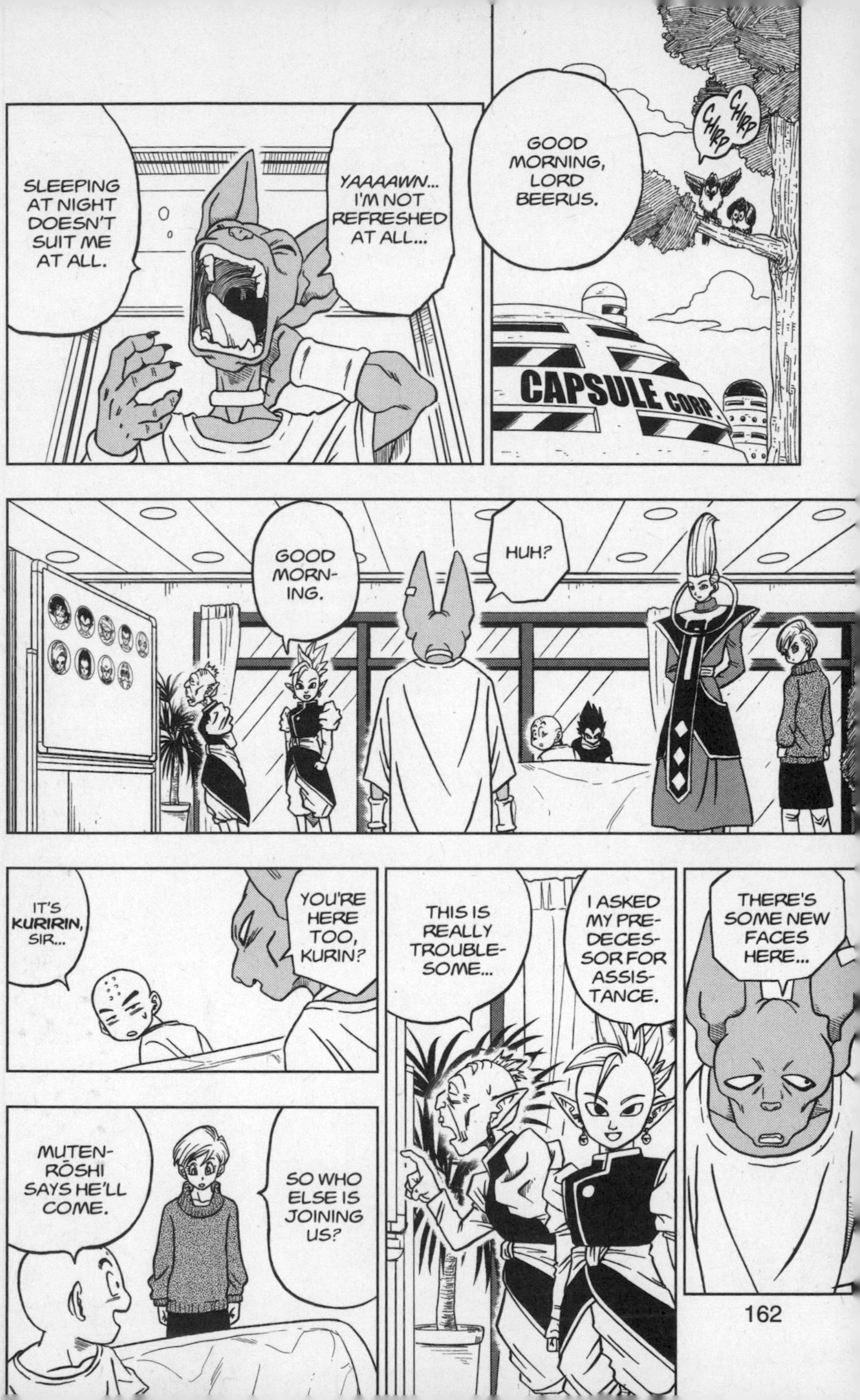
CHIRP
CHIRP
GOOD MORNING, LORD BEERUS.
YAAAAWN... I'M NOT REFRESHED AT ALL...
SLEEPING AT NIGHT DOESN'T SUIT ME AT ALL.
HUH?
GOOD MORNING.
THERE'S SOME NEW FACES HERE...
I ASKED MY PREDECESSOR FOR ASSISTANCE.
THIS IS REALLY TROUBLESOME...
YOU'RE HERE TOO, KURIN?
IT'S **KURIRIN**, SIR...
SO WHO ELSE IS JOINING US?
MUTEN-RŌSHI SAYS HE'LL COME.
CAPSULE CORP

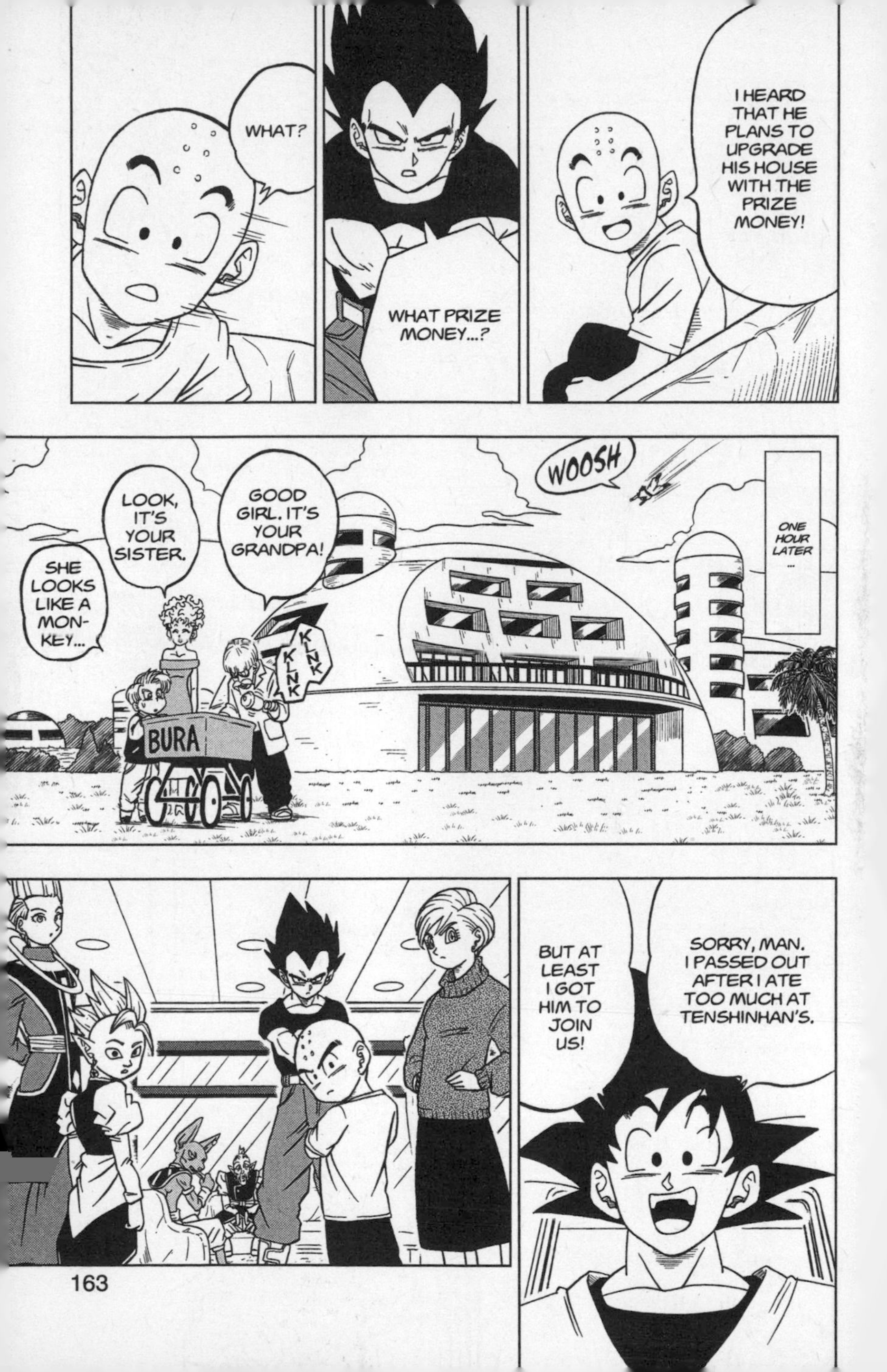
I HEARD THAT HE PLANS TO UPGRADE HIS HOUSE WITH THE PRIZE MONEY!
WHAT PRIZE MONEY...?
WHAT?
ONE HOUR LATER ...
WOOSH
GOOD GIRL. IT'S YOUR GRANDPA!
LOOK, IT'S YOUR SISTER.
SHE LOOKS LIKE A MON-KEY...
KLNK KLNK
BURA
SORRY, MAN. I PASSED OUT AFTER I ATE TOO MUCH AT TENSHINHAN'S.
BUT AT LEAST I GOT HIM TO JOIN US!

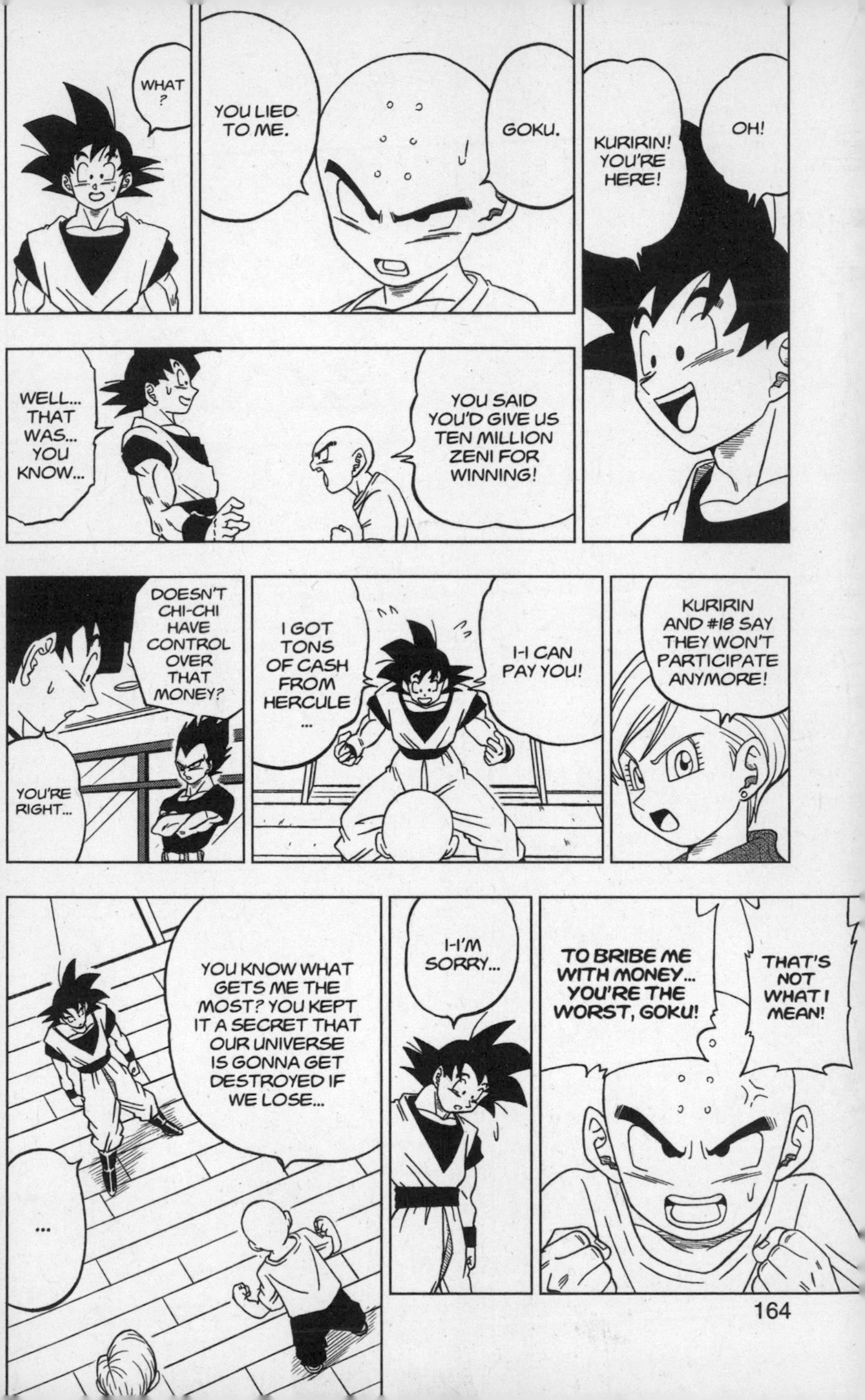
OH!
KURIRIN! YOU'RE HERE!
GOKU.
YOU LIED TO ME.
WHAT ?
YOU SAID YOU'D GIVE US TEN MILLION ZENI FOR WINNING!
WELL... THAT WAS... YOU KNOW...
KURIRIN AND #18 SAY THEY WON'T PARTICIPATE ANYMORE!
I-I CAN PAY YOU!
I GOT TONS OF CASH FROM HERCULE ...
DOESN'T CHI-CHI HAVE CONTROL OVER THAT MONEY?
YOU'RE RIGHT...
THAT'S NOT WHAT I MEAN!
TO BRIBE ME WITH MONEY... YOU'RE THE WORST, GOKU!
I-I'M SORRY...
YOU KNOW WHAT GETS ME THE MOST? YOU KEPT IT A SECRET THAT OUR UNIVERSE IS GONNA GET DESTROYED IF WE LOSE...
...

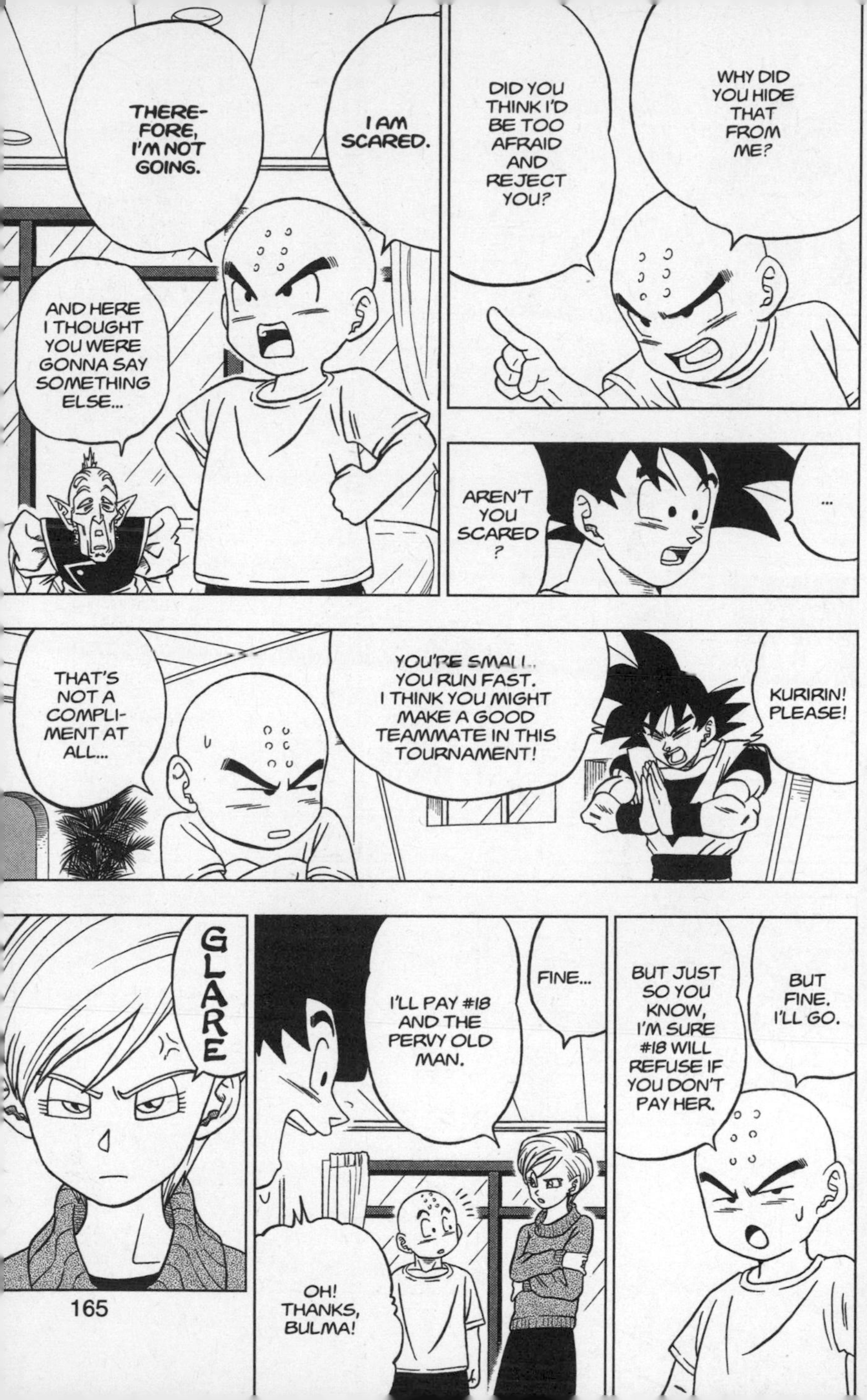
WHY DID YOU HIDE THAT FROM ME?
DID YOU THINK I'D BE TOO AFRAID AND REJECT YOU?
...
AREN'T YOU SCARED?
I AM SCARED.
THEREFORE, I'M NOT GOING.
AND HERE I THOUGHT YOU WERE GONNA SAY SOMETHING ELSE...
KURIRIN! PLEASE!
YOU'RE SMALL.. YOU RUN FAST. I THINK YOU MIGHT MAKE A GOOD TEAMMATE IN THIS TOURNAMENT!
THAT'S NOT A COMPLIMENT AT ALL...
BUT FINE. I'LL GO.
BUT JUST SO YOU KNOW, I'M SURE #18 WILL REFUSE IF YOU DON'T PAY HER.
FINE...
I'LL PAY #18 AND THE PERVY OLD MAN.
OH! THANKS, BULMA!
GLARE

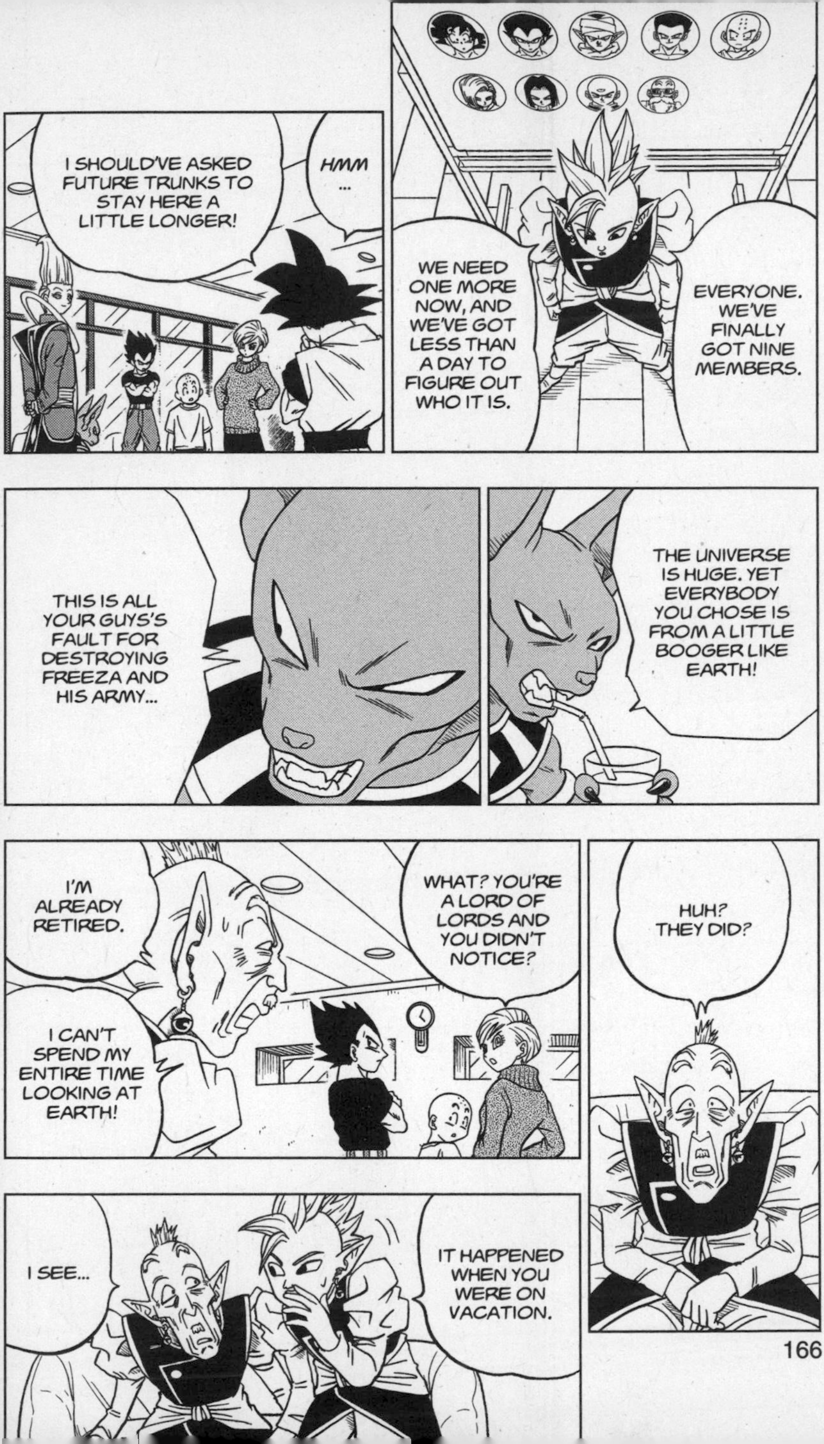
EVERYONE. WE'VE FINALLY GOT NINE MEMBERS.
WE NEED ONE MORE NOW, AND WE'VE GOT LESS THAN A DAY TO FIGURE OUT WHO IT IS.
HMM ...
I SHOULD'VE ASKED FUTURE TRUNKS TO STAY HERE A LITTLE LONGER!
THE UNIVERSE IS HUGE. YET EVERYBODY YOU CHOSE IS FROM A LITTLE BOOGER LIKE EARTH!
THIS IS ALL YOUR GUYS'S FAULT FOR DESTROYING FREEZA AND HIS ARMY...
HUH? THEY DID?
WHAT? YOU'RE A LORD OF LORDS AND YOU DIDN'T NOTICE?
I'M ALREADY RETIRED.
I CAN'T SPEND MY ENTIRE TIME LOOKING AT EARTH!
IT HAPPENED WHEN YOU WERE ON VACATION.
I SEE...

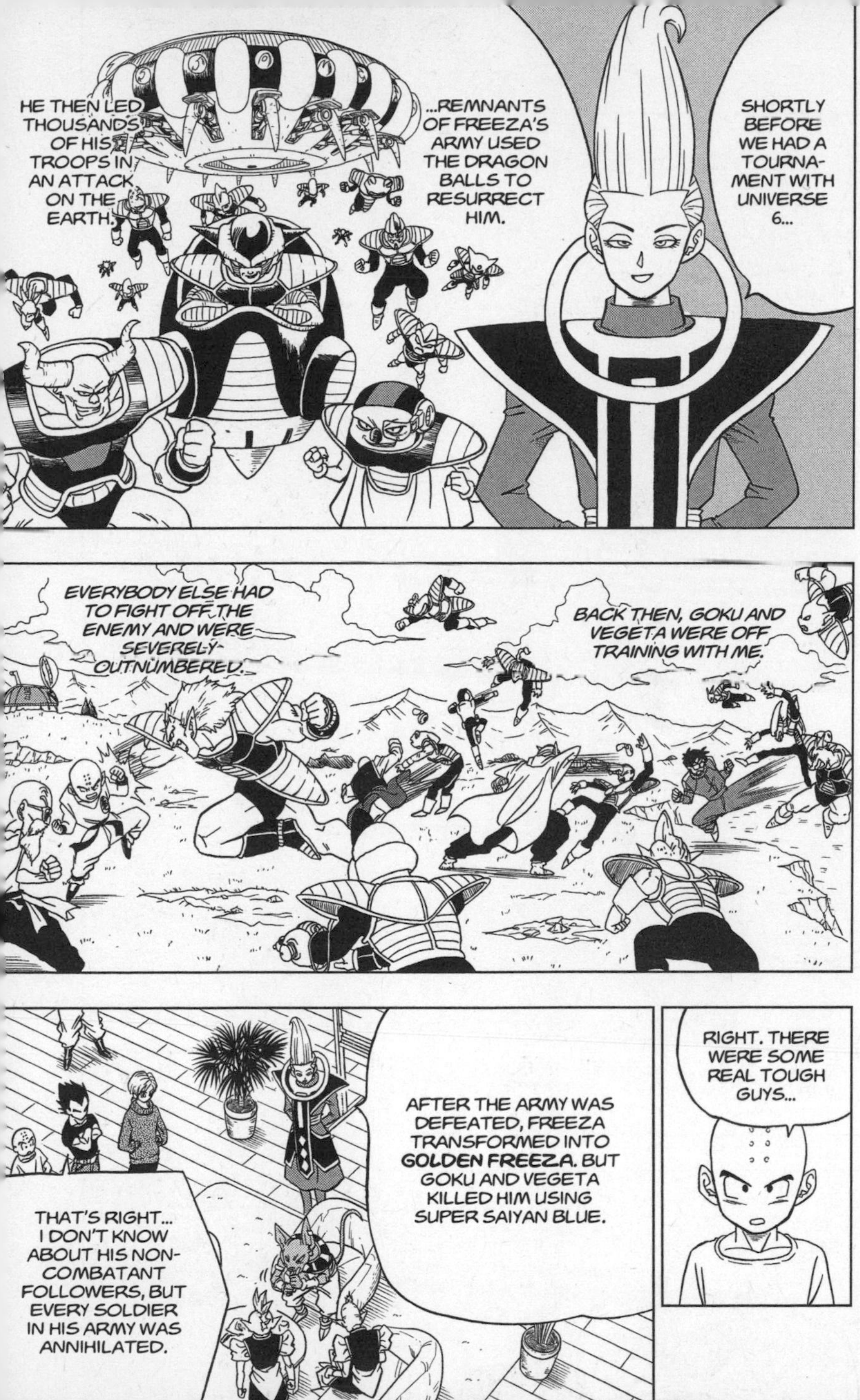
SHORTLY BEFORE WE HAD A TOURNAMENT WITH UNIVERSE 6...
...REMNANTS OF FREEZA'S ARMY USED THE DRAGON BALLS TO RESURRECT HIM.
HE THEN LED THOUSANDS OF HIS TROOPS IN AN ATTACK ON THE EARTH.
BACK THEN, GOKU AND VEGETA WERE OFF TRAINING WITH ME.
EVERYBODY ELSE HAD TO FIGHT OFF THE ENEMY AND WERE SEVERELY OUTNUMBERED.
RIGHT. THERE WERE SOME REAL TOUGH GUYS...
AFTER THE ARMY WAS DEFEATED, FREEZA TRANSFORMED INTO **GOLDEN FREEZA**. BUT GOKU AND VEGETA KILLED HIM USING SUPER SAIYAN BLUE.
THAT'S RIGHT... I DON'T KNOW ABOUT HIS NON-COMBATANT FOLLOWERS, BUT EVERY SOLDIER IN HIS ARMY WAS ANNIHILATED.

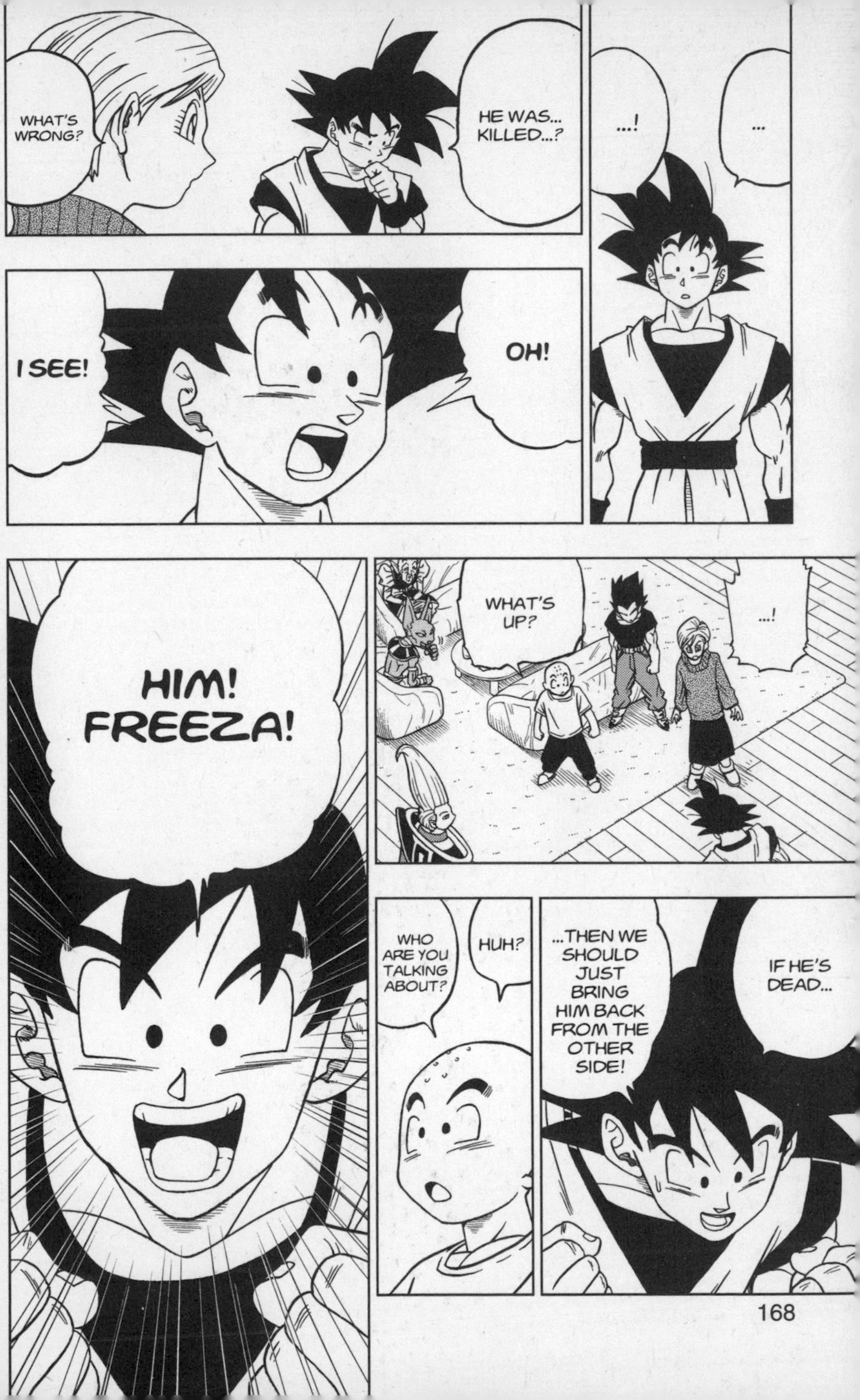
...
...!
HE WAS... KILLED...?
WHAT'S WRONG?
OH!
I SEE!
...!
WHAT'S UP?
IF HE'S DEAD...
...THEN WE SHOULD JUST BRING HIM BACK FROM THE OTHER SIDE!
HUH?
WHO ARE YOU TALKING ABOUT?
HIM! FREEZA!

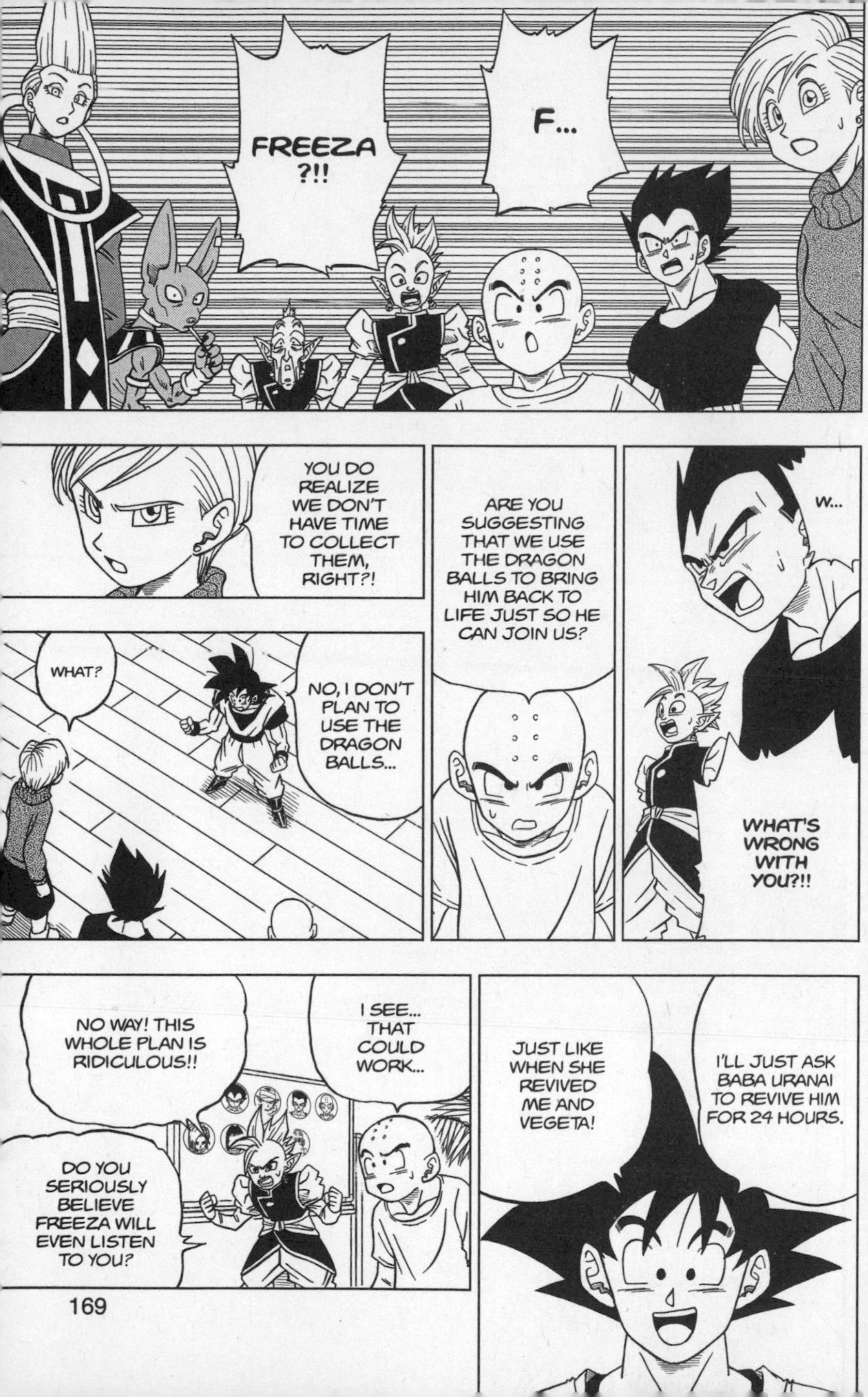
F...
FREEZA ?!!
W...
WHAT'S WRONG WITH YOU?!!
ARE YOU SUGGESTING THAT WE USE THE DRAGON BALLS TO BRING HIM BACK TO LIFE JUST SO HE CAN JOIN US?
YOU DO REALIZE WE DON'T HAVE TIME TO COLLECT THEM, RIGHT?!
NO, I DON'T PLAN TO USE THE DRAGON BALLS...
WHAT?
I'LL JUST ASK BABA URANAI TO REVIVE HIM FOR 24 HOURS.
JUST LIKE WHEN SHE REVIVED ME AND VEGETA!
I SEE... THAT COULD WORK...
NO WAY! THIS WHOLE PLAN IS RIDICULOUS!!
DO YOU SERIOUSLY BELIEVE FREEZA WILL EVEN LISTEN TO YOU?

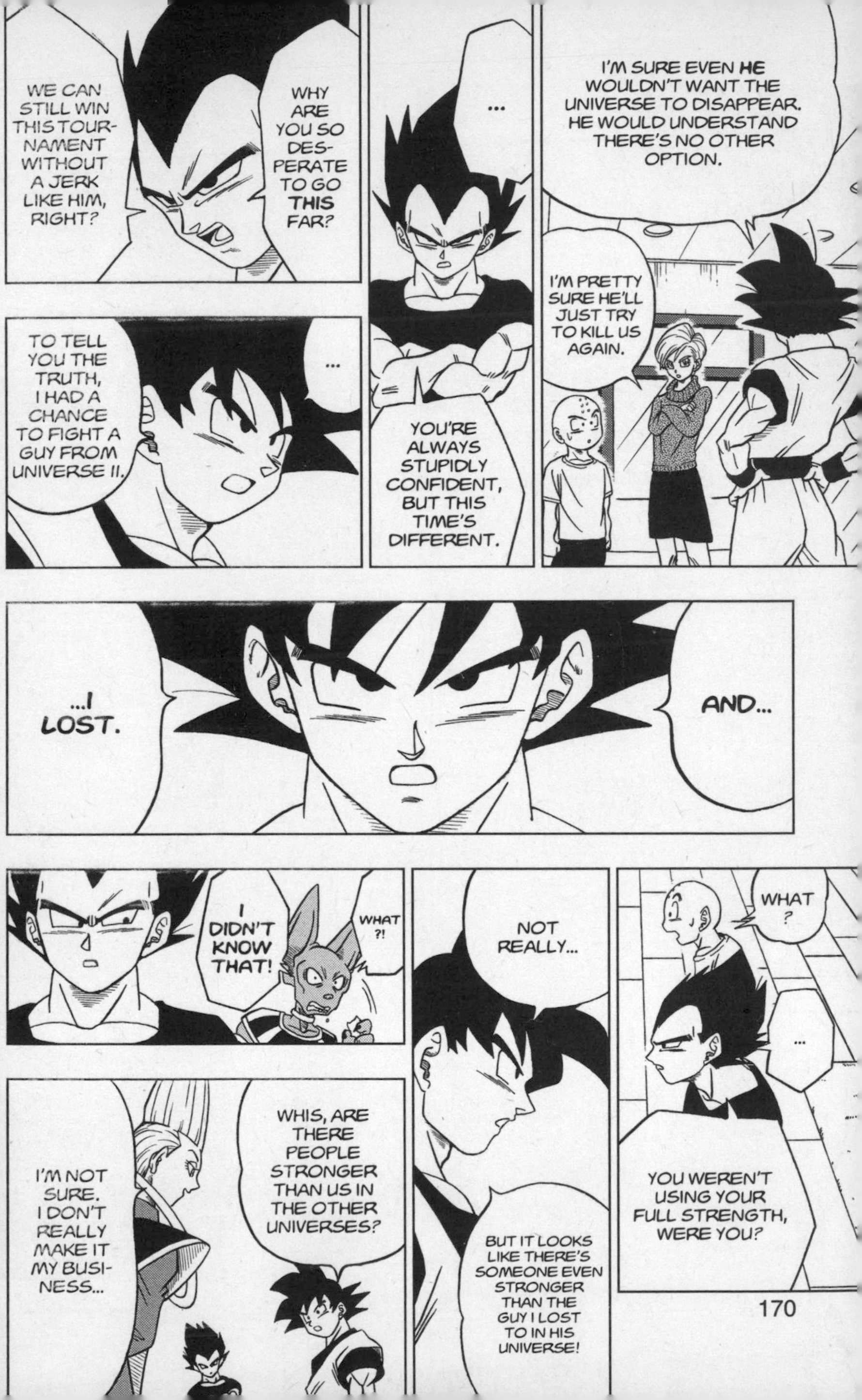
I'M SURE EVEN HE WOULDN'T WANT THE UNIVERSE TO DISAPPEAR. HE WOULD UNDERSTAND THERE'S NO OTHER OPTION.
I'M PRETTY SURE HE'LL JUST TRY TO KILL US AGAIN.
...
YOU'RE ALWAYS STUPIDLY CONFIDENT, BUT THIS TIME'S DIFFERENT.
WHY ARE YOU SO DESPERATE TO GO THIS FAR?
WE CAN STILL WIN THIS TOURNAMENT WITHOUT A JERK LIKE HIM, RIGHT?
...
TO TELL YOU THE TRUTH, I HAD A CHANCE TO FIGHT A GUY FROM UNIVERSE 11.
AND...
...I LOST.
WHAT ?
...
YOU WEREN'T USING YOUR FULL STRENGTH, WERE YOU?
NOT REALLY...
BUT IT LOOKS LIKE THERE'S SOMEONE EVEN STRONGER THAN THE GUY I LOST TO IN HIS UNIVERSE!
WHAT ?!
I DIDN'T KNOW THAT!
WHIS, ARE THERE PEOPLE STRONGER THAN US IN THE OTHER UNIVERSES?
I'M NOT SURE. I DON'T REALLY MAKE IT MY BUSINESS...

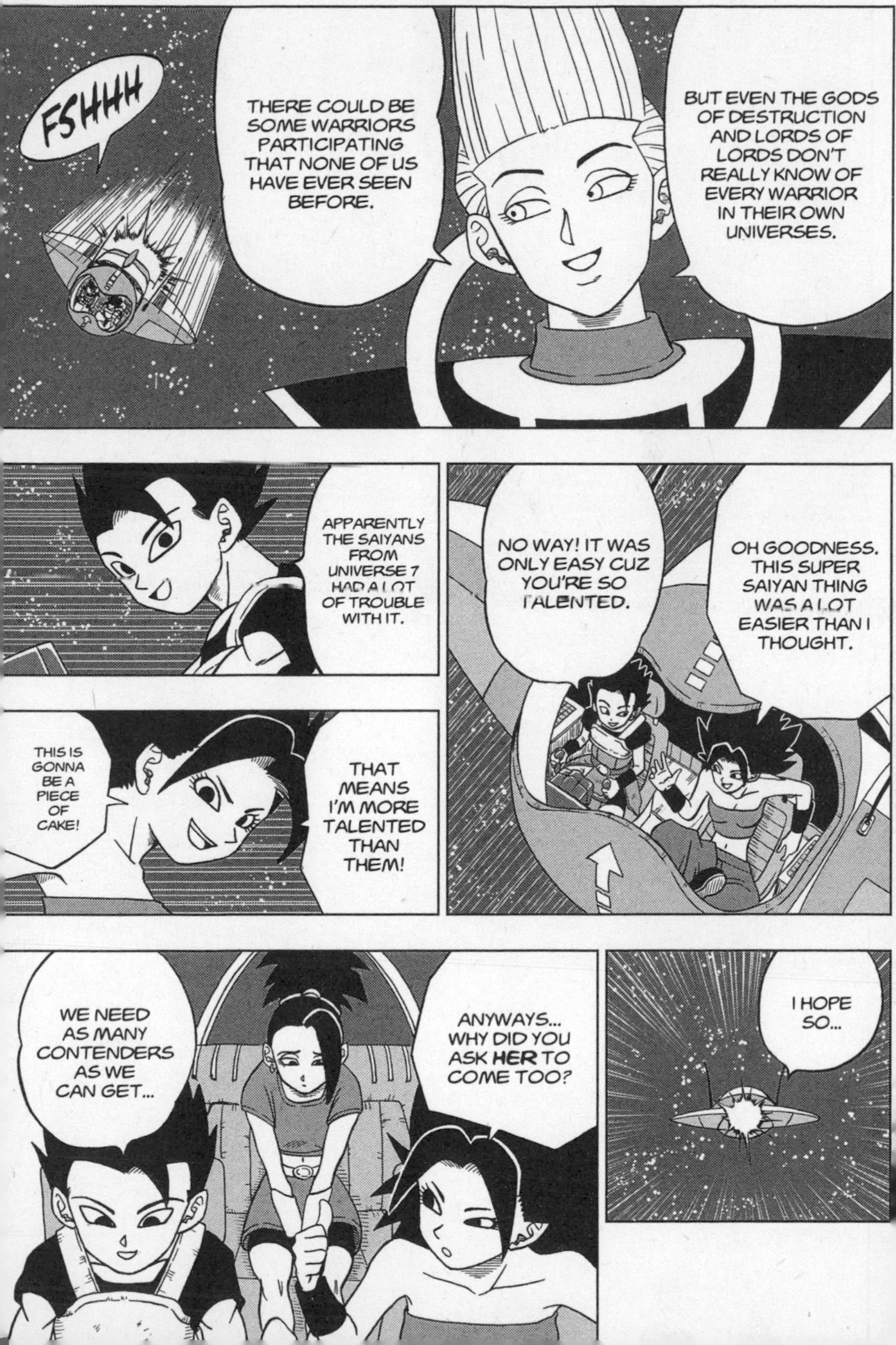
BUT EVEN THE GODS OF DESTRUCTION AND LORDS OF LORDS DON'T REALLY KNOW OF EVERY WARRIOR IN THEIR OWN UNIVERSES.
THERE COULD BE SOME WARRIORS PARTICIPATING THAT NONE OF US HAVE EVER SEEN BEFORE.
FSHHH
OH GOODNESS. THIS SUPER SAIYAN THING WAS A LOT EASIER THAN I THOUGHT.
NO WAY! IT WAS ONLY EASY CUZ YOU'RE SO TALENTED.
APPARENTLY THE SAIYANS FROM UNIVERSE 7 HAD A LOT OF TROUBLE WITH IT.
THAT MEANS I'M MORE TALENTED THAN THEM!
THIS IS GONNA BE A PIECE OF CAKE!
I HOPE SO...
ANYWAYS... WHY DID YOU ASK **HER** TO COME TOO?
WE NEED AS MANY CONTENDERS AS WE CAN GET...

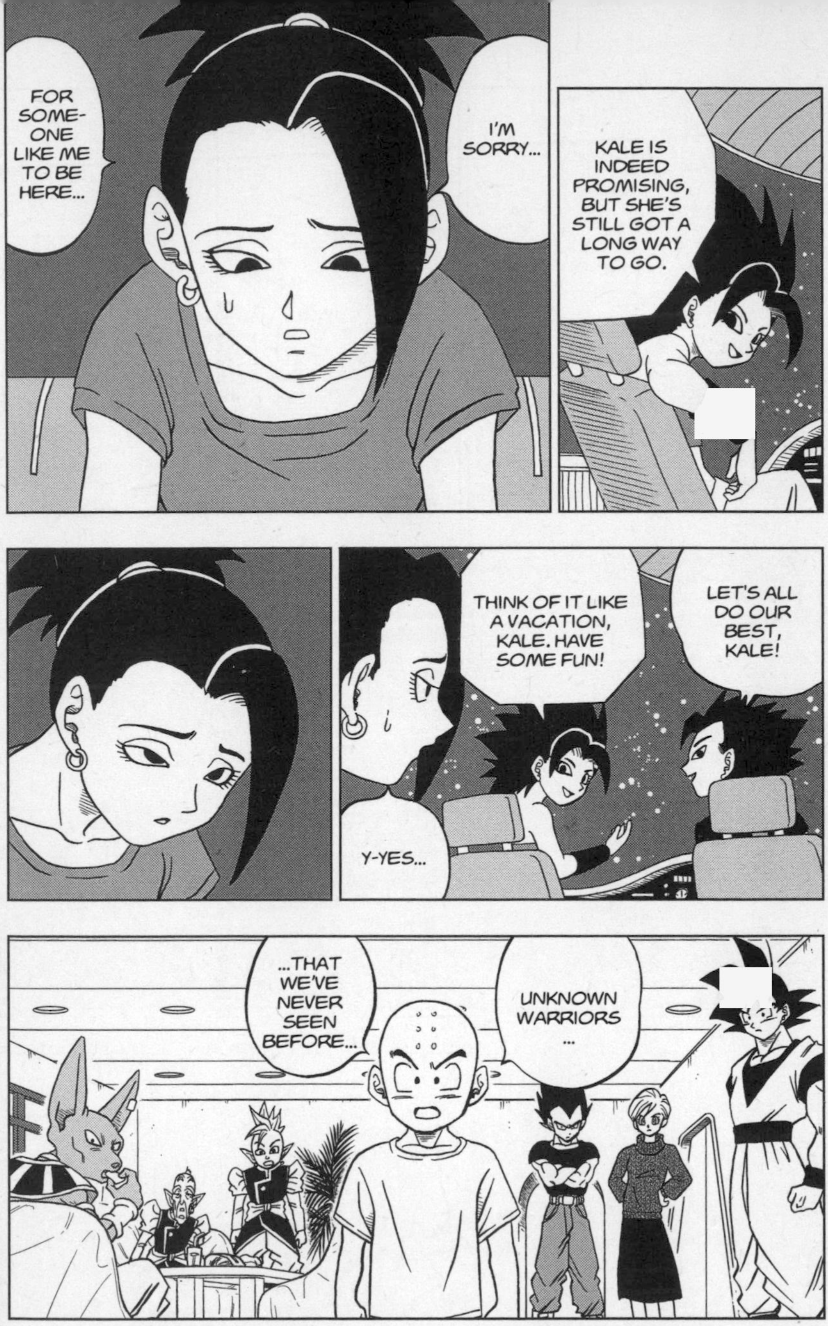
KALE IS INDEED PROMISING, BUT SHE'S STILL GOT A LONG WAY TO GO.
I'M SORRY...
FOR SOME-ONE LIKE ME TO BE HERE...
LET'S ALL DO OUR BEST, KALE!
THINK OF IT LIKE A VACATION, KALE. HAVE SOME FUN!
Y-YES...
UNKNOWN WARRIORS ...
...THAT WE'VE NEVER SEEN BEFORE...

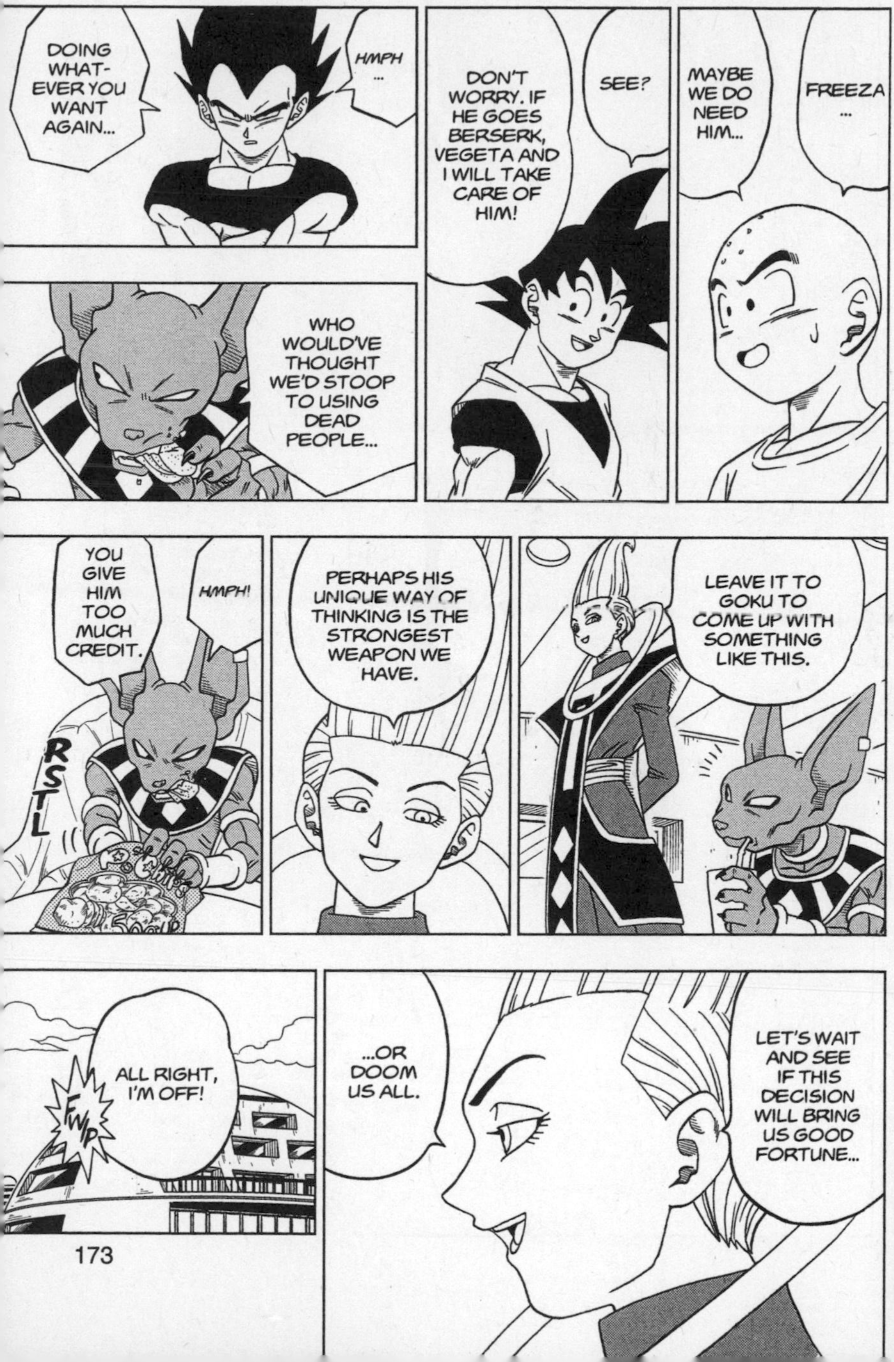
FREEZA ...
MAYBE WE DO NEED HIM...
SEE?
DON'T WORRY. IF HE GOES BERSERK, VEGETA AND I WILL TAKE CARE OF HIM!
HMPH ...
DOING WHAT-EVER YOU WANT AGAIN...
WHO WOULD'VE THOUGHT WE'D STOOP TO USING DEAD PEOPLE...
LEAVE IT TO GOKU TO COME UP WITH SOMETHING LIKE THIS.
PERHAPS HIS UNIQUE WAY OF THINKING IS THE STRONGEST WEAPON WE HAVE.
HMPH!
YOU GIVE HIM TOO MUCH CREDIT.
RSTL
LET'S WAIT AND SEE IF THIS DECISION WILL BRING US GOOD FORTUNE...
...OR DOOM US ALL.
ALL RIGHT, I'M OFF!
FWIP

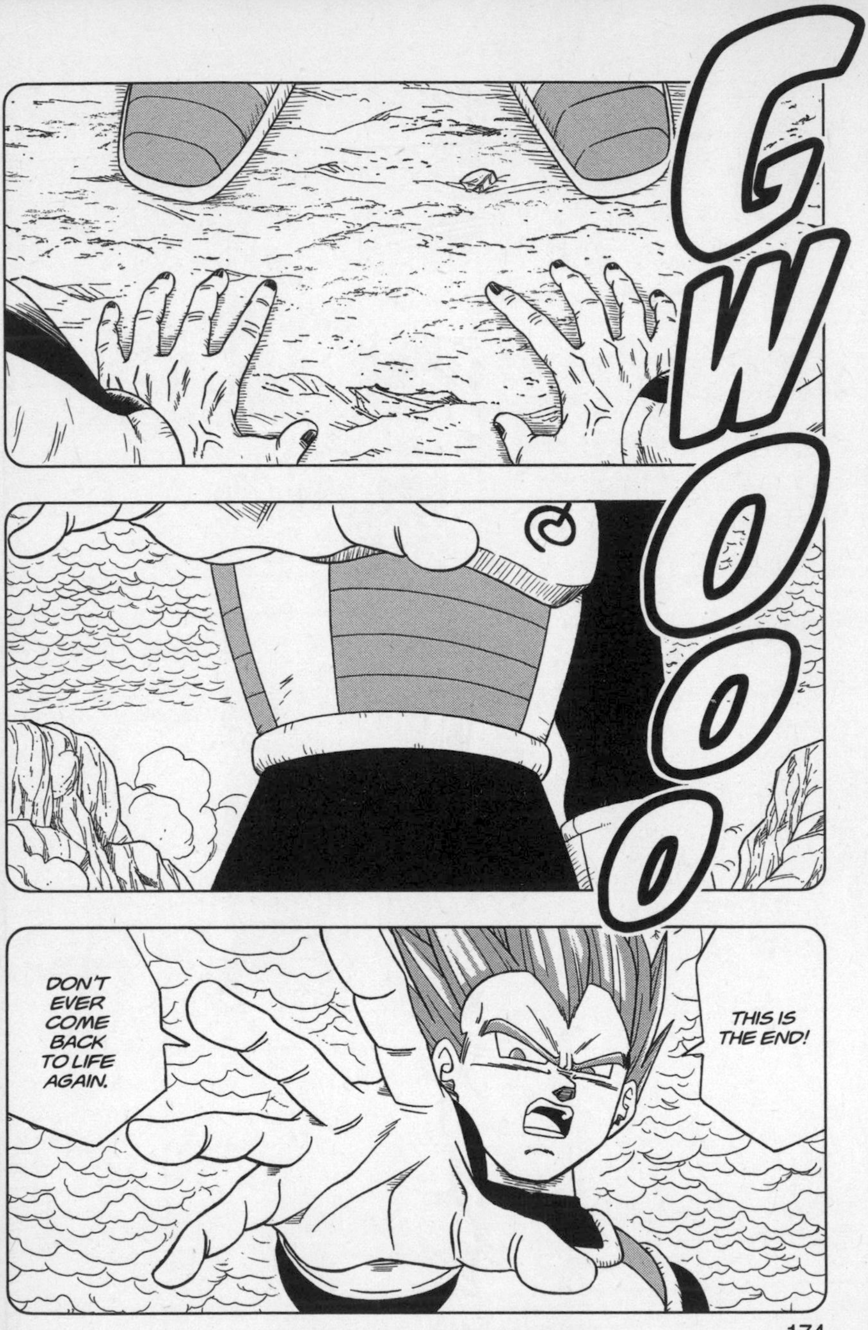
GWOOOO
THIS IS THE END!
DON'T EVER COME BACK TO LIFE AGAIN.

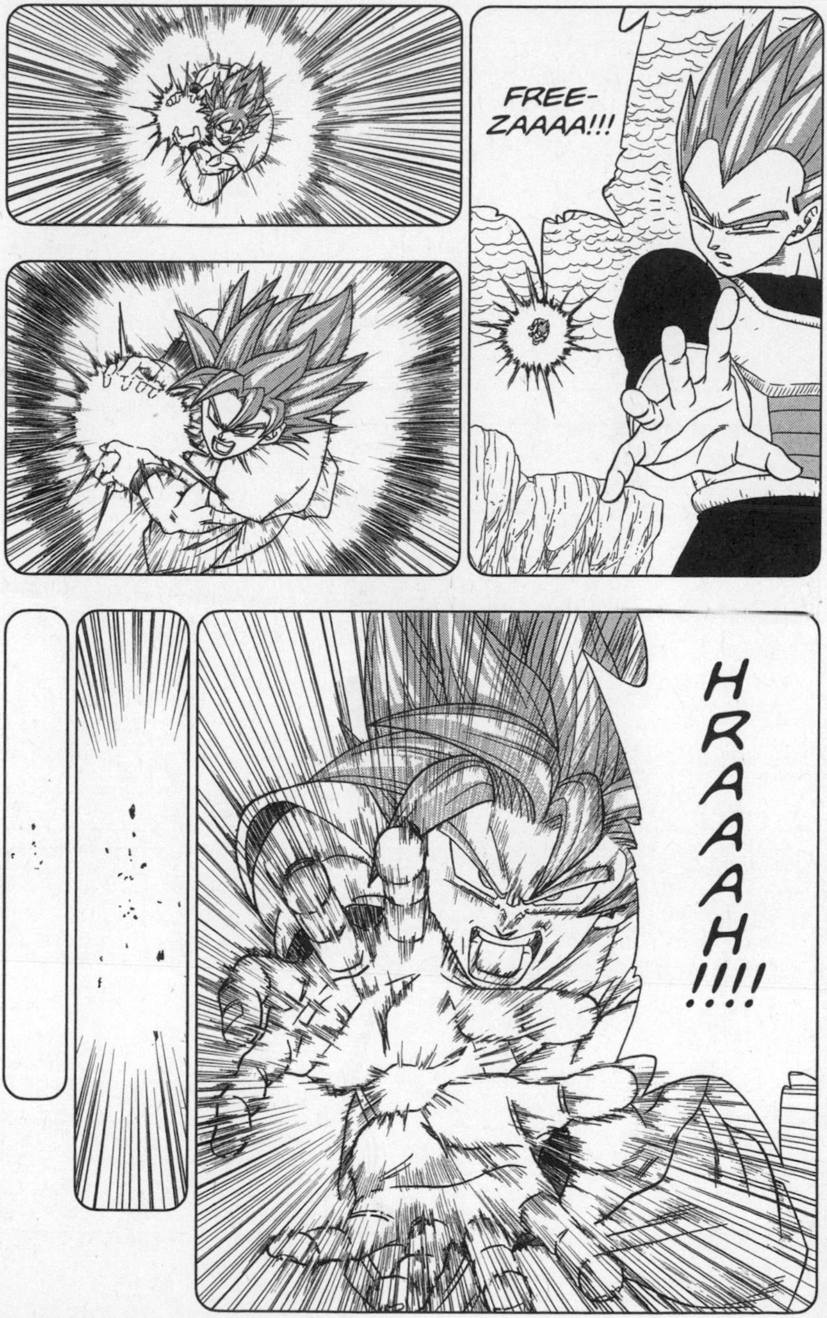
FREE-
ZAAAA!!!
HRAAAAH!!!!

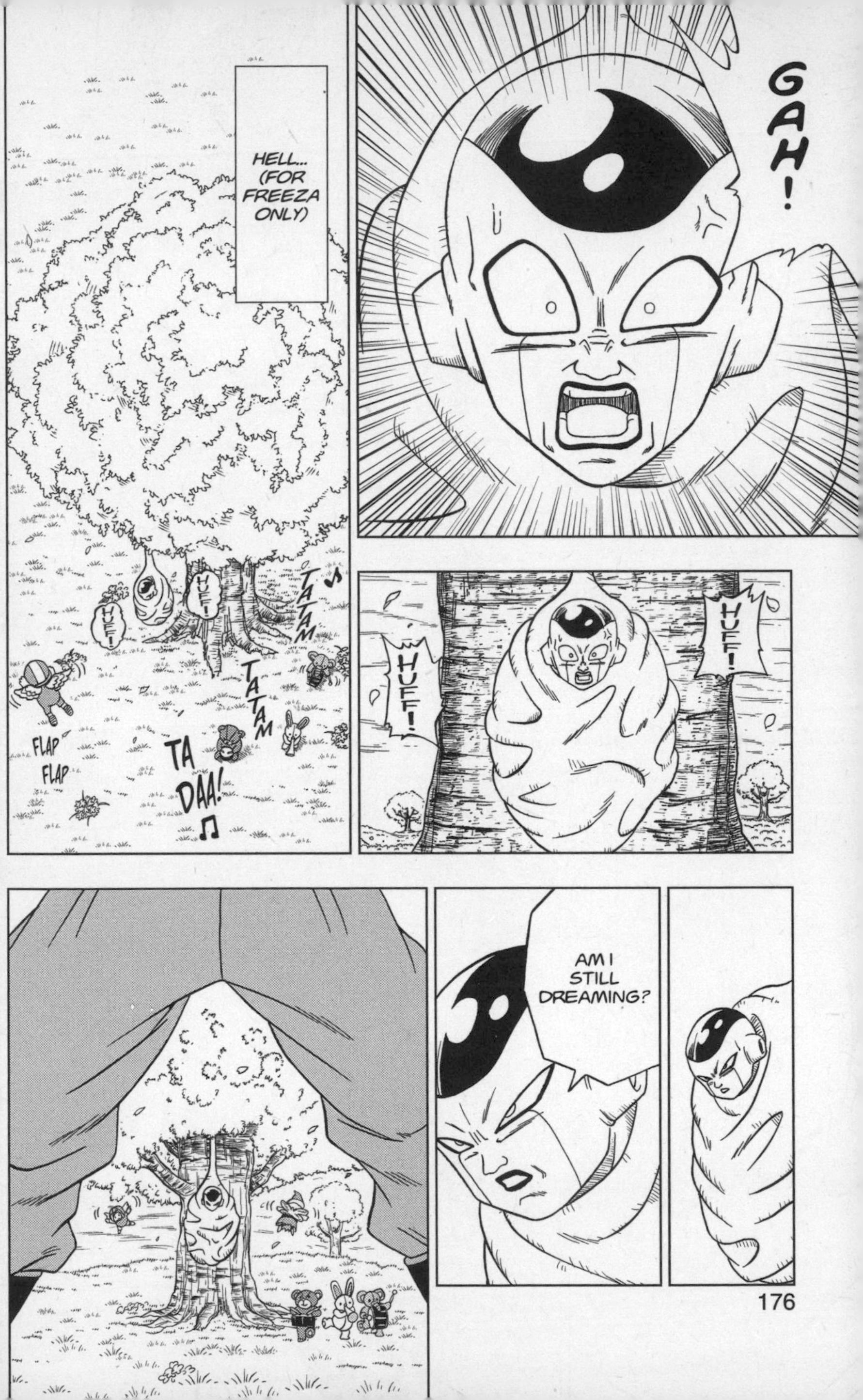
GAH!
HUFF!
HUFF!
HELL... (FOR FREEZA ONLY)
HUFF!
HUFF!
TATAM
TATAM
TA DAA!
FLAP
FLAP
AM I STILL DREAMING?

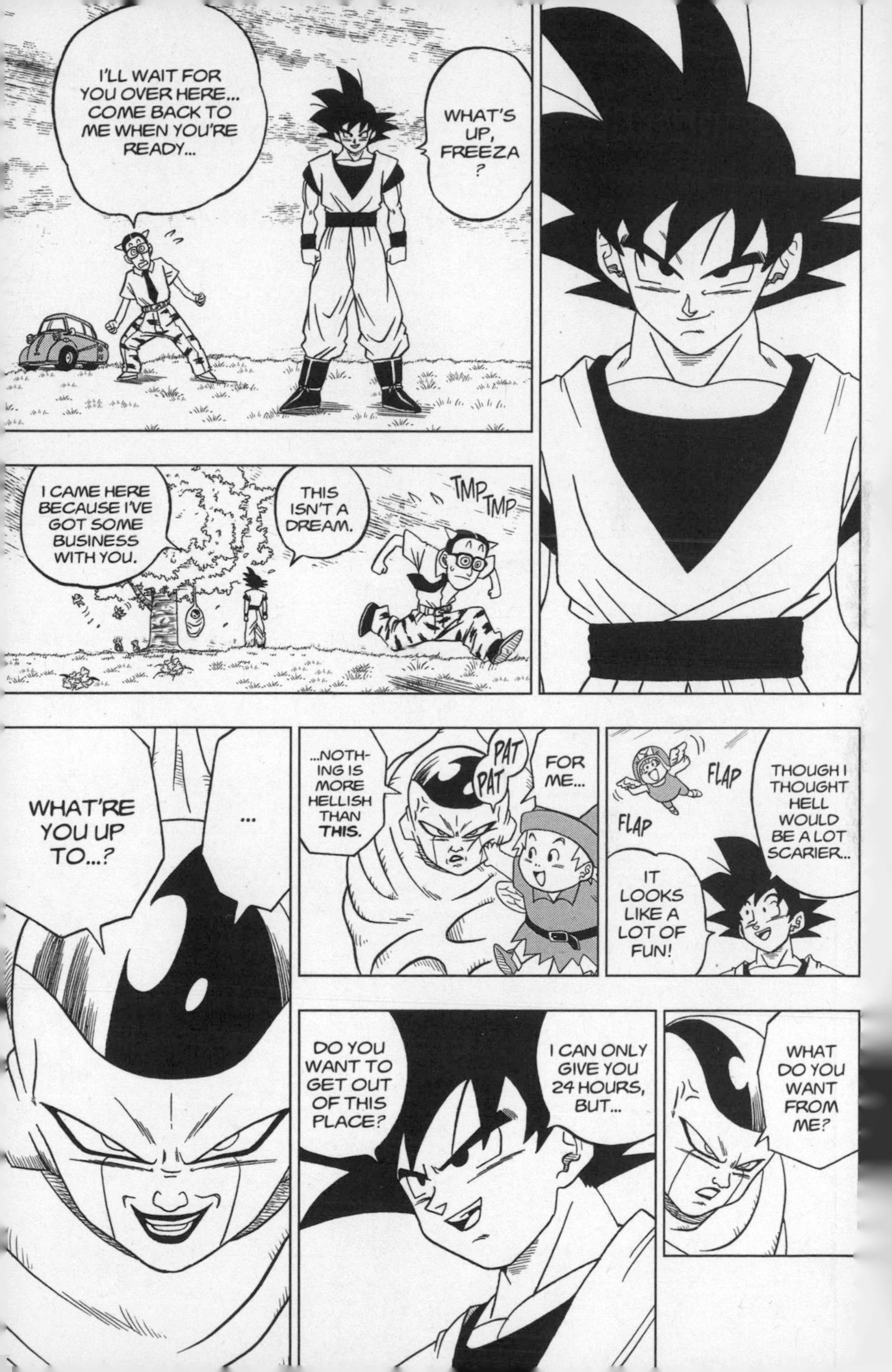
WHAT'S UP, FREEZA?
I'LL WAIT FOR YOU OVER HERE... COME BACK TO ME WHEN YOU'RE READY...
TMP TMP
THIS ISN'T A DREAM.
I CAME HERE BECAUSE I'VE GOT SOME BUSINESS WITH YOU.
THOUGH I THOUGHT HELL WOULD BE A LOT SCARIER...
FLAP
FLAP
IT LOOKS LIKE A LOT OF FUN!
FOR ME...
PAT PAT
...NOTHING IS MORE HELLISH THAN **THIS.**
WHAT DO YOU WANT FROM ME?
I CAN ONLY GIVE YOU 24 HOURS, BUT...
DO YOU WANT TO GET OUT OF THIS PLACE?
...
WHAT'RE YOU UP TO...?

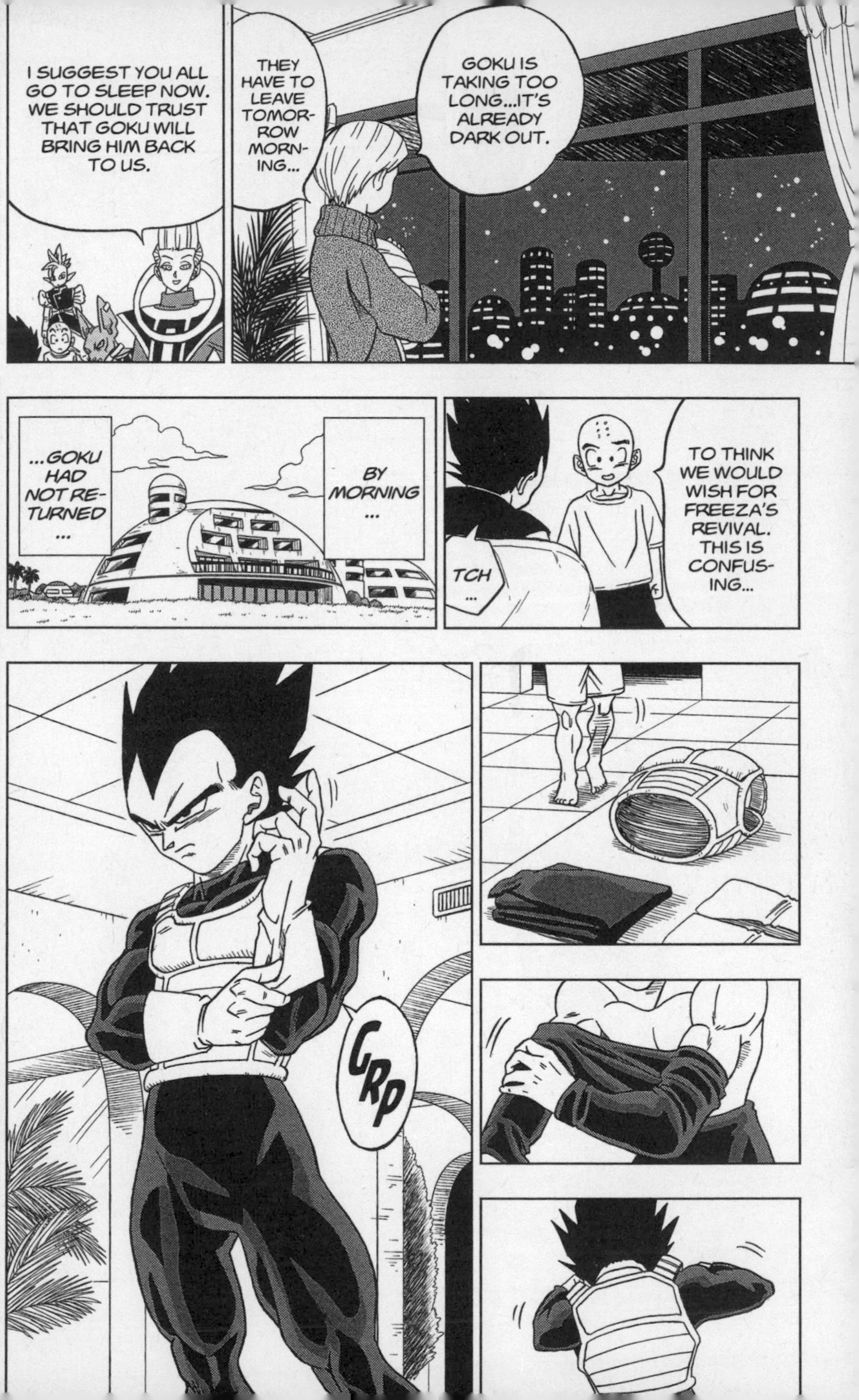
GOKU IS TAKING TOO LONG...IT'S ALREADY DARK OUT.
THEY HAVE TO LEAVE TOMORROW MORNING...
I SUGGEST YOU ALL GO TO SLEEP NOW. WE SHOULD TRUST THAT GOKU WILL BRING HIM BACK TO US.
TO THINK WE WOULD WISH FOR FREEZA'S REVIVAL. THIS IS CONFUSING...
TCH...
BY MORNING...
...GOKU HAD NOT RETURNED...
GRP

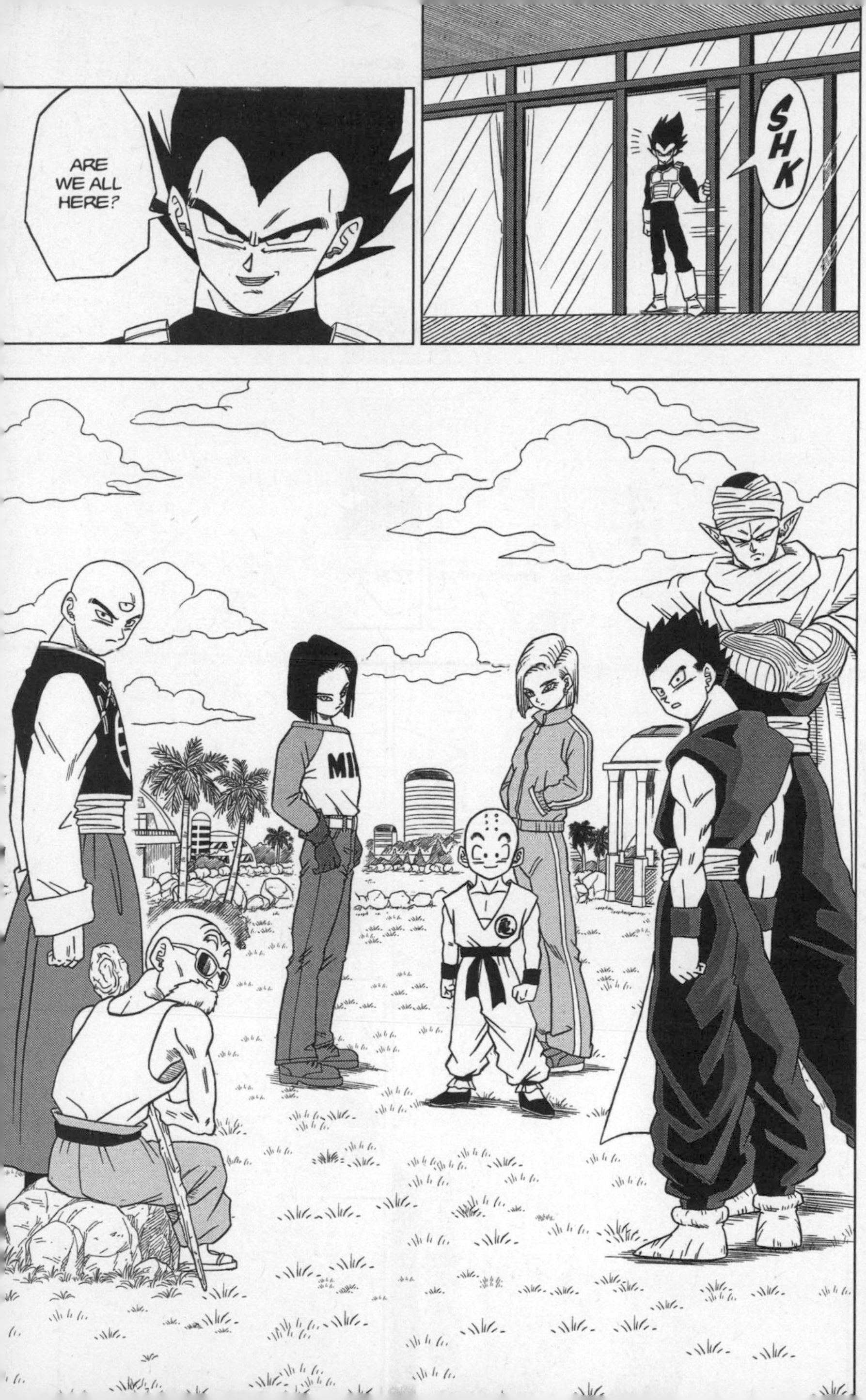
SHK
ARE WE ALL HERE?

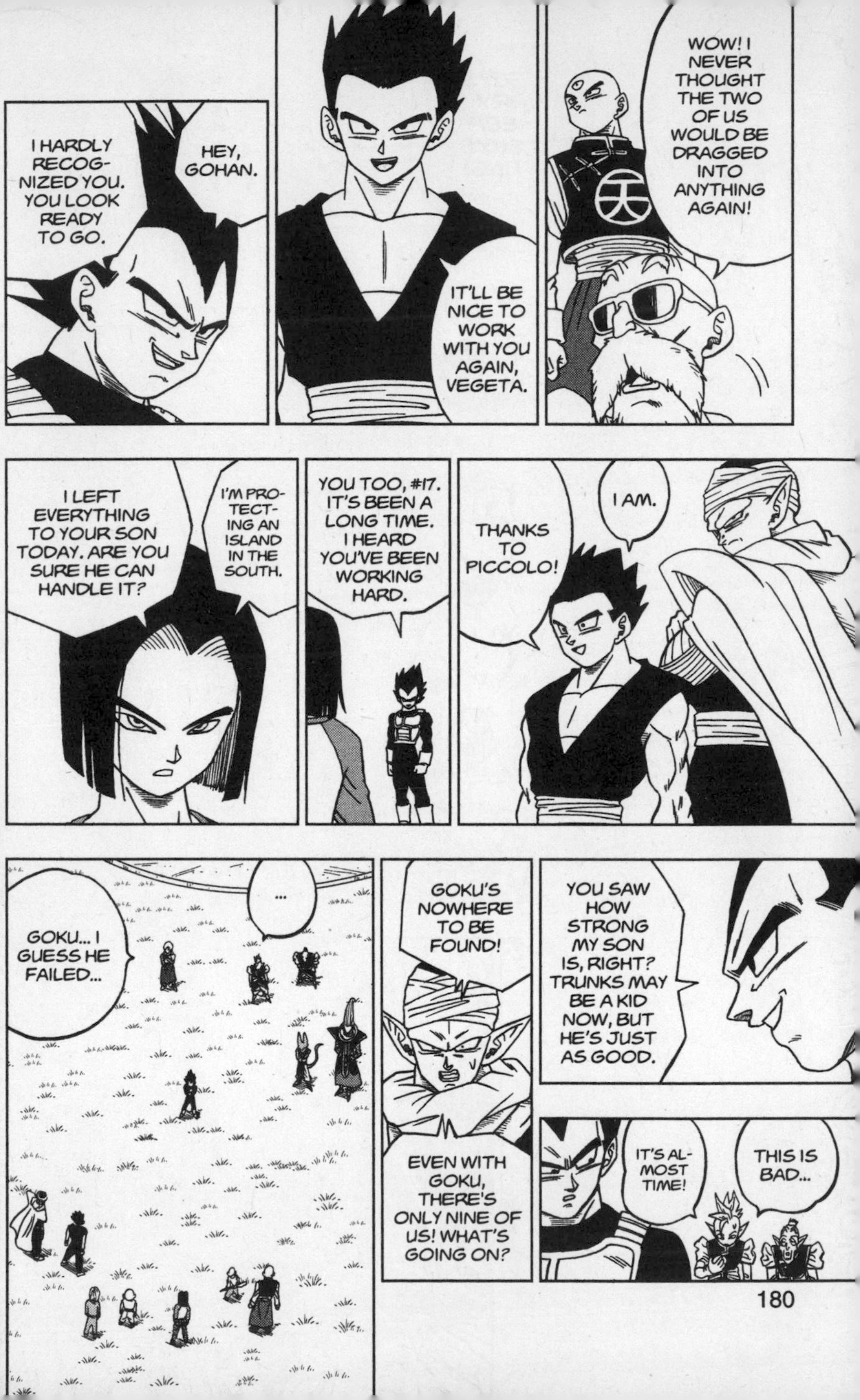
WOW! I NEVER THOUGHT THE TWO OF US WOULD BE DRAGGED INTO ANYTHING AGAIN!
IT'LL BE NICE TO WORK WITH YOU AGAIN, VEGETA.
HEY, GOHAN.
I HARDLY RECOG-NIZED YOU. YOU LOOK READY TO GO.
I AM.
THANKS TO PICCOLO!
YOU TOO, #17. IT'S BEEN A LONG TIME. I HEARD YOU'VE BEEN WORKING HARD.
I'M PRO-TECT-ING AN ISLAND IN THE SOUTH.
I LEFT EVERYTHING TO YOUR SON TODAY. ARE YOU SURE HE CAN HANDLE IT?
YOU SAW HOW STRONG MY SON IS, RIGHT? TRUNKS MAY BE A KID NOW, BUT HE'S JUST AS GOOD.
THIS IS BAD...
IT'S AL-MOST TIME!
GOKU'S NOWHERE TO BE FOUND!
EVEN WITH GOKU, THERE'S ONLY NINE OF US! WHAT'S GOING ON?
...
GOKU... I GUESS HE FAILED...

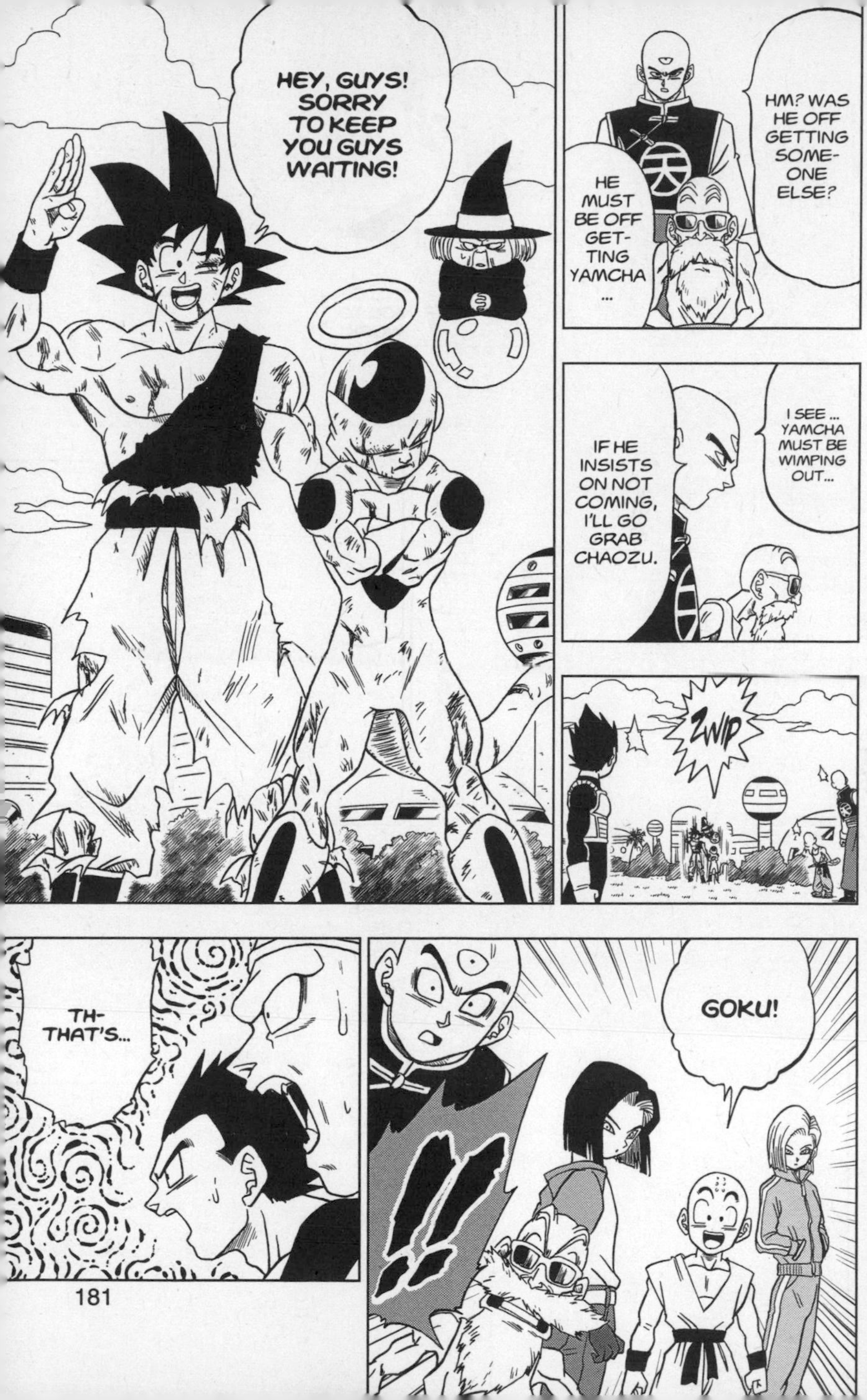
HM? WAS HE OFF GETTING SOME-ONE ELSE?
HE MUST BE OFF GET-TING YAMCHA ...
I SEE ... YAMCHA MUST BE WIMPING OUT...
IF HE INSISTS ON NOT COMING, I'LL GO GRAB CHAOZU.
ZWIP
HEY, GUYS! SORRY TO KEEP YOU GUYS WAITING!
GOKU!
TH-THAT'S...

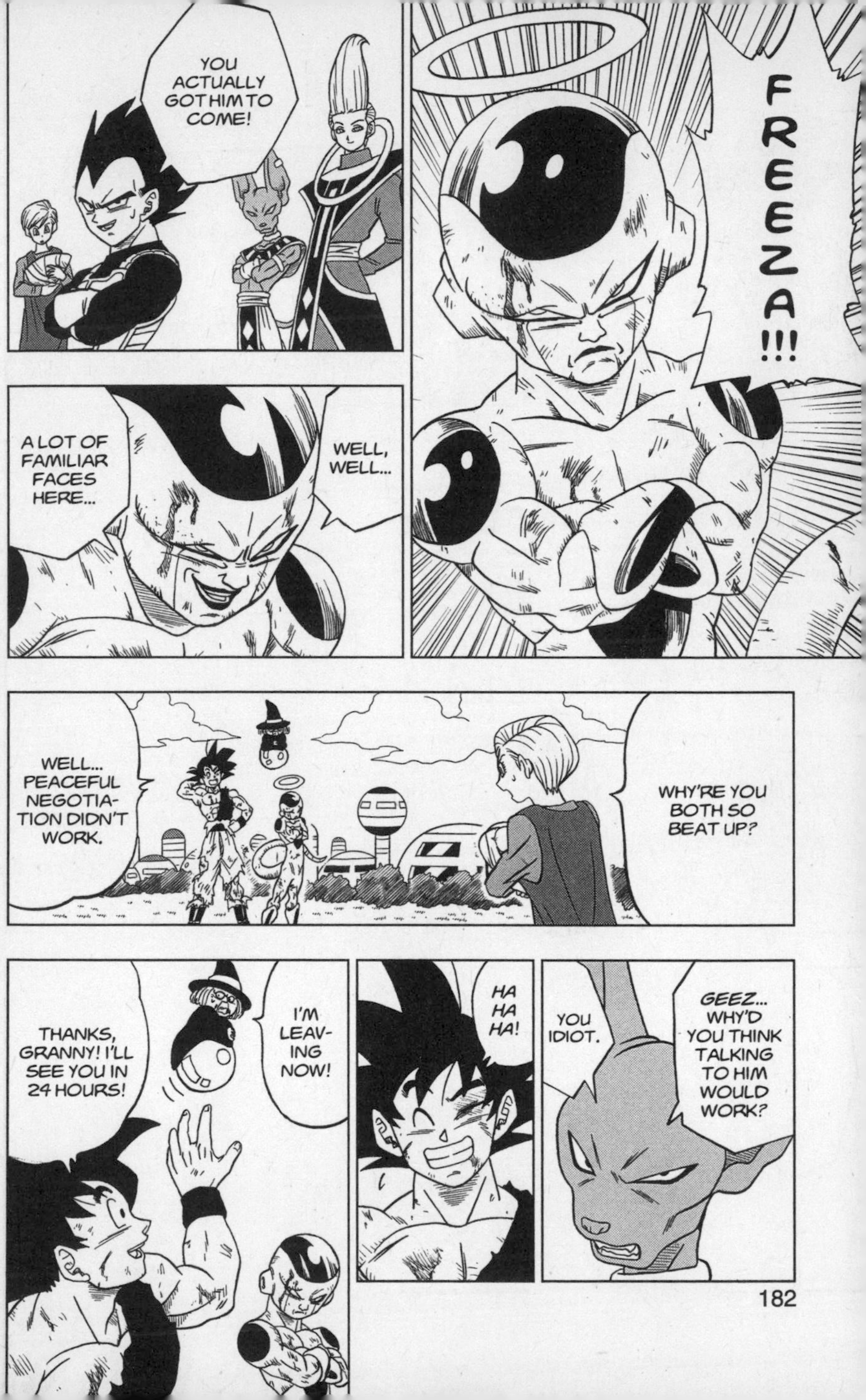
FREEZA!!!
YOU ACTUALLY GOT HIM TO COME!
WELL, WELL...
A LOT OF FAMILIAR FACES HERE...
WHY'RE YOU BOTH SO BEAT UP?
WELL... PEACEFUL NEGOTIATION DIDN'T WORK.
GEEZ... WHY'D YOU THINK TALKING TO HIM WOULD WORK?
YOU IDIOT.
HA HA HA!
I'M LEAVING NOW!
THANKS, GRANNY! I'LL SEE YOU IN 24 HOURS!

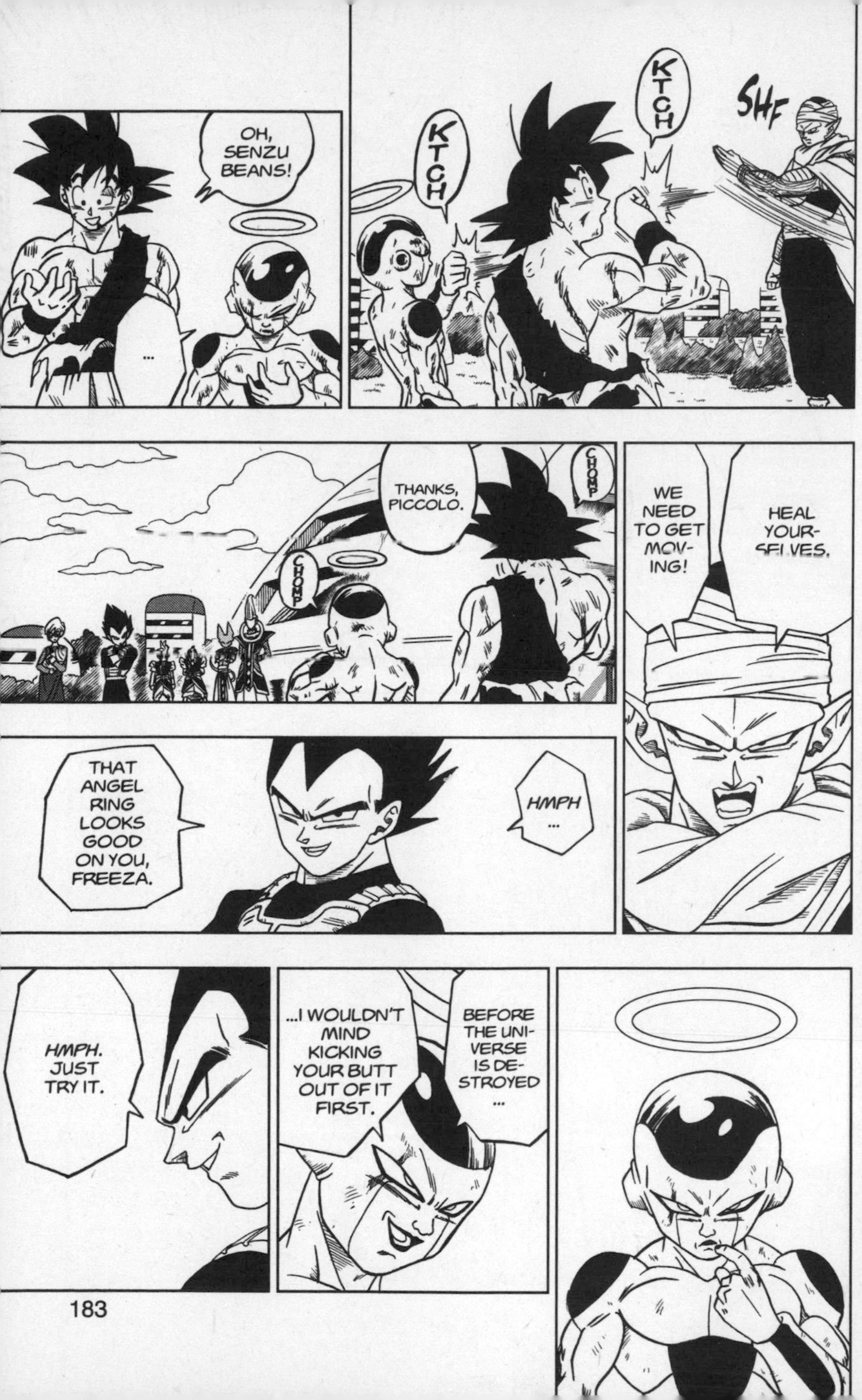
SHF
KTCH
KTCH
OH, SENZU BEANS!
...
HEAL YOURSELVES.
WE NEED TO GET MOVING!
CHOMP
THANKS, PICCOLO.
CHOMP
HMPH...
THAT ANGEL RING LOOKS GOOD ON YOU, FREEZA.
BEFORE THE UNIVERSE IS DESTROYED...
...I WOULDN'T MIND KICKING YOUR BUTT OUT OF IT FIRST.
HMPH. JUST TRY IT.

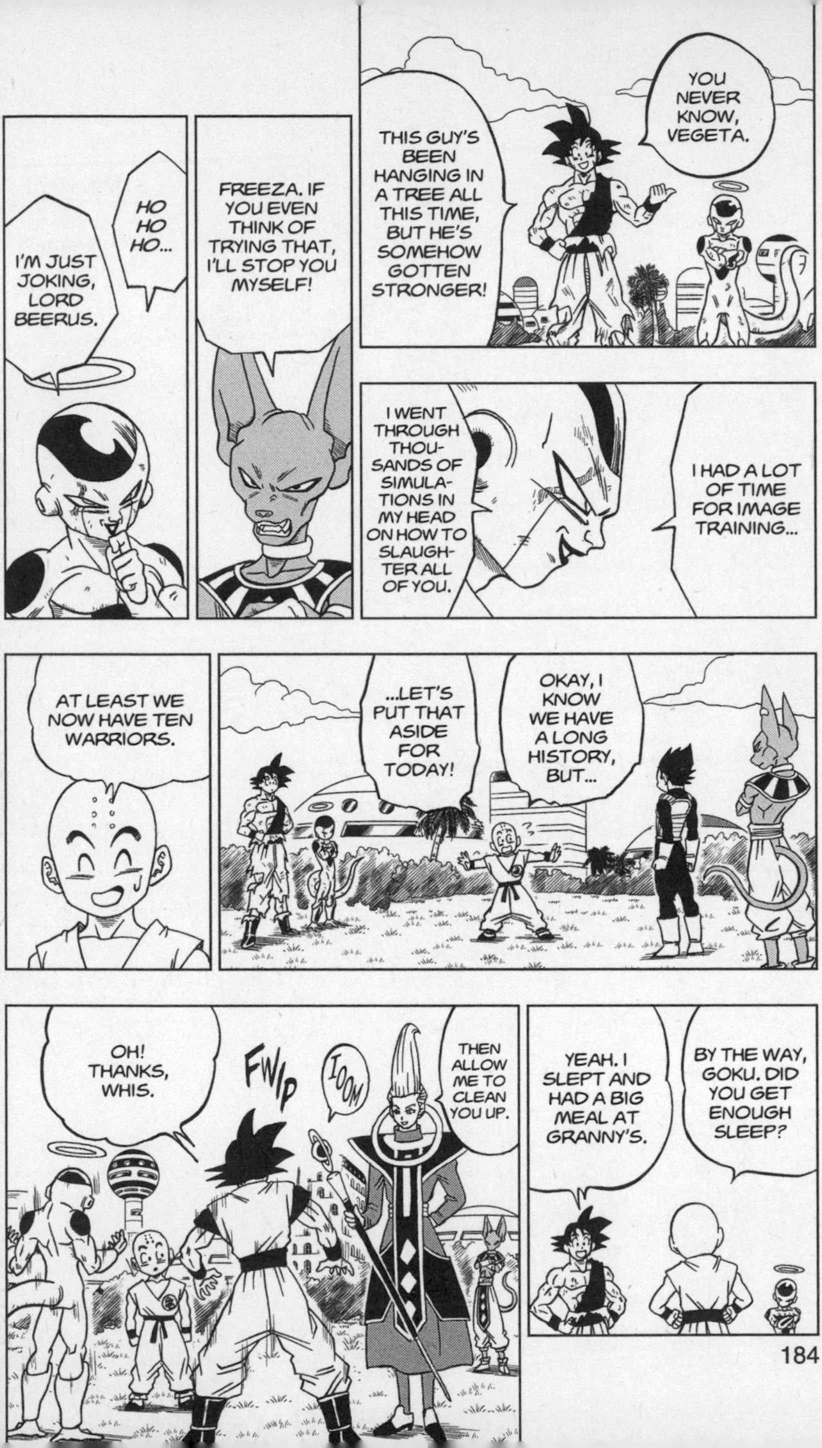
YOU NEVER KNOW, VEGETA.
THIS GUY'S BEEN HANGING IN A TREE ALL THIS TIME, BUT HE'S SOMEHOW GOTTEN STRONGER!
I HAD A LOT OF TIME FOR IMAGE TRAINING...
I WENT THROUGH THOUSANDS OF SIMULATIONS IN MY HEAD ON HOW TO SLAUGHTER ALL OF YOU.
FREEZA. IF YOU EVEN THINK OF TRYING THAT, I'LL STOP YOU MYSELF!
HO HO HO...
I'M JUST JOKING, LORD BEERUS.
OKAY, I KNOW WE HAVE A LONG HISTORY, BUT...
...LET'S PUT THAT ASIDE FOR TODAY!
AT LEAST WE NOW HAVE TEN WARRIORS.
BY THE WAY, GOKU. DID YOU GET ENOUGH SLEEP?
YEAH. I SLEPT AND HAD A BIG MEAL AT GRANNY'S.
THEN ALLOW ME TO CLEAN YOU UP.
IOOM
FWIP
OH! THANKS, WHIS.

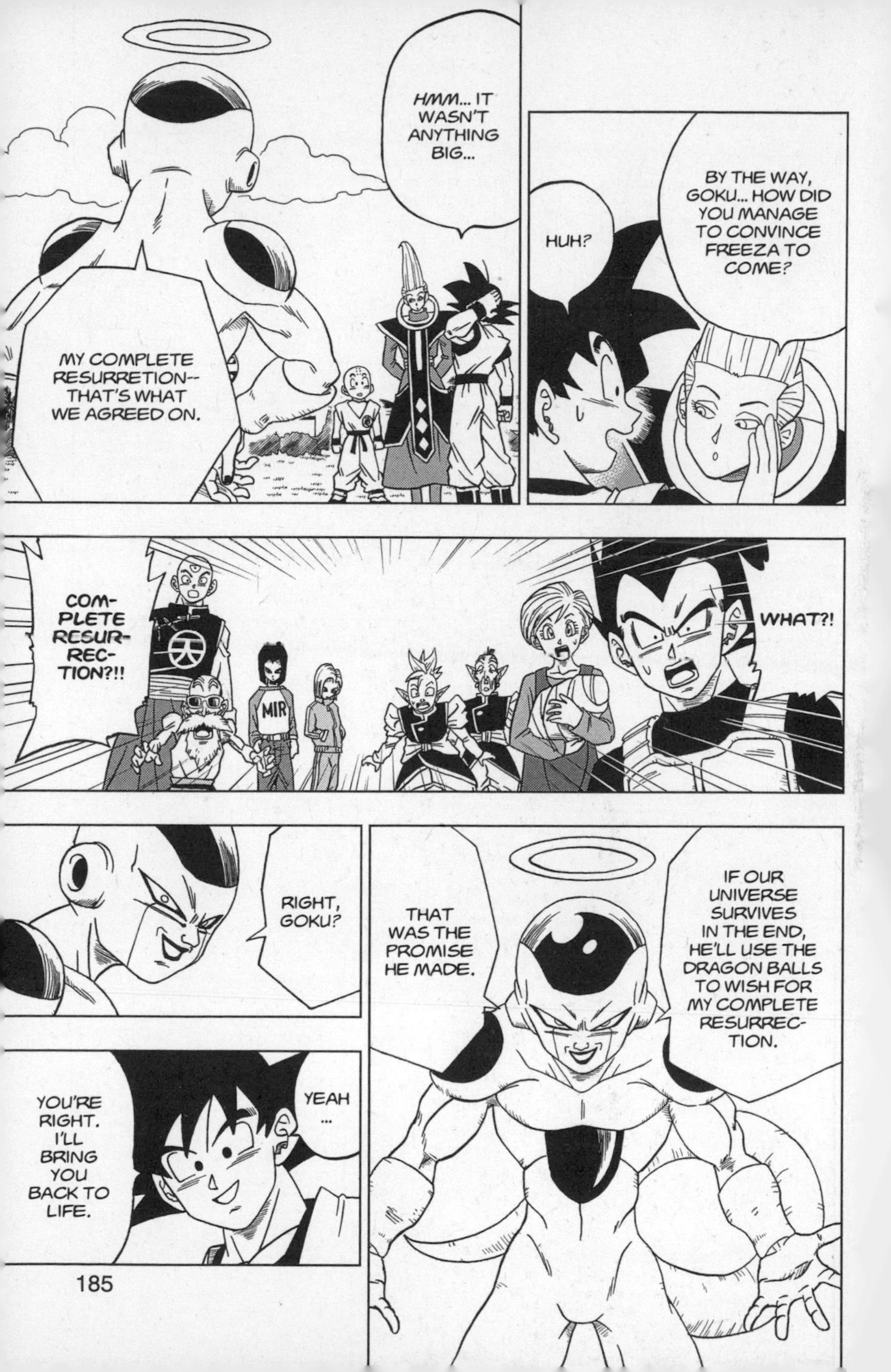
BY THE WAY, GOKU... HOW DID YOU MANAGE TO CONVINCE FREEZA TO COME?
HUH?
HMM... IT WASN'T ANYTHING BIG...
MY COMPLETE RESURRETION-- THAT'S WHAT WE AGREED ON.
WHAT?!
COM-PLETE RESUR-REC-TION?!!
IF OUR UNIVERSE SURVIVES IN THE END, HE'LL USE THE DRAGON BALLS TO WISH FOR MY COMPLETE RESURREC-TION.
THAT WAS THE PROMISE HE MADE.
RIGHT, GOKU?
YEAH ...
YOU'RE RIGHT. I'LL BRING YOU BACK TO LIFE.

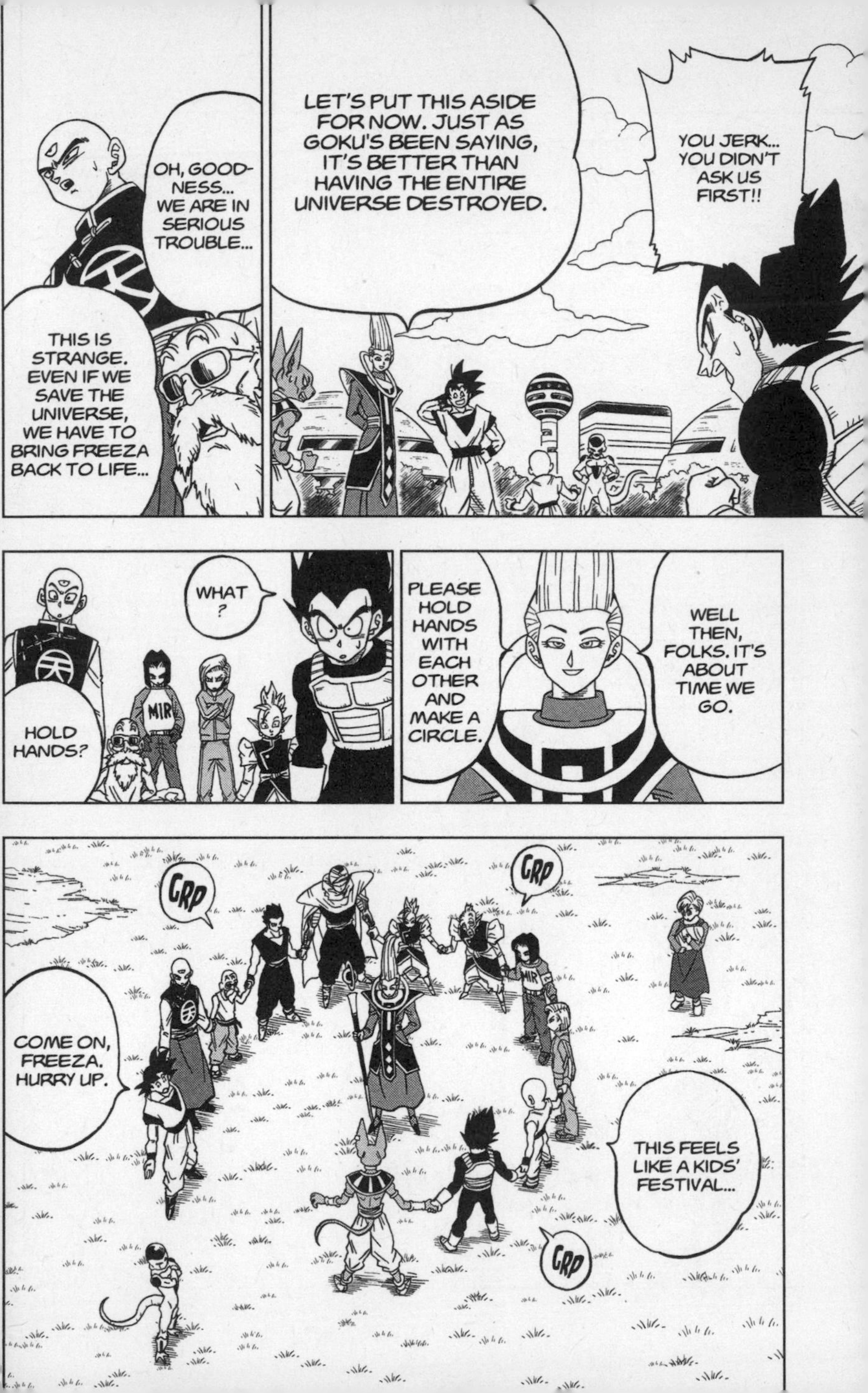
YOU JERK... YOU DIDN'T ASK US FIRST!!
LET'S PUT THIS ASIDE FOR NOW. JUST AS GOKU'S BEEN SAYING, IT'S BETTER THAN HAVING THE ENTIRE UNIVERSE DESTROYED.
OH, GOODNESS... WE ARE IN SERIOUS TROUBLE...
THIS IS STRANGE. EVEN IF WE SAVE THE UNIVERSE, WE HAVE TO BRING FREEZA BACK TO LIFE...
WELL THEN, FOLKS. IT'S ABOUT TIME WE GO.
PLEASE HOLD HANDS WITH EACH OTHER AND MAKE A CIRCLE.
WHAT?
HOLD HANDS?
GRP
GRP
THIS FEELS LIKE A KIDS' FESTIVAL...
COME ON, FREEZA. HURRY UP.
GRP

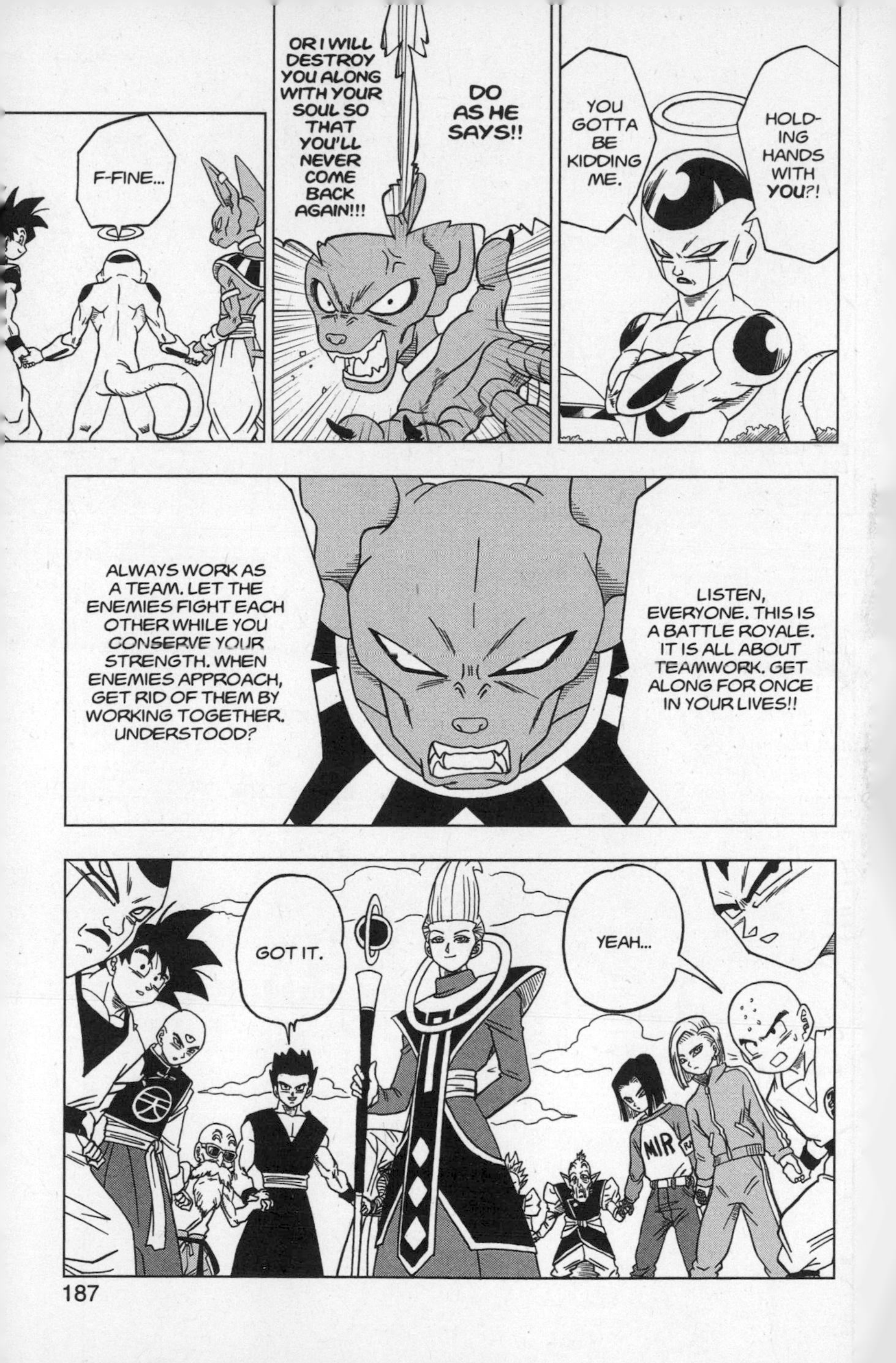
HOLD-ING HANDS WITH YOU?!
YOU GOTTA BE KIDDING ME.
DO AS HE SAYS!!
OR I WILL DESTROY YOU ALONG WITH YOUR SOUL SO THAT YOU'LL NEVER COME BACK AGAIN!!!
F-FINE...
LISTEN, EVERYONE. THIS IS A BATTLE ROYALE. IT IS ALL ABOUT TEAMWORK. GET ALONG FOR ONCE IN YOUR LIVES!!
ALWAYS WORK AS A TEAM. LET THE ENEMIES FIGHT EACH OTHER WHILE YOU CONSERVE YOUR STRENGTH. WHEN ENEMIES APPROACH, GET RID OF THEM BY WORKING TOGETHER. UNDERSTOOD?
YEAH...
GOT IT.

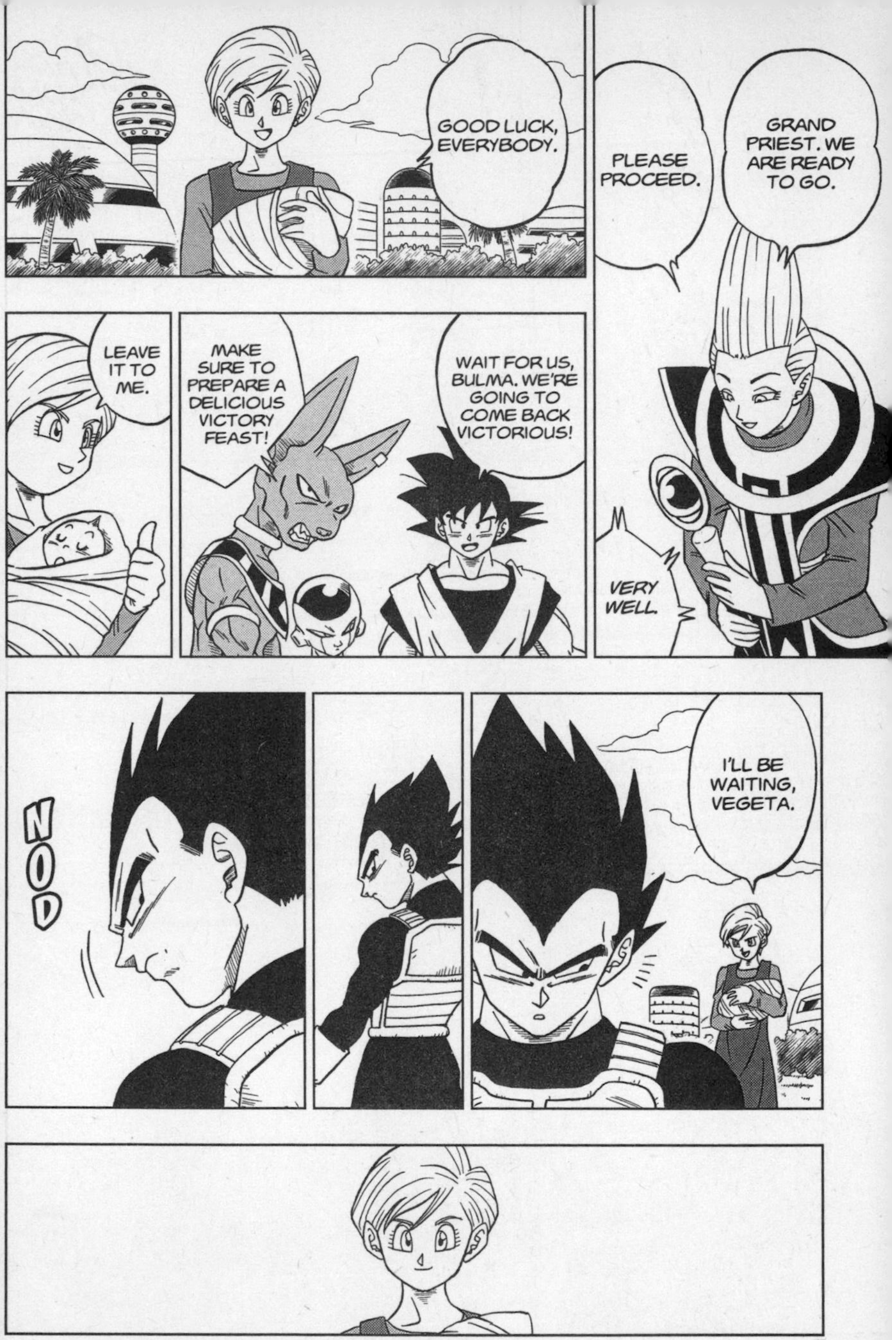
GRAND PRIEST. WE ARE READY TO GO.
PLEASE PROCEED.
VERY WELL.
GOOD LUCK, EVERYBODY.
WAIT FOR US, BULMA. WE'RE GOING TO COME BACK VICTORIOUS!
MAKE SURE TO PREPARE A DELICIOUS VICTORY FEAST!
LEAVE IT TO ME.
I'LL BE WAITING, VEGETA.
NOD

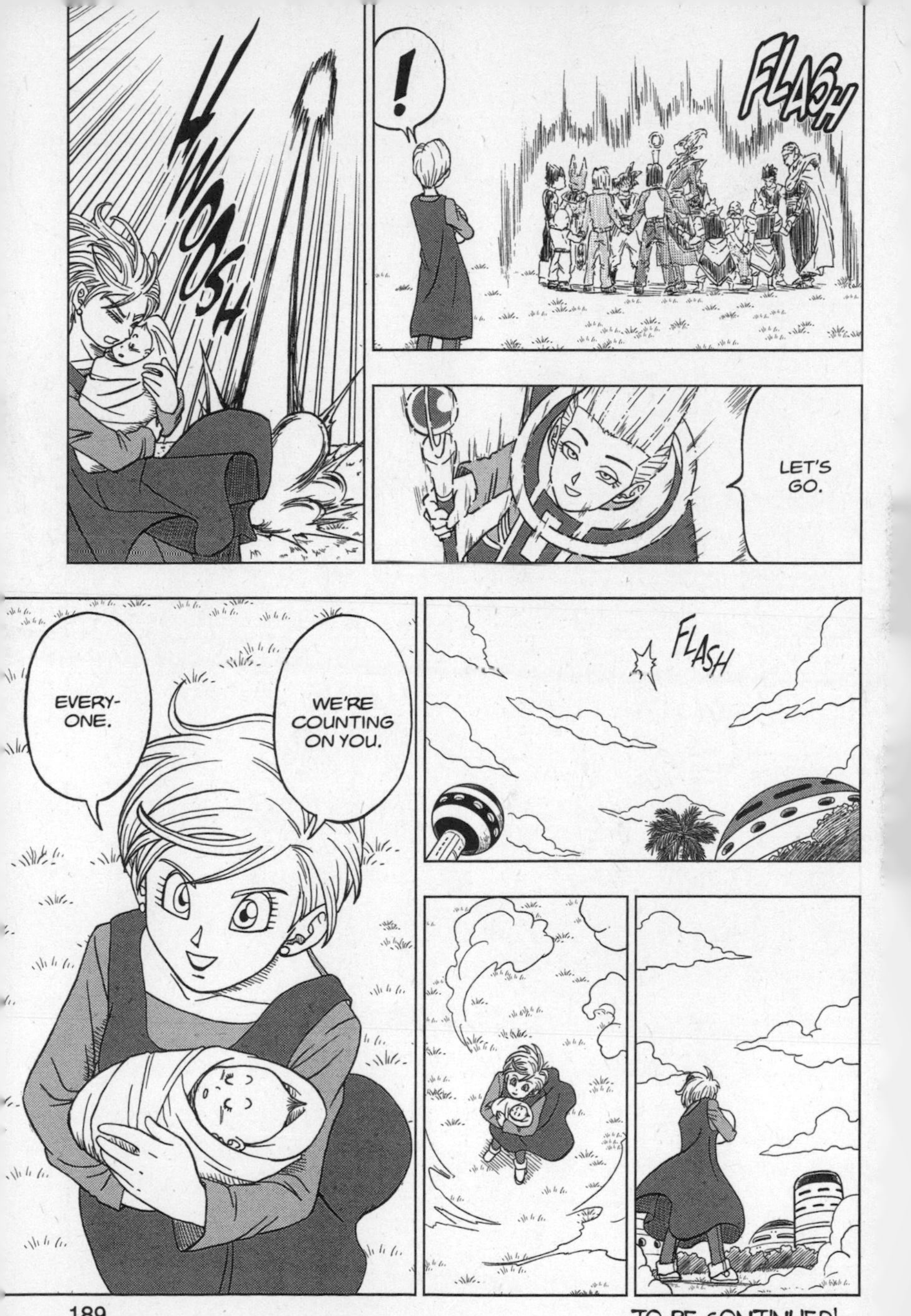
FLASH
!
LET'S GO.
WHOOSH
FLASH
WE'RE COUNTING ON YOU.
EVERY-ONE.

TO BE CONTINUED!

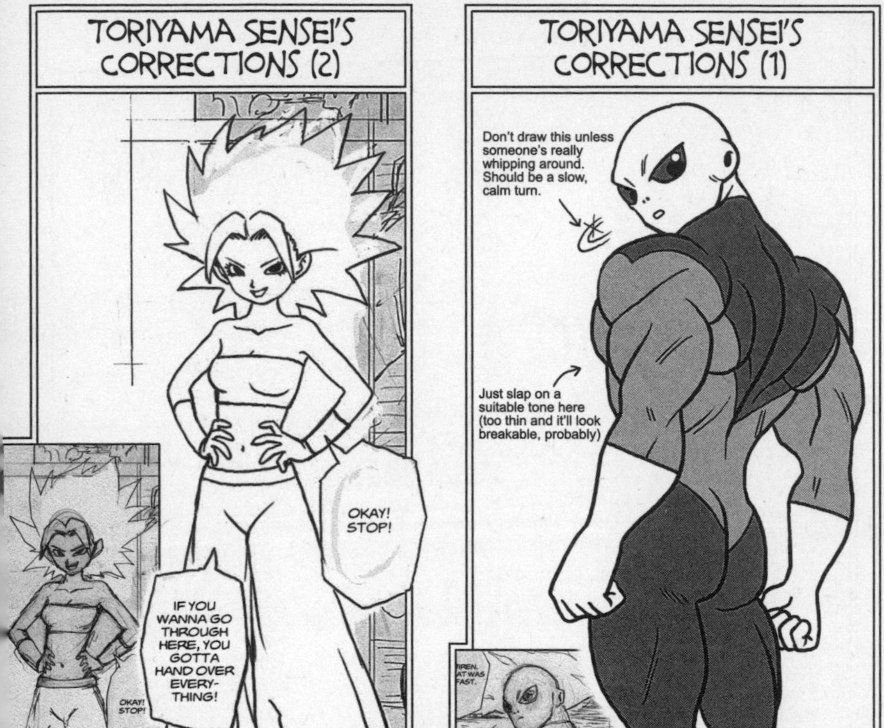

TORIYAMA SENSEI'S CORRECTIONS (1)
Don't draw this unless someone's really whipping around. Should be a slow, calm turn.
Just slap on a suitable tone here (too thin and it'll look breakable, probably)
When someone's floating there without a background, show them from a lower angle, so it's crystal clear that they're floating.
*TOYOTAROU'S ORIGINAL VERSION
TORIYAMA SENSEI'S CORRECTIONS (2)
OKAY! STOP!
IF YOU WANNA GO THROUGH HERE, YOU GOTTA HAND OVER EVERY-THING!
OKAY! STOP!
IF YOU WANNA GO THROUGH HERE, YOU GOTTA HAND OVER EVERY-THING!
*TOYOTAROU'S ORIGINAL VERSION
SENSEI DREW THESE VERSIONS OF THE NEW CHARACTERS' DEBUT SCENES FOR ME.

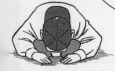

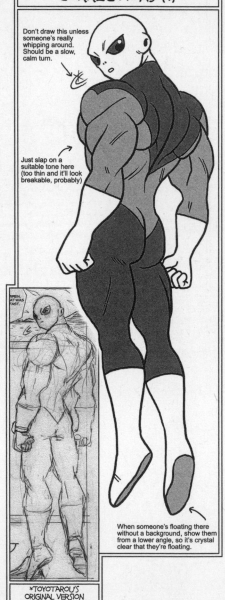

TORIYAMA SENSEI'S CORRECTIONS (3)

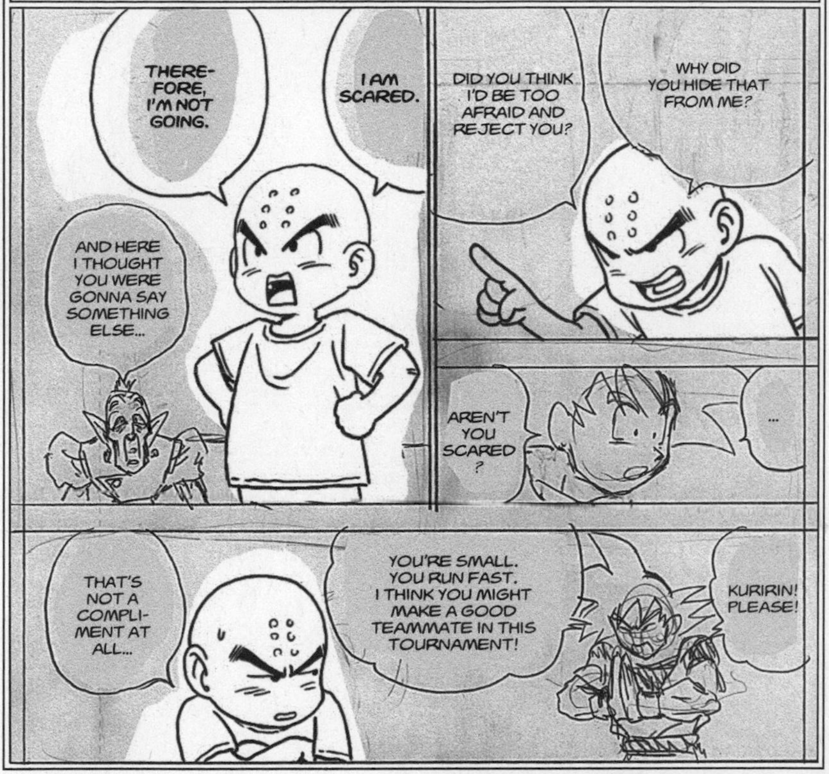
WHY DID YOU HIDE THAT FROM ME?
DID YOU THINK I'D BE TOO AFRAID AND REJECT YOU?
...
AREN'T YOU SCARED?
I AM SCARED.
THEREFORE, I'M NOT GOING.
AND HERE I THOUGHT YOU WERE GONNA SAY SOMETHING ELSE...
KURIRIN! PLEASE!
YOU'RE SMALL. YOU RUN FAST. I THINK YOU MIGHT MAKE A GOOD TEAMMATE IN THIS TOURNAMENT!
THAT'S NOT A COMPLIMENT AT ALL...

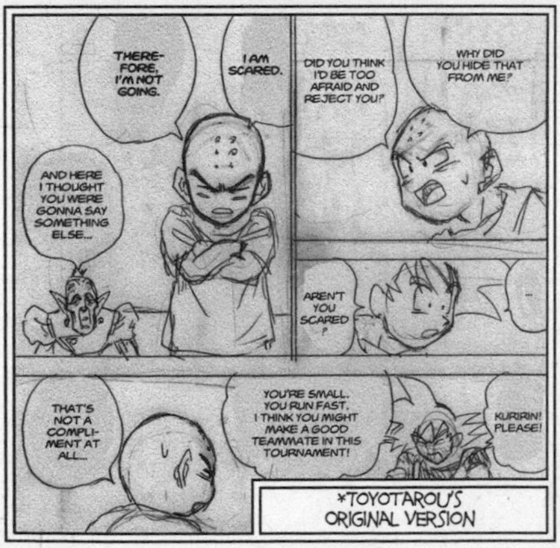
WHY DID YOU HIDE THAT FROM ME?
DID YOU THINK I'D BE TOO AFRAID AND REJECT YOU?
...
AREN'T YOU SCARED?
I AM SCARED.
THEREFORE, I'M NOT GOING.
AND HERE I THOUGHT YOU WERE GONNA SAY SOMETHING ELSE...
KURIRIN! PLEASE!
YOU'RE SMALL. YOU RUN FAST. I THINK YOU MIGHT MAKE A GOOD TEAMMATE IN THIS TOURNAMENT!
THAT'S NOT A COMPLIMENT AT ALL...
*TOYOTAROU'S ORIGINAL VERSION

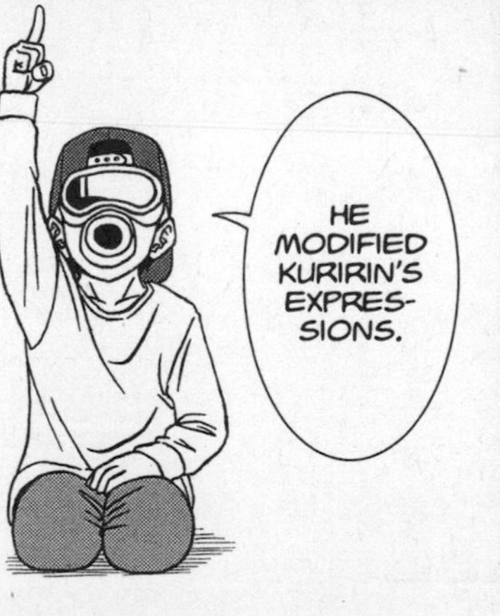
HE MODIFIED KURIRIN'S EXPRESSIONS.

YOU'RE READING
THE WRONG WAY!

Dragon Ball Super reads from right to left, starting in the
upper-right corner. Japanese is read from right to left,
meaning that action, sound effects, and word-balloon
order are completely reversed from English order.